CHARITY AND SYLVIA

Charity and Sylvia

A SAME-SEX MARRIAGE IN EARLY AMERICA

Rachel Hope Cleves

OXFORD
UNIVERSITY PRESS

OXFORD
UNIVERSITY PRESS

Oxford University Press is a department of the
University of Oxford. It furthers the University's objective
of excellence in research, scholarship, and education
by publishing worldwide.

Oxford   New York
Auckland   Cape Town   Dar es Salaam   Hong Kong   Karachi
Kuala Lumpur   Madrid   Melbourne   Mexico City   Nairobi
New Delhi   Shanghai   Taipei   Toronto

With offices in
Argentina   Austria   Brazil   Chile   Czech Republic   France   Greece
Guatemala   Hungary   Italy   Japan   Poland   Portugal   Singapore
South Korea   Switzerland   Thailand   Turkey   Ukraine   Vietnam

Oxford is a registered trade mark of Oxford University Press
in the UK and certain other countries.

Published in the United States of America by
Oxford University Press
198 Madison Avenue, New York, NY 10016

Library of Congress Cataloging-in-Publication Data
Cleves, Rachel Hope, 1975-
Charity and Sylvia : a same-sex marriage in early America / Rachel Hope Cleves.
pages   cm
Includes bibliographical references and index.
ISBN 978-0-19-933542-8 (hardcover); 978-0-19-062731-7 (paperback)
1. Same-sex marriage—United States—To 1865.   2. Bryant, Charity.   3. Drake, Sylvia, 1784–1868.
I. Title.
HQ1034.U5C54 2014
306.84'8—dc23

2013050416

Frontispiece: Silhouettes of Charity Bryant and Sylvia Drake, framed in their braided hair.
Courtesy of the Henry Sheldon Museum of Vermont History, Middlebury, Vermont.

Contents

Bryant Family

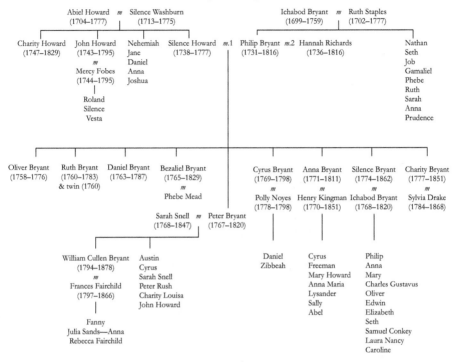

Abiel Howard *m* Silence Washburn
(1704–1777) (1713–1775)

Ichabod Bryant *m* Ruth Staples
(1699–1759) (1702–1777)

Charity Howard (1747–1829)

John Howard (1743–1795)
m
Mercy Fobes (1744–1795)
|
Roland
Silence
Vesta

Nehemiah
Jane
Daniel
Anna
Joshua

Silence Howard *m.1* Philip Bryant *m.2* Hannah Richards
(1738–1777) (1731–1816) (1736–1816)

Nathan
Seth
Job
Gamaliel
Phebe
Ruth
Sarah
Anna
Prudence

Oliver Bryant (1758–1776)

Ruth Bryant (1760–1783) & twin (1760)

Daniel Bryant (1763–1787)

Bezaliel Bryant (1765–1829)
m
Phebe Mead

Sarah Snell *m* Peter Bryant
(1768–1847) (1767–1820)

Cyrus Bryant (1769–1798)
m
Polly Noyes (1778–1798)

Anna Bryant (1771–1811)
m
Henry Kingman (1770–1851)

Silence Bryant (1774–1862)
m
Ichabod Bryant (1768–1820)

Charity Bryant (1777–1851)
m
Sylvia Drake (1784–1868)

William Cullen Bryant (1794–1878)
m
Frances Fairchild (1797–1866)
|
Fanny
Julia Sands—Anna
Rebecca Fairchild

Austin
Cyrus
Sarah Snell
Peter Rush
Charity Louisa
John Howard

Daniel
Zibbeah

Cyrus
Freeman
Mary Howard
Anna Maria
Lysander
Sally
Abel

Philip
Anna
Mary
Charles Gustavus
Oliver
Edwin
Elizabeth
Seth
Samuel Conkey
Laura Nancy
Caroline

Note: The names of Charity's cousins and grandnieces/nephews have been included selectively, focusing on relations mentioned in the book.

Drake Family

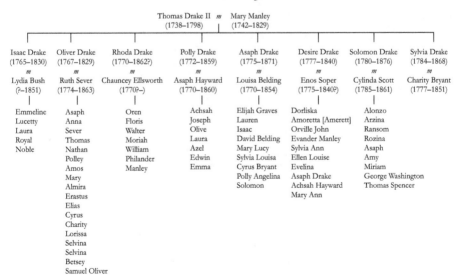

Thomas Drake II *m* Mary Manley
(1738–1798) (1742–1829)

Isaac Drake (1765–1830)
m
Lydia Bush (?–1851)
|
Emmeline
Lucetty
Laura
Royal
Noble

Oliver Drake (1767–1829)
m
Ruth Sever (1774–1863)
|
Asaph
Anna
Sever
Thomas
Nathan
Polley
Amos
Mary
Almira
Erastus
Elias
Cyrus
Charity
Lorissa
Selvina
Selvina
Betsey
Samuel Oliver

Rhoda Drake (1770–1862?)
m
Chauncey Ellsworth (1770?–)
|
Oren
Floris
Walter
Moriah
William
Philander
Manley

Polly Drake (1772–1859)
m
Asaph Hayward (1770–1860)
|
Achsah
Joseph
Olive
Laura
Azel
Edwin
Emma

Asaph Drake (1775–1871)
m
Louisa Belding (1770–1854)
|
Elijah Graves
Lauren
Isaac
David Belding
Mary Lucy
Sylvia Louisa
Cyrus Bryant
Polly Angelina
Solomon

Desire Drake (1777–1840)
m
Enos Soper (1775–1840?)
|
Dorliska
Amoretta [Amerett]
Orville John
Evander Manley
Sylvia Ann
Ellen Louise
Evelina
Asaph Drake
Achsah Hayward
Mary Ann

Solomon Drake (1780–1876)
m
Cylinda Scott (1785–1861)
|
Alonzo
Arzina
Ransom
Rozina
Asaph
Amy
Miriam
George Washington
Thomas Spencer

Sylvia Drake (1784–1868)
m
Charity Bryant (1777–1851)

Miss Bryant and Miss Drake were married to each other.

—DIARY OF HIRAM HARVEY HURLBURT JR. (1897)

Preface

THEY POSE GAZING at each other: two silhouettes, eyes level, chins uplifted, elegant. The portraits are cut from two thick cream mats set against a black cloth background and framed by a window of fine paper, pinkened at the edges. Around the paired images a thin braid of blonde hair loops and curls, coming together in a little heart nestled between their twinned bosoms. The woman on the right is slightly larger, her neck is thicker, and she has the slightest trace of a double chin. The woman on the left seems petite in comparison. Her jaw protrudes a little; her gaze is cast slightly downward. Both women have sharp pointed noses. They wear identical buns, perhaps the trademark of the cutter. Two twists of hair perch atop their foreheads and two wisps curl down the napes of their necks. They are mirror images, striking in their similarity, but the more you look the more their distinctions emerge. Their sameness is misleading, a misapprehension that obscures their differences from each other, and their difference as a pair from others at the time.[1]

The silhouettes are labeled Charity Bryant and Sylvia Drake, although no indication remains of which profile matches which name. It seems likely that the figure on the right with the beginning of a double chin is Charity, the older of the two. Born in 1777 in North Bridgewater, Massachusetts, south of Boston, Charity was nearly thirty when she met Sylvia, her companion in the portrait and in life. Her first three decades had included a great many painful experiences, mixed with brief interludes of joy. She lost her mother and five of her nine siblings to early deaths, suffered the rejection of her father and stepmother, experienced lengthy bouts of ill health, and endured vicious rumors about her character. Yet in the midst of these misfortunes she traveled throughout Massachusetts, fell repeatedly in love, wrote sheaves of poetry, and became expert in the valuable trade of tailoring. To Sylvia, seven years her younger, Charity appeared worldly and accomplished. Twenty-two when they met, Sylvia had little knowledge or experience of the world. She was born in Easton, Massachusetts, a town on North Bridgewater's western border, but insolvency drove Sylvia's family to resettle a decade later in remote Addison County, Vermont. Sylvia came of age in rural isolation, dissatisfied with her circumscribed opportunities and searching for a path to satisfy her spiritual inclinations.

Charity opened the door to a different life. She struck an astonishing contrast to the women in Sylvia's family, who were all mothers to large and growing families. Sylvia ultimately had sixty-four nieces and nephews; one sister-in-law gave birth to eighteen children, ten by the time Sylvia and Charity met. Sylvia's female relatives were tied to their homes by the constant labor of making food, nursing children, and keeping house. Charity had no house; she lived with family members, or at times paid for her board, earning her way by teaching school. She had pledged at age twenty-three to never get married. Instead, she pursued passionate romantic relationships with women, who found her masculine independence and authority attractive. Charity poured her creative energies into writing verses, not birthing children. Charity's singularity and singlehood were intoxicating to Sylvia, who had very little interest in marriage herself. Sylvia dismissed the men who courted her without consideration. The Drakes could not make sense of Sylvia's aversion. But in Charity, Sylvia finally found a kindred soul.

What an irony that these two marriage-averse women ended up forming such a remarkable union. They met in 1807, when Charity traveled to Weybridge, Vermont, to pay a visit to her friend Polly, Sylvia's older sister. Charity intended to visit Vermont for only a few months, but meeting Sylvia changed her plans. Once Sylvia and Charity found each other, they were never willing to be parted. Charity described their encounter as "providence." After a lifetime of troubles, God had given her a "help-meet."[2] A few months after they met, Charity rented a room in Weybridge, and on July 3, 1807, Sylvia came to join her. For the rest of their lives, the two women would celebrate this date as the beginning of their union. Over the next forty-four years they remained mutually devoted to each other through the tribulations of ill health, overwork, and spiritual doubt. To all who knew them, it seemed they passed their time together happily.[3]

Although Sylvia and Charity lived a quiet life, far from the bustle and commotion of the nineteenth century's growing cities, they did not live in secret. Everyone who knew them understood that they were a couple and viewed their relationship as a marriage or something like it. One man from a neighboring village, Hiram Harvey

Hurlburt Jr., recalled in his memoir that in town he always heard "it mentioned as if Miss Bryant and Miss Drake were married to each other."[4] His words offer the plainest statement that Charity and Sylvia's relationship was viewed as a marriage. Charity's nephew, the poet William Cullen Bryant, came close when he described the relationship as "no less sacred to them than the tie of marriage."[5]

One reason people viewed Charity and Sylvia's relationship as marital was that the women divided their domestic and public roles according to the familiar pattern of husband and wife. Throughout their lives together Charity always served as head of the household. Her name came first in public documents, such as tax records and census records. She handled the money and took the leading role in all of their business. Sylvia performed the wifely work of cooking and keeping house. In some ways, she did not live all that differently from her sisters after all. She even cared for the children who frequently visited the house, nurturing her many nieces and nephews as well as the young assistants who lived with the women. As Hiram Hurlburt explained in his memoir, "Miss Bryant was the man" in the marriage. And Sylvia, according to William Cullen Bryant, was a "fond wife" to her "husband."[6]

Charity and Sylvia also seem to have viewed their relationship in these terms. Charity portrayed herself as a husband when she called Sylvia her "help-meet"—a common early American synonym for wife, adopted from the Bible, Genesis 2:18. Sylvia fantasized about taking Charity's name for her own. On an archived scrap of paper, in Sylvia's handwriting, there survives a list of names that looks like practice toward a signature, with big loops on the capitals and flourishes on the final letters. The list begins with the name "Bryant," followed by "Bryant Charity," then plunges into the sequence "Bryant Sylvia Bryant Sylvia Bryant Charity Bryant Sylvia." Excluded from the legal form of marriage, it appears that Sylvia, in a romantic gesture, once inscribed her desire to become a wife in name as well as practice.[7]

According to English common-law tradition, wives assumed their husbands' names because marriage transformed spouses into a single person. Genesis 2:24 states that "a man shall cleave unto his wife: and they shall be one flesh." The idea that a husband and wife became one person, in spirit, body, and law, lay at the heart of early American ideas of marriage. The eighteenth-century English jurist William Blackstone described husbands and wives as *one person* in the law.[8] Charity shared Sylvia's evident wish for marital oneness. "May we pass our whole life," Charity serenaded Sylvia in an 1810 poem, "and our minds be united in one."[9] Her language echoed an early nineteenth-century English treatise, which defined husbands and wives as "*united in one* body out of two by God."[10]

Many friends and relations believed that Charity and Sylvia achieved this marital status. Charity's sister-in-law, and good friend, Sally Snell Bryant, wrote to the women in 1843, "I consider you both one as man and wife are one."[11] Sylvia's brother

Asaph, who was also close to both women, told Charity that "I consider you and My Sister Sylvia Happely one."[12] Charity's former lover Lydia Richards, a lifelong friend to both women, saw Sylvia and Charity as so powerfully united that it was impossible to divide them. She wrote that "you are indeed in many respects so much <u>one</u> that a separation can scarcely be made."[13] When the women finally were divided by Charity's death in 1851, many of their friends and relations found it impossible to imagine Sylvia continuing on alone. Seventeen years later, after Sylvia's death, her relations erected a common headstone over the two women's mortal remains in the graveyard on Weybridge Hill. They were buried together like any other married couple.

Yet everyone recognized that Charity and Sylvia's marriage was not like every other. They were "nerely one" according to friend Anna Hayden, they were "almost as one," but they also remained separate.[14] Sylvia never did take Charity's last name. Both women kept their identities as single women in name and law. Both their names appeared in the tax records, and Charity's name did not cover Sylvia's, as a husband's would according to the laws of coverture that governed spousal property in the nineteenth century. Charity and Sylvia did not want it that way. They believed that they each deserved equal claim to the wealth produced by their shared labor.[15] Charity and Sylvia forged a union that was like a marriage but that was also unlike a marriage in fundamental ways related to their sex. By binding herself to another woman, rather than to a man, each woman enjoyed a degree of independence that she could not have otherwise maintained.

But by forming a marriage of two women, both Charity and Sylvia also risked reprobation they would not have otherwise received. Early Americans defined marriage as a sexual institution, and sexual relations between people of the same sex were both legally and socially proscribed in early American society. How did Charity and Sylvia manage their reputation as "husband" and "wife" without sparking the condemnation of their families, friends, and neighbors? Like queer people in many times and places, Charity and Sylvia preserved their reputations by persuading their community to treat the matter of their sexuality as an open secret. Although it is commonly assumed that the "closet" is an opaque space, meaning that people who are in the closet keep others in total ignorance about their sexuality, often the closet is really an open secret. The ignorance that defines the closet is as likely to be a carefully constructed edifice as it is to be a total absence of knowledge. The closet depends on people strategically choosing to remain ignorant of inconvenient facts. In this light, Charity and Sylvia's acceptance within their town should be understood as the result of their success in persuading others to choose ignorance by not asking questions about their sexuality. No matter what the answer, the very act of being questioned would have damaged the women's respectability.[16]

The open closet is an especially critical strategy in small towns, where every person serves a role, and which would cease to function if all moral transgressors were ostracized. Small communities can maintain the fiction of ignorance in order to preserve social arrangements that work for the general benefit. Queer history has often focused on the modern city as the most potent site of gay liberation, since its anonymity and living arrangements for single people permitted same-sex-desiring men and women to form innovative communities. More recognition needs to be given to the distinctive opportunities that rural towns allowed for the expression of same-sex sexuality. For early American women in particular, the rural landscape rather than the city served as a critical milieu for establishing same-sex unions. Women of Charity and Sylvia's generation spoke far more often of their desire to retire together to a little cottage in the countryside, than of their urge to move together to the city.[17]

Charity and Sylvia gave a lot to their family, faith, and neighbors, which encouraged the community to keep their open secret. Sylvia's brother Asaph captured this delicate balance in his brief handwritten memoir. Likening the women's relationship to a marriage while simultaneously maintaining its distinctiveness, Asaph explained that "my sister Sylvia has not Married," having instead spent her life "in company with Miss Charity Bryant." Asaph's relationship with Charity and Sylvia was rocky at times, but for many years he paid frequent visits to their house and accepted them into his own. His children spent countless days and nights with their aunts; he named Charity as godmother for one of his sons. Asaph accommodated the women's relationship, which sometimes troubled him, because he saw both Charity and Sylvia as moral buttresses who upheld the community. "To say the least," he observed approvingly, they "have done as much to build up and keep society to gather considering thier means as aney other two individuals."[18]

Charity and Sylvia gained the toleration of their relatives and community not by hiding away but by being public-minded. "Be useful where thou livest, that they may both want + wish thy pleasing presence still," Sylvia began her diary for 1835. She copied the words from George Herbert, a seventeenth-century minister famous for his devotion to his parishioners.[19] Herbert's words captured the combination of faith and practicality that inspired Sylvia and Charity's service. During their long lives together in Weybridge they taught Sunday school, cleaned the church, organized charities, supported their nieces' and nephews' educations, hired local women to work in the tailor shop they ran, and wrote epitaphs for the village graveyard. They became "Aunt Charity" and "Aunt Sylvia" to the whole community. When a former worker asked Charity to take on her younger sister as an apprentice, she explained that it was "the union which exists between Miss Drake and yourself" that made their home such a desirable situation for the young girl.[20] Charity and Sylvia's relationship, far from hidden, was widely known and respected. In fact, the absence of a man in their household allowed the women's marriage less privacy than traditional unions received. In a male-dominated world, two women could not claim the same freedom from public interference that a man could for his home.

The women's union was so public that even in their own time they appeared as subjects in print. Charity's nephew Cullen published the first account of their remarkable marriage in his newspaper, the *New-York Evening Post*, in 1843, and later included that account in an 1850 book of letters.[21] Cullen had a deep affection for his aunt Charity, who lived with his family on several occasions during his childhood. Charity supported Cullen's poetic talent from the time he was young. She copied out poems he wrote as a child that are now the only extant manuscript versions of those works.[22] Once grown up, Cullen remained a loyal nephew to Aunt Charity and Aunt Sylvia. He wrote them letters and even paid them several visits.

His published account of their marriage began with praise for the edenic beauty of the landscape where they lived. Traveling across the Champlain Canal from upstate New York to the Vermont border one summer, Cullen passed by "fields heavy with grass almost ready for the scythe, and thick-leaved groves of the sugar-maple and the birch." He rode through meadows luxuriant with white-flowered clover, which filled the soft summer air with a sweet perfume, before arriving at their cottage door. Copying the sequence of the popular marriage ceremony from the *Book of Common Prayer*, Cullen's paean to his aunts continued:

If I were permitted to draw aside the veil of private life, I would briefly give you the singular, and to me most interesting history of two maiden ladies who dwell in this valley. I would tell you how, in their youthful days, they took each other as companions for life, and how this union, no less sacred to them than the tie of marriage, has subsisted, in uninterrupted harmony, for forty years, during which they have shared each other's occupations and pleasures and works of charity while in health, and watched over each other tenderly in sickness; for sickness has made long and frequent visits to their dwelling. I could tell you how they slept on the same pillow and had a common purse, and adopted each other's relations, and how one of them, more enterprising and spirited in her temper than the other, might be said to represent the male head of the family, and took upon herself their transactions with the world without, until at length her health failed, and she was tended by her gentle companion, as a fond wife attends her invalid husband. I would tell you of their dwelling, encircled with roses, which now in the days of their broken health, bloom wild without their tendance, and I would speak of the friendly attentions which their neighbors, people of kind hearts and simple manners, seem to take pleasure in bestowing upon them, but I have already said more than I fear they will forgive me for, if this should ever meet their eyes, and I must leave the subject.[23]

Far from feeling offended by Cullen's disclosures, Charity and Sylvia treasured his poetic description of their marriage. When Sylvia died, her will directed that a copy of Cullen's 1850 book of letters be left to a favorite niece.[24]

The poet's account won the favor of his aunts because, although evocative, it avoided giving the women's names. This was a matter of great importance to Charity, whose early life was marred by vicious rumors about her character. Unfortunately for the historian, such concerns led Charity to seek the destruction of her own most personal writings, including her diary and letters, to protect them from prying eyes. Over the course of her life, Charity probably wrote more than fifteen hundred letters. She wrote two hundred letters to her friend Lydia alone, in a correspondence that lasted from 1799 to 1846. According to a letter record that she kept in a ledger, Charity continued to write nearly twenty letters a year up until the end of her life.[25] And yet only thirty-six of her letters in total still remain.[26] The rest were, presumably, turned to ashes. Traces of those burnings remain. For example, Lydia's sister Sally wrote to Charity, after Lydia's death, promising to destroy her half-century's correspondence if so directed:

> The trunk containing your letters was given to me before my sisters death with the request to keep it unopened until I had order from you which request has been strictly complied with notwithstanding it would be highly gratifying to me and my daughters to peruse them It would be hard for me to commit them to the flames even if you should desire it. But they are yours and your wish respecting them shall be granted if it is in my power.[27]

The fact that Charity's reply is missing offers strong proof that she instructed Sally to burn all the pages. Exchanges with other friends tell a similar story. When her correspondents died she worked diligently to ensure that her letters to them were destroyed. She even got into a quarrel with one sister's widower after he refused to confirm the destruction of her letters.[28]

After her own death, however, Charity lost the power over the disposition of her property. Sylvia, who took control of the papers that the women had accumulated throughout their lifetimes, did not wish to see them all destroyed. Gossip had never blighted her early years. Although the women did encounter some negative reactions from hostile family members and neighbors, overall Sylvia derived a positive reputation from her union with Charity. Being connected to this brilliant and charismatic figure elevated Sylvia from the anonymous station into which she was born, the youngest daughter of a bankrupt living on the provincial frontier. The last thing that Sylvia wished was to eliminate the evidence of her lifelong companion.

Instead, Sylvia preserved the poems her partner wrote, as well as many years from her own diary, their business papers, the correspondence they received, and countless little scraps that had once been deemed important enough not to throw into the fire (including the page where she practiced signing Sylvia Bryant). She kept the papers in a trunk and left them to posterity. Sylvia had many years following Charity's death to weed through the papers and remove anything she deemed too private. Many papers are missing. Although both women appear to have kept journals throughout their lives, only a few years of Sylvia's diary remain and none of Charity's do.[29] Very few letters written by Sylvia survive, only fifteen mostly archived among the papers of her relations. Following some lost logic, Sylvia preserved the papers that she saw as the most fit memorial to her and Charity's lives. Her desire to have the relationship publicly acknowledged in her own lifetime, and memorialized after her death, has made this book possible. After Sylvia's death, her family gave the trunk to a local history collector; the papers are now archived at his namesake museum, the Henry Sheldon, in Middlebury, Vermont. These writings provide the most significant sources for this book.

Charity and Sylvia would not have been shocked by readers' interest in their story. Before their deaths, Cullen's account had already demonstrated that curiosity about their lives extended beyond their circle of immediate acquaintances. However, they could hardly have expected anyone to study their marriage in the fashion that follows—our culture and preoccupations have been revolutionized since their lifetimes. Sylvia's sensibility would have been offended by the brazen indiscretion of this book. While Cullen felt a certain modesty about drawing aside "the veil of private life," I do not share his restraint. Historians, unlike poets, are not content with evocative imagery. We have a ravenous appetite for the factual. This book investigates all the details of Sylvia and Charity's relationship, even asking the question that they worked so hard to forestall: did the women share a sexual relationship? Many other questions also drive the pages of this narrative. How did their childhoods prepare the women to fashion such a divergent life path? What sorts of relationships did Charity form with the women she met before Sylvia? What resistance did she encounter? How did Charity and Sylvia persuade their traditional, rural, nineteenth-century community to accept them as a married couple? How did they reconcile their romantic relationship with their religious faith? How did Sylvia's family relate to Charity, and vice versa? How did the women earn a living? And how were they remembered after their deaths?

To answer these questions I draw on a wide range of materials. In addition to the papers at the Henry Sheldon Museum, I have found primary sources related to Charity's and Sylvia's lives scattered across archives in Massachusetts, New York, Illinois, California, and Washington. At many points in the research I was amazed by the richness of the surviving documentary record about the ordinary women and men who people these pages. I am thankful for the verbosity and historical-mindedness of eighteenth- and nineteenth-century New Englanders that gifted me with sources such as the receipt for Sylvia's gravestone, the diary of Charity's sister-in-law, and the memoir of a man who knew Charity and Sylvia when he was a child. The variety of the historical record has allowed for a far more intimate perspective on the lives of my subjects than I ever could have dreamed possible at the project's outset.

Of course, the historical record of Charity and Sylvia's relationship is also notable for its silences. Not only have few of the women's letters survived, the documents that do remain are mostly silent on the subject that first sparked my interest and probably the interest of most readers: the women's sexuality. Some of the strongest evidence for the women's sexual relationships appears in their religious writings, where they struggled with the burden of secret sins that left both women feeling uncertain about their redemption. Romantic letters and poems hint at more positive aspects of the women's physical relationship. In both these sources, references to sexuality take the form of allusions, not direct statements. Respectable nineteenth-century women rarely wrote directly about sex of any sort, but this silence is especially characteristic of the history of same-sex intimacy.[30] For many centuries, sex between women or between men was referred to as "the mute sin" or the "crime not fit to be named."[31] As late as the 1890s, Oscar Wilde's lover Alfred Douglas dubbed their passion "the love that dare not speak its name."[32] Such locutions have led historians to argue that what is not said must be an important conceptual tool for writing lesbian and gay history.[33] The research for this book has required me to read the silences in documents where they speak loudly.

Thankfully, I have had the works of other scholars to guide me safely along the shoals of speculation. It would be impossible to write such an intimate portrait of two individuals without the contextual research and theoretical insights provided by generations of scholars. Hundreds of works ranging from nineteenth-century genealogies to twenty-first-century queer studies have helped me to place Charity and Sylvia in their time and to make sense of their lives. The book owes its greatest debt to scholars in early American history who have investigated everything from the development of the tailoring trade in the eighteenth century, to patterns of friendship among young people after the Revolution, to the growing rates of single-hood in the nineteenth century. The end result of my investigations, I hope, will contribute to this archive of knowledge and support new understandings of the past as well.

Charity and Sylvia's story reveals that there was more opportunity for the expression of erotic love between women in early America than has previously been believed. The earliest inquiries into lesbian and gay history recovered an oppressive record of religious codes, civil laws, and scientific thought directed against people who had sex with members of their own sex. When evidence was first discovered that romantic relationships between women were common in early America, historians believed that nobody could have seen those relationships as sexual. Otherwise, they would have been taboo. Any sex that did take place, it was assumed, must have been shrouded in complete secrecy.[34] But Charity's and Sylvia's lives tell a more complicated story, revealing the gap that existed between prescription and practice, the rules that govern society and how societies actually operate. Early Americans did understand the potential for a sexual element within women's friendships. Several of Charity's early intimacies were gossiped about for this reason. More astonishing still, society could also tolerate such sexual possibilities through manufactured ignorance, creating opportunities for same-sex sexuality that should ostensibly have been impossible.

The potential for toleration of same-sex sexuality extended so far that even same-sex marriage did not lie outside the boundaries of possibility in early America. Same-sex marriage is not as new as Americans on both sides of today's debate tend to assume; it is neither the radical break with timeless tradition that conservatives fear nor the unprecedented innovation of a singularly tolerant age that liberals praise. It fits within a long history of marriage diversity in North America that included practices such as polygamy, self-divorce, free love, and interracial unions. Many queer scholars today criticize the mainstream gay rights focus on same-sex marriage for being "homonormative," or an attempt to secure respectability for privileged lesbians or gay men based on their similarity to straight people. But Charity and Sylvia's history reveals how same-sex marriage can challenge society's rules of respectability as well. Through their union, Charity and Sylvia undermined the conventional definitions of womanhood and manhood that ordinary marriages reinforced. They staked out new claims to familial, economic, and spiritual authority that were denied to their conventionally married sisters. It seems reasonable to hope that same-sex marriage has the same potential to reshape acceptable sex roles today.[35]

Ten years ago I walked in the door of the Henry Sheldon Museum on a sunny summer afternoon. The entrance way was unremarkable, but something in the air set my senses tingling. You know, I said, there are great treasures waiting to be discovered in local museums like this. It was entirely by accident that I stumbled across the story of Charity and Sylvia a year later, and I found out that their papers were archived at the Sheldon. Putting together the story of Charity and Sylvia's marriage has been like building a jigsaw puzzle, made more difficult by all the missing pieces. But the research process has left me more sure than ever that there are countless pieces remaining to be found, if not from Charity's and Sylvia's lives then from the lives of other lovers who lived outside the norms. Their stories have been hard to see because they confound our expectations. We see each story as one of a kind, defying categorization. Taken together they tell a history we are only beginning to know. The most remarkable element of Charity and Sylvia's life together, in the final assessment, may be how unremarkable it was.

1

A Child of Melancholy

1777

CONFINED TO HER bed, where she had remained since the birth of her daughter Charity a month before, thirty-nine-year-old Silence Bryant lay dying. The weight that disease brought to bear on her chest was compounded by the pressing considerations of the spiritual fate awaiting her and the temporal fate awaiting her children. Silence's strict Congregationalist faith directed that she prepare her soul to meet her maker, but that blessed reunion would leave her children motherless. The survival of her sickly infant hung tenuously. Outside the rectangular windows of the colonial house, the fields of North Bridgewater, Massachusetts, were green with early summer grass. Inside, a gaunt-faced woman, grown old before her time, succumbed to consumption. The infant daughter she left behind never knew her mother and never ceased mourning her death.[1]

Silence's life ended amid a scene of destruction. Beyond the sickroom walls, the nation entered the third year of a terrible war for independence. At the front, Washington's continental army pursued Hessian soldiers across central New Jersey, leaving the wool-clad corpses of mercenaries scattered along the roadsides.[2] Off the coast of New York, captured American sailors lay dying from disease and malnutrition on British prison ships.[3] Close to home, in Massachusetts, a smallpox plague raged through private homes, sweeping away whole families.[4] Silence's death was only one among thousands in June 1777, hardly worthy of notice outside the family circle. Her death was not even the first within the family since the war began.

Signal guns from Lexington and Concord were heard in North Bridgewater, twenty miles south, within hours of the Revolution's opening battles on April 19, 1775. That afternoon, several of Charity's uncles marched north with the minutemen.[5] They led the way in a parade of local citizens who volunteered to fight throughout the eight-year war. The Bryants' fourteen-year-old neighbor Hezekiah Packard volunteered two months later when the cannon shots from the Battle of Bunker Hill echoed through the village.[6] North Bridgewater men played a critical role in the Battle of Dorchester Heights, the following March, which enabled the patriots to recapture Boston.[7] A month later, Silence's oldest son, Oliver, volunteered for Captain Elisha Mitchell's Plymouth County company of the Massachusetts militia.

Oliver's enlistment period was probably shorter than a year, since the patriots were still wary of creating a permanent army at that early stage in the war. But he did not live to finish his term. Exactly how Oliver died is uncertain. Charity was in error when, many decades later, she told her nephew John that her oldest brother had died in June 1776, two months after his enlistment.[8] The State Library of Massachusetts holds a rations receipt made to Oliver Bryant dated August 9, 1776, in a camp "near New York."[9] This places him in proximity to the Battle of Long Island, which makes sense since Bryant served in Col. Simeon Cary's regiment that fought there.[10] According to a family genealogy he died in the battle, but his gravestone records his death date as August 24, three days beforehand.[11] A camp disease may have taken his life before the fighting broke out.

Silence was already in a weakened state when she heard the news. The birth of Oliver eighteen years before had been the first in a nonstop sequence of pregnancies and parturitions that absorbed her entire adult life. Five months' pregnant when she married Philip Bryant at the age of nineteen, she gave birth to Oliver in March 1758.[12] Ruth and a twin who died followed in 1760. Another son may have been born in 1761 and died in infancy. More surviving children were born in 1763, 1765, 1767, 1769, 1771, and 1774.[13] At some point in this history, Silence developed consumption. The wasting disease caused severe respiratory distress, fever, exhaustion, and weight loss. Silence was harrowed and spent when, pregnant once again, word of Oliver's death reached her. A bleak season followed, while Silence struggled through the grief of losing her oldest son, the ravages of a terminal illness, and the needs of a household of young children plus one more on the way.

Her difficulties were compounded by the closely concurrent deaths of her parents and her mother-in-law, which deprived Silence of both practical and emotional support when she needed it most. Her father and mother, Abiel and Silence Howard, figured largely in their daughter's and grandchildren's lives. Abiel played an instru-

mental role in orchestrating Silence's marriage to Philip Bryant, who had come to
live with the Howard family in order to train as a doctor under Abiel's guidance. In
a story common to the eighteenth century, the apprentice fell in love with the master's daughter—or at least made her pregnant. The match, if precipitous, seems to
have been welcome. As Silence and Philip's family swiftly grew in the years that followed, the children frequently visited their grandparents who lived nearby. Abiel
lent his grandchildren books from his extensive library and encouraged their love of
poetry; Silence, a pious woman, nurtured the grandchildren's faith.[14] Silence
Howard's death in August 1775 and Abiel Howard's death in January 1777 seem to
have come as a surprise. Abiel died intestate, prompting the court to appoint Philip
Bryant to administer his estate.[15] Philip's own mother, Ruth Staples Bryant, died
two months later, increasing the family's grief.[16]

The deaths of so many beloved relations so close in proximity struck a terrible
blow to Silence. When spring arrived in North Bridgewater in 1777, the rejuvenation
in the fields hardly reflected the spirit within the Bryant household. By the time of
Charity's birth, on May 22, 1777, consumption had reduced Silence to a shadow of
her former self. It came as no surprise when she passed away a month later. Silence is
only a ghost in the records of Charity's life, legible in her absence, which so strongly
defined Charity's sense of self. Charity believed her mother's death destined her to
become a "child of melancholy," as she titled an 1800 poem recounting her origins.
In Charity's retelling, there is no backdrop of war or disease. Her mother's death is a
singular irony, intruding on a pastoral scene, bringing grave consequences to her
unfortunate daughter:

As the sun rising pleasant in May
Seems to promise new life to the lawn
Even such was my youth's early day
And as fair and serene was its dawn;
But clouds have o'ershadow'd the scene
And tempests continue to blow,
While to think on the days that have been
But serves to embitter my woe.

And say, was I wrong for to dream
That fortune upon me would shine?
When friends to me smiling did seem
And the tend'rest of Mothers was mine
But Heaven too soon of its boon

Repenting, nounc'd it again
While I am left poor, and alone
By remembrance to double my pain.[17]

Despite Charity's complaint, it is unlikely that she had any "remembrance" to double her pain. Her description of Silence as "the tend'rest of Mothers" is so formulaic as to be almost empty, although Charity did have the memories of her older siblings to draw on when she chose the word *tender*. Her sister Anna Kingman, who was six when their mother died, used the same word to describe Silence in a poem she wrote in 1800 that recounted Charity's infancy. In Anna's words, Charity had been deprived of a "<u>Mother's</u> tender anguish." Silence's death left the baby with "no <u>Mother's</u> care no fond maternal love / No <u>Mother's</u> rising hope or boding sigh."[18] Silence appears in Anna's words, like in Charity's, as a broken promise of love. Of course, Anna remembered their mother dimly if at all.

No other description of Silence has survived to support Charity's and Anna's poetic renderings. A gravestone bearing her name and the words "wife of Dr. Philip Bryant" stands in an old cemetery in North Bridgewater (renamed Brockton more than a century ago). As a prominent medical man, Philip earned biographical entries in books of local history and an epitaph on his gravestone. But Silence Bryant, like so many women of her generation, was never memorialized. In death she stayed true to her name.[19]

The one word in Silence's own voice that she left behind was the name she chose for her infant daughter. She called the girl after her youngest sister, Charity Howard. By choosing this single sister as a namesake Silence pointed her daughter to a model of womanhood that differed significantly from her own.[20] Charity Howard, who alone among her sisters never married, earned a reputation during her life as an accomplished seamstress. A set of decorative bed drapes that she stitched before Silence's death, from silk she dyed herself, are so expertly embroidered that portions of the work have been preserved by two different museums.[21] Charity Howard survived her married sisters by many decades, living well into her eighties.[22] She became for her niece an example of both the creative rewards that might derive from a single life and the financial vulnerabilities that long-lived "spinsters" faced.

Whatever dreams Silence held for her daughter's future, there was good cause to worry whether Charity would survive to fulfill them. She was a very sickly baby. The infants of tubercular mothers are often born small and are sometimes infected by the disease. Charity's chances for survival worsened after Silence's death, when she lost the opportunity to nurse. There is no evidence that she was nursed by a surrogate. Her father did hire a caretaker for Charity named Grace Hayward, but she was an unmarried woman in her forties who would not have been able to breastfeed.[23] Instead, she likely fed Charity on a pap mixed of flour, water, cow's milk, and bread, which would have distressed her immature digestive system. Long after Silence's death, Charity's survival remained uncertain. Even decades later, her infant suffering haunted her older sister Anna's memory:

> You drew in trouble with your earliest breath,
> And liv'd the long expected prey of Death!
> For wasting sickness nipt your infant bloom
> And mark'd you out a victim for the tomb.[24]

One stroke of luck saved Charity from following her mother to an early grave. Grace Hayward came to love her charge. In later writings, Charity celebrated Grace as a "generous" woman of "kind compassions" who "nursed my helpless infancy" and whose "affection, by me, can never be forgotten."[25] She looked after Charity, both body and soul. Grace's dedication to nourishing the struggling infant, to easing her discomfort when she cried, and to protecting her from the "unwholesome winds" that doctors of the era blamed for disease restored Charity's physical health from the assault of the "wasting sickness" that had taken her mother's life.[26] The "affection" with which she performed her duties also nurtured Charity's heart.

Unfortunately, Grace could not be a constant presence throughout Charity's childhood. Philip Bryant remarried when Charity was two, and his new wife, Hannah Richards Bryant, who was notoriously frugal and unsympathetic to her stepchildren, dismissed Charity's nurse when she got the chance. Still, Grace remained in the Bridgewater area, and she stayed close to the girl whose infancy she had watched over. She returned to work for the family at times when sickness required, which was unfortunately frequent, and she became known to the other siblings in the family as Aunt Grace, but Charity regarded her as an "ever-kind mother."[27]

The affectionate indulgence of Charity's numerous older brothers and sisters also helped to soften the blow of her early orphanhood. The Bryant siblings were close-knit, united by their common love of poetry and their common dislike for their stepmother. Charity, as the baby, was cosseted by her big brothers and sisters. But this intimacy came at a cost. The Bryants were an unlucky family, shadowed by early death. From watching her older siblings, Charity came to expect death's imminent grip on her own shoulder.

Charity was six when her oldest sister Ruth died from the same wasting disease that had killed their mother, who probably infected her. Consumption frequently passed between family members living in close quarters, devastating entire households. Ruth's sickly appearance was guaranteed to terrify a child Charity's age. The skeletal bodies of consumption victims, and their symptomatic bleeding from the mouth, appeared monstrous to many adults (there are even scholars who connect consumption to myths about vampires). Ruth's presence in the home during Charity's early years acted as a warning to the sickly child of that painful end that possibly awaited her.[28]

Ruth's death released Charity from witnessing a terrifying spectacle of suffering, but it cost her sister a great potential ally. Ruth was an extraordinary young woman. When the battles of Lexington and Concord shook the village soon after her fifteenth birthday, she embraced the cause of American independence with a passion. Unable to shoulder a gun like her uncles and older brother, Ruth instead picked up her pen and began writing poems in support of the war. The poems made her family proud—the only surviving copy of her work is copied out in the hand of middle brother Peter. Ruth's voice was valorous, brave, and dedicated. She had an unusual fascination with warfare for a female poet, especially for an unmarried girl. Sometimes her verses assumed the identity of a valiant soldier. These poems, among the first that Charity read, set an example of the risks an unconventional young woman could take on the page.[29]

Although Ruth's death deprived her youngest sister of her stewardship, Charity fortunately found another protector within the family circle. Her sister Anna was only six years older than Charity, but like many older siblings in difficult conditions, she became her baby sister's caretaker. Anna was "lovely."[30] Gentle, kind, and nurturing, she shied away from conflict, having "as great an aversion to strife as ever any body had."[31] And she loved Charity without judgment or restraint, more than she loved any of her other brothers or sisters. Her "partiality," she explained, was owing to the "peculiarness of [Charity's] situation."[32] Deeply compassionate, Anna's soul ached for her unfortunate sister who, she commiserated in a poem, had been unlucky from the beginning:

> To be wretched you were surely born
> The sport of fortune + of fools the scorn
> For all your days in one sad tenor run,
> And pass in sorrow as they first begun.[33]

As a little girl, Charity counted on Anna to console her in the face of sorrow. Anna became another mother to her little sister, willing to provide the nurturing that Grace, during her absences from the household, could not and that their stepmother, Hannah, despite her presence, would not. Anna, in Charity's words, acted

> Kind as a sister, and thy feeling heart
> In all my cares has borne a mother's part
> No grief's distress'd me but thy generous soul
> Gave all her powers my bosom to console[34]

Requiring from Anna "all her powers" of consolation betrayed a certain selfishness on Charity's part. Anna too suffered through the grief of early orphanhood, the premature loss of beloved siblings, and the entrance of an unsympathetic adult into the family home. But during childhood, Anna and Charity set a pattern of protector and protected that lasted into adulthood. Anna indulged Charity in a sense of distinctive misfortune that was not entirely accurate.

The losses in the Bryant family did not distinguish Charity or her surviving siblings from many other youths of the era. High mortality rates in the late eighteenth century caused many of those born during the 1770s and 1780s to share Charity's experience of early orphanhood. In fact, orphanhood can be seen as the archetypal experience of the era. In declaring independence, the colonies enacted metaphorical matricide against Mother Britain and patricide against King George. The Revolution overturned colonial patterns of life and unleashed a series of profound economic, religious, and social transformations. A whole cohort came of age culturally as well as biologically orphaned, forced to find their own way in a new world. This experience, it has been argued, inspired the individualist cast to early national American society.[35] Charity's sense of distinctiveness ironically likened her to many in her generation. It helps explain how she became willing to behave in a manner that challenged traditional expectations. Like the individualistic men of her generation who threw off the old habits of deference to pursue their own self-interest, Charity felt enabled to break from the past and pursue a life more radically dissimilar from her mother's, or even her aunt's, than Silence Bryant could ever have imagined.

And yet Charity remained defined by her family background. Charity took no joy in recollecting her childhood, but she would not have traded her family for another. A person's family explained who she was. When a young boy named Hiram Hurlburt Jr. stepped into Charity and Sylvia's shop in the fall of 1835, Charity pointed a finger at him and announced, "Your mother was a Bullard, she came from Athol, Mass."[36] That genealogy defined the boy in her eyes. Likewise, the fact that she was a Bryant meant a great deal to Charity and to the people she knew. The family had a cultured reputation that generated respect within New England society. Long after Charity left Massachusetts, she kept careful tabs on the family. And when her nieces and nephews had questions about their family history, they turned to Aunt Charity for answers. Responding to their inquiries was as likely to cause her consternation as give her pleasure. When her nephew John asked for a catalog of the birth and death dates of his grandparents, uncles, and aunts, Charity obligingly replied to his request, but she morosely proclaimed "of almost all it is said that they are dead!"[37] She was proud to be a Bryant, but recalling her family history brought her grief.

2

Infantile Days

1784

MARY DRAKE GAVE birth in a house that was not her own, or not for long. It was
the last day of October in the year 1784. It had been a fine fall so far, but even a
pleasant October in Massachusetts carries a chill.[1] Mary's good health fitted her to
hold her new daughter close and shield her from any drafts that filtered in from
outside. Unfortunately, Sylvia would receive no further inheritance than the
warmth of her mother's love and an affectionate family circle. Like the Bryants, the
Drakes were swept up by the winds of war. In one key regard they were set down
rather easier—all the members of the family survived; still, the Revolution took a
high toll. The financial chaos of the period bankrupted the family and left them
homeless.

Mary's husband, Thomas Drake II, was a good patriot. He served on the wartime Committee of Correspondence and Inspection in their town of Easton, on
Bridgewater's western border, and also enlisted for repeated brief stints in the
local militia.[2] He spent December 1776 in Rhode Island, guarding against British
landings; another five days in August 1778, doing the same; and finally three
months in late summer 1780 reinforcing the Continental Army. He survived
these enlistments unscathed. As a local historian of Easton put it, the military
experience of many men in the town was "limited to frequent trainings and an
occasional march to Rhode Island on an 'alarm.' Some of them never saw a Red-
coat." Thomas Drake fit that description to a tee. In a great military tradition of

the ages, he spent a good deal of time marching around, battling mosquitoes and boredom.[3]

His luck extended to the next generation. Sylvia Drake was the youngest of eight siblings. With birthdates beginning seven years after those of the Bryant children, her brothers were just a bit too young to fight in the war. Isaac, the oldest brother, born in March 1765, was only sixteen when the Battle of Yorktown effectively ended the Revolution. By the time he turned eighteen, the Treaty of Paris had been signed. Sylvia's next oldest brother, Oliver, was born in July 1767 and remained a child throughout the war years. Many Drake cousins and uncles joined the fight, marching alongside Thomas to the shores of Rhode Island. But Sylvia's siblings stayed home and passed the war years in physical safety.

The postwar years dealt the Drake family a more treacherous hand. Along with thousands of their countrymen, the Drakes were hit hard when Massachusetts entered a severe depression during the mid-1780s. The severity of this nationwide economic crisis compared in scale to the Great Depression of the 1930s. At the time, many politicians blamed small landholders for their own suffering, accusing farmers of overindulging in luxury goods and acquiring too much debt. The end of the war had reopened trade between America and Europe, and Massachusetts stores were crowded with European imports. Merchants filled the newspapers with advertisements for sumptuous goods, such as pink satin cloaks trimmed with fur and lace, silver-plated shoe and knee buckles, black silk gloves, velvet caps, bolts of Irish linen, squirrel muffs and tippets, wine glasses, brass candlesticks, pianofortes, German flutes, harpsichords, Japann'd teapots, genteel fans, Turkish figs, and leather-bound multivolume book editions. The appeal of these items after years of sacrifice and penury must have been powerful.[4]

Yet frugal Massachusetts farmers, who learned during two decades of boycotts against England to embrace thrift as a virtue, frequently resisted the allure of such temptations. Many families continued to make do in the mid-1780s with homespun and other domestic manufactures. These ordinary people blamed the economic crisis on wealthy investors who manipulated the state government in order to enrich themselves. Under the influence of securities traders, the Massachusetts state legislature passed a requisition bill in 1785 that forced ordinary farmers to pay high taxes in order to fund the interest on state debts that had been issued during the war years. Initially used to pay ordinary soldiers and farmers for their labor and goods, these securities had suffered deflation and were purchased by speculators at an extreme discount. After the war, the speculators pressured the state government to pay interest on the face value of the deflated securities. To make the full payments to bondholders the state had to raise high taxes on ordinary people, and to compound that injustice, the state demanded that the people pay their taxes in specie (silver and gold) rather than use the deflated securities as currency. By 1786, Massachusetts taxation rates were four or five times higher than they had been under British rule. According to ordinary farmers, this outrageous taxation was the cause of the state's financial distress.[5]

Whoever was to blame, Easton was hit particularly hard by the depression of the 1780s. Not a wealthy town to begin with, the Revolution had reduced Easton residents to meager circumstances. In 1775, an influx of propertyless refugees from British-occupied Boston drained the town's resources. Throughout the war years, an epidemic of thievery plagued Easton, and impoverished neighbors took each other to court over the loss of even minor property. When the depression of the 1780s hit, the people of Easton became desperate. The town soon developed a bad reputation among its neighbors. A gang of horse-thieves made their headquarters in the village, stealing from area homes and shops and then fencing the goods in Canada. The local constabulary took part in the scheme. Most of the town did not turn to larceny but simply suffered in penury.[6]

At that time, the Drakes lived in the poorest and most isolated part of Easton, along its southeastern border with West Bridgewater. Separated by a large "cranberry meadow" from the wealthier northern reaches of the town and by the enormous Hockomock Swamp from communities to the south, the family lived in an insular settlement with their near neighbors, most of whom were relatives.[7] Unfortunately, Sylvia's father could not hold on to even this marginal property. Before the Revolution, a tax valuation put Thomas Drake II's annual worth at only £. 3, well below average for the town of Easton. Thomas's small property could support only one cow, and he grew just three bushels of grain per year. These assets placed him at the very bottom of what was then called the "middling" ranks, a status defined by a head of household's possession of land or skills that earned him a competence, or freedom from wage labor under a master.[8] By contrast, Charity's father's farm was twice the size, with an annual worth of £. 6, pasturage to raise two cows, and a yearly grain yield of thirty-one bushels; her well-established grandfather, Abiel Howard, owned real estate with an annual worth of £. 25, pasture to feed twelve cows, and fields capable of producing 132 bushels of grain per year. At the outset of his professional life in 1771, Philip Bryant had good reason to expect his wealth to improve over time and his place in the middling ranks to be secured. Thomas Drake, on the other hand, stood at great risk of losing his purchase altogether.[9]

Thomas Drake was not to blame for his meager landholdings. He faced a common dilemma among New England families with many children. Both the Drakes and the Manleys, Sylvia's mother's kin, were original founders of Easton in the 1690s, and both families had produced a great number of children over the previous eight decades.[10] As the generations multiplied, each subdivided their property among their heirs into smaller and smaller parcels until the inheritors were left without sufficient land to make a living. At the time of the Revolution, this dynamic reached a critical point not only in Easton but also in villages across New England, launching a generation of migration to the west.[11]

Thomas started his adult life with only two small plots, and as his own family grew he recognized that he could not support very many mouths from those parcels. After his fourth child was born, he decided to sell his eastern inheritance and buy a larger tract in the less-expensive west. The plan was good, but the timing turned out to be poor. Thomas sold his land during the Revolution for currency that swiftly lost its value, leaving him without land or capital. He tried to stay solvent. He looked for wage labor, but the wrecked economy made it difficult for him to find paid work, and the high tax rate made it impossible to extricate himself from debt. The year that Sylvia was born, 1784, marked a low point in the condition of the people of Easton. Debt cases flooded the Court of Common Pleas. Many Drakes and Manleys were among the plaintiffs and defendants. Sylvia's father Thomas won a judgment of £. 8 in default from a fellow townsman, but it is unlikely that he collected any money from the debtor. Lawsuits could not redeem the family's circumstances.[12]

The death of Sylvia's grandfather, Thomas Drake senior, in 1788 brought a better opportunity for the family to regain their place. Thomas II served as the executor of the estate, but his father did not leave much to be sold or divided. The inventory of Thomas senior's household reads in sharp contrast to the list of luxuries advertised in the newspapers. When Sylvia's grandfather died he left behind no wine glasses or silver candlesticks, only six wooden dishes, one old pewter plate, and a pewter porringer. Instead of pink silk and satin, he left two old flannel shirts and two linen shirts. Instead of a Japann'd teapot, there was an "old iron kittle." The probate record reveals a standard of living far rougher than the genteel fantasy peddled by the newspapers. And the thirty acres of land Thomas Drake Sr. owned were sold off to settle the estate's accounts.[13]

If the Drake family had reached this impasse a couple decades later, they might have joined the great migration of landless New Englanders into early nineteenth-century factories. But New England's first successful cotton mill did not open until 1793, and mill work did not create many jobs until the nineteenth century.[14] When the Drakes went bankrupt they followed a more traditional pattern of survival: the family split up. The older children were sent to work for relatives. Nineteen-year-old Isaac went to his Uncle Joseph, seventeen-year-old Oliver went to Nathaniel Manley in Bridgewater, and ten-year-old Asaph went to Benjamin Hayward, also in Bridgewater. It seems likely that Thomas Drake II also left the family to seek work, judging from the lack of younger siblings who followed Sylvia.

What happened to Sylvia and her sisters is less clear. Fourteen-year-old Rhoda and twelve-year-old Polly were likely put out to work as domestic servants in the households of neighbors or family. Even New England families with adequate resources frequently hired their daughters out to other homes during their adolescent years. Domestic work gave daughters the housekeeping experience they would need as wives, the opportunity to accumulate resources for starting their own households after marriage, and an escape from generational conflict with their parents. An infant like Sylvia, however, could not have been separated from her mother. Sylvia, her nearest sister, Desire, and her mother, Mary, probably lived together in the homes of family members for the next several years.[15]

Sylvia's extreme youth at the moment of the family's dissolution protected her from being sent away. But Sylvia also suffered for being the youngest in the family. Unlike her older siblings, Sylvia could never clearly remember the days when her family lived all together. Instead of memories, she substituted a halcyon fantasy of togetherness, establishing a standard that ordinary life could hardly attain. An acrostic poem that Sylvia later wrote for her sister Polly—one of the few nonreligious compositions she ever penned—described the family's dispersal as an exile from Eden.

> Sister + friend the child of my mother
> I often reflect on my infantile days
> Surrounded by Parents by sister + brother
> Taught by their kindness + won by their praise
> Endear'd was this family band to each other
> Reluctant we parted delighted we met
> Parents + children + sisters and brother
> O sweet were the hours no painfull regret
> Love sat on the features, while each strove to smother
> Lifes parting pang, as they left their dear home
> Years past away, they remembered each other.
> How sweet was the thout that they no more should roam

Unable to remember the ordinary daily conflicts that no doubt arose when the family lived together, Sylvia believed that her brothers and sisters should always be close, and she grew upset when, as adults, tensions arose among them.[16]

Sylvia's older siblings may not have looked with the same honeyed gaze on their early years, but they shared her desire to keep the family together. After bankruptcy split the young family, the Drakes sought whatever opportunities they could to rejoin each other. Eventually, Sylvia's intrepid middle brother Asaph found a new place for the family to take root. Born a month after the battles of Lexington and Concord, Asaph lived and breathed the "spirit of '75." Independent-minded, entrepreneurial, and self-sufficient, Asaph personified the charter generation of Americans who shaped the new republic. Nearly a century later, when Asaph was a devout old man, he confessed to being "a very unfaithful boy" who was "always building castles in the air."[17] But his childhood inconstancy had less to do with weakness of spirit than with the age of man. Asaph personified the restless spirit that made the post-Revolutionary era a period of profound transformation in the United States.[18]

Like many boys of his generation, Asaph felt little obligation to remain with masters who did not suit him. The apprenticeship system in North America had never been as restrictive as its European counterpart. Young children, and even infants, entered into contracts to exchange their labor for room, board, and training, until they turned twenty-one, but they frequently broke those contracts. Court records from the eighteenth century are filled with disputes between masters and apprentices. Sometimes masters regained the services of errant young workers through the courts. But after the Revolution masters found it increasingly difficult to keep any hold on their apprentices. All the political talk of rights and liberties filled boys with ideas, and made public and legal opinion unsympathetic to the claims of masters. In fact, even the word *master* fell out of favor after the Revolution for being too servile. The new generation of Americans started to call their employers *bosses* instead, a Dutch word that did not carry the same subordinate connotations.[19]

Asaph was the sort of ungovernable youth who gave all apprentices in the post-Revolutionary era a bad name. When he was ten he left his first place, working on Benjamin Hayward's farm, before a year was out because he did not like it. He returned to stay with his parents until he turned thirteen, when he and his older brother Oliver went to work for Barnabas Howard at his tavern in North Bridgewater. The boys were paid only a dollar a month at the tavern. Two years later, both boys left because of the terrible conditions.

According to the 1790 federal census, the Drake family was reunited for a short spell. The census taker recorded eight residents in Thomas Drake's household, including four males below the age of sixteen and three females altogether (most likely Mary, Desire, and Sylvia).[20] But the situation did not last. In 1790 more than one-third of Easton's population was officially "warned out" of town, a strategy that early American municipalities used to avoid responsibility for providing relief to the poor.[21] Warned-out families were not always forced to leave town, but they had received notice that they could expect no support from local authorities. Propertyless and bankrupted, the Drake family may have been among those warned out in 1790. The reunited parents and siblings soon dispersed again.

At age fifteen, Asaph apprenticed himself to Eliphalet Leonard, a well-respected Bridgewater blacksmith. From early childhood, Asaph had wanted to apprentice as a smith, but this career required a lot of physical strength, and a boy could not begin training until he reached a certain size and demonstrated a strong build. Finally, Asaph had reached sufficient maturity to join Leonard's shop. In a previous age, Asaph would have remained for at least five years at Leonard's. He was happy in this full household and developed close friendships with the other apprentices. But the Revolution's disruptions, while bankrupting the older generation, had unleashed the ambitions of the younger. Disliking his master's governance, Asaph and two other apprentices ran away in the middle of the night and headed for the new state of Vermont, where they had heard there was a great deal of iron ore (and thus smithing opportunities). Asaph asked his father not to follow them; at age seventeen he was ready to declare his emancipation. "I had by this act broken my self loose and [flung] my self upon the wide world with out an individual to protect provide or care for me," Asaph later reflected.[22]

Asaph's choice proved decisive for his family. As he journeyed through New England, Asaph encountered multiple opportunities for work. Tired of being a "cringeing submissive servant," he turned down an offer of a new blacksmithing apprenticeship near Worcester, Massachusetts. In Swanzey, New Hampshire, he signed on to join a "troop of young men" who were going to build a forge in the wilds of Vermont. After being on the road for several months, he arrived in January 1793 in Weybridge, a new settlement in Addison County, on the far western border of the state, squeezed between the Green Mountains and Lake Champlain.[23] Although an initial wave of settlers had arrived in the town during the 1760s, they were chased out by Indian raids during the Revolution, and a new wave of settlers did not arrive until the mid-1780s.[24]

In Weybridge, Asaph found an opportunity to escape from the condition of servitude that had confined him since age ten. After two years of work building a grist mill on Otter Creek, which ran through Weybridge, Asaph saved enough money to buy his first fifty acres of land.[25] In another canny decision, he began courting the daughter of the mill's owner, David Belding. On December 15, 1796, twenty-one-year-old Asaph married twenty-six-year-old Louisa Belding; their first son, Elijah Graves Drake, was born seven-and-a-half months later. The marriage was not always happy, and Asaph often found fault with his wife. But the match was very advantageous to the poor young man. His father-in-law, David Belding, was the town clerk of Weybridge, and in 1797, at age twenty-two, Asaph was named as a town proprietor, joining the public body responsible for approving land claims in the village, a profitable as well as respectable appointment.[26]

After becoming a proprietor, Asaph summoned his parents and siblings to come join him in Weybridge. His father, Thomas, once a constable and now a bankrupt, saw a chance to restore the family fortunes in Vermont.[27] Accompanied by one of Asaph's brothers, Thomas set out in January 1798 with a team of horses to make the two-hundred-and-fifty-mile journey to Vermont while the sleighing was good. But barely thirty miles north tragedy struck. In Charlestown, Massachusetts, Thomas suddenly sickened and died. His son brought his body back home to Easton. Thomas Drake II was buried in the town of his birth, leaving his sons and daughters to restore the family's shattered fortunes. The following year, fifteen-year-old Sylvia and her widowed mother, Mary, finally joined Asaph's household in Weybridge.[28]

The contrast to Easton could hardly have been more profound. Easton may have been disreputable in the late eighteenth century, but it had been settled for over a century and its proximity to Boston and Providence conferred a level of sophistication that would not soon be found in Vermont. Standing on a hill overlooking Easton in the late 1790s, a spectator saw miles of farms, forests of steeples, and the furnaces of industry. The new mills of Pawtucket were less than twenty miles south. If Sylvia could have beaten a path through the thick trees and undergrowth to clamber to the top of Weybridge's Snake Mountain soon after her arrival, she would have seen a very different landscape—just a single rough-cut road along Otter Creek leading to a few scattered farms carved out of the woods. The natural landscape, of round and jagged mountain tops, dark forested hillsides, and green valley floor leading to magnificent Lake Champlain, may have been sublime. But man-made impressions on the landscape were few and far between.[29] The town had a population of fewer than five hundred. The new settlement was more than a little rough around the edges. The townspeople had little time for religion, education, or culture. Settling a new area meant clearing trees, building houses, and constructing mills. Weybridge did not even have a separate church building until 1802.

The abundance of land on the frontier created an opportunity for a young man to advance from runaway apprentice to town father in five years. It also held plentiful opportunities for a young woman to become a wife. In towns like Weybridge, couples often married young and had large families. But, as Louisa Belding learned every time her husband Asaph picked at her faults, marriage did not offer women the same release from "cringeing submissive" servitude that it brought to men. Through her older brother's initiative, Sylvia regained the family togetherness that the Revolution and its consequences had so long disrupted. But she lost the new opportunities that were opening for women at the century's close in the longest-settled villages of New England. Gazing from the top of Snake Mountain, it was hard for a young woman to find a path to independence in the wilds of Weybridge.

3

O the Example!

1787

THE MISFORTUNES OF the Bryant family did not end with the Revolution. Before the new United States constitution could be ratified, another sibling lost his life, and Charity learned, in no uncertain terms, about the great dangers that shadowed youth's passage to maturity even during peacetime. Her oldest brother Oliver's death in the army had come as a predictable blow during wartime. Ruth's death at the Revolution's close followed a long illness. But Daniel's death arrived out of nowhere. His prospects appeared rosy in the spring of 1787 when he completed his medical training and was appointed to be a tax assessor for North Bridgewater. He began courting a young woman in town and prepared to start his own family. Following his father's path, Daniel seemed poised on the brink of established respectability. But along the final stretch of his passage into manhood, something terrible went wrong. Before Thanksgiving, Daniel was dead, leaving his family in shock.[1]

In the decades following the Revolution, the "rising generation" became a subject of great concern to their elders.[2] Youth of the postwar era approached adulthood across a landscape that had transformed from the time their parents were young. The war for independence had not only broken the political bonds of empire, creating a new nation, it had torn the social fabric of the colonial world, birthing a new American culture. The authority of the older generation fell under attack; their models for maturity seemed antiquated. This cultural revolution freed American youth to craft original visions of manhood and womanhood, but their innovations came with uncertainties. New freedoms led to possibilities for phenomenal success or for crushing failure.[3] As the youngest sister in a large family, Charity grew up observing her siblings' complicated journeys into adulthood, witnessing both fore-warnings of the dangers and hints of the pleasures that awaited her. As the decline in parental authority heightened the significance of sibling relations in the post-Revolutionary era, the experiences of Charity's brothers and sisters played a pro-found role on shaping her coming of age.[4]

Daniel was the first of the Bryant siblings to reach maturity after the Revolu-tion. His service in the war itself was almost a lark. He enlisted in 1781 at age eighteen as a member in Col. Abram Washburn's "beef squad," traveling the New England countryside from Cape Cod to the westernmost settlements, requisi-tioning cows and driving them to Cambridge for slaughter to feed the troops.[5] The worst of the fighting had ended by then. Serving in the army gave Daniel an enjoyable opportunity to escape the confines of the family home and the heavy load of farm work demanded by his parents, while exposing him to little physical danger.

Daniel's real difficulties began when he returned home. His grandfather's and father's examples pointed Daniel toward an obvious choice of profession as a doc-tor. But to become his own man, Daniel would have to establish himself as an independent citizen. During the colonial period, manhood in New England had been associated with possessing a competence. By transforming subjects into citi-zens, the Revolution added a new political dimension to the requirements of manhood. During the 1780s and 1790s, it became necessary for young men to dem-onstrate their ability to act as members of the body politic and enter into civic association with fellow manly citizens. Success in this political sphere required a reputation for possessing the republican virtues of public integrity, personal honor, and fraternal loyalty.[6]

Daniel, like many of his generation, found the opportunity to demonstrate his political virtues within the realm of masculine friendship. The Revolution had polit-icized a style of friendship first made popular by the mid-eighteenth-century litera-ture of "sensibility." Novels and poetry within this genre encouraged women and men to demonstrate deep feelings, often within friendships, as a sign of their refine-ment. In the early republic, close connections between men became regarded as not only refined, but a necessary ingredient for national unity. Political thinkers argued that republican politics required social affections to replace the tyrannical bonds of monarchy and combine individualistic Americans into a political community. Modeling themselves on the famous friendships of the classical republican era, American friends adopted Greek and Roman names for each other and boldly declared the permanency of their mutual affection.[7]

Most young people found personal as well as political satisfaction in these connections. Friendship was more than necessary hardtack to feed the body politic: it was ambrosial manna for a person's soul. In Daniel's case, pursuing friendships served both the political goal of defining his civic worthiness and the personal purpose of arming him against the depressive tendencies that shadowed many members of the Bryant family. Writing to his cousin and close friend Gideon Howard in the fall of 1786, Daniel described friendship as his "most sovereign antidote against lowness of spirit." Echoing the popular beliefs of the day, Daniel praised the "free Communication of Sentiments between two friends without Reserve" as "the greatest pleasure that we Enjoy upon Earth." He ranked the emotional satisfaction of friendship even above courtship, an activity that occupied a great deal of his attention as he completed his medical training.[8]

Historians of friendship often regard the early national era as a golden age, when men and women could express same-sex affections unshadowed by the suspicions of sexuality that scared later generations away from physical closeness and declarations of mutual love.[9] This claim contains more than a germ of truth, but its nostalgic perspective overlooks a less pleasant aspect. Freighting friendship with intense emotions made it ripe for negative feelings like jealousy, envy, resentment, and rage, as well as for positive feelings. For Daniel, friendship went from boon to curse with remarkable speed in the spring of 1787, when he received an upsetting letter from Gideon Howard. The argument that followed revealed how the "free Communication of Sentiments" that Daniel celebrated could lead to "infinite pain," as well as the "greatest pleasure."[10]

Like so many fights, the rift between Daniel and Gideon began over a woman. Gideon had caught wind of rumors that were circulating about a young woman "friend" of Daniel's, presumably somebody he was courting. Although cross-sexed friendships were not unknown at the time, the word "friend" was used as a common synonym for lover—husbands and wives often referred to each other by the name.[11] Any ambiguity about the nature of the connection between Daniel and his female friend contributed to the circulating rumors, reported by Gideon, that the young woman in question was leading Daniel on by pretending to have stronger feelings for him than she really possessed. The rumor blemished the girl's reputation by suggesting she was a coquette or flirt, but more seriously for Daniel, it called his own manliness into question. His culture defined masculinity by the qualities of clear-sighted reason and good judgment. If Daniel had been fooled by a flirtatious young woman, it spoke poorly of his character.

Gideon was probably trying to save his cousin from further public humiliation by relaying the gossip, but Daniel did not take the letter in that spirit. Instead, he accused Gideon of betraying him by failing to defend the young woman's character and, through extension, his own. "A person that can [be] contented and easy in company where the character of one that he calls his friend is treated with disrespect, and not endeavor to defend it deserves not the name of friend," Daniel berated his cousin. He pledged to defend his female friend, demonstrating the loyalty that Gideon lacked. He swore that her character was as "spotless" as "the Robe of Moses worn at the transfiguration" and that she had never misled him. "From a long and intimate acquaintance with her I can aver that I have ever found her agreeable and entertaining possessed of sentiments that can fully justify my friendship for her," he asserted. "Far from receiving any ill treatment from her, I have ever been used by her with all the sincerity and openness that characterizes sincere friendship," and "I have neither been Decieved nor Imposed upon." For Gideon to repeat the circulating rumors implied that Daniel was a "fool" who lacked "discernment"—in other words, the very opposite of a worthy republican citizen. If he entertained Gideon's warnings, Daniel argued, he did not deserve to be called a man: "Good Heaven! That I should arrogate to myself the name of man and yet suffer the character of my friend to be stigmatized to my face without complaining or even defending it." It was a matter of public honor for Daniel to defend the young woman he had been courting.[12]

Once Daniel had declared true friendship to be the greatest antidote to low spirits that he knew; now "false" friendship proved as terrible a source of misery. Gideon's letter, Daniel wrote, "cut me to the heart," "wounded my feelings," and "injured" the "tender & delicate fibres of a feeling Heart." Although he declared himself above the "judgment of the Rabble," the idea that his fellow townsmen had his affairs "constantly in their mouths" drove him crazy, making him appear a "madman" in some people's eyes.[13] Looking back on this period many decades later, Charity misremembered herself as much younger than ten years old at the time.[14] It was as if the spectacle of Daniel's unraveling made adulthood appear so terrifying for a girl on the brink of adolescence that she willed herself to return to childhood.

No record remains of the cause of Daniel's death, only meager clues. It seems unlikely to have been the consumption that killed his mother and older sister. Daniel's energy and activity in the year before his death, finishing his medical studies, receiving election to a town office, and courting a potential wife, do not suggest a man suffering from the slow wasting that gave consumption its name. Additionally, while family records indicated consumption where it was the cause of death, they left the reason for Daniel's death unnamed. The speed and silence surrounding his death, coupled with the evidence of his emotional distress in the months immediately beforehand, suggest another possibility: suicide.

Suicidal tendencies ran in the Bryant family. Charity would suffer from them in her twenties. Her nephew Edwin Bryant ended his own life in 1869. The most famous poem that William Cullen Bryant wrote in his youth, the death-themed

"Thanatopsis," was inspired at least in part by his morbid impressions following the suicide of a young honeymooner in his village.[15] The rupture in Daniel's friendship with Gideon, the insinuations against his manliness, and perhaps the failure of a much-desired courtship could all have contributed to a suicidal depression in the young man. At the time, critics of the culture of sensibility worried that the intense emotional style could inspire suicides. Only months after Daniel's death, a newspaper essay warned readers of the dangers that disappointment in courtship posed to young people of "sensibility." In "many instances," the author warned, a coquette's "unmeaning and ungenerous conduct has cost a worthy man his happiness and his life." When there was an "excess of sensibility," like Daniel revealed in his letters, even "irreproachable" characters could be driven to take their own lives.[16]

Popular novels of the early republic echoed the notion that the wrong choice of friends could have fatal consequences. Problematic friendships catalyze the suicides of several of the young male characters in the novels of Charles Brockden Brown, published in the 1790s. Young women in the era's novels are more likely to die from illegitimate childbirth following seductions engineered by false friends. But both types of stories highlight the profound dangers of misdirected sociability.[17] In the view of period novels, the crises in Daniel's friendship and courtship were sufficient cause for suicide. On the other hand, it is possible that Daniel died from a swift-moving disease (such as typhus) to which he was exposed in the course of his medical practice. His family's failure to record his cause of death could be an oversight, not an act of concealment.

Either way, it would not be strange if Charity associated Daniel's demise with the crisis in his relationships immediately prior. Daniel's sufferings served as a clear warning about the perils of friendship. At least the lessons from this incident were counterbalanced by the contrasting example from another of Charity's siblings, her third oldest brother, Peter. Light-spirited and witty, perhaps immune to the depression that afflicted Daniel, Peter enjoyed his own boisterous friendship with their cousin Gideon during the same year that Daniel and Gideon's friendship imploded. While Daniel wrote to rebuke Gideon for his lack of loyalty, Peter wrote him praising the pleasures and advantages of social gatherings. Peter was so committed to the precept that "the love of society is natural to mankind," that his father, Philip, had to scold him for "carry[ing] on very high" at nighttime "frolicks" involving alcohol and dancing. "O the Example, the Example!" Philip bemoaned. Indeed, through Peter's example, Charity received a sense of the pleasures that friendship could yield, as well as the perils.[18]

Peter was born in 1767. Too young to serve in the Revolution, he had even greater need than Daniel to demonstrate his manly virtue through his friendships. He modeled his intimacy with his cousin Gideon on the classical story of Damon and Pythias, a favorite in the eighteenth century. The Ciceroan tale, about two young students of

Pythagoras who proved their willingness to sacrifice their lives for one another, was retold in Benjamin Franklin's classic *Poor Richard's Almanac*.[19] In the same season that Daniel was lobbing furious accusations of betrayal against Gideon, Peter was pledging his loyalty to Gideon. "My dear lov'd friend," Peter addressed Gideon in a 1787 poem, "Damon can never prove a treach'rous friend." Peter swore his "heart" was "unsuspicious and sincere," that he would never mix "flattery with falsehood" or "cheat his friends with one Dissembld tear." Unlike his brother, Peter promised never to let a woman come between himself and Gideon. He swore that if a girl whom Peter admired proved "unkind," still "Damon and YOU must never, never, part." Six years younger than Daniel, and not yet ready to marry, Peter treated courtship as a laughing matter. "I stole a kiss," Peter teased, from the "ruby lips" of a young maid Gideon admired. But he laughed "there is no danger; this is only rallery."[20]

If Peter made friendship seem untroubled, his progress to maturity presented its own warning lesson to Charity. The problems for Peter arose not in his friendships but in his relations to his parents. His experiences typified the larger generational struggle between those who came of age before and after the Revolution, but they were also particular to dynamics within the Bryant family. As a younger son in a large family, Peter was born to limited advantage. Although oldest sons did not inherit all the family property in eighteenth-century New England, where primogeniture had never taken hold, they typically had access to more material support than younger brothers.[21] After Oliver's death during the Revolution, Daniel as the next oldest brother received his parents' support for his medical studies. But Peter, who followed both Daniel and another brother, Bezaliel, did not receive the same advantage. Despite his desire to study medicine, Peter's father, Philip, and stepmother, Hannah, insisted that he stay at home and work on the family farm.

If Peter had been born to an earlier generation, he might have put up with the unfortunate consequence of his birth order. But Peter was a child of the Revolution, determined to establish his independence. Already, at age nineteen, he had a strong political voice. In the heady days of February 1787, as tax resisters led by Daniel Shays battled Massachusetts forces and calls circulated for a national political convention to be held in Philadelphia, Peter took eager part in the public discussion. Gathering with other men at a local shop to talk politics, Peter would hold forth on his views, "silencing" the other men, he joked, "with the thunder of my eloquence!" In his typical jocular fashion, Peter drew a picture of himself for cousin Gideon: "strutting across the floor with cane in hand, stretching up and stroaking my belly; assuming a big look, a look of infinite importance, and attacking those conceited dabblers in politics, with which that climate abound." Joke as he might, Peter's ambitions were no laughing matter. Eventually, he would serve for a decade in the Massachusetts state legislature as an influential leader of the Federalist Party.[22]

Peter's independent spirit, so typical of his generation, would not submit to parental authority. He complained bitterly about his parents' demands for his labor. While Peter personally identified with Damon, student of Pythagoras, his parents had forced him to follow the example of another classical Damon: the shepherd-hero of Virgil's pastoral poems. "Mourn thy Damons lot unkind," Peter wrote sorrowfully in his poem to Gideon. He had to "Exchange the Studies pleasing to his mind / For rural toils and labours of the field." The choice was not his own. "He heard his sentence pass'd with sad regret," for his parents condemned him to "leave of thy studies." Instead "the rural task now his hands Employments / And to the fields his cares must be confin'd." While Gideon and Daniel were at their studies, Peter complained, "Brown exercise must be thy Damons lot."[23]

Peter's disappointment did not last for long. The next season, following Daniel's death, Peter went to study medicine with a French doctor, Lewis Leprilete, in the nearby town of Norton. But the breach between Peter and his parents was never entirely resolved. Peter remained resentful that Philip and Hannah had put him to work rather than send him to school. After his medical training, Peter moved away to the far western frontier of Massachusetts. He maintained a cordial correspondence with his aging parents, but he rarely returned to North Bridgewater for visits.[24] More than a century later, his descendants kept alive the memory of Hannah Richards Bryant as a "dour, domineering" "taskmaster" who "kept him at farm labor until he rebelled."[25]

The generational conflict between Peter and his parents afflicted the other siblings within the Bryant family as well. Charity's brother Bezaliel (Beza for short), born in 1765, disappeared from the family circle as an adult, moving to New York State to work as a merchant. Beza rarely contacted his parents after the move, although for a time he kept in touch with Peter, his nearest-aged sibling. Peter forwarded the little information he had from Beza to his father and stepmother in yearly letters.[26] When Philip died in 1816, Beza had been entirely out of touch for many years.[27] Interestingly, his parents' decease seemed to reopen the door to his involvement with the family. In the remaining decades of his life Beza spent time with his surviving siblings and nieces and nephews and kept in touch by letter when they were separated.[28]

No evidence remains of the relationship between Charity's parents and Cyrus, the youngest brother in the Bryant family, who died in 1798 when he was still in his twenties, but the generational conflict that divided Peter and Bezaliel from their parents seems to have afflicted older sisters Anna and Silence as well. The evidence suggests that both young women were driven by the same desire to escape the family home as their brothers. Unfortunately, the range of choices available to the Bryant sisters was far more restricted than the possibilities available to their brothers. The

Revolution had opened the door to new demands for education by young women of the rising generation, but few new social freedoms accompanied the broadened scope of learning. This gap between expanding intellectual aspirations and limited freedom of action created a dangerous climate for young women in the late eighteenth century. If they pursued their own interests too avidly, they risked sullying their reputations and destroying their futures.[29]

The well-known story of Elizabeth Whitman, a Connecticut woman who died in 1788, pointed out the dangers of too much intellectual ambition to young women in Anna and Silence Bryant's generation. Born in 1752 into a prominent family, Whitman came of age during the Revolution. Her parents arranged an unwelcome engagement for her to a respectable minister, but his death before the marriage took place prompted Whitman to forge an independent identity for herself as a writer. Through epistolary relationships with prominent authors of her generation, including the poet Joel Barlow, Whitman succeeded for a while at establishing a literary persona. However, like Daniel Bryant, she ultimately paid a terrible cost for her friendships. In her mid-thirties Whitman became pregnant. The identity of the father remains unknown (in addition to Joel Barlow, people have suggested future vice president Aaron Burr or his cousin Pierrepont Edwards as candidates). Whoever the father was, he would not or could not marry her. Perhaps seeking to hide her condition, Whitman traveled to a tavern in Massachusetts where she gave birth to a stillborn child, then died. Whitman's family's importance made her death a public scandal, the subject of both gossip and newspaper reportage. A decade later, her story served as the inspiration for one of the first American novels, Hannah Foster's bestselling *The Coquette* (1797).[30]

As Anna Bryant entered her teens in the late 1780s, she showed the same interest in poetry that had inspired Elizabeth Whitman to seek an independent life. But rather than delay marriage, like many intellectual women who sought a window of unfettered adulthood before confining themselves to the domestic labor of eighteenth-century maternity, Anna moved quickly into courtship with Henry Kingman, marrying at age twenty in January 1792. Younger sister Silence, who did not share her sisters' poetic tendencies, settled into marriage even earlier, becoming the wife of her cousin Ichabod Bryant in December 1792, when she was only eighteen years old (even younger than her mother had been at her marriage to Philip Bryant).[31] Both women moved to distant towns with their new husbands. When financial hardships forced Anna and her husband to move back in with her father many years later, she was eager to leave again as soon as possible, saying that she would regret "a few good friends whom I shall leave behind," but remaining notably silent on the subject of her aged parents.[32]

Anna's and Silence's marriages in 1792 left Charity, aged fifteen, the only child in her parents' home. Her situation was uneasy. In Charity's words, she never experienced any "Domestic peace" under her parents' roof.[33] The generational conflict that drove her brothers and sisters from home reached a crescendo in the relations between Charity and her parents. The trouble began between Charity and her stepmother. "The old lady," according to Charity, seldom thought "favorably" of her.[34] It is unsurprising that Hannah's domineering personality clashed with Charity's emerging assertiveness. By her teens, Charity had already begun to express her characteristic sharp wit, self-confidence, and authoritative demeanor. Charity's more accommodating and gentle sister Anna called her youngest sibling "your ladyship" in jest.[35]

The personality conflict between stepdaughter and mother was likely complicated by Hannah's demands for Charity's time and Charity's resistance to accommodating her. Maintaining a rural household in the late eighteenth century required a nearly endless routine of domestic labor, from hand washing and sewing to gardening, preserving, baking, weaving, and quilting. Many households hired young women to assist with these numerous tasks. Hannah undoubtedly expected Charity to devote her days to laboring for the good of the family. But Charity had a powerful aversion to domestic work.[36] As Charity entered her late teens, her drive for greater learning likely added to the household conflict. Many New England women born before the 1760s were not even literate; and most who could read and write, like Hannah Bryant, considered literacy a tool for household management rather than a means of self-actualization.[37] When Charity opted to spend her time reading or writing rather than washing or cooking, Hannah probably grew even more frustrated with her disobedient stepdaughter.

Discouraged at home, Charity, like her brothers, sought out friendships in which to express her emerging sense of self. During her teens, she found a twin soul in a young woman named Mercy Ford who came from the nearby town of Pembroke. The girls shared an interest in literature, especially the verses of Edward Young, author of the ten-thousand-line *Night Thoughts*, a gothic poem about youth, friendship, and early death. The poem held special significance for Charity.[38] The first edition of *Night Thoughts* was published in North America in 1777, shortly after Charity's mother's death. Subsequent editions coincided with additional losses within the Bryant family. Young's themes of mortality and loss resonated with Charity's experiences.

Charity found solace from her family troubles in reading poetry with Mercy, but as for her older brother Daniel, friendship also became a source of trouble. When Charity turned twenty in 1797, and showed more interest in pursuing her friendship with Mercy than in marrying like her sisters had done, her situation at home became even more difficult. Charity's father, Philip, who had offered his daughter a modicum of protection from her stepmother's cruelty, grew disapproving. Philip Bryant was not the easiest man to get along with. Although one biographer described him as possessing a "calm and even temper," his children saw a different side of his personality at home.[39] He could be harsh and withholding, especially to Charity. After one dust-up, Anna wrote consolingly to Charity that she was "much chagrined and mortified at the conduct of the Old Esq. but I hope that his crabbed temper will meet with something to humble it that he may treat his fellow creatures with a little more decency and respect."[40] As Charity came of age and developed into a different sort of woman, her father withdrew his support for her. Shortly after her twentieth birthday, Philip demanded that Charity leave the family home.

His rejection cut Charity to the quick. The early loss of her mother stamped Charity with a sense of abandonment, making her especially vulnerable to her father's hostility. In her autobiographical poem, "A Child of Melancholy," Charity voiced her heartbreak over the loss of her father's love:

> A father too once have I known
> In whom were affection and truth
> But his truth + affection have flown
> Away, like the breeze of the South'
> He has driven me far from his door,
> Without home, without friends and forlorn
> The thought of which tortures still more
> A heart that already is torn.[41]

Anna pitied her sister's "situation—cast upon the wide world without protection—and presented with the malevolence of one who ought to love and cherish you."[42] Charity poured out her despondence on paper, "Oh I reflect how hard my fate / And almost meet despair!"[43]

As Charity faced her own crisis on the passage into adulthood, the specter of her older siblings' troubles cast a grim shadow over her future. But if Charity, like many of the Bryants, tended toward depression, her morose character was limned with steely resolve. Her father's rejection led her to "almost meet despair," but she did not succumb. Instead, she packed her bags and set off to find refuge in Anna's home. Over the following decade, Charity's resolute determination to be true to her own desires caused challenges far beyond her family circle. Her passion for making friends with other young women became the cause of tensions in a number of the communities where she resided during her twenties. The intellectual aspirations and uncompromising spirit that provoked the anger of her parents drew the great admiration of other young women in her generation, and eventually their admiration drew talk.

4

Mistress of a School

1797

A SEA OF faces stretched before Charity's eyes. At the front of the class sat the little ones, barely able to work a slate. The children in the middle rows were old enough to have mastered forming letters, but most, she wrote to a friend, were too "dull and lazy" to put them to good use. The children in the back could hardly be called by that name; some were taller than Charity. The thought of trying to instill learning in any of their cloudy minds made Charity feel "perplex'd, sick, and discouraged." There were only a few weeks left in the term, but Charity's patience was running thin. She dismissed the children to play outside, sat down at her table, and pulled out the piece of paper and pen that she had tucked away earlier that morning.[1]

What Charity appreciated most about teaching were the solitary moments before the students arrived or after they went out to play. In those quiet times she could devote her attention to her own writing. Sometimes she worked on poems; other days she wrote correspondence. Both required deep concentration. Charity crafted her letters with great care, trying to strike the right tone of intimacy without overreaching, to find a sympathetic ear for her grief without sounding pathetic. There was also penmanship to consider, and attention needed not to smudge the wet ink on the page. Good writing required focus. It took time and space free from the demands of others. The schoolhouse without its children met those needs.

Teaching rescued Charity from domestic tyranny. Expelled from home for her independent-mindedness, Charity relied on her strong intellect to support her new situation. By age twenty, Charity had acquired sufficient learning to teach a district (elementary) school. Like most girls of her generation, Charity probably did not receive any formal education past the district-school level, but she grew up in a literary family and received a strong education at home. Charity's well-developed mind represented her family's most lasting legacy. Although she never knew her doctor-poet grandfather Abiel Howard, who died before her birth, she probably grew up reading from his library, which her father, Philip, executor of Abiel's estate, had the opportunity to acquire. Philip was a book collector himself and had even bought and sold books in the 1750s to help finance his medical education. During Charity's childhood, he served several terms on North Bridgewater's school committee. Charity's well-formed mind, if not her determination to flex it, was the product of design.[2]

Many of Philip and Silence's children, including Charity's older siblings Ruth, Peter, and Anna, followed their grandfather's example by writing poetry. Charity probably learned the craft of writing from Peter and Anna, who were her closest friends in the family.[3] To later generations, this family skill at writing letters and poetry became known as a Bryant trait. P. P. Kingman, a grandniece descended from Charity's sister Anna, once complained that "there is not Bryant enough about me to make me a good penman or a fast writer." Charity, on the other hand, embodied that Bryant characteristic. As her grandniece put it, Charity could fill a sheet of paper in "fifteen minutes" since "Charity is a Bryant and the Bryants are a family to whom the muses are peculiarly propitious."[4] As another distant relative put it, the Bryants were "natural poets."[5]

Charity taught her first class in the winter of 1797–98 in Dartmouth, Massachusetts, near the Rhode Island border, where she had traveled to live with her married sister Anna Kingman after she was driven from home. Boarding with the Kingmans and teaching at the district school gave Charity her first taste of independence. Although she did not much like the students, Charity stuck with teaching on and off for nearly a decade. Compelled by circumstances to return to Bridgewater in the summer of 1798, Charity discovered her beloved brother Cyrus and his wife, Polly, both sick with consumption and living with her parents. Charity remained home long enough to nurse the couple until Polly's death after which Cyrus departed to join his brother Peter in Cummington, in the Hampshire Hills of western Massachusetts (he died upon arriving).[6] Within months, Charity moved to Cummington as well, where she began teaching in the neighboring Plainfield district during the summer of 1799. The year after she taught in Pelham, toward the middle of the state, where Anna and her husband had since moved. Forced by ill health to return to her parents' home again in the fall of 1800, Charity took a break from teaching. But she returned to the classroom on numerous occasions during the years that followed.[7]

The wages were never high. One summer she received only six shillings a week (roughly the price of three gallons of beer). The summer that Charity taught in Pelham, Anna and her husband did not charge for boarding, letting Charity keep her full pay of eight shillings six pence per week. In addition, the couple allowed Charity to control her own time "before and after school." This situation, Charity wrote, was "a better chance than I ever had before." The students were "dull and awkward and very trying to the patience." The long walk from Anna's house to the school was grueling on a hot day. But the job gave her a freedom that was rare for a young unmarried woman of the time. She had time to write.[8]

The limited self-determination that Charity achieved through teaching during her twenties reflected an important development in American society. Prior to the Revolution, the most common waged employment for young unmarried women was domestic service, which offered little independence or mental challenge.[9] Some married women ran "dame schools" in their homes, where they taught little children to read, but very few women taught in the district schools. (Girls were not even admitted to many Massachusetts district schools until shortly before the Revolution.) Luckily for Charity, teaching opportunities for single women expanded after independence. The Revolution had inspired a movement to improve education for girls, creating a generation of young women with the skills to instruct children in elementary education. Towns across New England soon recognized these women as a potential labor force. State laws mandated that towns maintain district schools for children, but anti-tax sentiment drove local authorities to run the schools at the lowest cost possible. Women became attractive candidates for district teaching jobs because, by virtue of being women, they could be paid far less than men. The meager wages did not prevent women from flocking to the work. By 1830, more than half of district-school teachers in Massachusetts were women; one in five Massachusetts women in the nineteenth century taught school at some point in her life. Charity stood at the vanguard of this trend.[10]

The educational reformer Horace Mann tried to explain the feminization of the teaching profession in terms of women's natural proclivities. A woman was suited to working with young children, Mann claimed, because "she holds her commission from nature. In the well-developed female character there is always a preponderance of affection over intellect."[11] But few women teachers saw the work that way. They often complained about their pupils' stupidity, loudness, and disinterest. Most women did not become teachers from a great desire to spend their days with children—they could achieve that goal by following the typical path of marriage and motherhood. Charity's decision to teach in the summer of 1799 indicated a rejection of childrearing responsibilities, particularly of the responsibility to care for Cyrus and Polly's orphaned son and daughter, work that traditionally fell on the family spinster.[12] Charity's refusal to assume responsibility for the children enraged her parents, who considered her decision selfish and expelled her from their home again. Teaching enabled her to live without their support and thus escape the fate of becoming a foster mother.[13]

Serving as a teacher offered middling-class young women a window of time in which to earn wages, live apart from their families, pursue intellectual interests, and still preserve their good names.[14] Other varieties of paid work, especially working-class city trades like operating a tavern, selling food in the public market, or sewing clothes for pay, were disreputable because they forced women to mix with men outside the home. Teaching offered a halfway point between the close oversight of domestic service and the promiscuity of urban labor. School teachers typically "boarded around" with students' families, spending two weeks at a time in each household. They were never out of the public eye, but neither did they answer to a single family. Teachers were everyone's responsibility, but no one's in particular. The situation did not free a young woman from surveillance, but as long as she acted within limits, a teacher could achieve a certain independence and keep her reputation intact.

When Charity's friend Nancy Warner began teaching at a school eleven miles from home, she wrote to Charity about her excitement at being "freed from parental restraints and commands" and gaining the opportunity "to enjoy true liberty."[15] Charity's friend Lydia Richards, who started teaching school when she was seventeen, also reveled in the "liberty" she gained through the job. "My circumstances were never so favorable to happiness," she wrote Charity. "I have been almost free from all cares except those which respect myself and school—have been at liberty to go and come when I chose." Her students often irritated her, and the schoolhouse could be stuffy and unpleasant, but the job was a great release from the work at home, where her duties included spinning, weaving, sewing, and knitting for her six younger siblings. Lydia had a happy and loving family, but she still jumped at the opportunity to escape their never-ending calls on her attention.[16] For Charity, whose home life was deeply troubled, the schoolhouse appeared doubly attractive.

Charity found more than refuge in the schoolroom; she discovered a place to flourish. During her teaching years, Charity matured into a highly respected correspondent and poet, crafting a persona as a writer that defined her until the end of her life. Beginning in 1797, she embarked on a series of epistolary relationships with fellow teachers and family members, some of which continued for fifty years. The early national era was a time when letters were high art, not simply a means of conveying information.[17] The great literary works of the age, such as Samuel Richardson's novel *Pamela* (1740), were often told through letters. People opened personal correspondence with high expectations, shaped by the superb examples they read in print. Charity's letters made good on that promise. Her friends heaped praise on the letters she wrote, even as they apologized for their own weak attempts. Mary Hovey, a schoolteacher, wrote regretfully to Charity that she could never "write with as much propriety, ease, and elegance, as *you* can."[18] Schoolteacher Maria Clark felt the same way: "I heartily wish that I could compose with that freedom and elegance that glows throughout the whole of your writings."[19] Lydia admired the "liberty and freedom" in Charity's letters and apologized that "my pen is not the pen of a ready writer."[20] Charity's skillfulness intimidated her. "I am unable to write suitably to such a person as yourself," Lydia told Charity. But she kept going anyway, in order to receive Charity's letters in return.[21]

Charity's letters shared more than a generic resemblance to the letters of *Pamela*. In her correspondence, Charity compared herself to the novel's tragic heroine. "My life has been from the beginning one scene of troubles, crosses, and disappointments and such it will continue undoubtedly to the End!" Charity began a letter to her sister-in-law Sally. She followed with a couple foreboding lines of poetry quoted from *Pamela*: "Who from the mornings brightest ray / Can promise what will be the day."[22] Charity identified with Pamela, who suffered at the mercy of forces far more powerful than herself but tried to maintain her virtue and faith in the face of tribulation. Like Pamela, Charity relied on writing as an escape from her sorrows. Charity could relate when Richardson's heroine declared that she could not "live without a pen in my hand."[23] By styling herself after this popular heroine, Charity wrote letters that brought the excitement of novel-reading into the realm of experience for her friends.

Their responses resonated with sympathy for her sufferings. "Your bosom should no more heave with sighs," Lydia wrote to Charity in 1800, "your heart should no more be oppressed with sorrow, and misfortune should no more be heaped on you, but, on *me* should they light, in my heart should the sorrow of affliction rest, and yours should no more be pierced with anguish."[24] Lydia cried along with Charity's letters just the way that many young women cried along to *Pamela*. The letters were absorbing to Lydia because they painted such a contrast to her own unremarkable life, living at home with her affectionate parents.

Charity's poems were as accomplished as her letters. She wrote her initial poems for other teachers who were her friends. Exchanging handwritten poems was a common practice among respectable young women in the late eighteenth and early nineteenth centuries. The tradition began in part as an adaptation to the social stigma against published women authors. Women exchanged handwritten poems and copied friends' compositions into their own commonplace books, so they could circulate their writings without offending propriety by having their writings appear in print. Friends valued these handwritten gifts for material and emotional reasons. The price of paper led many letter-writers to cram as many words as possible onto each sheet, often turning sheets ninety degrees and penning a second page crosswise over the first. But in a poem given as a gift the words were permitted to luxuriate in space. A poem's visual appeal mattered, and letters were illustrated with great swoops and swirls of ink to make each line beautiful. Poems were also valued as gifts because they required a high expense in time, a precious commodity among young women whose daylight hours were busy with work. Writing during the evening required candles, another pricey commodity. Most of all, poems had value as gifts because they signaled emotional intimacy and trust between the giver and the getter. Poems symbolized a connection that ran deeper than superficial pleasantries.[25]

Even copying out the work of a famous author for a friend was a sign of emotional intimacy. Choosing just the right lines required familiarity, a knowledge of poetry, and good taste. Writing personalized verses required something more—creativity, of course, but also the willingness to pin your heart on your sleeve. Fashionable ladies of the time might have breezily composed poems for each other without much effort. But the daughters of ordinary families in rural Massachusetts assigned a great deal of importance to the task. They wrote poems to amuse each other, but also to convey true sentiments and to establish lasting intimacies. To make the task easier, most aspiring poets chose to write in an established genre like the acrostic, where the first letter of each line spelled out a name. More confident poets wrote rebuses, or poems that contained secret messages to be decoded.

To write a good rebus took an extra-clever mind. Charity's friends and family esteemed her especially good at this task. "I wish you would write me a Rebus on my name," Charity's friend Lavinia, a fellow teacher, beseeched her. "I love to read your poetry." Lavinia was a self-assured woman who founded her own female seminary in South Carolina, then later in life married an artist (who invented the squeezable paint tube) and moved to London. Despite her courageous character, she felt nervous about sharing her own writing with Charity. "I have written a Rebus + if it was not quite beneath your attention I would send it to you," she wrote hesitantly.[26] It does not seem that Lavinia ever worked up the courage to send her rebus to Charity, since no signed poems by Lavinia are preserved in Charity's and Sylvia's papers. Maybe the rebus simply went missing, but Lavinia's example follows the model for Charity's other friendships. Charity wrote many more acrostics and rebuses than she received in return.

She set to work on her rebuses and acrostics by assembling a list of words whose first initials spelled out her subject's name. Charity began an acrostic for Lydia Richards by jotting the words "Love Youth Death Innocence Aurora Religion India Charity Happiness Adversity Reason Delight Sorrow" down on a scrap of paper.[27] The final poem is missing but the list of words, almost a poem in themselves, succinctly captures the pleasure that more-experienced Charity took in her emerging friendship with younger, innocent Lydia. The words also revealed Charity's skillfulness by seamlessly working her own name and feelings into the acrostic.

By her early twenties, Charity was a nimble enough poet to venture a wide variety of poetic genres Some of her works made only the slightest reliance on the acrostic form. "A Poem to a friend," which Charity wrote while teaching in Dartmouth in winter 1798, repeated the initials A S, three times for her friend, but was formally structured into quatrains of iambic pentameter following an ABAB rhyming scheme.[28] Charity also used Isaac Watts's familiar hymn meter (quatrains of alternating eight- and six-syllable lines, following an ABAB rhyme scheme) to write devotional poetry and adapted hymn meter for her autobiographical poetry, an innovation later credited to Emily Dickinson. Charity's poems may not have the incandescent spark that makes Dickinson's poetry so timeless, but they are undoubtedly clever.[29]

Few of her contemporaries could rise to Charity's standard. Unwilling even to try, several of her correspondents repaid her acrostics with elegantly copied poems from published works. The right choice of lines could still be personal, even if they were not composed specifically for the recipient. A friend named Mary Barron gave Charity two beautifully scripted poems to express her regard. The first, "Queen Mary's Lamentation," was a traditional song about Mary Queen of Scot's imprisonment. The queen in the poem is both a tragic figure, whose vain sighs are echoed back by the stone prison walls, and a powerful figure, condemned to death for the threat she poses to the English monarch, Queen Elizabeth. Charity's decision to preserve the poem in her papers throughout her life testifies to the wisdom of Mary Barron's choice of subject. Queen Mary's mixture of power, charisma, and misfortune echoed Charity's own qualities and made for a pleasing comparison.[30] The second poem Mary Barron selected, a set of love verses from Tobias Smollet's novel *Roderick Random* (1748), also featured a tragic heroine, Monimia (originally from Thomas Otway's 1680 play *The Orphan*). Monimia's parentless misfortune again was well calculated to appeal to Charity's sense of melancholy and distinctiveness.[31]

When Charity's correspondents dared to share their own poetry, they typically embedded these gifts in apologies for their inadequacy, and acknowledgments of Charity's natural superiority. Mary Hovey, who praised Charity's writing so effusively, hesitated to send Charity any of her own poetry. But when the two women had a disagreement, Mary sent an apologetic acrostic on Charity's name to prove the depth of her regard. The poem expressed awe for Charity, whom she described as a nearly heavenly creature: "Charity prolific grace / High in the Heavens she reigns / And when on Earth she finds a place / Raps the soul in Heavenly strains." What the lines lacked in finesse they made up in devotion.[32]

Many of Charity's fellow teachers praised her writing in adoring terms. The heightened quality of their language was typical of the eighteenth-century culture of sensibility. Charity, who kept a handwritten copy of British author Helen Maria Williams's influential paean "To Sensibility" among her papers, shared her brothers' appreciation for this ardent style.[33] Sensibility, however, does not explain the expressions of self-abasement that Charity's correspondents frequently added to their effusions. Mary Hovey, for example, did not stop at telling Charity how marvelous her writing was; she continued by acknowledging her recognition of "*my* inferiority to *yourself*."[34] Such apologies reveal how Charity's brilliance both attracted and intimidated her friends.

Maria Clark also cast herself in a subordinate position to Charity, whom she addressed by the pet name "Ermina." Like Mary Hovey, Maria acknowledged Charity's superior writing skills and declared "I aspire not to an equality with Ermina."[35] Instead of sending Charity poems of her own composition, Maria copied out a poem from Sarah Fielding's 1749 book *The Governess, or The Little Female Academy*, the first English novel written for girls, which told the story of a boarding-school teacher's relationships with her young charges. The poem, praising virtue over wealth as the only balm for sufferings, was very well chosen. The book's plot, about a teacher, obviously connected to Charity and Maria's shared profession, while the consoling quality of the lines spoke to the sorrows that haunted Charity throughout her young adulthood.[36]

Lydia Richards initiated her relationship with Charity on similar terms. "It must be condescension in you to hold correspondence with one as unworthy as myself," Lydia wrote modestly to her impressive new acquaintance.[37] In truth, Lydia had a sharp intellect of her own; she was an avid writer, composing not only acrostic poems but also pastoral verses and devotional poetry. Her love for writing immediately attracted Charity's attention, and Charity soon asked Lydia to write a poem for her. In her second letter to Charity, written only days after their first encounter, Lydia admitted that she had attempted to write an acrostic for her new friend, but she felt daunted by the thought of showing off the composition: "[I] so sensibly felt my inabilities that I almost gave up the idea." Braver than Lavinia, Lydia decided to enclose a few lines in her letter, "it comes so far short of what my heart would dictate that I hesitate whether I should send it, but imperfect as it is in every respect I now submit it to your candor."[38]

Lydia's original acrostic to Charity is missing, but a later acrostic, dated 1806, may be an improvement on those early lines:

Could friendship give what friendship would bestow
Her worth in each descriptive line should flow
And all that's good or graceful I would show:

Recount those virtues which tho rare they blend
In her unite and form the perfect friend
To her ascribe each soft attractive art
Yet artless and sincere her generous heart.
But O! my pen unequal to the task
Resigns its theme since justice more would ask
Yet in this heart shall injur'd goodness find
A friend to justice nor to merit blind
No more kind Heav' let grief pervade her breast
To her restore health, happiness, and rest.
Let this my dear till life and friendship end
Remind thee of thy true and faithful Friend.[39]

Lydia's poem was more skillfully written than Mary Hovey's apologetic acrostic to Charity, but it matched the former's worshipful tone. Charity appeared in Lydia's words as the "perfect friend," while Lydia described herself as "unequal" to the task of description. Unable to match intellects with Charity, Lydia offered instead her loving "heart" and sincere "friendship."

The persuasively self-deprecatory tone of Lydia's acrostic was a fine accomplishment, considering the skillful iambic pentameter and rhyming couplets that structured the composition. Charity encouraged Lydia's writing. Over the following decades, Lydia sent Charity many more poems, and Charity took pleasure in copying out versions in her own hand. Lydia's example raises the question of whether her fellow schoolteachers' declarations of unworthiness were entirely sincere or simply gestures toward the era's expectations of modesty from young women. If confessing their inadequacies was routine good manners, it is even more remarkable that Charity never followed her correspondents' examples.

There are no apologies enfolded within Charity's lines. Her poetic voice was robust and confident. She prefaced her acrostics with straightforward directives, rather than apologies. "Accept these lines with every wish sincere / That you may spend in joy the new-born year," she opened a typical poem. The opening lines to another acrostic asserted the worthiness of the lines that followed: "Accept my dear the tribute of a Friend / Not pay'd by flattery but sincerely pen'd." Charity stood by her poems, which she credited to her "muse." But her self-regard did not interfere with her admiration for her subjects. Her acrostics were highly complimentary. Charity praised the women she befriended for their "youth, ease, and mildness," "faith, love, and kindness," "lively and cheerfull Innocence," "sincere" hearts, "native artlessness," "kindness," "pleasing virtues," "goodness," "unsullied" souls, purity, and generosity. Her poems were gallant, charming, and romantic.[40]

Charity's poems counted modesty very high in the echelon of virtues. She appreciated women who dressed plainly. She was dismissive of fashion. She did not like trifling conversations. She was suspicious of flattery. She scorned flirts. In her papers she preserved a riddle about modesty that first appeared in a 1779 almanac:

What's fickle as the wind the French delight
A small disease thats hurtfull to the sight
These words when put together will express
The greatest charm a female can possess.[41]

Mode, a French fashion, plus sty, an irritation of the eye, spelled modesty, a woman's greatest charm. In short, Charity agreed with the standards of polite gentility that restrained the freedom of her friends' pens. She simply did not apply them consistently to herself.

Charity protested any claim that she had ever overstepped the bounds of propriety. And by most measures she had not. There is no suggestion that she ever dressed immodestly. She did not toy with the affection of suitors, like the coquette in Hannah Foster's novel. She did not behave boisterously in public. She was serious about religion. She established friendships with other serious young women, teachers and ministers' daughters. She read polite literature and wrote poems solely for private consumption. But something in Charity's persona still caused tongues to wag. She could not see it, but her self-confidence and assertiveness lacked the modesty expected from young women. They distinguished her as unwomanly. Charity began her twenties seeking a means to become a masterless woman; in the process she came into touch with her own mastery. This quality opened her to suspicion. Her relationships with men might have offered no just cause for rebuke, but her friendships with women soon struck a nerve.

5

So Many Friends

1799

FOUR YOUNG WOMEN sat in Deacon Richards's front parlor. Lydia Richards served the tea to her three guests, most likely Maria Clark, Nancy Warner, and Charity Bryant. The lively conversation among the women gathered around "the social board" erased any reservations Charity may have had about attending the gathering. Lydia and her guests had a great deal to discuss: the schools they were each teaching for the summer, the freedom of governing their own hours, the pleasures of writing. Charity discovered kindred spirits among her fellow teachers. When the meal ended, she rose to join the others on a walk through the orchard under the summer sky. For a brief moment, the pleasure that came from making new friends drove away the loneliness that so often haunted her. This perfect day shone in Charity's memory for the next fifty years.[1]

If Charity did not fall in love with teaching as a job, she did fall in love with many of her fellow teachers. Several of these teachers, like herself, never acquired a husband or married late in life. Together they constituted a loose network of bookish young women who formed primary romantic relationships with each other. Their intimacies had a powerful physical dimension, evident in the women's pleasure at having the opportunity to share a bed and embrace during overnight visits. But the intellectual dimension of their intimacies was just as powerful. Their affections for each other were wrapped up in words and writing. Charity's ability to evoke feelings on the page enamored her to many friends. As one admiring correspondent wrote her, "to describe my feelings is impossible unless I had your pen." Within their circle, the women created an affective world of language and ideas, taking part in an emotional repertoire far removed from the domesticated wifely and maternal love expected of early American women.[2]

It was no coincidence that Charity met such likeminded women through the schoolhouse. Since teachers boarded round, school districts typically sought out unmarried women for the job.[3] The vanguard generation of women who flocked to teaching in the post-Revolutionary era included many who aspired to freedom, at least temporarily, from the ordinary constraints of marriage and motherhood. They came not only to earn a respectable source of independent income but also to participate in a new youth culture of intellectually ambitious and assertively unmarried women that was emerging in New England in the 1790s. Becoming teachers, they joined the likes of Sarah Pierce, founder of the first institution of higher education for girls in the United States, Connecticut's Litchfield Female Academy, who wrote verses about her dream of building a house with her friend, Abigail Smith, and exchanged letters with Abigail's brother Elihu, founder of an early New York City literary society and a committed bachelor, discussing her opposition to marriage.[4]

Charity and many other women teachers, including Pierce, may have been attracted by the schoolroom's reputation as a place where women could form intimacies with other women. Polite literature described these relationships in platonic terms, but reform tracts, medical texts, pornography, and certain risqué novels described the schoolhouse as a place where girl students and teachers exchanged dirty stories, taught each other to masturbate, pleasured each other, and even shared dildos.[5] The school was a potential sexual training ground in the imagination of the post-Revolutionary generation. Fictional accounts of notorious prostitutes featured the boarding school as the place of their corruption.[6] One quasi-pornographic newspaper published in New York City in the 1840s even ran an advertisement for a girls' boarding school in its classified section.[7] The reputed erotic atmosphere within schools was not solely the fantasy of male writers. Infrequent evidence survives that when boarding-school girls or women shared beds, some kissed, caressed, and even brought each other to orgasm.[8]

If Charity was not aware of the schoolroom's underground salacious reputation, she had another proximate reason to identify teaching as an opportunity to meet out-of-the-ordinary women. During her childhood, a school ten miles away was taught by Deborah Sampson, who became famous for having served crossdressed in the American Revolution. (Sampson was in fact a distant relation by marriage, having married a man from neighboring Easton.)[9] An account of

Sampson's wartime exploits, supported in part by subscriptions from the people of Bridgewater, was published in 1797, the very year that Charity entered the teaching profession.[10] Sampson's example suggested, at the least, that teaching offered refuge to nonconformists.

The promise of female companionship served as an important motivation for Charity's decision to accept her first teaching job in Dartmouth, following the breach in her relations with her parents. Charity's sister Anna lured her to Dartmouth by promising that "my friend Eliza," another teacher in the district, "would make you pleased."[11] Anna knew her younger sister very well. Within weeks of Charity's arrival in town, Eliza was sending her letters addressed to "my dear dear friend."[12] Their intimacy set a pattern. Over the next couple years, as Charity traveled to work at schools across Massachusetts, she embarked on a series of passionate friendships with her fellow teachers. After Eliza, she met Maria, Lydia, and Nancy, opening her heart to each woman in turn, searching for that moment of mutual recognition between likeminded souls, and learning too late that these intimacies came at a price.

Often, Charity's friendships began with a spark, a bright moment of electric exchange that passed between herself and another woman. Maria Clark told Charity that "from the first moment that I had the happiness of seeing you I felt myself drawn by some powerful attraction."[13] Another time she told Charity that "I have loved [you] with the most sincere affection from the first moment the kind heavens presented you before my eyes."[14] The connection between the young women went far beyond ordinary acquaintance. Maria treated Charity as an object of singular devotion. "I know of no person living with whom I should more delight to contract an intimacy than with my lovely Ermina," Maria wrote in her first letter to Charity, calling her new friend by a pet name taken from a widely reprinted 1772 sentimental novel, *Ermina, or the Fair Recluse*.[15] In Maria's eyes, Charity was as charming as that novel's unfortunate heroine. "O tell me, my lovely girl, what endearing charm it is that binds me so close to you," Maria gushed in a later letter.[16] She answered her own question with compliments on Charity's appearance, poetry, and character: "in you I see all that is amiable and lovely summed up into one being every way calculated to inspire my heart with love and gratitude."[17] When the friends were separated, Maria dreamed about Charity. At night, Maria wrote, "my Ermina" is "constantly before my eyes—in my nocturnal visions." But dreams were not enough, she wanted to have Charity physically with her. "I gaze upon the visionary luster," Maria wrote, but "I mourn the absent substance." Waking up from dreams about Charity filled Maria with a keen sense of longing.[18]

A strong physical sensation passed between Charity and Lydia when they first touched on the afternoon of Lydia's tea party. As the two clasped hands during their walk in the orchard, Charity felt that "round my heart was cast [a] silken band."[19] Lydia felt it too. In the first letter she wrote to Charity after that summer afternoon, she described her desire to again "take you by the hand and embrace you as a friend."[20] The physical intimacy between the friends intensified over the next several months. Soon Lydia was writing to Charity about her longing to sleep with her. "In the visions of the night you are present with me—and I in reality imagine myself embracing my dear friend," Lydia wrote in November 1799, after Charity had left Plainfield for her brother's house in nearby Cummington. Lydia begged Charity to come for a long stay in her home so the two could be together.[21] Rather than "sleep alone," Lydia wanted to be "happy in the arms of my dear friend."[22]

Lydia's physical desire for Charity is almost palpable from the early letters between the women. She and Charity found pleasure in each other's bodies, and especially in each other's breasts. An early acrostic poem that Charity wrote for Lydia began with praise for her physical charms; the "L" in Lydia stood for "Lovely in person." The poem admired how Lydia's "generous bosom glows in friendship pure as the first opening rose." Charity conveyed a powerful erotic attraction by comparing her young friend's new breasts to budding flowers.[23] The language drew on a lesbian landscape tradition made popular in the sonnets of Anna Seward, a British poet well known in 1790s New England.[24] Lydia, for her part, liked to imagine Charity tucking the letters she sent into her "bosom."[25] The pages acted as a conduit of their mutual desire.

A similar physicality permeates Eliza's letters to Charity. Thoughts of Charity gave Eliza an "agitated bosom."[26] And Eliza wrote that Charity's letters had the power to "awaken all my feelings."[27] Like Lydia, Eliza found that paper was not adequate to the task of expressing her feelings. She longed for intimate time together. She wanted "hours alone with you my dear," Eliza wrote to Charity while the two both lived in Dartmouth.[28] After Charity left the village, Eliza wrote of her longing to "imbrace you this moment."[29] Charity's letters to Eliza seem to have been equally passionate. Eliza responded to one letter: "You say my dear if you dare freely to express the feeling of your heart you could rite till the day dawnd but you fear you should make work for repentance."[30] Charity's insistence that it would take all night to express her feelings to Eliza carried an erotic charge, especially given the suggestion that acting on those desires would supply cause to repent.

Considering the intensity of their feelings, it is no surprise that Charity's friends felt jealous of each other at times. The culture of sensibility prized devoted pairs, like Damon and Pythias, rather than widespread circles of acquaintance. Charity's very first friend from home, Mercy Ford, offered repeated reminders of the singularity of true friendship as Charity traveled from town to town. "I had a little conversation with our folks last Sunday about friendship," Mercy wrote to Charity when she had moved away for a teaching job. "You cannot think how ignorant they talk—I believe you would laugh to hear them—They supposed that a person was their friend that received them into their house and did not turn them out—then I have a great many friends however the subject was a very laughable one but of short duration, for I perceived their opinion was very different from mine therefore we could not agree, and it was a subject too tender to disagree upon, therefore we quit without being convinced upon either side." Mercy chose not to press the matter with her parents, but she explained her views more fully to Charity: "if they suppose they have so many friends why are they not happy, I have but one and when I am with her I think I am so."[31] Mercy, who never married, spent her youth devoted to her one true friend, until Charity left Massachusetts for good in 1807.

While Mercy feared that Charity would be distracted by new women she met in her travels, those new friends felt jealous of the first friend Charity had at home. When Charity left Dartmouth to return to North Bridgewater, her friend Eliza wrote how she could almost imagine "the happyness you felt when you had your friend [Mercy] coming towards you."[32] The tinge of envy in Eliza's sentiments is clear from her later mournful plea not to "forget your lonely Eliza."[33] As Charity continued moving throughout the state she made more new friends and made more old friends jealous. Maria Clark, whom Charity met in Cummington, grew jealous when Charity moved to Pelham and developed a new connection. After congratulating Charity on this new friend, Maria wrote, "I almost envy her the happiness which she enjoys."[34] Maria, like Mercy, reminded Charity that true friendship was a singular relationship. Charity agreed, but the intensity of her pleasure upon making new friendships made it hard to obey this rule.[35]

It may seem surprising that Charity had such freedom to form so many passionate relationships with other young women during her early twenties, but these "romantic friendships" received full sanction within the culture of sensibility, especially during the second half of the eighteenth century.[36] The relationships fit well within the new middle-class culture of love-matches then redefining courtship and marriage. Sentimental novels like *Ermina*, read by Charity and her friends, used the device of intimate letters exchanged between same-sex friends to advance their marriage plots.[37] In everyday life, parents looked to their sons' and daughters' intimate friendships as promising connections for introducing their children to potential spouses. Friends provided introductions to unmarried sisters and brothers, passed letters between courting couples, and helped friends to make sound judgments about potential lovers. Foolish friends might lead youth into bad marriages, but virtuous friends were instrumental in arranging good marriages. Same-sex intimacies were generally viewed as instrumental, rather than oppositional, to courtship.[38]

The compatibility between friendship and marriage does not mean that same-sex intimacies were always platonic. Romantic friendship created scope for a wide variety of strong feelings, including trust, pity, love, jealousy, happiness, and eros. Historical research reveals that the intimacy between female friends could extend to sex. The most overt record of lesbian life available from the period, the diary of English gentlewoman Anne Lister, shows that women looking for sexual intimacy with other women found ample opportunities within the framework of romantic friendship. Lister used a secret code derived from algebra and ancient Greek to record her orgasmic sexual encounters with a number of friends, one of whom eventually became her life partner. Romantic friendships were so popular among literate young women of Lister's generation that it would have been strange if her sexual relationships took place outside their context. It was sensible for a young woman seeking sexual encounters with other young women to do so within a popular form of relationship marked by physical intimacy, declarations of love, and elevated sentiments.[39]

Charity's world was not blind to the sexual possibilities within romantic friendships. Parents and youth knew that a "carnal act between two of the same sex," in the words of a religious text from the era, was possible.[40] Ministers, doctors, and legal authorities decried the so-called sin against nature, while many readers of sensationalistic literature took secret pleasure in imagining it. This knowledge extended to the possibility for sex between women.[41] But romantic friendships did not often provoke a community's concerns about illicit sexuality, in part because sexual feelings were not strictly coupled with romantic feelings the way they would be later in the nineteenth century. Men and women could experience and express emotional intimacy in a wide variety of relationships. In addition, sexuality figured into a lot of nonromantic relationships. The bonds of authority were just as likely to lead to illicit sexuality as were the bonds of romantic love. Society saw no more reason to link same-sex sexual behavior with romantic friendships than with the relationships between master and apprentice or teacher and student. Plenty of masters made unwanted advances on the apprentices they hired, but early Americans did not cast a suspicious eye on all employers and workers. Likewise, friends who expressed passionate love for each other were free from suspicion unless they gave reasons for concern.

Concerns arose when friendships seemed to interfere with marital futures. Young people might become so devoted to each other that they dreaded to be divided. Educated young men sometimes worried that they would not find the same communion of souls with lesser-educated women that they shared with their male peers. Young women sometimes feared marriage as a traumatic event that would draw a curtain over the friendships of their youth by restricting their time and resources.[42]

Most young people put those fears behind them, because they saw marriage as the central pillar of adult life. But when friends became reluctant to separate, their elders sought to intervene. Community suspicions also arose when youth behaved contrary to norms considered proper to their sex. Anne Lister, who cut her hair short, aroused the suspicions of her friends' parents.[43] Charity likewise caused concerns in the communities where she worked as a teacher, and the concerns grew the longer she remained within them. Although social sanction made it easy for her to enter into intense friendships with the women she met while teaching, something about Charity troubled onlookers as those intimacies developed. Within months of her arrival in each town where she taught, Charity became the subject of vicious gossip.

The rumors about Charity likely concerned her sexual propriety. Gossip, which played a prominent role in regulating early national society, scrutinized various aspects of men's behavior, including their financial dealings, their treatment of subordinates, and their relations within the family. Gossip about women, however, focused with singular attention on sexual behavior.[44] Because women had limited roles in the public sphere, their public reputations depended on how well they performed the modesty and chastity demanded from their sex. Women who carried on even innocent flirtations with men could acquire poor reputations, as in the example of Charity's brother Daniel's female friend. However, there is no indication that flirtations with men provoked the gossip about Charity. There is no record that she engaged in any flirtations with men at all.

Instead, the rumors appear to have been tied to Charity's masculine demeanor and her relationships with other women. Far from a coquette, Charity dressed with a notable lack of adornment and avoided superficial chatter.[45] Her appearance struck some who knew her as mannish. She did not wear her hair short or have her garments tailored like a man's, as the independently wealthy Anne Lister did. Charity strove to preserve the feminine respectability that secured her teaching positions, but she still managed to convey a certain masculinity. Lydia commented more than once on Charity's resemblance to her brother Peter, both in "countenance" and "motions."[46]

Eighteenth-century culture regarded masculine women with deep suspicion. Social critics often attacked outspoken women as mannish in order to silence them. English satirists depicted American "daughters of liberty" during the Revolutionary era as mannish-looking.[47] Likewise Mary Wollstonecraft, author of the early feminist text *A Vindication of the Rights of Woman* (1792), was caricatured wearing a bowler hat. As one early acolyte complained, "I wish [Wollstonecraft] were better understood, and read to more purpose; but our women fear to be masculine."[48] Americans adopted Shakespeare's insult against women who were "impudent and mannish growne" as an aphorism to rebuke those who challenged their subordination within a male-dominated culture.[49] Underlying this hostility was the strong association between female masculinity and lesbianism, although eighteenth-century writers would not have used this term. Instead they might refer to sex between women as "tribadism," another classically derived term, directed against mannish women, who supposedly used their oversized clitorises to rub against, or even penetrate, other women.[50] A woman who cultivated her masculine charms could be seen as hoping to attract a female lover. Charity's resemblance to her brother, both in the way she looked and, perhaps more significantly, in the way she held her body, aroused suspicion.

Charity's emerging identity as a single woman tipped the scale against her. Like mannish women, spinsters were objects of derision in eighteenth-century America, especially in family-oriented New England. As Charity advanced through her early twenties without entering into courtships with men, her single status became more notable. Again, she stood at the vanguard of a tremendous shift in American culture. During the colonial period, no more than 2 or 3 percent of women remained unmarried for life, but after the Revolution an increasing number of women, like Charity, began to choose singlehood in order to preserve their autonomy. As rates of female singlehood surpassed 10 percent in the antebellum era, new suspicions about spinsters emerged, including a recognition of their affinity to lesbians. A groundbreaker for this demographic transformation, Charity experienced the full force of negative opinion leveraged against single women. She considered this bias a primary reason for leaving Massachusetts later.[51]

Within the context of Charity's masculinity and single status, the intense intimacies she pursued with other women alarmed many onlookers and spurred gossip against her. Records of the specific contents of the rumors that circulated about Charity are muffled by the restraint that governed personal correspondence during the period. The belief that "gossip should never be written" ruled the honor culture of the 1790s, which regarded a person's good name as their most valuable and fragile commodity.[52] In Charity's case, this precept was strengthened by the habitual silencing that enveloped same-sex sexuality, known commonly as "the crime which could not be named."[53] Charity's friends avoided committing the specifics of the gossip about her to paper, exercising wise caution during an age when letters that circulated by hand were at constant risk of exposure. Charity wrote often about her sufferings from malicious tongues, but she remained just as elusive about the particulars. Interpreting the gossip requires reading the silence surrounding it as characteristic to sources concerning lesbianism.[54] Considering the dangers of writing down rumors, it is remarkable that written evidence of the gossip campaign against Charity survives at all. The existence of remaining traces of the rumors can be attributed in large part to Charity's character as a writer. Caution could not stifle her fierce urge to commit pen to paper. Probably the only relief she found from the sting of slander was through writing in self-defense.

The gossip about Charity began while she held her first teaching job in Dartmouth, in the winter of 1797. The talk became so vicious that after six months her sister Anna sent Charity back to North Bridgewater in the hope that old friends there might "counterbalance the disagreeable sensations arising from the...disagreeable circumstances."[55] Unfortunately, Charity's removal did not stop the rumors. Even after her departure, her Dartmouth friend Eliza reported that "your friend Eliza and Sister are still the topic of conversation but I try to be both deaf and blind to all they can say and follow my own inclination feeling my self so innocent of what I am accused with." Eliza shied away from committing the rumor's details to the letter. She wished she could "open my whole mind to you on paper," but regretted "how much I cannot say."[56] Although Eliza did not provide specifics, her letters made it clear that the accusations concerning her were connected to Charity. When Anna left Dartmouth several months later, Eliza wrote hopefully to Charity, "I do not expect I shall be the subject of conversation so much as I have been—now the cause is removed."[57] The gossip was more focused on Charity (and Anna by proxy) than on Eliza, who declared herself estranged from fellow villagers because she would not join their gossip. When a new family arrived in Dartmouth, Eliza comforted Charity that now "your pain will lay dormant a while" since "at present they are the subject of conversation."[58] But the gossip did not dissipate as quickly as Eliza hoped. Even a year later Eliza claimed to have no real friends in Dartmouth.[59]

The gossip devastated Charity. During her stay in Dartmouth, she began to write bleak, morose poems, the first that she ever saved. She adapted a published rebus on the theme of darkness.[60] Another original poem juxtaposed good wishes for a friend's birthday with dark forebodings of "rude gusts" and "threatening clouds."[61] Forced to return to North Bridgewater in 1798, Charity found little relief in her parental home. She continued to vent her misery on paper, copying out a scene from a recent play entitled "The Suicide" about a young man's desire to kill himself because of his shame for his sexual sins.[62] The scene resolved with the would-be suicide's brother persuading him to return to the family home and ask for forgiveness, much as Anna had prompted Charity to do. Sadly, Charity's parents were not the forgiving sort. After living at home for six months and taking care of her brother Cyrus and sister-in-law Polly during their fatal illnesses, Charity and her parents had a falling out over her refusal to take on responsibility for Cyrus and Polly's two orphaned children. In January 1799, Charity left home again to join her brother Peter and his wife, Sally, in Cummington.

It did not take long for gossip about Charity to surface there. At first, Charity established a good reputation and received the offer of a teaching job in nearby

Plainfield. She began to forge friendships with other young teachers in the vicinity. But, just as in Dartmouth, Charity soon became the subject of rumors. They may have originated in reports from back east. By late summer, the gossip had spread wide. Charity grew depressed. Some of her new friends turned a deaf ear to the talk. Maria Clark assured Charity that "the lips that would insinuate so much as a hint against my dear, ought to be sealed in everlasting silence."[63] Lydia Richards pledged never to listen to the "calumny and detraction" against Charity.[64] But Nancy Warner proved less faithful.

Nancy and Charity's falling out reveals how risky the intense emotionality of romantic friendship could be. The conflict stemmed from Nancy's aversion to Charity's passionate courting of her affections. Unlike Maria or Lydia, Nancy married not long after meeting Charity, and she may not have sought the deep relationships with other young women that teaching enabled. Nancy's initial encounters with Charity were restrained. A deacon's daughter, Nancy filled her letters to Charity with spiritual meditations. Even for a religious age, Nancy's piety was distinctive. A minister she knew later in life described her as a "sainted" woman wholly dedicated to God's work. Charity, who had been swept up in the wave of religious revivals that marked the beginning of the Second Great Awakening, encouraged Nancy's letters, and soon the two were engaged in a serious exchange on the subject of faith.[65] But when the women spent time together in person, their intercourse apparently did not stick to celestial matters. Regrets gnawed at Nancy after each of her visits with Charity. She felt that she should be spending their time together encouraging Charity toward spiritual rebirth, but somehow their conversations strayed from the proper course. Leaving Charity's house one evening, Nancy rode through a frightening storm. She made it home safely but saw a message in the experience. Providence was warning her of the wickedness of her ways. "Had I according to my wish spent the evening with you and your company I fear the consequences would have been severe," Nancy wrote to Charity.[66] She had just escaped punishment.

At first, Nancy blamed herself for her and Charity's failure to spend their time together in a godly fashion. She expressed doubts about the wisdom of writing to Charity when "I am sensible that my feelings are entirely wrong and consequently think it would be wrong to blot my paper with them."[67] But at some point Nancy shifted the blame. She began to think it was "strange" that Charity wrote to her so frequently, when her own letters were neither instructive nor elegant. She pulled back from the friendship, telling Charity that perhaps they did not deserve to spend time together if they did not use the time for religious improvement. Sensitive to slights, Charity felt hurt by this seeming rejection. Nancy tried to smooth the situation. "You have misunderstood me," she declared, insisting that she remained Charity's sympathetic friend. Not long later, she attempted to break off the friendship altogether. Nancy claimed her parents were responsible for the move, telling Charity that she had to "deprive myself of your company," or "if I enjoy it sacrifice my peace and comfort at home which is a painful thought." Worries about her parents' disapproval, she explained, "would overbalance the pleasure of seeing you." In a telling farewell, Nancy recommended that Charity turn her faith to God rather than feel angry that "we cannot enjoy all that our craving natures desire."[68]

The gossip about Charity played an important role in Nancy's withdrawal from the friendship. Unlike Maria and Lydia, Nancy never assured Charity of her disbelief in the public talk. Instead she chose more ambiguous expressions of comfort, such as "may the troubles that you are meeting with in this world all work together for your good."[69] Still, it came as a shock when Charity learned from mutual friends that Nancy had joined in spreading the rumors about her. The betrayal by someone who had been a friend hurt worse than the talk of strangers. To cope with this grief, Charity again turned to her pen, writing a series of linked acrostics about Nancy that gave vent to her feelings.

Charity took freedoms in verse that she never could in ordinary correspondence. The worst name she called Nancy in her letters was an "incomprehensible character." She criticized Nancy for her instability as a friend, surely a cutting insult for a culture that idolized Damon and Pythias, but a far cry from the attacks on her own character.[70] In her poems, under dictate from her muse, however, Charity made harsher rebukes. The first acrostic for Nancy, titled "Winter," compared her former friend to the barren landscape outside:

Nature, dear Nancy, clad in mourning lies!
And every bird for gayer refuge fly's
Nor will her robes of white here fancy charm
Cold is her breast, and pitiless her storm
Youth fly's her presence for a shed more warm
Who now will bear a sympathizing part?
Age sure will feel the moral in his heart!
Revolving years have whiten'd o'er his head
Nights darkest glooms have laid his glories dead
Each fleeting day. He like the naked trees,
Returns a hollow sound, and whistles in the breeze.

The poem burned with anger. "Cold is her breast, and pitiless her storm," Charity wrote in the poem's most direct indictment. The poem inverted the lesbian landscape genre, using images of deadened "naked trees" to symbolize the ugliness of its female subject. The acrostic, which Charity and her friends had always used to flatter and compliment each other, became a medium for the most stinging lacerations. Nancy and Charity had connected over their common religious devotion. Now Charity questioned her friend's faith. Nancy's professions of devotion, her "robes of white," could not disguise the inhospitable frigidity of her heart. Rather than compassionately shelter Charity through her trials, in true Christian spirit, Nancy had cast her off. But time would take its revenge, Charity hinted. As Nancy cast away her friend, so she herself was left alone. The passing of years would lay bare Nancy's "hollow" soul.[71]

Charity continued on the theme of time's revenge in her next acrostic for Nancy, titled "Spring." Lydia had once written to Charity that "envy and malevolence shall not always triumph" and that "the innocent and the guilty shall both meet their reward."[72] Charity took strength from Lydia's promise of celestial justice. In "Spring," Charity compared Nancy's youthful appeal to the short-lived flowers of spring. They charmed the eye for a spell, then wilted and fell away. Her mother's death had long ago taught Charity about May's false promises. Youth's beauties soon gave way to maturity, mortality, and judgment. Nancy would be stripped of her superficial charms, and if she did not repent, she would be punished according to her true nature:

Nature is dress'd in all her gay attire
And earth again receives her wonted fire
Nurtures each plant, and all the flowers inspire
Cares fly the scene—yet still the vision says
Youth, learn a lesson while you fondly gaze
What do these scenes to thy gay mind impart
Are they not emblems of the youthfull heart
Revolving years shall strip thee of thy prime
No wreaths of flowers thy temples shall entwine
Early then learn the lesson to be good
Reason will guide thee in bright virtue's road

Despite its caustic sentiments, "Spring" revealed a subtle softening in Charity's feelings, as Charity extended the possibility that Nancy might change, following "virtue's road" and the path to redemption.[73]

The final poem in the cycle, which Charity left untitled, offered both the most straightforward testimony to her falling out with Nancy and the most firm expression of her own will to recovery. The poem describes Charity's grief over the conflict, her recovery from the trauma, and her determination to avoid false friends in the future:

Now sinks my soul! Fond Nature drops a tear
And mourns the loss of friendship once so dear!
No, Heav'n forbids! My soul again revives
Casts off her chains, and sinking nature lives,
Yes, even nature this hard stroke forgives!
Where is the breast whose adamantine heart
And frozen bosom no kind words impart!
Resolving still the bleeding heart to tear
No friendships ever found a mansion there;
Enthrond' alone in hearts where kindness glows
Rejoicing still to heal the wretch's woes!

"The loss of friendship once so dear" had plunged Charity into a deep depression. But over time her feelings recovered, and her "sinking nature revived." Charity found a way to forgive even the "hard stroke" of Nancy's defection. She came to recognize that Nancy had never been a true friend; no true friend would "tear" a "bleeding heart." (This language of tearing a bleeding heart is the same that Charity used in her poem "A Child of Melancholy" to describe her father's betrayal.) True friendship could only be found in sympathetic hearts that sought "to heal the wretch's woes." In the future, Charity would be more cautious about the friends she pursued. Charity's experiences in Cummington curbed her voracious appetite for new relationships. But she did not close herself off altogether. She would not turn a "frozen bosom" or "adamantine heart" to the world, like Nancy had. She would have a heart "where kindness glows."[74]

Charity would even offer to forgive Nancy a few years later. When she heard from her sister-in-law Sally that Nancy, now married, had given birth to a child, Charity wrote a poem to congratulate her former friend. "Dear N---y still my fond affections fly / To hail you happy with your infant joy." Some simmering anger might be read into a verse of the poem that advised Nancy to teach her child "to venerate the Truth." But overall, the poem seemed to reflect Charity's desire to make peace and forgive past wrongs.[75] Ironically, Nancy's daughter Philena Fobes grew up to become a woman who expressed the same qualities that caused Nancy's suspicions of Charity in the first place. A well-known Illinois educator who never married, Philena's statue once stood on display in the Illinois State Historical Library. Memorials describe Philena as a "blue stocking with a love of learning and high academic standards."[76]

The rapprochement between Nancy and Charity came after years. In the short term, the atmosphere in Cummington became so poisonous that by early 1800, Charity decided to move again. This time she went to Pelham, in the middle of the state, where her sister Anna had relocated with husband, Henry, to join their middle sister Silence and her husband, Ichabod. Among the women who gathered for tea and a walk on a glorious summer's day the year before, only Lydia remained Charity's constant friend. She continued writing letters after Charity left Cummington, assuring her friend that "in vain do the malevolent hurl their darts at your character." Pained by the rumors, Lydia promised "I <u>will</u> maintain my sentiments of friendship amidst the boisterous ocean—<u>This bosom</u> shall ever shelter you, my lovely girl." She offered to intercede with friends who heard the gossip, however difficult that task proved. Lydia's good will, however, could not stop the new wave of gossip from destroying many of the friendships Charity had established in Cummington. Although Charity sent letters to the women she had befriended, they did not write back.[77] Even Maria, who had promised in 1799 that gossip could have no effect on her feelings, stopped writing in 1800. Charity gave Lydia a letter for Maria, but Lydia could not find a way to deliver it so she "fed it to the flames according to your request."[78]

Resettled in Pelham, Charity found no respite from the rumors now raging against her in Cummington. The Bryants were not the only family with branches in both towns. The frequent passage of people and letters between the villages guaranteed that opinions in one locale would travel to another. By late summer 1800, Pelham became as inhospitable as all the previous towns that Charity had inhabited since first leaving home three years before.[79] The full weight of her situation pressed down upon Charity. Her only surviving sibling whose hospitality she had not exhausted, brother Bezaliel, had moved to New York State and maintained infrequent communication with the family. With nowhere left to move, Charity took to bed in deep despair.

6

Discontent and Indifferent

1800

SYLVIA DRAKE HAD her place at the back of the one-room schoolhouse in Weybridge, farthest from the coal-burning stove. At sixteen, she was one of the oldest students, more capable of enduring the Vermont winter cold than the little ones. Most young women her age found better ways to occupy their time than attending school, such as preparing the linens they would need to begin their own households, working for wages to buy other necessities, or even marrying and caring for their own children. Sylvia chose to spend her second winter in Vermont focused on improving her mind. She had arrived in Weybridge already well educated for the daughter of a landless laborer, able to both read and write well. Plenty men of her station could do neither. Nonetheless, when the winter school session began in 1800, Sylvia insisted on returning for yet another season of instruction.[1]

Weybridge offered only a basic village school for Sylvia to attend. Winter sessions at village schools tended to deliver more advanced instruction in writing than the reading and math basics taught during the summer, but even the winter schools offered little beyond the elementary level.[2] As limited as Sylvia's educational opportunities were in Weybridge, Easton had not been much better. Sylvia's birthplace had repeatedly flouted the Massachusetts law that directed towns to operate common schools for local children. Local leaders preferred to pay fines rather than undertake the expense of hiring a schoolmaster. Although it had been settled in the 1660s, Easton had no school until the 1740s, and the town's girls were probably not admitted until the 1760s.[3]

The year that Sylvia left Easton a new private academy opened in nearby Bridgewater that admitted young women and offered instruction in history, geography, and *belles lettres*.[4] The Bridgewater Academy was part of a movement, sweeping Massachusetts at the end of the century, to offer a more advanced education to female students. The level of instruction did not match the schooling offered to young men preparing for college work, but it marked a radical divergence from a time when, in the words of a snippet of doggerel that appeared in a Vermont newspaper in 1805:

> ...a good old grannam
> at fifty pounds, *old ten* per annum
> Was hir'd to keep a village school;
> To learn the girls to knit—the boys to read
> And teach the little children, all the creed.[5]

By 1798, the early feminist writer Judith Sargent Murray, who resented being deprived of an education in her youth, noted ecstatically that "female academies are every where establishing." Sylvia, only seven years younger than Charity, belonged to a post-Revolutionary generation of women raised with newly broadened horizons. But the timing of her move to Weybridge excluded her from sharing the benefits.[6]

Unfortunately, Judith Sargent Murray's "every where" did not yet extend to new villages like Weybridge, where townspeople were more concerned with clearing land than with filling minds. Weybridge, resettled following the Revolution, established its first school in a log cabin at the top of Weybridge Hill in 1791. The structure doubled as a meeting house for the tiny town. After lightning burned the cabin down, the town rebuilt a new one-room schoolhouse on the village green in 1801.[7] Sylvia had to make good on the new educational possibilities open to young women of her generation within the frontier conditions of Weybridge. She might stay in school longer than her sisters, but she could not attend an academy.

Sylvia's situation hardly improved when she and her mother moved from her brother Asaph's home in Weybridge to live with her brother Oliver in neighboring Bristol. The town sat at the base of Hogback Mountain, and the entire terrain was hilly and forbidding. Settled at the same time as Weybridge, Bristol still did not have a single framed house by the turn of the century. The town was made up of log homes and tree stumps where forest had recently stood. There was not even a grist mill.[8] To an enterprising poor young man, Bristol's lack of development represented opportunity. Oliver not only followed Asaph to Vermont; he followed Asaph's example, taking advantage of the town's nascent condition to establish himself within the local hierarchy. He soon became an important man about town, acquiring the economic wherewithal to support his aging mother and baby sister as well as a growing family. But Sylvia found as limited educational prospects in Bristol as in Weybridge.

Middlebury, the nearby market town, would in short time become associated with precisely the model of female education that Sylvia craved. In 1800, the town fathers wrote to Sarah Pierce, founder of the Litchfield Female Academy, seeking assistance in establishing their own academy. Pierce sent them her twenty-five-year-old niece, Idea Strong, who had taught at Litchfield. Soon Strong was instructing girls in the Middlebury courthouse.[9] In 1802 she opened the "Young Ladies' Academy," bringing female education to Middlebury on the Litchfield model, offering instruction in subjects ranging from classical literature to the decorative arts.[10] Strong's premature death from consumption in 1804 opened the door to an even more challenging vision of women's education, when a young woman named Emma Hart arrived in town to take charge.[11] Hart moved away from the ornamental arts education offered to genteel girls, substituting rigorous training in fields like algebra, Latin, and philosophy. Under Hart's direction, the Middlebury school became a great success, and she continued to direct its operations after her marriage to Dr. John Willard. At the renamed Middlebury Female Seminary, Emma Hart Willard stood at the forefront of the women's education movement. The seminary's success transformed Willard into a celebrity, leading the governor of New York, DeWitt Clinton, to invite her to open a new female seminary in the city of Troy in 1819. Later Willard traveled through Europe and was feted by fellow female educators.[12] Today, Middlebury celebrates its connection to Willard; a marble memorial commemorating her educational vision stands at the entrance to town.

Sylvia followed Willard's career with interest, reading her books and commenting enthusiastically in her diary.[13] But Willard arrived too late to be of any use to Sylvia. Even had Sylvia been a few years younger, her background would likely have prevented her from attending either Strong's or Willard's school. The academies recruited girls from privileged families that had the capital both to pay the fees and to forgo the value of their daughters' labor.[14] Although the Drakes' fortunes took an upward turn with the move to Vermont, the family was too newly settled to send Sylvia to school in Middlebury. The possibility of an academy education shimmered like a mirage on Sylvia's horizon, alluring to behold but impossible to grasp.

The impossibility represented by the new academies only reinforced the bleakness of Sylvia's actual schooling opportunities when she arrived in Weybridge. Sylvia conveyed her deep unhappiness over her circumstances in a letter that she wrote during her second winter in Vermont to her sister Polly, who had married a North Bridgewater man, Asaph Hayward, and was still living in Massachusetts.

Her sympathetic brother-in-law wrote back affectionately, "I conclude you are very discontented in Vermont." Asaph sympathized with Sylvia, but he could hardly understand the depth of her discontent. Barely educated himself, Asaph felt puzzled by Sylvia's fierce desire to continue her schooling so long past the point at which most girls stopped. "I hear that you go to scool this winter which I am glad of althou you had good larning befour yet it is a difficult thing to get too much larning if you make a good improvment of it which I hope you will." He did not disapprove of Sylvia's strange decision, but he struggled to understand her rationale. What use, he wondered, could she make of extended learning?[15]

Asaph Hayward's gentle bemusement at Sylvia's peculiar desire for advanced learning was kinder than the reaction of many observers to the growing intellectual ambitions of American women. Many believed that the shift threatened women's place in the family and left them ill-equipped to perform the work required by a farmwife in the early nineteenth century. The *Middlebury Mercury* published a satiric notice in 1806, shortly before Emma Hart's arrival in town, advertising the opening of "an Academy for the education of YOUNG LADIES in the useful, though unfashionable art of HOUSEWIFERY." Ridiculing the academy-style education that taught girls "embroidery, fillagree, rhetoric, and dancing" but left them unable to "milk a coo," the new academy promised instruction in

> *Spinning, Weaving, Knitting, Darning, Sewing, Bleaching, Washing, Starching and Folding; Cutting and making up shirts for both sexes. Milking, making Butter and Cheese; White and Brown Bread; most kinds of Pies, Tarts, Custards, and Jellies, Pancakes and Slapjacks. Boiling, Codling, Roasting, Broiling, Frying, Fricasseeing, Alamoaning and Smothering* all kinds of *Flesh and Fish* with the construction of other necessary *Sauces and Gravies. Ragauts*, from the luscious haggis down to the simple shin of beef, turtle and rat soups inclusive. *Salting beef and pork, making Sausages, Pickling and Preserving* in general, *Drying apples, Curing Tobacco and Dying Blue* with an introduction to the nature of roots and herbs.[16]

The satire, intended to amuse, brought to light the disruptive nature of the move toward female education. Sylvia's insistence on remaining longer in school than usual challenged her family's expectations for her future. But affection for the baby in the family persuaded her older siblings to make allowance for her oddities.

The Drakes found some logic for her unusual path in the observation that Sylvia was a Sabbath child.[17] In the eyes of eighteenth-century New Englanders, being born on a Sunday conferred evidence of God's favor. Samuel Hopkins, a preeminent eighteenth-century minister, placed a special stake in his identity as a Sabbath child. His parents, he recalled in his memoir, always "considered it as a favour that I was born on the Sabbath," and from early childhood he knew that he was chosen to become a "minister or a sabbath-day-man."[18] Sylvia could not become a minister. During her childhood, women were discouraged from speaking in the Congregationalist church, let alone preaching. Men and women did not even sit together during meeting.[19] Nonetheless women were encouraged to read their Bibles, and from childhood onward Sylvia expressed a singular devotion to religious study that helped her family to rationalize her choice to go to school when other girls were marrying.

There may have been a cause besides intellectual curiosity and religious fervor that led Sylvia to cling to the schoolroom past her time. Polly's husband noted in his letter to Sylvia in February 1801 that her older siblings in Vermont reported there were many worthy young gentlemen who were "paying their respect to you," but Sylvia was "very indifferent" to all of them. Expressing a desire to remain in school longer gave Sylvia an acceptable explanation for her aversion to courtship. A sheer lack of romantic interest in her suitors could not provide the same justification. Courtship and marriage were matters that transcended romantic feeling. Families encouraged young women to judge their suitors on practical grounds such as their frugality, industry, piety, kinsmen, and property. Unions should be bound by affection, but passion need not play a role. The young men who courted Sylvia were "worthily deserving of your regard," Asaph Hayward advised Sylvia, and she should listen to their suits.[20] Their qualities, however, made little difference to Sylvia. Farmer or smith, resident of Bristol or Weybridge, tall or short, it is unlikely that any young man was pleasing to Sylvia.

Instead of expressing an interest in the villages' young men, Sylvia sought connections with other young women, relationships that marriage would impede with its heavy demands on a wife's time. There were fewer young women to befriend in frontier Vermont than in long-settled Massachusetts. According to the federal census, only thirty-six women between the ages of sixteen and twenty-six lived in Weybridge in 1800, and forty-three in Bristol.[21] The towns' widely spread residences, minimal educational opportunities, and early age of marriage for girls sharply reduced the number within this greater set who were suitable to become Sylvia's intimates. But Sylvia was not dissuaded.

The closest friend Sylvia made in Vermont, Lovina Wheeler, was four years younger than herself, which meant she remained unmarried later than many of Sylvia's nearer contemporaries. In other ways, Lovina represented a good candidate for Sylvia's affections. She came from a privileged family that valued education. With a girl like Lovina, Sylvia might be able to share the elevated style of romantic friendship just becoming popular among more genteel young women. Most farm girls in a town like Weybridge had too many daily concerns to waste their time in composing poems and letters to their female friends. Fit candidates for such intimacies were rare on the early national frontier.

Lovina's rare qualities also made her desirable as a wife, and sooner than Sylvia would have liked, Lovina accepted an offer of marriage from Jonathan Wainwright, the owner of an iron business in Middlebury.[22] The marriage created a distance between the two young women that could not be bridged. Like other wives of the era, Lovina's identity became subsumed by her husband's, and she was compelled to put away girlish things. When Lovina died in 1821, the Middlebury newspaper paid respect to the Wainwright family by printing a notice of her passing, with the succinct description: "Mrs. Lovina Wainwright, wife of Mr. Jonathan Wainwright, aged 33 years."[23] But in her diary, Sylvia would choose to remember Lovina as an unmarried girl in addition to a wife. "Hear of the death of Mrs. Wainwright nee Lovina Wheeler," Sylvia noted. By recording her friend's maiden name, Sylvia ascribed an unconventional significance to her friend's premarital identity, one not reflected in the newspaper obituary. "Companion of my youth, thou are no more," Sylvia continued, using the archaic familiar form of the second person. *Thou* denoted the closeness that had once existed between Sylvia and her cherished friend. Lovina's marriage had separated the women, but Sylvia's affections endured:

> I mourn thy early exit tho' thou hast long ceased to be my intimate. Early a wife + mother, thy residence at a distance I seldom saw thee: but never forgot thou existed. Thy image was imprinted so deeply on my memory that whenever recollection presented thee I beheld thee with pleasure + fondly hop'd some future period would favor us with a long interview. That hope which ever reviv'd at the recollection of that lov'd form, is now utterly extinguished.[24]

Sylvia's memorial to her friend suggested the physical dimension to her love for the "companion of my youth." Lovina's "image," not as a wife and mother but as a girl, remained permanently "imprinted" in Sylvia's mind. The contours of her "lov'd form" were etched so clearly in Sylvia's memory that any recollection of Lovina resurrected the old feelings and led Sylvia to long for her friend's presence beside her. Sylvia's diary entry captures the evidence of youthful romantic feelings that were lacking in her relations with male suitors.

Those feelings alarmed her siblings. Her sister Polly, who had received reports from the family in Vermont that Sylvia was refusing to entertain male suitors, wrote to Sylvia in June 1801 advising her to avoid excessive intimacies with other young women. Polly framed her letter "in answer" to a letter from Sylvia that had worried her, and that likely discussed Lovina. "I would give you a word of caution and my best advice, and hope your good sense will lead you to profit by it," Polly embarked on this sensitive subject, in notably more refined writing than her husband's. "You are now in the bloom of youth. Now indeed is the most dangerous time of your life—you are expos'd to a thousand unseen snares," Polly warned. Some snares were well understood by young women, such as the risk of forming a connection to a man who promised marriage, made you pregnant, and then breached his promise. "You are expos'd to the deception and the flattery of the other sex," Polly conceded, but she had another stronger concern for her little sister. She worried about

> the impositions of the false friendships of your own [sex]—you may believe me when I tell you that there are but few real friends—many proffes, but few know the meaning of friendship.—They know nothing of it but the name, and are entire strangers to that heartfelt bliss which takes place in the union of virtuous souls'—and you may often find, my dear, under the mask of friendship the most completed treachery.

Polly's own growing friendship with Charity Bryant, back in Massachusetts, may have influenced this warning to her little sister. Hearing of Charity's tribulations could have inspired Polly to try to save Sylvia from suffering the same sorrows.[25]

A few months later, in a letter to mark Sylvia's seventeenth birthday, Polly reiterated her concerns that her little sister was entering a "dangerous period" in which her hopes for redemption might be destroyed by the "snares temptations and enemies" that the devil enlisted to deceive humanity. This time, Polly called on a terrible example to drive home her point: the story of Sodom. "Lot chose to reside in Sodom because it was a pleasant country and well watered," Polly began, suggesting an analogy to the Drake family's removal to the green hills of western Vermont. But the "sins of the inhabitants soon made him forget the advantages of the place." The "ungodly deeds" of the men of Sodom caused a "righteous soul" to tremble. Polly exhorted her younger sister to avoid ungodly deeds and begin her new year in the awareness that it might be her last. Using Lot's story emphasized the critical importance of her message at the same time that it discreetly raised the dangers of the specifically sexual sins that might tempt a young woman entering the most "dangerous period" of adolescence. The sin of sodomy, as defined by traditional New England Protestants, encompassed a variety of non-procreative sexual acts, ranging from bestiality and masturbation to same-sex encounters.[26] Polly suggested a range of possible sexual sins tempting Sylvia when she called on Lot's example, but she may have had the danger of excessive physical intimacy between friends particularly in mind. Again, one wonders whether Polly's friendship with Charity brought this danger to mind.[27]

Sylvia shared Polly's religious sensibilities, which bound the sisters in affection despite their twelve-year difference in age. But if Polly hoped that an early marriage would rescue Sylvia from the perils of Sodom, she was bound to be disappointed. Polly married immediately after her twentieth birthday. Her sisters Rhoda and Desire had been unable to find husbands in Massachusetts, as their father's bankruptcy gave them little to offer suitors. But Desire married the owner of a grist mill in Bristol, Enos Soper, immediately upon removing to Vermont. Rhoda married a landowner from the same town.[28] Sylvia had the luck to come of age in a frontier community where men outnumbered women, and girls with domestic skills, like those Sylvia possessed, were in high demand. But despite Asaph's and Polly's urgings, she remained single.

Sylvia's aversion to courtship appeared evident even to Asaph and Polly's young daughter, Achsah, who began exchanging letters with her aunt in 1803, when she was ten. Achsah looked up to her clever aunt, whom she remembered from before the move. No doubt at her mother's urging, Achsah began to send letters to Sylvia with news from Easton and Bridgewater, copies of her school lessons, and snippets of poetry.[29] Achsah took after her aunt Sylvia. A precocious poet and a sly observer of the adult world, she was a very clever girl. Sylvia encouraged her niece's letters and wrote back with words of support for Achsah's studies. But Sylvia did not offer the same sort of gossip that her niece reported. In particular, Sylvia neglected the subject of marriage. Achsah's letters kept Sylvia apprised of the constant whirl of courtships and weddings in Massachusetts. "Miss Mehitebel Dalie is married to Mr Daniel Manley," she informed Sylvia in her first letter; in a later letter, "Uncle Manly Hayward is a courting Aunt Mary Monk and Clement Bryant is a courting Miss Phebe Perkins."[30] Exasperated with Sylvia's silence on these matters, Achsah pestered her "there don't any of the girls get married"?[31]

By 1804, Polly may have begun to suspect that Sylvia was not the marrying type. When their last single sibling, middle sister Desire, became engaged, Sylvia wrote to Polly that she expected soon to be "left alone." Polly understood that Sylvia's solitary station might be long-lasting. "If so," Polly wrote, "I hope you will be a comfort to our Mother in her declining age, as she has been the faithfull guide and protectress of your infant days."[32] Seemingly unwilling to begin her own family, Sylvia's siblings assumed that she would remain living among them, helping the family. No one could foresee a future in which their unmarried sister lived outside the family circle.

When Polly and Asaph moved with their children to Weybridge in 1805, all the surviving Drakes were finally reunited. Oliver, Isaac, Solomon, Rhoda, and Desire lived in Bristol; Asaph and Polly lived in Weybridge. Sylvia and her mother split their time living with different siblings. By then Sylvia had ended her attempts at further schooling. She took a great deal of responsibility for her mother. True to her sister's wishes, Sylvia treated Mary Drake as her "dear maternal friend," giving the aging matriarch the emotional (and later material) support that her married sisters found harder to spare.[33] The two women often spent time in Polly's household. Sylvia shared a religious vocabulary with her pious sister, and an interest in poetry with her clever niece, which made living among them comfortable. In Mary, Polly, and Achsah's company, she passed her early twenties without feeling the need to take on a new name.

Sylvia's closeness to the women in her family shaped her character. Her years among them trained her to be as proficient at the "unfashionable art of housewifery" as any curmudgeon could desire. She learned how to bake pies and cookies, to sew shirts, to make sausages, and to dry apples. Her upbringing instilled Sylvia with a sense of family loyalty and devotion to the well-being of the next generation. She was very much like the other women in her family, except for her lack of desire to get married and begin her own household. The significance of that peculiarity appeared great at some moments, and unimportant at others.

An aphorism of Alexander Pope's, often repeated in early New England, sagely declared "'tis education forms the common mind; just as the Twig is bent, the Tree's inclined." Thousands of school children, including Sylvia's own nieces and nephews, transcribed Pope's words into their copybooks as a reminder about the importance of learning.[34] The Drakes' history of hardships and migration to western Vermont denied Sylvia the formal education that she wished to "form" her mind, but her family's experience "bent" her growth in lasting ways. The depression of 1784, the division of her family, and the hardships of frontier life taught her thrift, industry, and endurance. Born a decade or two later, Sylvia may have had an easier childhood. Her intellectual inclinations would have found more avenues for development; her early years may have been less marked by desperation. But Americans of the next generation often felt impoverished for having missed the experience of the Revolution. Their experiences seemed trivial in comparison.[35] Sylvia's birth at the end of the Revolutionary era subjected her to deprivations but also inclined her to become a self-determined young woman. To extend Pope's metaphor, Sylvia was like a bonsai; raised under harsh conditions, pruned close as a twig, she adapted and became a hardy tree, crabbed in some respects, but beautiful to those who appreciated such qualities.

7

Never to Marry

1800

CHARITY'S HANDS WERE weak, but her sense of purpose was strong. For two months she had been laid low by ill health. Much of that time, she felt so unwell she could barely sit up. She had exhausted her sister Silence's hospitality, who—though only three years older than herself—had four young children to care for. The oldest, seven-year-old Phillip, was sick with dysentery, and the two-year-old, Mary, was ailing as well. Silence's youngest, Charles, was only three months old and required his mother's constant attention. The last thing that Silence needed was another person to look after, especially one who had become the target of such ill will in town. Holding the pen as best she could, Charity wrote to her sister-in-law Sally back in Cummington to inform her of the painful decision she had made. "I find it not convenient for me to tarry here," she wrote, "and think it rather prefferable to return to the intolerable scene that I quited than to live here any longer." Charity was going home.[1]

Sally opened the letter with calloused fingers. A busy farmwife with three young sons of her own, Sally supplemented the household income by sewing clothes for paying customers in the community, a skill that she had taught Charity during her stay with the family the year before. Between Sally's sewing and her housework, which included ironing, washing, quilting, spinning, weaving, breaking wool, knitting, making cider, churning butter, baking, and teaching her young sons how to read, she had no time in her life for friendships. She made her only exception for Charity, the one person to whom she wrote letters. Sally had come to love this little sister who so resembled her big brother, Sally's husband, Peter. Sally tried to capture the resemblance by drawing a profile of Charity the previous spring. This escapade into artistry represented one of the few moments of leisure that she recorded in fifty-three years of daily diary-keeping.[2]

If Sally was surprised by Charity's news that she intended to return home to North Bridgewater, she was even more surprised by the information that came next in the letter. Even the most capable hands might tremble when holding a letter from a twenty-three-year-old woman that boldly announced the intention never to marry. "You say that you hear I am going to be marrie'd," Charity wrote to Sally. "It is a false report and should you ever hear any more of the kind you may venture wholly to disbelieve them, for it is my settl'd and candid opinion that such a thing will never take place." Knowing that her unlikely decision to foreclose any future possibility of marriage would be hard for her relatives and friends to accept, Charity tried to demonstrate her seriousness of intention: "thousands in the world may call me a <u>fool</u> but I do not feel that their different opinions would add to my internal felicity." Confined to bed for two months, sick with mourning over the loss of her reputation in one town after another, Charity had come to realize that her happiness could not be dependent on the opinions that others expressed about her. She would have to live life on her own terms.

Still, Charity owed the people who loved her an explanation for why she was so certain that marriage would not improve her "internal felicity." Explaining this in writing proved a struggle, since anyone might read the letter and her words could enflame the gossip that continued to surround her. Charity pondered her dilemma, "could I see you I could tell you much, but write I can not." Doing her best, she explained her reasoning to Sally: "while I cannot form that connexion upon the only principle which I think will be productive of hapiness, I shall, <u>solemnly</u> never engage, and I <u>positively</u> think that <u>that</u> will never be the case." Charity presented her decision as a matter of "principle."[3]

The choice not to marry required a strong justification in the pro-marital culture of the early American republic. During the Revolution, young recruits had marched to war singing a popular tune that bid their "sweethearts" farewell, but pledged "when we've drubbed the dogs away / We'll kiss it out with you."[4] Many made good on that promise when they returned. Post-Revolutionary culture idealized marriage and motherhood as not only women's natural life path, but as their civic duty. Political writers asserted that women needed to embrace the roles of "republican wives" and "republican mothers" in order to promote the virtue of the male citizens who ran the new political system. At the same time, poetry and fiction promoted emerging romantic ideals about marriage, which pictured connubial love as critical for individual happiness.[5]

Charity's older siblings, with the exception of black sheep Bezaliel, all took the message to heart, marrying young and immediately starting their families. As Charity entered her mid-twenties, the pressure within her family to follow suit became intense.[6] Her siblings had a direct interest in Charity's marital future, since unmarried women could pose a real burden to their families. Charity's own Aunt Charity became such a weight to family resources that her nieces and nephews were eventually forced to place her in the poorhouse.[7] Charity's siblings had her interests in mind as well as their own when they encouraged her to marry. Unmarried adults were treated as objects of pity and ridicule in the popular culture. Satirists depicted spinsters as sharp-tongued hags who lived "sad" lives because they were unable to find men willing to marry them. Charity's family could not wish that fate for her.[8]

Yet an increasing percentage of women in the early republic were choosing that fate for themselves. The public enthusiasm for marriage in the post-Revolutionary era has made it difficult for historians to recognize that many in this new generation of spinsters did not remain single because of unfortunate circumstances or because of personal defects, but because they did not wish to marry. Marriage offered more woes than joys, it seemed to many. One of Charity's nephews inked this sentiment into his journal, copying a snatch of doggerel that captured the wisdom of spinsters succinctly:

When girls do get married their pleasures are <u>gone</u>
Their parents forsake them + trouble comes on
Their husbands will scold their children will cry
And that will make the girls faces look rincled.[9]

Some women were frightened of childbirth and the demands of raising a family; they were driven by the same individualism that characterized so many men in the early republic, and which was denied to women who occupied the relational statuses of wife and mother. Some women chose to remain single because they disapproved of women's traditional subordination within the marital union. Certain elite women chose to remain unmarried in order to retain control over their inherited property, a right that women lost under the coverture laws that governed early American marriage. There were pious women who chose to remain single in order to consecrate their lives to God. Others avoided marriage because of their aversion to men.[10]

Charity's claim that her decision to remain single was a matter of "principle" raises several possibilities. The first is that Charity had a specific man in mind as the only "principle" according to which she would marry. In other words, a failed courtship could have turned her against marriage for good. Another possibility is that by "principle," Charity meant what she said: an abstract logic governed her rejection of marriage. This could have been the principle of female obedience and masculine domination, which several of her contemporaries rejected. Or it could have been the fundamental principle that marriage united a husband and wife, which Charity knew by age twenty-three did not suit her. Our modern cultural assumptions about the naturalness of marriage between women and men, which were shared by Americans in the eighteenth century, make the failed-courtship explanation seem the most likely. But there are strong reasons, most significantly the forty-four-year marriage that Charity eventually formed with Sylvia, to believe that the last explanation makes more sense.

Charity did not reject marriage in principle for everyone. Unlike Sylvia, whose disinterest in courtship so irritated her cousin Achsah, Charity kept careful tabs in her correspondence on her friends' and family members' marriages. A year after her declaration to Sally that she intended to remain single, Charity wrote a poem celebrating marriage as both a holy institution and an earthly pleasure. The verses, probably composed as a gift for her sister Anna and Anna's husband, Henry, following a visit to their house, praised the marital household. "Blest be this Mansion long may it be blest," the poem began, "And every blessing on its Owners rest." The opening lines have the simple cadence of classical English poetry, that familiar iambic pentameter rhythm so soothing to the ear. It is easy to imagine the rhyme stitched onto an embroidery sampler, set below a simple house against a background of twining leaves and blossoms. But if the poem's opening lines looked back to traditional ideas of marriage as a holy household, the poem's heart evoked the new romantic ideal of marriage as a communion of souls. The peaceful home was a setting where the couple could find "pleasures" together, "while undivided all their moments move / Their hearts united in the purest Love." Charity closed the poem by beseeching God to preserve the couple from any discord or strife. The verses show Charity's support for marriage, at least when it came to other people.[11]

She believed in marriage, just not for herself. Charity desired intimacy, but her very belief in marriage as a romantic institution made it impossible for herself to participate. She could not settle for a marriage that generated a productive household, that gave her children and social standing, without also nourishing her affections. She wanted a marriage that united two souls, and for a reason that she could not state explicitly on paper, she knew that such a marriage would be impossible for her.[12]

That impossibility might have been caused by Charity's inability, for some reason, to marry the man of her choice. As Charity traveled through Dartmouth, Cummington, Plainfield, and Pelham, she met plenty of young men as well as young women. Her friend Maria from Cummington thought that Charity was courting. She wrote to Charity in the summer of 1799 to ask whether "Philanders addresses are received as usual." After Charity fled Cummington to stay with her sisters in Pelham and failed to write for several months, Maria wrote wondering whether the delay was caused by the "busyness" of a new status: "how do I know by ere now you are join'd with some happy swain in the sacred bonds of matrimony." But Charity's delay in communicating with Maria stemmed from old miseries rather than newfound joys. And despite her probing, Maria knew that Charity was unlikely to have gotten married since her last letter. In fact, Maria knew that marriage was a sensitive subject for Charity. She pleaded with Charity to "not be offended" that she asked, "though it is a delicate question."[13]

Who was Philander? Maria might have been using the name as a pseudonym, the same way that she called Charity by the name Ermina. Like Ermina, the name Philander had a classical ring and appeared in contemporary literature. In a 1797 memoir of Deborah Sampson, Charity's celebrated neighbor who had passed as a man to fight in the American Revolution, a character named "Philander" seduces and abandons a beautiful young woman named Fatima, leaving her to pine away in seclusion until Deborah encounters and romances her while in her male disguise. The memoir's ghostwriter, Herman Mann, suggests that the affair between Deborah and Fatima was sexual but harmless.[14] If Maria had Sampson's popular memoir in mind when she asked Charity about Philander, Maria could have been comparing Charity to Fatima, subject to some man's untrustworthy addresses, and comparing herself to Deborah, romancing Fatima/Charity in an erotic but acceptable fashion.

It is also possible that Maria was not using a pseudonym. There were numerous Philanders living in the towns where Charity resided between 1797 and 1801. Charity knew at least two Philanders in Dartmouth in 1797. In later years, Eliza sent her news of both young men's courtships and marriages, but on neither occasion did Eliza seem concerned about causing distress to her correspondent.[15] Charity also knew a young man named Philander Fobes in the Plainfield-Cummington area, where she was living when Maria sent her letter inquiring about Philander's addresses. Charity and Philander were close enough that she asked him to carry a letter to her sister Anna in the summer of 1799.[16] Philander Fobes married Nancy Warner in 1801, which might have been a cause for the split between the two young women. In this familiar narrative, two women fight over a man, and when one woman wins his affections, the friendship ends and the spurned woman swears off men for good. However, the timing is not right to support this seemingly persuasive narrative. As late as November 1800, *after* Charity declared her marriage embargo, Charity was under the impression that Nancy was engaged to a man named William Bodman. She did not learn about Nancy's marriage to Philander Fobes until a year later.[17]

The most suggestive evidence that there may have been a real Philander whom Charity wished to marry is in the same letter where Charity declared her marriage embargo. Charity opens the letter with the lament that her "life has been from the beginning one scene of troubles, crosses, and disappointments." No trust could be placed in good appearances. Dark clouds might suddenly overshadow any sunny day. And so, Charity wrote, were "my brightest prospects cut off in a moment, and my fondest hopes blasted in the twinkling of an eye." Charity's language raises the possibility that she might have found someone whom she wished to marry (her "fondest hopes"), but that the courtship came to an abrupt end.[18]

It is possible that the gossip spreading about Charity prompted her desired suitor, maybe Philander, to break off their courtship. Gossip disrupted many romantic relationships. Her brother Daniel's courtship was threatened by gossip, although he refused to believe the public talk. Even if a lover maintained faith in his intended, as did Daniel, family pressure could force an engagement to be broken. John and Abigail Adams pressured their daughter Nabby to break off an engagement with Royall Tyler, a young lawyer and writer who had a reputation as a rake, despite her love for him.[19] If Charity had become engaged to a lover before the rumors about her character circulated, it is entirely possible that her marriage plans could have been aborted and her "fondest hopes" shattered. There is even a scrap of poetry in Charity's papers copied out from a popular romantic epic titled "Henry and Emma," that voices a woman's lament over being suspected by her lover of sexual improprieties:

> Did e'er my tongue speak my unguarded heart
> The least inclin'd to act the wantons part
> Did e'er my heart one secret tho't reveal
> Which Angels might not hear or Virgins tell
> And have you Henry in my conduct known
> One fault but that which I must never own
> That I of all mankind have lov'd but you <u>alone</u>

Like the Charity–Nancy–Philander love triangle, this story is very believable. It fits another familiar narrative trope: a woman loses her reputation and is condemned to spend the rest of her life alone. It is the story of Fatima and Philander; it is the plot of half the romantic novels of the era. It resonates with our beliefs about the prudish past, when women waited to have sex until marriage, and if they became damaged goods their lives ended. It is a deeply compelling and satisfying answer to the puzzle of why Charity did not marry. And yet it is wrong. The story of Charity being doomed by rumors about her character to spend her life alone is historically unpersuasive for a number of reasons.

First, the early American republic was not nearly as sexually prudish as people imagine from reading period novels. Stories like Philander and Fatima's, where a girl's deflowering led to dire consequences, were aspects of a cultural reaction to the very high rate at which premarital sex actually took place. The novels were prescriptive, not descriptive. In fact, in the late eighteenth century some 30 percent of New England girls were pregnant at the time of marriage.[20] In most of those cases, premarital sex and the ensuing pregnancy probably contributed to the marriage rather than impeded it. Charity's mother was pregnant when she got married. So was Charity's sister-in-law Polly.[21] Charity's sister Silence had her first child eight months after her wedding.[22] Anna did not get pregnant until after marrying Henry, but that could have been by luck rather than abstinence.

Although women's sexual behavior was carefully scrutinized in the honor culture, being the subject of sexual gossip did not necessarily leave a permanent disability. Women could regain their social standing with proper application. The records of the church Charity attended as a young woman are filled with evidence of premarital pregnancies. When parents who had conceived a child before marriage wanted their child to be baptized they first had to make a formal apology for fornication. This might appear to be evidence of a harsh social stigma, but it is really the opposite. The pattern of confession-baptism was so routine that the church records used the same stylized language to record the process each time. It is just what people did. They courted, had sex, got pregnant, got married, had children, confessed, and had their children baptized, in that order. Cyrus and Polly never went through the formal confession process because they died too soon. But the church recorded their children Zibby and Daniel's baptism on their grandfather's account.[23]

There was more trouble when a girl became pregnant and the father did not marry her. But, again, there were routines for dealing with this common situation. The county courts routinely handled "prosecutions" for fornication that were really glorified legal proceedings to secure child support. An unmarried mother would appear before the court, confess herself guilty of fornication, name the father, and the court would assign financial obligations to him.[24] Sometimes the mothers were fined small amounts, but the proceedings were less about punishment than arranging matters to prevent an infant from becoming financially dependent on the town.

If sexual gossip about Charity prompted a suitor to break off his engagement, that does not explain why Charity did not eventually marry a different man. The gossip would not have been a permanent disability. Royall Tyler's rakish reputation disrupted his engagement to Nabby Adams, but he went on to marry another young woman shortly afterward. Despite becoming a subject of gossip because of her romance with Royall, Nabby also married soon after their engagement ended.[25] Whatever were the nature of the sexual suspicions that Charity came under, no one expected the gossip to permanently impair her ability to marry. If they had thought so, they would not have kept questioning her about her marriage plans. If she did not have a "sweetheart" she was about to marry, Peter wrote to Charity in 1804, "I have one in my eye for you."[26] As late as 1809, rumors circulated around Dartmouth that Charity had gotten married. Anna, who had already met Sylvia and welcomed her as Charity's "constant companion," wrote in astonishment to ask Charity if it was true. Anna knew better, but the people of Dartmouth believed the rumor.[27]

A failed engagement would not have taken Charity out of the marriage market. Many engagements were broken and the separated parties moved on to new courtships. Charity's cousin Ira courted a young woman named Fanny for two years, announcing to his family members that he planned to marry her, then left her at the last moment when he fell in love with someone else. The family was horrified by his behavior. But they forgave him. As Anna wrote, "Ira's conduct is indeed strange—but no more so than what frequently happens in the world."[28] Couples announced their intention to get married, then split for reasons of incompatibility, poor health, loss of reputation, bankruptcy, or any of the other routine traumas that afflicted people. And then former lovers moved on. In a society where marriage was ubiquitous, people found ways to overcome potential disabilities and get married. If Charity had a suitor who rejected her and left her bereft, leading her to swear at age twenty-three that she would never get married, that still would not explain why she made good on her promise.

The most likely explanation for Charity's fealty to her unusual promise to remain single is that she had a consistent aversion to having romantic relationships with men. It is striking that Charity preserved no letters from male friends during the decade before she met Sylvia. There are letters from male relatives, but not a single piece of correspondence with any man who could possibly be construed as a suitor. It is possible that she never received any letters from men (a strong point in favor of the argument that she never had suitors). It is also possible that she eliminated the letters in her possession to erase any suggestion of heterosexual romance in her life. This is not the behavior of someone whose engaged lover died prematurely. It is not even the behavior of someone who was slighted by a fickle lover. It is the behavior of a woman who recoiled at the suggestion she might be romantically involved with a man. Anne Lister, the English gentlewoman whose coded diaries provide such excellent insight into early nineteenth-century lesbian life, purged her correspondence of any traces of heterosexual courtship. She burned a love letter she received from a man, noting in her diary "It is not for me. I love and only love the fairer sex and thus, beloved by them in turn, my heart revolts from any other love than theirs."[29] Charity seems to have felt a similar revolt against marriage to men. She wrote in praise and admiration of other people's marriages, but there are no love poems in her own voice except those addressed to women. The overwhelming evidence is that Charity loved only the fairer sex.

Who then was Philander? Maria's inquiry into Philander's addresses might have conferred nothing at all about Charity's marital desires. If at one point a man did court Charity, it does not mean that she received him with interest. When Maria asked if Philander's addresses had been received "as usual," she did not indicate whether the usual was good or bad. "Usual" might have been careless disregard, or even angry rejection. There is a thread of fury that runs through Charity's correspondence when suggestions arise about her relationships to men. She seemed to foreclose all discussion of the matter in the strictest terms. Both Anna Kingman and Charity's friend Anna Hayden had to apologize when their husbands made remarks to Charity about courtship. Anna Hayden tried to defend her husband: "he only ment to rally you a little about being Married in hopes to keep up your Spirits, as you was a going off; little thinking of hurting your feelings in the least degree."[30] Charity did not want to hear anything on the subject of courtship. In 1802, when a letter from Anna suggested that in Pelham Charity's name was being spoken in connection with a merchant named Ormston, Charity firmly informed Anna that she "never wish[ed] to hear his name mentioned again."[31]

Anna and Peter sustained their hopes longer than Charity liked that their little sister would eventually marry. But at least one family member accepted Charity's disavowals of marriage when she first made them. Grace Hayward, Charity's motherly nurse, put enough faith in the young woman's intentions to worry about the consequences. Unlike Anna and Peter, Grace had never married and could easily anticipate a husbandless future for her former charge. Grace could also anticipate the difficulties, primarily financial, that Charity would encounter as a consequence of her chosen life path. Charity sweetly tried to comfort Grace and "dispell her needless fears," but the words failed to impress.[32] When Grace died in July 1802 she left the largest bequest from her estate—a fifty dollar note—to Charity. Smaller sums went to other members of the family. Charity's orphaned nephew Daniel, whom Grace had helped raise, received nine dollars. But the greatest portion went to help establish Charity on her solitary path.[33]

8

Charity and Mercy

1805

A YOUNG WOMAN living in a small house had few good places in which to keep her secrets safe from a suspicious family. Mercy Ford searched her sleeping chamber for a place to put the box she held. She had locked all of Charity's letters within it, but such a simple mechanism was inadequate protection for the dangerous words the box contained. Mercy's sister Thankful, who sometimes shared her bed, might discover the box; even worse, Mercy's mother could come across it. Unwilling to burn the pages because of their sentimental value, Mercy poured out her distress in a letter to Charity:

> I have fixed a little box and locked [your letters] all up in it and made them as secure as possible but if I should be taken away suddenly I don't know how they would fare if not I shall commend them to you without opening it—them others I would not have exposd for nothing that ever I see but in looking them over I see I was chargd not to destroy them and I feel but a wish to keep them sacred but for the world would not they should be exposed as I fear if I should have <u>them</u>[1]

Gripped by panic, Mercy could hardly voice her fears in coherent sentences. On calmer occasions, she was capable of writing clear letters. But faced with the threat of her mother, who had grown increasingly suspicious of Mercy and Charity's relationship, Mercy's words jumbled altogether. Still, her message was clear: she desperately needed Charity's help.

Charity knew a lot about the agony of exposure. Nearly five years earlier she had returned home to her parents after the spread of malicious rumors about her character made it impossible to live away any longer. Her parents offered her a home, but they could not stop the rumors from following her to North Bridgewater. The young women in her own village treated her like an "unwelcome guest" when she returned to town.[2] Under the strain of serial mistreatment, Charity's health collapsed. During the winter of 1800–1801, Charity suffered recurring bouts of a "paralitic disorder" so alarming that even her irritable stepmother tried to avoid their customary conflict. Laid low by despair and illness, Charity felt grateful for this unusual season of "domestic peace."[3]

She felt even more grateful for the nurturing attention of the one old friend who refused to abandon her; that was Mercy Ford. Born in 1778, a year after Charity, Mercy grew up in the neighboring village of Pembroke. Although Charity had numerous relations in Pembroke (one neighborhood in town was known as Bryantville), the difference in circumstances between the Bryant and Ford families made the young women unlikely friends. While the Bryant daughters wrote poetry and the sons pursued professional careers, the Ford family's limited resources forced Mercy and her older siblings to seek wage labor. Mercy's brothers traveled all the way to the South American sugar colony of Guyana to make their fortunes, and both died there young.[4] Mercy and her sisters were saved by their gender from this miserable fate; instead they worked in service for local families to earn their keep. Charity probably met Mercy when both girls were in their teens, while Mercy was working for a North Bridgewater family.

What drew Charity and Mercy together is not clear. Mercy's work in service differentiated her from the independent teachers whom Charity befriended during her travels. Mercy's mother ruled her life. She determined where and when her daughter could go, limiting the girl's daytime visits with Charity to brief interludes between work obligations. Mercy's letters to Charity apologized because "Momma said I must come home as soon as I could get there," or "Mother said I could not come after today," or Mother placed "strick orders for me to come back."[5] This maternal domination extended to work opportunities as well as friendships. When an employer invited Mercy to move to a different town, her mother would not hear of it. Mercy's brother insisted that she "had an undoubted wright to do as I liked," but Mercy had a hard time laying claim to that right. Like most young women of the period, she felt compelled to submit to the domination of more powerful parties.[6]

The common streak of independence that drew Charity and Maria Clark together cannot explain the connection between Charity and Mercy. Mercy, who wrote in the vernacular with frequent misspellings, did not share the skill for writing poetry that bound Charity and Lydia Richards. Nor did religion provide the glue for their early friendship, as it did for Charity and Nancy Warner. Later in life, Mercy became quite pious, and it is possible that the two girls initially met at church or a prayer meeting. But the girls' early correspondence lacks the sustained attention to matters of faith that characterized letters between Nancy and Charity. Instead of an intellectual or spiritual connection, something more visceral drew the young women together.

After the first season of their friendship, the girls remained close during Charity's years away. During the brief period in 1798 when Charity returned to North Bridgewater, she nursed Mercy through a long illness in the Bryant home. In the fall of 1800, when Charity came home again to convalesce herself, Mercy returned the favor. She spent hours by Charity's bedside reading her poetry. Immobilized by sickness, Charity threw herself into writing. Laments about the suffering caused by gossip served as a common theme throughout many of her pieces. Even a birthday poem that Charity likely wrote for Mercy warned that gossip haunted the "steps of youth," and "reputation by a breath is lost / While we on Life's tempestuous tide are tost / Subjected to the scorn of idle fools." The sentiments seem ill-suited to a day of celebration, but Charity sought to give her friend a present with lasting value: advice on the fragility of women's reputation.[7]

The pain of having her own character exposed to public scorn inspired Charity with tremendous sympathy for other young women who became the targets of gossip. When Charity heard during the fall of 1800 that a former friend in Cummington had borne a child out of wedlock, she extended sympathy, not judgment, to the unfortunate girl. "I am indeed sorry for my poor Jane," Charity wrote to her sister-in-law Sally. She had heard a relative talking about Jane, "and I must confess that it made my heart bleed to hear her [revel?] in the poor girls calamity, how strange it is that people can harbour such a spirit of malice and revenge!" Feeling sorry for both Jane, who was being frozen out by townspeople, and the "innocent babe," who suffered under the same prejudice, Charity refused to join in the talk about them.[8] And yet her defense of Jane committed the girl's shame to paper, an interesting broach of the rule against writing gossip. This frankness stands in contrast to Charity's elusive references concerning the gossip about herself and adds evidence that the talk about Charity centered on her suspicious relations with other young women. The "sin that could not be named" could not be discussed with the same clarity as an ordinary sin like fornication.

Charity did not judge Jane for her unwise choice in love. After the attacks on her own reputation she had come to scorn the small-minded folks who would "fain judge us by their riggid rules."[9] But during her convalescence, she was forced to acknowledge the power of gossip over the life of young women like herself. She emerged from this period of ill health resigned to remain living at home and to steel her reputation against further assaults by refraining from the promiscuous pursuit of new female friends that had gotten her into trouble before. Mercy, who for years had insisted in her letters that any person could have but one true friend, finally received the reward of Charity's devoted attention. Charity sharply curtailed her correspondence with other women. She tried to live her life in private. Even her brother Peter complained that she had become "distant and reserved." In frustration, he teased, "I wonder where you have buried yourself. I can hear no more of you than if you was on the other side of the Atlantic, or had made a visit to our antipodes."[10] His letter gave proof that Charity had found a winning formula for escaping gossip.

But as long as she lived at home, Charity could not escape her parents' surveillance. Charity's retreat from the public eye only disguised her "craving nature," as Nancy once put it. Despite her public "reserve," she remained, in private, the same passionate woman she had ever been. She did her best to confine those passions within the privacy of her relationship with Mercy, but eventually her parents and Mercy's parents grew suspicious, so deeply suspicious that Mercy decided to take the precaution of locking away all of Charity's letters.

The full story of Mercy and Charity's friendship can never be told because the women burned most of their letters to each other following 1805. These things we know—their friendship was passionate, physically intimate, had secretive dimensions, and lasted in an attenuated form throughout their lives. Although the majority of the letters that might offer more particulars of their relationship were destroyed, the few that survive contain evidence that Charity and Mercy maintained a frequent and explicitly erotic correspondence that they struggled to protect from prying eyes.

For many years the women appear to have carried on two separate correspondences—one for public sharing and one for private pleasure. Few of the private letters remain, but there is evidence they existed from two incongruent systems of numbering that Mercy used on her letters to Charity (sending letters 9 & 11 during the same window of time that she sent letters 27 & 28). There are also references to private letters that pop up in the surviving public letters. For example, in one exchange Mercy wrote to Charity that she would try to send a letter by the hand of Mr. Leonard, who was traveling between Pembroke and Bridgewater. Yet, she dared not send a second private letter she had written. "I much fear it will not be a safe chance and I dare not send the other [letter] for it is so particular and it will do by no means for the world." Mercy continued her public letter, giving ordinary news about the comings and goings of family members—Peggy had gone berrying with Capt. Sauer, sister Thankful had been away too long and angered their mother—but then returned to the subject of the private letter she wished to send. "I long you should have this other letter for it holds all—but it will never do," she complained. In closing she promised that "you shall have it soon perhaps I shall come and bring it." Mercy ended with an admonition to "write every day till then and I will if possible."[11] The next surviving letter in the correspondence is dated two months later. Any that came in between were destroyed.

In one of the few letters that survives from the young women's private correspondence, written in 1801 soon after Charity recovered her health, Mercy gushed about the intensity of her feelings for her friend:

> in what unknown reigeon shall I ever find thy equal. Surely to my heart there is none that can supply thy place—is there indeed such a friend besides on earth! So kind, so good so disinterested as my lovely sister! No surely I have found the <u>perl</u> then let me prize it—O my friend how shall I ever reward your goodness to me; with astonishment and wonder I view your unbounded goodness towards me! And to see it daily increasing strikes me silent—when I might think it could reach no further, and it could never be displayed more fully—to see it rise above every self gratification and to know my happiness was considered as the chief and only object, what must my heart be made of if it be not melted into unfailing gratitude...O my dear girl never die nor never do I expect to find that tender friendship in any other earthly object that I have proved in thee—well doest thou say many profess it but few know what it means—astonishing it is my dear to see how few know what it means—how can they profess it when they remain so far from what it realy is—when they know nothing of it but the name—my dear how much I want to see you I cannot tell you.[12]

Mercy's words explode with passion and desire. She loved Charity with an intensity that she knew exceeded the ordinary dimensions of friendship. She called Charity her "sister," to capture the inseparable bond that united them, but the letter suggests a more than sisterly connection between the women.

Mercy's specific wording hints that a sexual relationship developed between the young women after Charity's return from her travels. When Mercy wrote of having "found the perl" and of her desire to "prize it," she intended to describe Charity as a treasure, but it is also plausible to read a sexual meaning into her language. At the time, pearl served as a euphemism for clitoris, rendering Mercy's words a possible allusion to her desire to make love with Charity.[13] So too, when Mercy described how Charity rose "above every self gratification" to pursue Mercy's "happiness," her words carried allusions to the practice of mutual masturbation; "self gratification" appeared in texts of the period as a synonym for masturbation.[14] Mercy's letter could be describing a sexual relationship in which Charity typically played the active or masculine role, as it was then understood, of pleasuring her receptive feminine partner. In both instances from the letter, Mercy's language deployed euphemism, the convention of polite nineteenth-century letter-writers, to imply sexual acts. Her use of language bears a strong resemblance to courtship letters between opposite-sex couples of the time.[15]

In other letters, Mercy voiced her intense desire to spend nights in bed with Charity alone, strongly hinting at a sexual relationship between the two. While living at home, Mercy shared a bed with her unmarried sister Thankful—small houses, big families, and the high cost of furniture made bed-sharing common during the period. If a friend came over, she could have squeezed in alongside the two sisters. But Mercy wanted nights with only Charity. She complained when Charity missed an opportunity to visit while Thankful was away. "I depended on a good visit from you while T was at Bridgwater and we all alone." Worrying that another opportunity would not present itself, Mercy wrote longingly "you know that is the way I always lay out for comfort is alone with you and such comfort I can never have here certainly—." It may have been easier for the two women to spend evenings alone in bed at Charity's house, since none of Charity's sisters then lived at home. "I shall come if ever I can run away in the night," Mercy promised. But that would not be easy. At the time, Mercy's labor was badly needed at home. She was responsible for feeding the farm animals and cutting the wood that her widowed mother depended on. Charity would need to find a way to come visit her. Deprived of time alone together, Mercy promised that the two women would "take what we can git and be thankfull for it." A stolen caress could not match a night alone, but it would be better than nothing.[16]

The erotic dynamic that can be deduced from Mercy's letters to Charity resembles the sexual pattern described by Anne Lister in her journals. Charity, who was masculine in demeanor and intellectually ambitious like Lister, may also have resembled Lister in her sexual proclivities. Typically, Lister played the penetrative sexual role during her sexual encounters with women, focusing on bringing her lovers to orgasm with her fingers. Like many butch lesbians in the mid-twentieth century, Lister did not wish to be touched genitally during lovemaking, which is not to say that she did not take pleasure from her body. Lister brought herself to orgasm by rubbing against her lovers, but the underlying sexual dynamic in her encounters had Lister pursuing her lovers' "happiness," as Mercy might put it.[17]

In another parallel, just as Anne's relationship with her romantic friend Marianne sparked the concern of Marianne's parents when it appeared to be interfering with her courtship and marriage, Mercy and Charity's connection grew alarming to their parents the longer that the two women remained single and devoted to each other. When Charity first returned to North Bridgewater, Philip and Hannah Bryant likely appreciated Mercy's devotion to their ailing daughter. After Charity recovered her health, however, and the women's devotion to each other persisted, their parents had reason for concern. As the two women entered their late twenties neither showing any desire to get married, but instead pursuing every opportunity to spend their time together, and alone, both Charity's parents and Mercy's widowed mother seem to have become suspicious of the connection. Mercy's apparent disinterest in men (she never married and poked fun at one suitor picked out for her by family) could have alarmed Charity's parents, while the vicious gossip that had once circulated about Charity gave Mercy's mother plenty of cause to worry.[18] By 1804, Mercy had become anxious about her mother's suspicions. At the close of a letter in September, Mercy warned Charity "Dia daimee soft we are acourting by letters she believes." The words "Dia daimee" are the way an untutored English speaker might transcribe the French words *dis à d'aime*, or speak of love. Speak of love softly, Mercy warned, because her mother was reading Mercy's letters.[19]

It was Charity's parents, however, who finally sought to break up the women's connection, apparently refusing by the spring of 1805 to accept any more visits to their house from Charity's oldest friend. Mercy became frantic at the forced separation. In desperation she wrote secretly to Charity, "I want to see you so much if it was not for the shame and know nobody there can want to see me I would walk up and see you————."[20] A few weeks later she wrote again of her desire to see Charity. "I had almost formed a resolution to come and see you last week but as I could but have seen you and no more I thought it would but aggravate my pain which was almost as I thought too great before."[21]

Whatever had inspired the Bryants to blacklist Mercy was causing her equal trouble with her own mother. In despair, Mercy wrote of feeling that she was worth "nothing and less." Her home life, she told Charity, had become insufferable. She discussed moving away to live somewhere on her own, beyond parental surveillance, but her mother warned her that "if I leave it I shall carry my evil heart with me and where shall I be any better with that." It was at this point that Mercy wrote to Charity asking what she should do with Charity's letters that she had saved. What "if I should be taken away suddenly" she asked. Mercy may have been considering ending her life.[22]

Charity found herself in just as impossible circumstances. By May of 1805, Charity reached the conclusion that she would have to leave home.[23] Mercy begged Charity to pay her another visit before she left, while Thankful was away from the house. "I am all alone Don't fail to come," she insisted. Mercy urged Charity to stay in North Bridgewater; despite everything she hoped that the women still had a future together. "I hope you wont go it seems to me you will not," she implored.[24] But her hopes went unfulfilled.

Charity did not leave because she stopped caring about Mercy. She sustained that affection until the end of her life. Mercy was the only lover besides Sylvia whom Charity mentioned in the brief memoir that she wrote in 1844, where she memorialized Mercy as a "dear friend"—a brief notice, but in only seven hundred and fifty words to describe a lifetime of movement and experience, it counted for a lot.[25] It is difficult to imagine that Charity would have left if she had any choice, but her father and stepmother must have insisted. How else to explain Charity's decision to set off for her siblings' homes in Pelham and Cummington at the beginning of 1806? When she had retreated from those towns half a decade before, the gossip concerning her had been so relentless that Charity saw no possibility she could ever return.

As late as 1804, Charity stood firm on her promise never to go back to Cummington or Pelham. Her brother Peter wrote urging Charity to put the past behind her and come for a visit. He promised, "you need not fear now to come out of Egypt for they are dead that sought your life—or to drop figure—I believe your enemies are ashamed of their conduct your character has stood the severest scrutiny and has come out of the fiery ordeal like gold seven times tried."[26] But Charity refused Peter's invitation until she had no choice. She probably suspected that Peter was being overly optimistic when he promised that the gossip about her had passed. Charity's sister Anna offered a more honest assessment in 1805 of what Charity would find when she returned to Pelham: "as you come along, be sure and step lightly over the hill, for it may be, it is enchanted ground,—at least it is venomous, and you may get stung by some of its serpents—I therefore recommend caution." Five years after her sister's last visit, Anna believed that the town's forked tongues still threatened Charity's well-being.[27] Nothing less than a closed door in North Bridgewater could have forced Charity back to the towns where she had so much to dread.

Once, when Charity was young and full of hope, she had set out into the world guided by a passionate desire to forge relationships with other intellectual young women. When her desire caused her trouble in town after town, Charity tried to find satisfaction living at home with one true friend to share her pleasures. That life proved just as impossible to maintain under the scrutiny of her elders. Now Charity set off again, twenty-eight years old, with no home, no illusions about the possibilities that awaited her, and no reason to hope for the future.

9

Charity and Lydia

1806

TWENTY-FOUR-YEAR-OLD LYDIA RICHARDS loved her liberty too well to hurry into marriage. She paid little heed to the "addresses" of the men who courted her.[1] Eager to be on her own, each summer she boarded with strangers and worked as a schoolteacher. In Cummington, Ashfield, Williamsburgh, and other towns in the Hampshire Hills, Lydia took on the responsibilities of the classroom. Although she considered the school "no very agreeable place" and she found teaching to be perplexing, she welcomed the wages as well as the precious freedom to read and write as she pleased during her nonworking hours.[2] She would never find that possibility in marriage, and so she continued steadfastly on her solitary path until, in 1806, Charity's return to the region planted a new desire in her heart. Marriage to a man held little appeal but, as Lydia wrote to Charity after their friendship renewed, "I could wish, if it were not in vain, to be your constant companion."[3]

From their very first touch, the bond between Charity and Lydia had a distinctive power. They met on a warm summer afternoon in 1799, when Charity was one of three women teachers invited by Lydia's father, Deacon Richards, to have tea with his daughters in the parlor. The party was a great success, and all the young women became fast friends. But the connection between Lydia and Charity had a special spark. After refreshments the women set out together to walk through Lydia's father's orchards. As they stepped into the woods, seeking relief from the summer heat under the shade of the dark green foliage, Charity hesitated in the unfamiliar terrain. Lydia reached out to take her guest by the hand. When the girl's lithe fingers clamped around her own, Charity felt a powerful stirring in her chest. The feeling of Lydia's first touch was so charged that the sense memory stuck with Charity for the rest of her life. Gathering her courage, Charity grasped Lydia's hand and together they plunged forward.

As they walked together on that summer afternoon in 1799, Charity admired her companion. Only seventeen, five years younger than herself, Lydia had a vibrant physique. She carried herself with the modest decorum expected from a deacon's daughter, but plain clothes could not hide her "healthfull form" from Charity's discerning gaze. As the slight effort of the walk brought a blush to Lydia's face, "the rose and lilly met" in perfect harmony on her cheeks. Glancing back at Charity, Lydia's soft eyes reflected the "kind affections" in her heart. In this perfect moment, Charity's melancholy condition escaped her mind. She felt peaceful in Lydia's presence; "with thee all troubles were forgot."[4]

If only Charity's appreciation for female charms ended there, her peace of mind might have lasted longer. However, Charity's irrepressible attraction to the other young women she met on the afternoon of Lydia's party guaranteed that her troubles would soon be renewed. Lydia felt forlorn when Charity was forced by the spread of rumors about her character to leave Cummington in the spring of 1800. Despite her insecurities about the skill of her own writing voice in comparison to the eloquence that her friend possessed, Lydia wrote Charity an impassioned poem after their separation. "My Charity, my dearest, loveliest friend," Lydia began a cascade of emotional lines that mourned the loss of the "lovely girl" who had become her "souls delight." The poem captured Lydia's consuming fear that their separation would be final as she imagined that "in blooming youth" death might snatch Charity "away." Undaunted by the force of nature that seemed to separate her from her friend, Lydia defied death its victim:

Unfeeling monster, thou don't dare divide
Those souls by nature, and by friendship tied
Thou unrelenting foe! How canst thou part
Such kindred souls and wound the tender heart.

If Lydia refused to permit death to sever the connection between herself and Charity, then gossip had no chance. Their "kindred souls" shared an unbreakable connection.[5]

As other friends dropped away during the early 1800s and Charity grew isolated in North Bridgewater, Lydia kept faithfully writing to the far removed woman who had made so profound an impression on her heart. After a couple of years, Lydia was the only friend from her travels with whom Charity still exchanged letters.[6] Lydia treated the letters that Charity sent her as sacred objects. When one arrived, she would run into the orchard to break the seal in solitude and read each coveted word beyond the "sight of evry human eye." Near the sacred spot where the women had first touched, she took her "pleasure" from Charity's "precious lines."[7] Later, after she had reread the letter a number of times and regained control of her feelings, she returned to her family and read select passages aloud.[8] Then Lydia tucked each letter away among the growing collection that she kept in her bed chamber.

Neither the lengthening separation nor the ongoing rumors about Charity's character seemed to diminish the ardor Lydia professed to feel. When Charity, depressed by her circumstances, let the correspondence slip, Lydia kept writing, assuring Charity, "my lovely girl, *that* friendship and affection which were once engrav'd on my heart for you, the hand of time, absence or silence has not erased."[9] Nor did time seem to lessen the attraction Lydia felt for her distant friend. Lydia likened that feeling to a flame that Charity had kindled within her; it remained burning brightly long after Charity had gone.

In an 1802 letter, Lydia rhapsodized about her physical longing for Charity, "'how sweet is mutual love'... Oh that *we* might once more experience its sweets, clasped in each others arms."[10] She repeated that desire in most of her letters, sometimes hinting at the forbidden quality of the love that the two women shared. "Why, alas! Are the dearest friends forbidden to enjoy the objects of their highest pleasure and most ardent affection," Lydia complained in the fall of 1803, three years after the women's last encounter.[11] Describing her "ardent affection" for Charity as forbidden associated their attachment with illicit relations, including sodomy, which was labeled a "forbidden love" in period works.[12] While Lydia's nearby friends married one by one, she remained committed to singlehood and a forbidden friend. Despite their distance from each other, Lydia pleaded with Charity, "let our hearts, my dear, be still united."[13]

After the fourth year of the women's separation had passed, Lydia still longed for the day to come that brought "to my vacant arms that lovely friend which I so long have wish'd, but wish'd in vain, to press to this still palpitating heart."[14] Unbeknown to Lydia, the shattering conclusion to Charity's relationship with Mercy Ford was bringing Charity's return to the Hampshire Hills a little closer. Too saddened to put pen to paper, Charity failed to inform Lydia of her declining condition in North Bridgewater. "Why, my dear, this silence, this long silence?" Lydia begged.[15] Having no honest way to answer Lydia's insistent question, Charity wrote nothing in reply. In silence, she packed her trunk to leave North Bridgewater.

In April 1806 Charity arrived in Pelham, where her sisters Anna and Silence lived.[16] For several months Charity enjoyed their hospitality. Despite Anna's warnings about the fork-tongued vipers who still inhabited the town, Charity found a kind reception from her family. Charity's situation, as her cousin Vesta Guild put it, called "forth all the tender feelings" from those who loved her.[17] At least it prompted such feelings in her sisters. Her parents were another story. Vesta had to admit that the obstacles impeding her happiness back home seemed insurmountable.[18]

In August, Peter Bryant sent a medical apprentice to Pelham to collect his long-absent sister and bring her to Cummington.[19] When he told the deacon's daughter the news that at last Charity was returning to the Hampshire Hills, excitement caused Lydia's "palpita'ing heart" to beat so hard that she left the second *t* out of palpitating on the first spelling, inserting it later at the top when she discovered the mistake. "My dear, with haste fly to your friend whose arms will be extended and waiting to receive you," Lydia commanded, "and whose bosom will feel a void till the return of her long absent friend." Having Charity within miles made it impossible for Lydia to wait a moment longer. "With what joy shall I again behold my dearest friend, with what friendly ardor press to my thrilling heart the object of my firmest attachment! The happy hour 'in prospect smiles,' and pleasure fills my heart," Lydia wrote in overheated excitement.[20] On August 14, nine days following her arrival in Cummington, Charity left the Bryants for Lydia's family home in neighboring Plainfield. After six long years, the kindred souls were reunited.[21]

In the first exhilarating evenings of their reunion, as Lydia took Charity into her arms in their bed at night, the mutual longing between the women must have overpowered any shyness between them. Lydia had written so often about her desire to press Charity to her bosom. Enacting this desired wish brought their warm bodies close together. Both women likely wore shifts to sleep, thin linen garments that hung thigh length, with loose drawstring necks that easily exposed their breasts. As Lydia took Charity to her "generous bosom" and Charity wrapped her arms around Lydia's body, bare flesh pressed bare flesh. The pleasure they shared in this embrace had sexual meaning in their time, as it would in ours.

Evidence of lesbian "bosom sex" practices in the early nineteenth century have been preserved in the rare correspondence of two African-American female lovers, schoolteacher Rebecca Primus and domestic servant Addie Brown. Separated by work, Brown wrote to Primus informing her that at the boarding school where Brown worked in service, several women sought to share her bed at night and fondle her breasts. Brown placated Primus that "I shall try to keep your f[avored] one always for you," but added "should in my excitement forget you will pardon me I know." When Primus apparently did not forgive her this excitement, but expressed jealousy over the thought of other women touching Brown's breasts, Brown backtracked. In her next letter Brown promised that when she slept with another woman "I can't say that I injoyed it very much," and she denied recollecting what she had meant by the word "excitement" in her previous letter. The exchange paints a vivid picture of a self-consciously sexual culture of breast play among women educators and school workers in the antebellum era.[22]

Straight couples in the nineteenth century also eroticized the act of embracing each others' heads to their breasts. "Could I but ley my head upon your bosom and whisper love to you," wrote one longing nineteenth-century wife to her absent husband, "I miss you in every thing—But the nights—to wake and find you gone." Expressions of desire for bosom embraces often served as polite means for couples to describe their other sexual longings, and it was understood that embracing a lover to one's breast led to further demonstrations of ardor. An eager young man writing to his fiancée described his wish to "squeeze her and hug her and kiss her forehead and eyes—yes I'll kiss them again and again, and when I have looked at them to my heart's content I'll kiss them again and her cheeks and lips and throat, and I'll take liberties with her back hair and pull out her hair pins, and tousle and tumble her up generally."[23] Breast play inspired many young couples to grow more heated in their embraces. Very likely, the bosom embraces that Lydia and Charity shared in their bed at night did not represent the full extent of the erotic pleasures they took in each other's arms.

By bringing their bodies together, Lydia and Charity opened the possibility of rubbing their thighs, knees, pelvic bones, and genitals together in the common pursuit of pleasure that led female lovers in the eighteenth century to be known as "tribades," derived from the verb to rub in Greek, and "fricatrices," derived from the verb to rub in Latin. Period texts depicted a range of possible sex acts between women including mutual rubbing and digital stimulation.[24] Depictions of cunnilingus are less common to the period, but that does not exclude its possibility. No sources exist that can answer the question of precisely which intimate touches Lydia and Charity shared in bed at night. It may even be possible that their embraces remained chaste. Lydia's surviving letters tell us only that she took enormous pleasure in sharing her bed with Charity and longed, when Charity was away, to have her return "to the arms of your friend."[25]

The pace of letters that Lydia wrote to Charity increased tenfold after their reunion, signaling the intensification of her feelings. When the first visit drew to a close after two weeks and Charity returned to her brother's house in Cummington, Lydia experienced an excruciating sense of loss. The first seven days of Charity's absence, she wrote to Cummington, felt as long as the previous seven years of separation. She begged Charity to return to Plainfield as quickly as possible, dreaming that "a few days will again restore you to my arms."[26] Soon her wish was granted. Over the following six months, the women contrived to spend most of their time together, staying either at Lydia's house, Peter's house, or with other friends. Even so, during their inevitable intermittent separations Lydia sent Charity twenty letters—compared to the average of two a year she had written during their long separation.

Lydia filled these letters with comments about the impossibility of writing openly about her feelings, echoing the complaints of Charity's previous lover Mercy Ford. Lydia's first letter following Charity's return from Plainfield to Cummington initiated this theme: "my dear, I must not write half I could say."[27] The next day she wrote another letter, although she knew better, and signed off with a plea to Charity to return as soon as possible "to your almost impolitical <u>friend</u>."[28] Lydia knew it was "impolitical" to commit the depth of her feelings for Charity to paper, as such repeated and passionate letter-writing had gotten Charity and her friends in trouble before, but the inflamed state of Lydia's feelings overcame her caution. She wrote again the next day.

Charity also acted more like a lover than was wise. Although her half of the correspondence does not survive, we can catch glimpses of her actions in Lydia's letters and in Charity's sister-in-law Sally's diary. In September, while Lydia taught at a school in nearby Goshen, Charity traveled to visit her sisters in Pelham again. Before leaving she sent Lydia a handkerchief pin. Gifts of jewelry, especially a piece of keepsake jewelry like a handkerchief pin, signaled courtship in the romantic culture of the nineteenth century. And a pin, with its penetrative qualities, had obvious symbolism for lovers. Lydia was delighted with the gift.[29]

When Charity returned later that month to Cummington she did not travel straight away to Lydia, but stayed for a couple weeks with Peter. Her delay may have been prompted by rising suspicions about the friendship within the Cummington community. The prolonged absence made Lydia distraught. She wrote to Charity complaining that she felt "cruelly depriv'd" of her company and that she had "a desire still unsatisfied which nothing but your presence and society can fulfill." Lydia begged Charity to send a new "token of your fidelity and friendship" to prove her love.[30] Charity responded with a batch of new letters, promising Lydia that she would return to Plainfield the following week. Lydia was somewhat mollified. "Six days will restore us to each other's arms," she sighed, and then they would have time and space to discuss the "many things which I wish to write, [and] must not." Worrying that the friendship was troubling people within the Bryant household, Lydia included in her letter a request that Charity come to do some sewing work at the Richards house. Work created a respectable need for Charity to visit, offering a more compelling rationale for the trip than the women's shared affection. Still, Lydia could not restrain herself from assuring Charity that what she really desired was her friend's companionship.[31]

At the beginning of November, Charity returned to Lydia's house for another two-week visit. Lydia then accompanied Charity back to Cummington and spent a night in the Bryant home, but she could not stay any longer.[32] Already, Charity's situation at Peter and Sally's was deteriorating. The family was living in the house of Sally's father and mother, Ebenezer and Sarah Packard Snell, old-fashioned, rigid Puritans who had taken a strong dislike to Charity.[33] Some of their antagonism may have rubbed off onto their daughter, who under the stress and physical discomfort of her seventh pregnancy had little patience to spare. Peter tried to excuse Sally's short temper: "You know the fair sex in certain circumstances are afflicted with a peculiar irritability."[34] Charity's lack of enthusiasm for helping Sally with her endless domestic tasks could only have aggravated the pregnant woman.[35]

Lydia worried about Charity's growing unhappiness in her brother's household. Sensibly, she advised Charity to "make your present home my dear as agreeable as possible, and let reason and fortitude assist you to support every trying scene."[36] Un-sensibly, she began to fantasize about creating a new home for Charity, by adopting her as a permanent companion within the Richards household. Lydia's family was a model of understanding and emotional support compared with the Bryants and Snells. Lydia's father had admired Charity since her first visit to the house, and he thought that an early set of verses she wrote "outdid all the female compositions he ever saw." Deacon Richards's affection for Charity encouraged Lydia to consider asking her parents whether her homeless friend might move in with the family way back in 1801. "I have at times thot of proposing to my parents that they should give you an invitation to come and make this your home and enjoy all the privilege which I am favor'd," Lydia wrote to Charity back in North Bridgewater. But the idea had then seemed too "impracticable" to put into effect.[37] Now, in the fall of 1806, the idea so possessed Lydia that she began questioning whether it could be made real.

For six years, Lydia had chosen to pursue a path unthinkable to young women in her parents' generation. By rejecting suitors and working for wages, Lydia had preserved her liberty to read and write, unlike her married friends. Sharing those rewards of singlehood with Charity promised an even greater happiness than she had previously contemplated. "If you had such a family and home as I am blest with, how would it add to our mutual happiness," she wrote. As Charity's constant companion, Lydia dreamed, she would be able "to share with you in reading those valuable authors which employ your leisure moments."[38] They would lead a life devoted to literature and the mind. The greatest obstacle to realizing this vision lay in a lack of the imagination, a deficiency that neither Lydia nor Charity suffered. "If our ideas are confin'd our thou'ts will consequently be confin'd likewise," Lydia wrote to Charity.[39] Alarmed that troubles in Peter's house would drive away her soul mate, Lydia set loose her thoughts and ideas.

The shared passion for reading and writing that first united Lydia and Charity held a key to imagining a new way of life together. Poetry and novels had taught the women most of what they knew about romantic friendship, and one of the most celebrated romantic friendships within the era's literature was the lifelong attachment between Eleanor Butler and Sarah Ponsonby. These two Anglo-Irish gentlewomen had run away from their families in 1778 to spend their lives together in the Welsh village of Llangollen. Their romantic manner of living and their charming home and gardens attracted many famous visitors who wrote about the relationship. William Wordsworth, Walter Scott, and Erasmus Darwin all commented on the relationship (Anne Lister visited as well).[40] Charity and Lydia most likely learned of the so-called Ladies of Llangollen in the works of Anna Seward, a celebrated British poet who devoted her pen to the subject of female friendships. Seward wrote several poems about the Ladies of Llangollen, whose style of living together she hoped to adopt with her own beloved friend Honora Sneyd.[41] Seward even named one of her books for the women, *The Vale of Llangollen and Other Poems* (1796).[42]

The surest clue that Lydia in particular liked the poems of Anna Seward lies in a strange stylistic tic. Lydia repeated the word "vale" in her poetry and correspondence in the same way that Anna Seward did, to convey her appreciation for the female form.[43] Vale, meaning valley, was an archaic word even in 1800, but it appeared frequently in Seward's writing. Not only did she title her most popular poem for Butler and Ponsonby "The Vale of Llangollen," but she also incorporated images of vales into many of her other poems, especially those devoted to her friend Honora.[44] Often pairing it with words like hill, mound, or cleft, Seward used the word *vale* as a euphemism for female genitalia. In a poem like Seward's 1806 "Song," dedicated to Honora, "the Syren of my soul," the poet used a description of nature to voice her pleasure in watching the morning light reveal her lover's body: "Oft I saw the rosy dawn / deck the hill, the vale, the lawn / Pleas'd I found them fair, and warm."[45] Seward's usage spread to other poets, who offered even more explicit depictions of the landscape to represent women's lovemaking. Estelle Anna Lewis's poem, "The Last Hour of Sappho" (1844), named for the famous lesbian poet, rhapsodized the sun that "kiss[ed] the sloping hills, and myrtle bows / And flowers, and streams, and Lesbian maiden's brows, / As they were warbling 'long the sultry vale."[46]

Lydia's poems adapted the word *vale* to the same purpose. An acrostic titled "Spring," which Lydia copied out for Charity while they were living together in January 1807, contained lines that could be interpreted as descriptive of a woman having an orgasm during oral sex:

Zephyrs gently wave oer field and groves,
While tuneful warblers breathe their pleasing notes
And rivulets murmur through the peaceful vale
Each tumult of the breast is hush'd to peace

The lover's zephyr breath, passing over her partner's lower groves, brings forth tuneful warblers and pleasing notes, until in the climactic moment rivulets murmur through the vale and the internal tumult is restored to peace.[47]

In Seward's poems, the vale represented not only a woman's body, but also a feminized physical space. In "the fairy palace of the Vale," Seward wrote, the Ladies of Llangollen devote their time "to letter'd ease" and "Friendship's blest repose." Lydia's fantasy of adopting Charity as her "constant companion" and, sharing "in reading those valuable authors which employ your leisure moments," sought to replicate the Ladies' famed arrangement. Waiting for Charity to return to Plainfield in November 1806, Lydia wrote a poem to her absent lover describing how her dreams of "promis'd pleasure" with Charity inspired her to build castles in the air.[48] Lydia desperately desired a home to shelter herself and Charity, like the gothic-Tudor fairy palace that Butler and Ponsonby renovated for themselves. Unlike those Irish gentle-ladies, however, Charity and Lydia had no inheritances to pay for their independence. A castle built from air, not bricks and mortar, was the best that Lydia could construct.

To be practical, Lydia dreamt that she and Charity might make their lives together in the bosom of the Richards family. In early December, she wrote to Charity that on her next visit to Plainfield "it will probably be convenient for you to bring your trunk—do bring every thing."[49] Never again, she hoped, would the women's bond be sundered. In her heart, Lydia had come to imagine herself and Charity as secretly wed. She wrote to Charity in a December 1 letter that soon "I hope my dear we shall 'take a sight of comfort.'" The quotation came from a popular play, Venice Preserv'd, which featured a secret marriage between two star-crossed lovers, Jaffeir and Belvidera. The line repeated Belvidera's promise to her secret husband that only when they were reunited would she glimpse "a sight of comfort." Placing herself in the role of secret wife and lover, Lydia begged Charity to bring her peace by making the move to Plainfield.[50]

On December 8, Charity arrived in Plainfield, trunk in tow. For nearly two months, the women shared their lives. As Lydia had desired, they spent many of their leisure hours reading and writing poetry together. Lydia presented Charity with a new year's poem voicing her wish that nothing might interrupt their future together. "May life's best joys distill like gentle dew," Lydia prayed, and "Thy friends prove constant and forever true."[51] But the idyll could not last forever. Narratives of secret marriages tend to end badly. Like Jaffeir and Belvidera, or the more familiar star-crossed couple Romeo and Juliet, Lydia and Charity could not protect their secret bond for long from the scrutiny of family.

Lydia's chamber, far from being a fortified tower, lay subject to the household authority of her parents. Under this parental roof, Charity and Lydia lived in constant danger of exposure. The tension proved unbearable. At the end of January, the two women traveled together to the nearby town of Worthington to pay a visit to a friend and escape familial oversight for a spell.[52] Soon the Richardses demanded Lydia return back home, alone. The pain "when I was torn from you," Lydia wrote to Charity, was "indiscribable." Apparently, her parents had discovered a reason to separate the friends. They may have become aware of the sexual bond between Lydia and Charity. Charity seems to have worried as much.

One letter hints that Charity feared Lydia's parents had discovered a secret sexual object she possessed, possibly a dildo. (Leather and rag-stuffed dildos were known objects at the time, and Charity could have used her sewing skills to construct one.) Whatever the secret object was, once Lydia returned home to Plainfield, she wrote to assure Charity of its safety: "the thing which you supposed you left I have found here." Lydia also promised that "your letter has never been expos'd." But Charity's greater anxiety, that Lydia's parents had discovered they were lovers, could not be swept away.[53] Lydia begged Charity to return to Plainfield, but Charity came only for a short while. Contrary to her lover's hopes, Charity made plans to leave the Hampshire Hills once again, accepting an invitation from her old Bridgewater friends Asaph and Polly Hayward to visit them at their new home in Weybridge, Vermont.[54]

On the wintry day in February 1807 that Charity made her final departure from Plainfield, Lydia stood crying at the window as she watched the sleigh pull away. Moments before her departure, Charity had scribbled out a last letter and handed it to Lydia, who tucked the page within the bosom of her dress. She was crying too hard to read it straight away. Only after Charity had disappeared from sight did Lydia pull the paper from her breast. Charity had written an acrostic on the word "adieu," five short sentences promising to love Lydia forever and to come back to her. At the bottom of the page Charity drew a dotted heart, along the outside she wrote her own name and inside she wrote Lydia's. It was a picture of an embrace, of Charity enfolding Lydia and of Lydia's name surrounding yet another vale. The gesture was deeply erotic, and consequently deeply dangerous. It was the sort of letter that, left in the wrong place, and seen by the wrong eyes, could get both writer and recipient in terrible trouble.

Alone in her bedroom that evening, Lydia felt a terrible loneliness take possession of her heart. After midnight, when she was sure her parents and siblings had gone to sleep, she scrawled out her feelings of abandonment in a letter to her absent friend, bemoaning her condemnation to "now sleep alone—not as formerly, when enclos'd in your friendly <u>arms</u>."[55] Thoughts of the physical intimacy she had lost plagued Lydia over the following months.[56] She dreamed about what it would have been like to join Charity on the trip. If only she could have come along, then at night Charity's head "should rest on my bosom, and at night you should repose in my arms!"[57] Time did not diminish Lydia's longing. She breathlessly counted the days until Charity's return, when she hoped they would be united for good.[58] She dreamed of Charity at night and thought of her by day. Lydia's thoughts turned so intensely toward Charity that she took several chances in her writing that she probably should not have.

A month after Charity's departure, Lydia sent Charity a letter in which she enclosed a poem written in red ink, a color typically associated with courtship. The poem, like so many of Lydia's letters, described her pleasure in Charity's love, her sorrow at their separation, and her longing for a physical reunion. Now Lydia imagined herself reclining on Charity's "gentle breast," and "guarded by her gentle hand." The poem skimmed the boundaries of polite speech, the red ink broadcasting the passion of Lydia's feelings. This was the twentieth letter she had written Charity since their reunion six months earlier. Read in sequence, the letters trace a rising crescendo of feeling, until Lydia's extreme and desperate longing for her absent lover drove her to the outer limits of propriety.

Thus it is striking that the next letter in the sequence of correspondence has gone missing from the archive.[59] The Henry Sheldon Museum, where Lydia's correspondence is stored, has a record of a letter Lydia wrote to Charity three weeks after the red-ink poem. But the letter itself has vanished. In the card catalog an archivist has written the simple word "missing." Sometime after the original indexing of the collection during the 1930s the letter disappeared. A missing document is hardly surprising in such an extensive collection. Researchers misplace documents in the wrong files. Papers get lost. But the context of this particular missing document, coming at the apogee of an arc of lesbian desire, arouses suspicion. The possibility exists that this particular letter spoke too transparently about a physical relationship between Lydia and Charity and was removed from the collection as a consequence. Many archival collections have been purged of homoerotic materials and other items deemed sexually inappropriate.[60] Lydia's missing letter is a silence that requires consideration.

In the spring of 1807, another silence troubled Lydia. At the time of her departure, Charity promised Lydia she would come back at the end of spring. Grieved at their separation, Lydia counted the days until Charity's promised return. After a month had passed, Lydia wrote to Charity that "at the most unfavorable calculation, the time of our separation is at least a third elapsed—the rest will soon be gone, long as it may seem." Only this reassuring thought preserved Lydia's peace of mind. Thoughts of Charity obsessed her: "you are not only almost constantly in my mind when awake, but I very frequently dream of you." She dreamed of Charity "returning from Vermont," and she dreamed of their physical reunion. Seductively, she informed Charity that her parents were leaving for a weeklong visit and "I shall be almost alone in the house. O that you could be here."[61] The image was designed to arouse Charity and hurry her home, but Lydia's confidence in the power of her physical charms to draw back her absent lover began to falter as May came and there was no word from Charity about her return.

Finally, in June, a letter arrived from Charity, written on her birthday, May 22, with the news that she intended to prolong her visit in Weybridge until the fall. Lydia wrote back sorrowfully, "I could earnestly have wish'd to see you before the expiration of so long a term." Lydia remained committed to her dream of making a life with Charity. She informed Charity that her younger sister Sally was getting married. In early America, the marriage of a younger sister before the older suggested that the firstborn was unlikely to marry.[62] By allowing Sally to marry out of birth order, the Richards family acknowledged Lydia's chosen identity as a single woman. Confirming her exceptional path, Lydia accepted another summer teaching contract and departed to board for the summer in Hawley. She would earn her own way until Charity's eventual return. "To your friendly bosom I commit everything," Lydia wrote in closing. And then a final hasty postscript: "writing my dear does not satisfy me—I want something more."[63]

The months stretched on. Lydia heard very little from Weybridge. She imagined that Charity must be living with Asaph and Polly Hayward, surrounded by their children, Achsah, Edwin, and Emma. She waited with "patience, resolution, prudence &c." until she could once again press Charity to her heart. She signed her letters to Charity "yours as ever in the bonds of friendship."[64] She waited for her lover's return. She fantasized about a device that could carry their voices to each other across the great space that separated them. How sad, she wrote,

> That this silent conversation cannot be convey'd to you with that rapidity with which sounds are convey'd in the vehicle of air—At the usual calculation, could any sound be heard at so great a distance, (and it is asserted that sounds may be heard 200 miles in cold countries) ten minutes would be sufficient to convey it from me to you.[65]

Denied the opportunity to speak into Charity's ear, she sent letter after letter asking when Charity was coming home.[66] She directed her thoughts north like arrows.

Charity sent a letter promising to come home in November, then another letter putting off the date again. When November came, Lydia heard from acquaintances who had visited Weybridge that Charity was living with a young woman apprentice. The realization of her betrayal fell like a blow. Earlier, she conceded, "I yielded a kind of unwilling consent to your longer stay in Weybridge," but she had not consented to a permanent separation. Now "you seem to express some doubt respecting your return in the winter." When, she asked, would their long separation come to an end? "When shall I once more clasp you to this palpitating heart?"[67] She followed this stinging letter with an even more powerful rebuke, copying out a plaintive poem from the 1791 seduction novel *Charlotte Temple* in which the title character laments her ruin and abandonment by her lover, Montraville. Like Charlotte, Lydia mourned that her "weary breast / can neither peace nor comfort find / Or friend where on to rest."[68] Charity's abandonment had left Lydia so bereft that she took the tremendous risk of sending Charity a letter that clearly identified herself as a forsaken lover.[69]

Still she hoped, waited, and believed against all evidence that Charity would come back to her. In January 1808, Lydia wrote to tell Charity that she had turned down another offer of marriage. She remained "yours as ever, L. Richards."[70] A year had passed since Charity's departure. "How little my dear, do we know of futurity! And how little did we see or know of it at the moment of our separation," Lydia wrote.[71] More months passed and no letters came from Charity. Lydia began to imagine that Charity had died. But she reassured herself that if Charity were dead, or even incapacitated by illness, people in Weybridge would write to let Peter know, and Lydia would hear it from him.[72] She wrote one more time, "if you ever write again my dear do tell me when I may hope to see you—how little did I believe when I parted with you that so long a separation would ensue."[73]

Only after Charity returned to visit Massachusetts in the spring of 1808 with her "apprentice" in tow did Lydia accept that her beloved companion had left her forever. Lydia recognized the time had come to write Charity a letter of farewell. To protect their privacy, Lydia enclosed the letter in a wrapper, an extra piece of paper intended to guard the contents within. Before the invention of envelopes in the mid-nineteenth century, letter-writers typically folded and sealed their pages, then wrote the address across a square left blank for that purpose. Lydia, who was an especially verbose letter-writer, never used wrappers and always squeezed as many words as possible into her correspondence. But on this occasion she took precautions, both covering the letter and asking Charity to "burn this if you please as soon as read."[74]

Even with those guards in place, Lydia chose her words cautiously. She tried to express her feelings in terms that might read clearly to Charity, but would be obscure to snoopers. Lydia acknowledged her agony over the change in the women's relationship. "Such fleeting hours and days I have indeed enjoy'd with you," Lydia wrote, "but they are gone." Then, intermixing her own words with a series of pointed quotations from the hymns of Isaac Watts, Lydia bid farewell to Charity as a lover:

> 'To boundless joy, and solid mirth, our nobler tho'ts aspire' And how often has our own experience witness'd the fallacy, and the vanity of earthly good— But to abandon all the pleasures of life, and deny that there is any earthly good worth possessing, would still, in my opinion, be unreasonable, and absurd— Can those who have ever enjoy'd the sublime pleasures of exalted friendship,

sincerely say, there is nothing in it <u>worth</u> enjoying? I think not. But alas, how many 'thorns' lie hid in this choicest 'rose'! 'Friendship divides the shares, and lengthens out the store' And I have sometimes for a moment almost doubted whether an affectionate and endearing friendship was productive, on the whole, of more real pleasure and enjoyment, than of pain and anxiety—at least in many instances—and indeed I <u>this moment</u> doubt it. But our life must be fill'd up with varieties—pleasure and pain must chequer the scene—And if this variety, this instability and insufficiency of sublunary things might lead us to the unchanging, the all-sufficient and inexhaustible Fountain of substantial happiness, we might then receive real benefit from them—But O, how much of my heart, and how many of my thoughts are engross'd by earthly friends and terrestrial enjoyments!—'How they divide our wavering minds, And leave not 'half for God.'—O my dear, I have become wholly undeserving of the blessing of friends, by too great an attachment to them, and forgetfulness of the great giver.

The passage may seem unremarkable to modern readers, but like a rebus it contains a hidden message that was clear to Charity, who knew the hymns of Isaac Watts as well as Lydia did. It begins with a quotation from Watts's poem "Parting with Carnal Joys." The term "carnal joy" referred to sexual or sensual pleasures in the Christian tradition. Lydia sent a clear message that their sexual relationship had come to an end by quoting this poem, which instructed Christians to bid farewell to the world's sensual pleasures.[75] Watts's hymn offered an ascetic rejection of earthly love as a "base" pleasure, but Lydia distinguished her own reasons for "parting with carnal joys" from the ascetic rationale. She refused to deny the "sublime pleasures" of friendship; instead she explained that it was the thorns hidden in the rose of friendship that drove her off. Again she was quoting Watts, referencing another of his poems rejecting sensual pleasures. This second poem, "Earth and Heaven," instructed Christians to beware "mortal joy" because every "pleasure must be dash'd with pain." Pleasure never came without a cost, "so roses grow on thorns, and honey wears a sting."[76] The pleasures of friendship were meaningful and good, Lydia insisted. Quoting Watts's elegy for his friend Thomas Gunston, Lydia wrote of how friendship lengthens out the store.[77] But the pains brought by friendship were real. Lydia wondered whether friendship's pleasures could really compensate for its pains. "Indeed I <u>this moment</u> doubt it," she reflected. Finally, Lydia expressed the hope that her disappointment in love might lead her to a renewed relationship with God. And here she quoted Watts one last time. Friends, she wrote, "divide our wavering minds, and leave not 'half for God.'" The line came from a poem Watts composed after a poetess named Elizabeth Singer turned down his proposal of marriage. His marital hopes dashed, Watts bemoaned that every "pleasure has its poison, too."[78] He never married. Lydia used this last Watts reference to identify herself as a rejected suitor. She had offered Charity companionship for life, but Charity rejected her offer. Now Lydia recommitted herself to God. Like Watts, Lydia turned away from dreams of companionship and devoted herself to religious causes.[79]

That Lydia chose to remain unmarried after her breakup with Charity, and did not simply fall into spinsterhood, is clear from the first letter that she wrote in the wake of this farewell missive. The close of Charity and Lydia's romantic relationship did not end their friendship. Perhaps this was one of the benefits of having a relationship that defied conventional categorization. Lydia could not claim the name of scorned woman, and Charity did not get marked down as a rake or seducer. When they ceased to be lovers the two women reinvented their relationship as friends instead of becoming litigants in a breach-of-promise suit. The first letter that Lydia wrote in her new capacity opened again with a quotation from Isaac Watts. "My dear," Lydia wrote, "Life's a long tragedy." This time she was quoting from the oddly titled "The Mourning-Piece," which Watts wrote to a friend shortly after the friend's marriage. The title foreshadows the antipathy toward marriage Watts expresses within the poem. Although he intended the lines to celebrate his friend's wedding, he did a better job describing marriage's pains than its pleasures. (Later Watts apologized in a prefatory "epistle" for the "mortifying lines.")

"The Mourning-Piece" opens with a character named Dianthe making a declaration of her decision to avoid marriage: "Dianthe acts her little part alone, / Nor wishes an associate. So she glides / Single thro' all the storm, and more secure." Dianthe rejects marriage because coupling exposes a person to too much pain. Although she is frequently pursued in love, "firm she stood, / And bold repulsed the bright temptation still, / Nor put the chains on." Dianthe, named after the Roman goddess of chastity Diana, rejects the chains of marriage on principle. Lydia's letter drew repeatedly from "The Mourning-Piece" in order to send a clear message to Charity. The references to the poem both offered recognition of the new relationship that Charity had formed and announced Lydia's own intention to remain unmarried. Life is indeed "a long and tumultuous scene, full of perplexity and care," Lydia wrote to Charity, echoing Watts's lines "What kind perplexities tumultuous rise, / If but the absence of a day divide / Thee from thy fair beloved!" Her own soft heart could not hold up under the pain of being divided from her lover, so she like Dianthe would remain unmarried on principle.[80]

Lydia could expect Charity to understand her meaning. Poetry was always their common language, from the first acrostics they exchanged in 1799 to the last poem Charity wrote for Lydia two months before Lydia's death in 1846. Reading poetry together was their favorite way to spend their time. Lydia never directly quoted Dianthe's pledge to remain single; the meaning would be too obvious to prying eyes. But she knew that Charity's brilliant mind could complete the lines that she began. Charity was as familiar with Dianthe's pledge as Lydia was; the lines had special meaning to her. Eight years earlier Charity had made the same pledge. It took meeting Sylvia Drake to change her mind.

10

Charity and Sylvia

FEBRUARY 1807

DESPITE THE TEARS of her friend, the strenuous objections of her brother, and the foreboding state of the weather, Charity mounted Dr. Shaw's sleigh one cold morning in February 1807 to set out on a 150-mile drive north.[1] She had little choice. Despite their best efforts, neither Peter nor Lydia could make Charity feel welcome in Cummington and Plainfield. The townspeople, Charity felt, treated "women in a single state" like herself with "contempt."[2] Peter could not even compel his own in-laws, whose house he shared, to be kind to his long-suffering younger sister. At Lydia's parents' house, Charity lived in a suspended state of anxiety, worried that one fatal slip would reveal her secrets. The pressure took a toll on her health. Once again, she felt the need to take flight.[3] Increasingly desperate to leave Massachusetts, Charity finally wrote a letter to Polly and Asaph Hayward accepting their longstanding invitation to Vermont.

The letter thrilled her old friends. "We shall all be glad to see you," Asaph wrote in reply.[4] The news would be especially welcome to his wife, Polly, who felt isolated in the rough little frontier house they had inhabited since moving from North Bridgewater two years before.[5] Charity's knowledge of poetry and her religious sensibility promised much-needed stimulation after the long months that Polly had spent cooped up with her seven young children. It was a particularly severe winter, with temperatures frequently far below zero. One evening the thermometer dipped to negative twenty-eight degrees.[6] The weather gave the Haywards cause to worry about their guest's safe arrival. Local newspapers carried stories of winter travelers and livestock who got lost in the snowdrifts and would not be discovered till the spring thaw.[7] But anticipation overcame these concerns.

Charity too must have felt some trepidation tempering her excitement as the sleigh completed the final leg of the journey. The little settlement at Weybridge barely left a smudge on the white blanket of snow that covered the valley.[8] If her destination looked unprepossessing from the outside, what reception would Charity find within Asaph and Polly's four walls? Back in Bridgewater, the couple had treated Charity as a member of their family. The Haywards were connected to Charity's mother's relations, the Howards, making Asaph and Charity distant cousins. Polly and Charity also shared a spiritual sisterhood stemming from their attendance at the same church.[9] In 1803 Polly asked Charity to be a godmother to her new twins, whom Charity named Edwin and Emma, after a poem about star-crossed lovers whose future was quashed by a cruel father.[10] Before the Haywards left Massachusetts, Charity would watch the babies when Polly left the house. But two years had passed since she had seen the little ones, leaving her a stranger in their eyes. Asaph reassured her that "our children talk about aunt Charity every day," but little children had such short memories.[11]

Even Polly and Asaph's oldest daughter, Achsah, with whom Charity had shared a special bond, would now be like a stranger, grown from a child into a fifteen-year-old young woman. Would Achsah still have the quick and curious sensibility that once endeared her to Charity, or would the pressures of maturity have tamed her spirit? Years before, Achsah had embraced Charity as a surrogate aunt to replace her beloved aunt Sylvia, who had moved with her mother's other siblings to Vermont. Achsah saw a strong resemblance between the two women. One afternoon in 1803, while Charity was watching the twins, Achsah wrote a letter to Sylvia describing "Aunt Charity" as the "nearest to me of any body about here" in filling Sylvia's absence. Charity was as "clever as the day is long and always ready to do anything in the world," Achsah reported. The young girl seemed to recognize that Charity and Sylvia shared a distinctive orientation to the world, a critical distance that made them unusual.[12] Achsah may also have made a silent comparison between Sylvia's and Charity's apparent shared aversion to marriage, for which Achsah had once rebuked her aunt.[13]

Overhearing Achsah and her younger siblings talk daily of Charity in the weeks before she arrived gave Achsah's aunt Sylvia some cause for anxiety as well. The visit of this purportedly clever and learned woman represented an exciting opportunity for Sylvia, who felt frustrated by the lack of opportunities for intellectual development in remote Weybridge. Residing for long stretches in the Haywards' home, Sylvia found a source of spiritual inspiration in her older and pious sister Polly and a source of juvenile companionship in her younger and witty niece Achsah. Charity's arrival at the Haywards' created the potential for Sylvia to form a new type of connection, an equal friendship with another single woman like herself given over to the love of learning and religion. At the same time, Charity's arrival threatened to expose the weakness of Sylvia's education, confirming the insecurities that she suffered over her poor schooling.

No record remains of Charity and Sylvia's first encounter. Sylvia may have been waiting at the Haywards' house when Charity first stepped through the door, or she may have later paid a visit to her sister's to be introduced to the much-anticipated guest. Sylvia was only twenty-two when she and Charity first met, but their meeting seemed ages overdue. Countless intersections bound their family histories in the previous decades. Sylvia's brothers Asaph and Oliver had worked at a tavern kept by Charity's cousin Barnabas; Charity frequently visited with her Howard cousins who lived in south Easton and were neighbors to the Drakes; Sylvia's oldest sister had married a man who was distantly related to Charity's mother and her foster mother; a relation of Charity's had married Sylvia's uncle Josiah. Sylvia's brother Asaph Drake alluded to these prior family connections when he described the women's relationship in a memoir of his life penned forty years later.[14] Perhaps he hoped to naturalize the relationship between the women with allusions to a family bond, because from the outset the spark between Charity and Sylvia was so romantic in nature.

The women's histories and personas complemented each other and compelled an immediate mutual attraction. If Sylvia felt insecure about her lack of sophistication, that youth and innocence endeared her to Charity, who had endured years of travail. Charity adored Sylvia as her "sweet girl."[15] If Charity worried about the burden of her past, her complicated history added to the aura of worldliness that attracted Sylvia. Charity's experiences of travel and friendship gave Sylvia access to a wider world beyond the boundaries of Weybridge. She was glad to become an "apprentice" to the older woman.

During the months after Charity's arrival, she and Sylvia had plenty of time to establish their intimacy. March and April continued the unusually snowy and cold weather that had gripped the region for months.[16] Confined within the frontier community's small houses, seated close to the open hearths that provided their heat, the women spent hours in close contact. Weybridge badly needed a tailor as skilled as Charity, and soon she had more work than she could handle by herself.[17] Sylvia began to help with the sewing.[18] Fingers kept busy by needle and thread, they made conversation to keep their minds occupied. At night they may have shared a bed and continued the conversation, but with their hands freed from work. The cold that permeated the bed chamber drew the women close together. By the time May warmed the Vermont air, Charity and Sylvia were in love.

Two poems reveal Sylvia's feelings during her first months with Charity. The first, a manuscript poem titled "Spring," was signed S. D. but left undated. A close reading suggests that Sylvia wrote the poem in the spring that she and Charity fell in love, but the timing cannot be confirmed. The second poem, titled "Ode to Spring," was published in the local *Middlebury Mercury* on June 10, 1807, and written during May of that year. The poem is signed "S. D.," like the manuscript poems Sylvia left behind. The author was local, since the poem appeared in no other newspapers or poetry collections, but Sylvia's authorship cannot be definitively established. Each poem follows a similar structure and incorporates similar imagery, suggesting one author for both. Taken together, these two poems illuminate the exuberance and anxieties that Sylvia felt as she fell in love.[19]

Both poems begin with a statement of the sheer joy that residents of a cold climate feel when winter's white shroud melts away and blossoms burst forth on the branch.

Spring	Ode to Spring
The beautifull season of spring	Winter, with her dismal train,
Has return'd to enliven the mind	Now has left the happy plain
The birds on the boughs sweetly sing	Genial Spring resumes her seat,
To teach us to be gentle & kind	Prolific queen of every sweet

The newspaper's "Ode to Spring," a much longer poem, next introduces the character of the "genial goddess, May!" who brings love to the land. Sylvia associated May with Charity, since it was her birth month.[20] When the goddess of May arrives, she introduces "*scenes of innocence and love*"; she "smiles / whilst love the passing hour beguiles" and "the am'rous plaintive dove, / murmurs music thro' the grove." The lines are Sylvia's love song to Charity.

The physical nature of the women's intimacy is hinted at by lines in both poems comparing spring romance to the freshets that break through the ice-choked river. May awakens new delightful feelings in the dormant body/earth.

All nature seems fill'd with delight	Bub'ling down the craggy steep,
The brooks softly murmur along	As chrystal clear the waters creep;
The sun moon & stars with their light	Which when the fruitful flat they gain,
Awaken each Heart to a song.	Glide smoothly thro' the spacious plain.
	Sweet the prospect—sweet the grove;
	Scenes of sympathy and love

This imagery participated in the long tradition of erotic landscape poetry that compared a lover's body to scenes from nature, familiar not only from the lesbian sonnets of Anna Seward but from the sonnets of Shakespeare. ("Shall I compare thee to a summer's day?") In Sylvia's odes to spring, suggestive images of murmuring streams passing over sweet groves "awaken each heart to a song" and give way to "scenes of sympathy and love." Recalling Seward's symbolism, Sylvia's published "Ode to Spring" describes a scene of "joy in the flow'ry winding vale." The line speaks to the possibility of the women's orgasmic fulfillment—their joy in the vale. The line also suggests that far from the judgmental surveillance of her Massachusetts connections Charity had discovered her own "vale of Llangollen" along the banks of Weybridge's Otter Creek.

Both of Sylvia's spring poems end on a similar foreboding note, observing that every birth or rebirth must be followed by decline and sorrow and that the knowledge of past and future sufferings haunts our most hopeful moments.[21] As Isaac Watts put it, sweet honey comes with a sting. Sylvia ends both "Spring" and "Ode to Spring" with pain and death:

But the hand that now holds the pen	But Autumn crops his fancied bloom
And endeavors to scribble in vain	Pointing, tho' slow, a certain doom;
Dreads the springs sad sickening return	He withers like the ripin'd corn,
That gives nothing but sorrow & pain.	And silver hairs his brows adorn:
	Unstrung each nerve, all vigor past,
	He yields to winter's chilling blast.

Even in love, Sylvia's Calvinist soul felt the weight of mortality and God's judgment bearing down on her. These sentiments were routine for strict Protestants of the era, but the young woman had a special reason to feel the cruelty of spring's arrival.

The end of May brought the date for Charity's promised departure from Weybridge. Charity had arrived in Vermont in February with the stated intention to remain for only three months before returning to Massachusetts.[22] Sylvia's poems suggest the pain she felt while falling in love as she watched her allotted time with her lover slip away. In pastoral poetry, the cycle of seasons stands as an allegory for man's long passage through life: spring's birth, summer's vigor, fall's senescence, and winter's cold death. For Sylvia the cycle accelerated mercilessly. Spring meant spring, a few months not a stretch of years, and sorrow loomed not at life's long end but in a handful of weeks.

For Charity, feelings of betrayal complicated the dread of separating from Sylvia. Throughout her late winter months in Weybridge, Charity received a steady stream of letters from Lydia bespeaking her longing for her absent lover and counting the days until Charity's return. In April, Lydia sent a letter reminding Charity of the promise she had made to return, and courting Charity with a poem about their love. "Lovely friend, forever true / My heart can never forget" Lydia wrote in red-inked lines, "For her I shed the silent tear / And wisk it from my eye / This painful absence too severe."[23] Charity knew that she did not deserve Lydia's flattery. She had not remained true but allowed Sylvia's warm proximity to distract her from the other woman waiting 150 frozen miles away. Charity's guilty conscience explains why she withheld mention of Sylvia from her letters to Lydia throughout the spring and summer of 1807.

As the final days of May slipped away, Charity decided to extend her stay in Weybridge through the summer, but her decision to remain did not resolve the problem of the women's looming separation.[24] In June, Sylvia left Asaph and Polly's home to spend some time with her mother in the nearby town of Bristol. Single women like herself needed to distribute the burden of their upkeep among the members of their families. After Sylvia's departure, Charity remained in Weybridge longing for the young woman to whom she had become so passionately attached. Though there were only ten miles from Weybridge to Bristol, still the distance overpowered Charity's common sense during the days they spent apart.

Before Sylvia's departure the women had agreed that Sylvia would write first. Charity knew from past experience that caution needed to be taken with personal correspondence. Letters passed between Sylvia and herself by the hands of Sylvia's relatives, who traveled often from Weybridge to Bristol. Too frequent or too demonstrative letters might alarm the Drakes. But if Charity were a cautious woman this history would never have been written. Her individualism and drive made her life notable. She was "enterprising and spirited" in the words of her nephew Cullen; "always ready to do anything in the world," according to Achsah.[25] Rather than sit quietly in Weybridge and wait for a letter, longing drove Charity to the pen. Sitting at a table in Polly's house, Charity wrote the first of only three letters that she apparently ever sent to Sylvia. The reason for this neglect is simple: the letters succeeded in bringing Sylvia back to her within a month. Never again over the following forty-four years would they be separated. From the moment that Charity and Sylvia met to the moment Charity died, the women spent only one month apart: June 1807.

"My dear Sylvia," Charity began. "It was not our agreement, nor was it my intention to have written to you, before I had the pleasure of receiving a letter from you. But notwithstanding, I feel an inclination not easily overcome to address a few lines to you at this time." The letter mixed caution with the evidence of desire. "I have often felt the want of your society since we parted," Charity wrote, and "often recollected the agreeable hours which I have passed with you." Soon, she wrote, "I hope they will be renewed." Couching her longing for Sylvia in familial terms, Charity wrote that everyone in the Hayward house was "anxious to hear" whether Sylvia intended to come back for the summer. But neither Polly and Achsah nor the children wrote to tell her so. Charity's letter is the only evidence of desire for Sylvia's return to Weybridge.[26]

On its surface, Charity's letter gives little evidence that she considered Sylvia a lover. The tone is resolutely friendly. Charity closes the letter with "ardent and sincere desire," but this signature is out of step with the temperate tone that precedes it. As typical with Charity's writing, however, close reading reveals hidden layers of meaning. While Charity communicated messages to Lydia in the language of poetry, she used biblical references for Sylvia. It is likely that Sylvia knew every verse of her King James Bible nearly by heart. (In later years she led the Weybridge Sunday school, training children to memorize the Bible verse by verse.) Charity counted on this knowledge when she wrote to Sylvia. After expressing her hope that Sylvia would soon return to Weybridge, Charity used biblical terms to reassure Sylvia about a possible cause for reluctance: the sexual potential within their intimacy.

If Sylvia returned, Charity promised, they could live together according to God's "dispensations" and improve their hours together "better than those already passed." Quoting from Paul's second epistle to the Corinthians, Charity promised Sylvia that even if Satan tempted them and made their flesh infirm, God would still love them in their weakness. When Paul asked God to relieve him of Satan's temptations, God promised "my grace is sufficient for thee." The Pauline verses that Charity quoted to Sylvia ended with a warning to church members who practiced "uncleanness, fornication, and lewdness," but gave hope to sinners who "repented."[27] In short, through the language of the New Testament, Charity promised Sylvia that God would forgive them their "uncleanness" and "lewdness" if they repented. God loved man *especially* in his weakness. The verse established a holy basis on which to establish their future together.

Sylvia missed Charity as terribly as Charity missed her. During their brief separation she wrote Charity many letters. Those pages are missing now, whether lost or purposely destroyed; we know of their existence only because Charity thanked Sylvia for the lines. Whatever Sylvia wrote must have revealed the strength of her feelings for Charity. The letters made Charity so confident in their shared love that she began to plan for their future.

First she needed to find a place to live in Weybridge. A decade of experience had taught Charity a clear lesson: her romantic attachment to another woman could never be secure under someone else's roof. In Massachusetts, Charity had little choice but to live with her family. To reside on her own in the same town as a brother, sister, or parent would indicate a shameful disorder within the family. In Weybridge, Charity's absence of true kin gave her no choice but to establish her own residence, which freed her to live the life she desired. She could not live forever on the hospitality of Asaph and Polly. Fortunately, the high volume of sewing work in Weybridge generated just enough income to live on her own. By the end of June, Charity had rented her own room in town.[28] Charity's proximity to the Drakes kept her within the fictive kinship network of a highly esteemed local family. The visit to Weybridge had reestablished all the old intimacy between Charity and the Haywards, allowing Charity to draw on her role as "aunt" to authorize her membership in the Weybridge community. Within careful limits, Charity had set up her own home for the first time in her adult life.

Afterward, Charity wrote to Sylvia in Bristol to make plans for the younger woman's return to Weybridge. Although she loved writing, Charity now declared that she looked "forward to that period as near at hand when the use of pen and paper will be needless to communicate our tho'ts, and express our feelings." Charity had run her course with love letters and their incumbent risks, lacunae, miscommunications, and disappointments. She and Sylvia would live together and love each other unattended by "those piercing thorns which the Rose conceals." Their relationship would defy Watts's claim that all pleasures come with pain. Charity called on the "*God of Love!*" to grace their future. Charity's second letter to Sylvia did not disguise the passion of her feelings as her first letter had. She begged Sylvia to come back to Weybridge straight away. "Do not wait," Charity implored her absent lover.[29]

The question remained of how to persuade Sylvia's family to let her go. The women found a convenient rationale in work. Charity proposed to hire Sylvia full-time as her assistant in the tailoring business. This arrangement suited the Drakes well. Nearly twenty-three, with no marriage on the horizon, Sylvia was poised to become a burden to her family. If she could earn her keep working for Charity she would save her family both expense and worry. On the afternoon of July 2, Charity wrote her last letter to Sylvia. "I am … feeling very anxious to have you *come* this week as I have much work on my hands," she began. But unable to repress her emotions, Charity soon slipped into a lover's tone. "Do not disappoint my hopes and blast my expectations. For I not only want you to come to assist me, but I long to see you and enjoy your company and conversation and tho' I feel very anxious to have you come for the first consideration, yet for the last, every delay excites anxiety in my bosom." Addressing Sylvia as her "dear girl," Charity closed the letter with an "ardent wish" for Sylvia's earthly and celestial happiness.[30] The next morning, Polly and Asaph's nineteen-year-old son Joseph traveled from Weybridge to Bristol to collect Sylvia and her trunk and bring them back to Charity.

On Friday, July 3, 1807, "I left my mother's house and commenced serving in company with Dear Miss B," Sylvia wrote in her diary decades later.[31] Through all the uncertainties of Sylvia's childhood, Mary Drake had tried her hardest to protect this cerebral youngest daughter from the world's bitter repast. Now Sylvia had to reassure her mother in the sober terms of work and faith that she was ready to leave the family. When Joseph arrived at the door with the horse and cart, she bid her mother a last farewell then climbed into the seat beside her nephew. The river road snaked south beside Otter Creek, crossing buzzing fields of flowering Timothy-grass and passing rough homesteads recently erected. Each heavy step of the horse closed the distance between Sylvia and her beloved. To think that only months before they had been strangers to each other and now each felt they could not live apart. The cart arrived at Charity's door. At last Joseph made his farewell and the door closed behind the two women.

Charity Bryant's family home in North Bridgewater, now Brockton, Massachusetts. This classic "New England large house," two rooms deep on both floors, is representative of homes built in eighteenth-century Massachusetts. The house was identified as the Bryant home by Gerald Beals, curator of the Brockton Historical Society. *Photo by author, July 2012.*

"A View from the Falls at Otter Creek," by Thomas Davies, 1766. The landscape surrounding Otter Creek remained rugged when Sylvia Drake moved to Weybridge, around 1799. *With permission of the Royal Ontario Museum © ROM.*

Silhouette of Asaph Drake (1775–1871).
Middle brother Asaph pioneered the Drake
family's removal from Massachusetts to
Addison County, Vermont. *Courtesy of the
Henry Sheldon Museum of Vermont History,
Middlebury, Vermont.*

Peter Bryant (1767–1820). Charity lived with
Peter Bryant and his family periodically
during her twenties, before she settled in
Weybridge, Vermont. *Bryant Family Papers,
Bureau County Historical Society, Princeton,
Illinois.*

Sarah "Sally" Snell Bryant (1768–1847).
Charity shared a close connection to her
sister-in-law Sally Bryant throughout the
women's long lives. *Bryant Family Papers,
Bureau County Historical Society, Princeton,
Illinois.*

Locks of hair cut from twins Edwin and Emma Hayward, 1803. Charity Bryant befriended Sylvia's older sister Polly Hayward in North Bridgewater, Massachusetts, during the early 1800s. The two became so close that Polly and her husband, Asaph Hayward, asked Charity to name their twins, who were born in 1803. *Photo courtesy of Randy Hayward.*

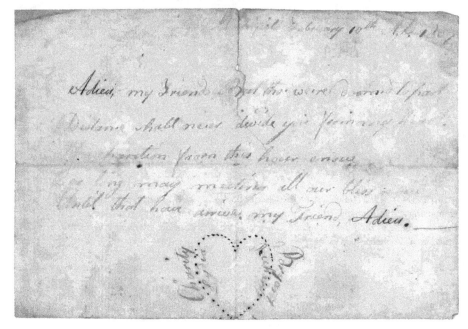

The poem presented by Charity to her lover Lydia Richards, before Charity departed Massachusetts to visit Weybridge in February 1807. Lydia and Charity had discussed establishing a home together in Massachusetts, but Charity abandoned the plan in order to stay in Vermont with Sylvia. *Courtesy of the Henry Sheldon Museum of Vermont History, Middlebury, Vermont.*

An acrostic for Sylvia Drake, written by Charity Bryant, August 17, 1807. Charity excelled at composing acrostic poems. This early acrostic was one of many Charity would write for Sylvia over the course of their lives together. *Courtesy of the Henry Sheldon Museum of Vermont History, Middlebury, Vermont.*

A page from Sylvia Drake's 1821 diary. Drake squeezed as many words as possible onto her diary pages, using shorthand for clothing items the women sewed and initials for frequent visitors. Both Sylvia and Charity kept diaries throughout their lives, but only five years of Sylvia's diaries are still extant. Charity's diaries were all destroyed after her death. *Courtesy of the Henry Sheldon Museum of Vermont History, Middlebury, Vermont.*

Charity Bryant and Sylvia Drake used this adult-sized cradle to treat their frequent ill health. They sometimes encouraged guests who were feeling sick to rest in the cradle as well. *Courtesy of the Henry Sheldon Museum of Vermont History, Middlebury, Vermont.*

A few years after Charity's death in 1851, Sylvia left their rustic cottage and moved into her brother Asaph's comfortable brick house in Weybridge, Vermont. She remained there until her death in 1868. *Photo by author, July 2012.*

Sylvia Drake and Charity Bryant are buried together in Weybridge, Vermont, under a single headstone. The Drake family showed respect for the women's union by not only burying them together, but also spending extra money to have the women's names embossed rather than carved into the monument. *Photo by author, July 2012.*

11

The Tie That Binds

"ON THE 3RD day of July 1807," Charity wrote in a brief 1844 memoir of her life, Sylvia Drake "consented to be my <u>help-meet</u> and came to be my companion ~~in labor~~."[1] In thirteen well-chosen words, two stricken out, Charity, master at rebuses, disguised a radical assertion: that she and Sylvia began their lives together by uniting in a marriage.

Each word built this astounding claim. To begin, Charity averred that Sylvia had "consented" to a union between the women. For nearly a millennium, "consent" had served as the touchstone of marriage in the European tradition. Neither a minister's presence nor a civil license was necessary if it could be proved that two people had consented to marry one another. The passage of the Hardwicke Act in England in 1753 imposed new licensing restrictions that cracked down on the problem of clandestine marriages.[2] But in the United States, nineteenth-century jurists continued to affirm that couples could establish common-law marriages legitimated by mutual consent alone, rather than civil or religious authority. This right to enter into marriage by consent could even override the rules that governed who was eligible to marry. At times, courts recognized consent-based common-law marriages in which one spouse had a civil disability, such as being enslaved or underage, which excluded him or her from marrying.[3] Charity and Sylvia's connection, which defied the legal definition of marriage as the "union of a man and woman," fell within this gray zone.[4]

Charity's next words, describing Sylvia as "my <u>help-meet</u>," built her claim that the women's relationship constituted a marriage. She adopted the phrase from the passage in the book of Genesis where God creates Eve as a help-meet to Adam (2:18). In the Protestant culture of early America, *help-meet* served as a common synonym for wife.[5] Charity's use of the pronoun "my" before the word "help-meet" further claimed Sylvia as a wife by taking possession of her. In his influential *Commentaries* (1765–69), jurist William Blackstone explained that under coverture law a wife's "very being" fell under the "protection" of her husband upon marriage; all her property, and to a large extent her body, became his. Ownership defined the relationship of husband and wife.[6] Although Charity and Sylvia, like many nineteenth-century feminists, would challenge Blackstonian doctrine by insisting on an equitable distribution of property in their own union, Charity used the semantic resonance of the possessive phrase "my help-meet" to establish the marital quality of her and Sylvia's union.

Charity followed her description of Sylvia as her help-meet with the elaboration that Sylvia "came to be my companion." The implication that Sylvia had left a prior home to join Charity established both that she and Sylvia began cohabitating on a specific date and that they resided under Charity's roof. These assertions contributed to the representation of the relationship as marital. Following English precedent, the early American legal scholar James Kent listed "cohabitation" as a primary evidence of common-law marriage, along with consent.[7] Equally important, in New England social practice couples typically marked their married lives as beginning when they went "to housekeeping" under the husband's roof.[8] Charity's memoir demonstrated that she and Sylvia had followed traditional practice.

Finally, by crossing out the words *in labor*—the only correction made to the 1844 memoir—Charity emphasized that her life with Sylvia originated in love, not in economic need. Their relationship fit the new nineteenth-century romantic definitions of marriage as a union of souls, as well as the earlier colonial understandings of marriage as a pragmatic partnership. Charity seemingly wrote the words *in labor* in order to strike them through and correct any misapprehension by future generations. The women worked together in order to live together, not the other way around. Sylvia's contribution to the tailoring business provided the couple with the combined resources they required to support themselves. Their longstanding union did not evolve out of a practical work arrangement.

By 1844, when Charity penned her memoir, her marriage to Sylvia had long since acquired social force, if not legal validity, within the Weybridge area. As one local man, Hiram Hurlburt, recalled from growing up during the 1830s, everyone in town regarded the women "as if Miss Bryant and Miss Drake were married to each other." Communal acceptance of the women's marital relationship did not come all at once, however. It took years for the women to make their private commitment to each other public knowledge. If in the summer of 1807 Sylvia and Charity had talked openly about their relationship as a marriage, the families would have been compelled to break the lovers apart. Social sanction extended to intense attachments between women only when those relationships did not interfere with conventional family structure. Forswearing traditional marriage to live their lives together broke that fundamental agreement. So at the beginning, Charity and Sylvia needed to preserve the fiction that their futures remained undetermined.

The day before Sylvia arrived at Charity's house in Weybridge, having "consented" to be her "help-meet," Charity wrote home to Massachusetts delaying her return until the fall and making no mention of Sylvia.[9] In her public correspondence that summer, Charity gave the impression that all her time was taken up by tailoring work and recovering her health, but in her private writings, Charity celebrated her new-formed union. An acrostic that she wrote for Sylvia in August suggested that the two women were joined in a spiritual marriage. Charity's poem called on the heavens to bless and "protect my lovely friend" and to "attune her heart to gratitude and Love." Grant Sylvia good health and a clear mind, Charity implored, and "espouse her cause, accept her as thine own."[10] By calling on Christ to *espouse* Sylvia in his role as a heavenly bridegroom, a common image in New England Puritanism, Charity herself spoke for Sylvia's well-being.[11] As Charity implored God's blessing on Sylvia in each loving line, she espoused Sylvia's interests as her own.

Despite her earlier promises, at summer's end Charity felt no more ready to forsake Sylvia and depart for Massachusetts than she had felt in the spring. At the beginning of October she mailed off a flurry of letters to the people waiting back home, postponing her return yet again. She blamed the delay on ill health and good work opportunities. Charity's brother Peter scolded her, "I consider you as a sort of runaway." He grumbled that he "did not much like your leaving us so abruptly last winter," but he was happy to "understand you or your services are at least in great demand." Concerned that money woes might be preventing her return, Peter offered to pay for Charity's passage back to the Hampshire Hills.[12] Lydia also felt dissatisfied with Charity's continuing absence. Perhaps to assuage her own guilt, Charity had suggested that Lydia was being "unconstant" and "unfaithful." The Plainfield teacher roundly repudiated this baseless accusation and reminded Charity that she had "yielded a kind of unwilling consent to your longer stay in Weybridge." Worried about Charity's "decaying health," Lydia begged her to return swiftly to Massachusetts.[13]

Charity did not tell either Peter or Lydia about the relationship that kept her in Vermont. She withheld the news from her brother because his household already deemed Charity suspicious on that account. She did not tell Lydia because the information would break her heart. Charity did finally mention Sylvia in her October letter to Lydia, but she wrote nothing about their intimacy, giving the impression that Sylvia, like Achsah, was just an innocent young friend. Only from acquaintances who had visited Weybridge did Lydia hear that Charity had taken on a live-in assistant to help with her sewing. "I conclude the apprentice is no other than Sylvia," Lydia guessed with the acute sensitivity of a lover.[14] Charity herself had not mentioned the arrangement.

Charity revealed her secret reason for not wanting to leave Vermont to only one person, her older sister and surrogate mother, Anna Kingman. More than anyone else in the Bryant family, Anna sympathized with her little sister, felt for the tribulations she had suffered, and wished for her future happiness. If anyone could accept the unconventional new life that Charity was attempting to build, it would be Anna. Charity's gamble succeeded. Although Anna reported back her "disappointment" over Charity's refusal to come home to Massachusetts, she expressed her pleasure—if a little confusion—in learning about Charity's new friend:

> You have introduced a character in your letter, my dear sister, but I am still at a loss who it can be, as you introduce her only by the name of Sylvia. But from your representations she appears to possess a degree of excellence which entitles her to a place in my heart.—your friends are mine—and whoever performs the offices of kindness toward you, does it to me also. Do be so kind as to present her my compliments and thanks.

Charity won Anna's approval for Sylvia by describing her as a nurse of sorts. Sylvia's willingness to perform the "offices of kindness," or in other words to care for Charity during the bouts of ill health she frequently suffered, endeared her to Anna. At the same time, Anna knew her youngest sister well enough to understand that the relationship probably extended beyond such offices. In her response to Charity's letter introducing Sylvia, Anna praised friendship as the "sweetest charm of life," conveying her approval for the female intimacies around which Charity organized her life, and by extension accepting her new relationship.[15]

Her excuses made, Charity retired into seclusion with Sylvia for the long winter. She wrote to no one in Massachusetts during the next several months, having no wish to disturb her present idyll with thoughts of the future.[16] But spring's return in 1808 renewed the specter of the women's separation. More than a year had passed since Charity first made the trip to Vermont with the intention to remain for a single season. She had exhausted the reasons she could offer to friends and family for her long absence, but the thought of leaving Sylvia caused Charity terrible distress. In March, Charity poured out her grief over this dilemma in a poem titled "On the Prospect of Separation":

O shall I still believe
My Sylvia will prove kind?
That she will ne'er deceive
This heart to her inclin'd
By every gentle tie
That binds the tender heart;
O Whether could I fly,
Should she from me depart!
Where could I rest my head
But on her friendly breast.
Short of the silent Dead!
Where all the weary rest.
How could I bear to see
Her from my bosom torn
Myself departed be
And left alone to mourn
O should my adverse fate
Endure this cruel blow
My heart beneath its weight
Must sink in pain and woe
But Hope shall still preside
Within my trouble'd breast
And paint the brighter side
TO soothe my cares to rest.[17]

The lines echoed Charity's August 1807 acrostic for Sylvia depicting the women's spiritual union. The two women, in Charity's words, were united "by every gentle tie / That binds the tender heart." The *tie that binds* was then, as it is now, a common expression for marriage, and the title of a hymn frequently sung at wedding ceremonies: "Blest be the tie that binds our hearts in Christian love."[18] The hymn casts Christ in the role of a heavenly bridegroom, joined by covenant with his community of believers. By laying title to the tie that binds, Charity claimed the language of marriage for her and Sylvia's relationship and invested their union with Christian authority.

Imagery of a spiritual marriage appealed to Charity and Sylvia, whose sex excluded them from entering a civil marriage. At the same time, Charity's lines illuminated the physical dimensions of the women's union by including imagery of bosom intimacy. How could Charity find ease if not on Sylvia's friendly breast, and how could she bear for Sylvia to be torn from her "bosom"? Charity dreaded "the prospect of separation" from Sylvia's body as much as from her soul.

Unwilling to be separated, but unable to defer her return to Massachusetts any longer, Charity arrived at the only possible solution—she would bring Sylvia back home with her. In April, the two women set off together to visit their friends and family to the south. The women's trip to Massachusetts resembled a conventional "bridal tour," an early American precursor to the honeymoon.[19] The trip gave Charity an opportunity to introduce her help-meet to her family and to establish the women's new identities as a fixed couple. Charity later claimed that she "returnd to Mass taking Miss D with me not knowing as I should return again to Vt."[20] At the time, however, she expressed little doubt that the visit to Massachusetts was just that and would terminate with her return to Vermont. Within a month of the women's arrival in Massachusetts, Charity informed her sister-in-law Sally that she planned to return to Weybridge in the fall.[21] Charity's friends and family members expected as much. Observing Charity and Sylvia together revealed what Charity had found so impossible to write: the two women were inseparable.

Charity and Sylvia began their tour in Pelham, reaching Charity's sister Anna Kingman's house in May 1808. Charity planned the trip with careful consideration. Anna's acceptance of Sylvia would smooth the path for her encounters with the rest of the Bryant siblings. The strategy succeeded. Observing her sister's happiness in this new companion persuaded Anna to endorse the relationship. Before their departure Anna gave each woman a letter, which they could share with other family and friends met later on the tour. Her letter to Sylvia overflowed with praise, bolstering the inexperienced young woman's confidence for the rest of the journey. "Language is unable to express how deeply my heart is affected by your benevolence, and how highly I appreciate your goodness!" Anna wrote. You leave behind a "name sweeter than the perfumes of Arabia, an impression of your goodness which the hand of time cannot ease."[22] Anna recognized Sylvia as a kindred soul: pious, giving, and devoted to Charity's well-being. Grateful for Anna's kindness, Sylvia wrote to her worried mother in Vermont, "you can hardly imagine what an agreeable instructing and entertaining woman Mrs Kingman is I take much satisfaction in her company."[23] The letter could calm any fears Mary Drake felt about her youngest daughter's reception within the elevated circle of the Bryant family.

Anna's letter to Charity performed an even more generous act, granting permission for Charity to pursue her new life in Vermont. "I trust it is needless to tell you how much I shall regret your absence," she wrote to her youngest sister, but "I am confident I need be under no apprehensions concerning your welfare while so dear and faithful a friend as Miss Drake is your constant companion, and I trust you are not insensible, my dear sister, how much you owe her fidelity and attachment."[24] By naming Sylvia as Charity's "constant companion" and adjuring Charity to "fidelity,"

Anna symbolically blessed the women's union. At Anna's house, the private commitment Charity and Sylvia had made began to assume a public shape.

Anna executed one more important office for Charity before their visit to Pelham ended: she played host to Charity's reunion with Lydia. Charity could not bring Sylvia to Lydia's parents' house in Plainfield, but she needed to meet Lydia in person to apologize for her abandonment over the past year. While Lydia waited for Charity in Plainfield, practicing "patience, resolution, prudence, &c.," Charity had rented a home for herself in Weybridge and invited Sylvia to join her.[25] While Lydia dreamed about Charity spending the evening surrounded by Polly's children, Charity and Sylvia had been spending their nights alone together.[26] While Lydia rejected a marriage proposal, Charity had asked Sylvia to be her help-meet.[27] While Lydia continued dreaming of the moment when Charity would return, Charity had put down roots in the town where she would live for the rest of her life. Charity owed Lydia an explanation that could never be entrusted to paper.

Lydia arrived in Pelham in the middle of May. The reunion demolished any dreams Lydia still preserved of spending her future with Charity. She learned that Charity was lost to her as a lover; the question now was whether the two women could remain friends. After returning home to Plainfield, Lydia wrote Charity a distraught letter acknowledging the end of their romantic relationship. Although she used a string of quotations from the hymns of Isaac Watts to encode her message, the "pain and anxiety" she expressed in the letter were so palpable that Lydia urged Charity to burn the pages after she read them.[28] Then Lydia put down the pen. Since Charity left Plainfield for Vermont in February 1807, Lydia had written to her every month, despite the long stretches in which she received no return of correspondence. The visit to Pelham stopped her hand. June, July, and August passed in silence.

Charity and Sylvia, meanwhile, set off for the next and perhaps most frightening stop on their journey—a visit to their birthplaces. Following Charity's departure from North Bridgewater in early 1806, her father, Philip, did not communicate with her for two years. Finally, in March 1808 he sent a letter to Weybridge inviting his estranged daughter home for a visit. At seventy-six years of age, Philip Bryant needed to reconcile with his daughter soon if he hoped to see her in this world again. The recent death of his brother Job, Charity's uncle, served as a grim reminder of his own mortality. At his side, he daily witnessed the sufferings of his wife, whom ill health had rendered "helpless." His letter to Charity carried a note of urgency, "I hope you will come + see ys as soon as you can."[29] Despite his plaintive tone, it took an act of great courage for Charity to return to North Bridgewater and bring Sylvia with her. If she hoped that old age had mellowed Philip and Hannah, she was sorely disappointed. Sylvia wrote back to her own mother in Weybridge that Hannah "knocks about like a house on fire," and she was a far cry from the "helpless" figure Philip depicted in his letter to Charity. Perhaps if he told the truth, Charity would not have come at all.[30] In the end, Charity had reason to be glad she made the visit. Her father and stepmother did not issue Sylvia a welcome to the family, like Anna had, but they agreed to open the house to Charity and her companion in the future.

Other visits in Bridgewater and Easton produced positive results. Charity introduced her new lover to Mercy, who extended her "best love" to "Silvia."[31] Charity also established friendships with relatives of Sylvia who had remained in Easton.[32] The 1808 tour set a precedent for return visits, establishing the women as a settled couple. Charity's peculiar desire to spend her life in the company of another woman was easier for North Bridgewater to accept now that she lived away than it had been when she tried to make the town her home. Traditional New England communities were built around the marital household: a husband, wife, and children represented the building block of social order.[33] Even in the early nineteenth century, single women were discouraged from living alone. After Mercy Ford's mother died in 1810, Charity's former lover found it difficult to leave her brother's house. Although she "had an idea of giting a chamber and being alone," she found she could not "git suited and suit others at the same time."[34] Charity escaped this bind by leaving home. Her move to Vermont relieved North Bridgewaterites of the obligation to regulate her domestic arrangements. Living in Weybridge smoothed Charity's relations in her native place.

Their reception in North Bridgewater and Easton encouraged Charity and Sylvia to brave Cummington as well. Traveling via Pelham, the women arrived at Peter and Sally Bryant's home on September 3, 1808. Sally's record of the visit in her diary was predictably terse. "Charity Bryant + Miss Drake come—quite warm," she recorded on the Saturday of their arrival. The following day, the family went to church and celebrated communion day. At the meeting, Sally had a chance to appraise Sylvia's piety, which she considered a matter of great significance. Sylvia must have made a good impression. The visit seemed to be going well on Monday, when Sally recorded that "Charity cut me out a gown + spencer of black lutestring." The women spent the following day at home together with the children, while Peter made a visit to Worthington. Rain kept them indoors in the afternoon, providing an opportunity to sit by the hearth and sew companionably. On Wednesday "Charity went away."[35] Sally didn't mark Sylvia's departure, but the visit laid the basis for a friendship between the two women. When Charity and Sylvia returned to Cummington two years later, Sally noted Sylvia's arrival by first name.[36] Afterward, her letters always directed Charity to "give my love to Sylvia."[37]

During their stay in Cummington, Charity and Sylvia also visited with Lydia.[38] Three months had passed since the women's encounter in Pelham, and the long silence had allowed Lydia to recover her equanimity. Now she renewed their correspondence on a new basis of friendship. Despite an episode of sickness in her household, Lydia found time to send Charity two letters in the days after the visit and to congratulate Charity on making her relationship with Sylvia public knowledge. "Much of my love attends Sylvia," Lydia wrote with warmth, "the world is no longer kept in ignorance."[39] A third letter swiftly followed, directed to Weybridge, blessing Sylvia as "the friend of your heart and partner of your cares. Her goodness I hope is rewarded, and kindness and friendship returned, may you long be happy in each other."[40] The language Lydia chose described Charity and Sylvia's relationship as a type of marriage. Expressions like *friend of my heart* and *partner of my cares* served as commonplace endearments for spouses. The phrase "may you long be happy in each other" were words that a well-wisher made to the newly married.[41] The benediction must have cost Lydia a few tears, but they preserved her friendship with Charity and enabled all three women to remain affectionate for the rest of their lives. Lydia, living as a single woman with her parents, ended her next letter to Charity with the dismal thought that "I must dismiss my pen and retire—but retire alone—may you, my dear, with our sister Sylvia, have undisturb'd repose."[42] Despite her palpable envy, Lydia acknowledged Sylvia as Charity's life companion.

Before their return to Weybridge, Charity took one more important action to establish the public face of their union. She asked her brother Peter to buy a ring for her on his next trip to Boston, where he served in the state legislature.[43] Rings had symbolized the bonds of matrimony in European culture since ancient times. Traditionally, only the bride received a ring.[44] Charity asked Peter to purchase her a single ring valued at four dollars, the cost of a hundred bushels of coal in Weybridge.[45] For a working woman like Charity, who kept her fingers busy every moment of the day just to pay for her subsistence, the expense was considerable. The ring was too valuable to be placed in the mail, so Peter held onto it until the women came for their next visit to Massachusetts.[46] For, as Charity noted in the record of her life, "after tarrying six months and not being willing to part with my friend I return'd with her" to Weybridge.[47] The task remained for the two women to persuade the Drake relatives, like the Bryants, that they were bound together for life.

12

Their Own Dwelling

1809

ON JANUARY 1, 1809, Charity and Sylvia awoke together for the first time in their own house.[1] The day before, they had moved into a new twelve-by-twelve-foot struc-ture built just for themselves.[2] The single room, which doubled as their living space and tailor shop, had plastered walls, a stove for cooking and warming the air, a single bedstead, a cutting table, and a couple of chairs. Despite its tiny dimensions, the crowded house seemed like a "mansion" to the women and their friends.[3] The struc-ture's significance far outsized its square footage. By building a home together, Charity and Sylvia laid the physical foundation to spend the rest of their lives together and symbolically announced the permanence of their union to all their neighbors and family in Weybridge.

Settlers who moved to a frontier village like Weybridge placed enormous signifi-cance on property ownership. Only a desperate thirst for land would drive them from the refined, long-settled communities of southern New England to the rough-hewn northwest. The Drakes, for example, left behind a dense network of relations, long-established churches, and well-stocked merchants when they migrated from Easton to Vermont. They made the move because it permitted Sylvia's brothers, who had been left landless by the economic disorder of the Revolutionary era, to establish them-selves as property owners. A man could not call himself a man unless he possessed a competency, or independent source of living, that preserved him from an effeminizing dependence on others. But acquiring farms in Weybridge and neighboring Bristol restored the Drakes' name and social position at a high cost to their comfort.[4]

The close association between land and masculinity made it very difficult for women to become property owners. Denied the appointments to land commissions granted their brothers and fathers, without landed inheritances or the wage-earning capacity to accumulate enough capital to buy land, women depended on men to provide them homes. This structural bias made it almost impossible for women to live on their own, although it was a dream of many female friends to set up a home together.[5] The biblical story of Naomi and Ruth modeled this desire for the Protestant culture of early America. "Where thou lodgest, I will lodge... where thou diest, will I die," Ruth pledged to Naomi, in words that held special resonance to generations of women friends.[6] Seldom could women follow their example.

In Charity and Sylvia's case, a fortuitous set of circumstances allowed them to prove the exception by entering into an unusual arrangement with the village's one female landowner, Sarah Hagar. The year that Charity arrived in Weybridge, Hagar, who was a neighbor of Sylvia's sister Polly, was deeded property from her father, Luther Martin, to hold in trust for her sons.[7] Martin probably designed this unusual transmission in order to keep the property out of the hands of Sarah's husband, Benjamin Hagar, a cobbler and merchant who had problems managing money. Martin acted wisely: a little more than a decade later Benjamin Hagar died from yellow fever while on a business venture in Surinam.[8] His wife's possession of the Martin property in trust for her sons protected it from her husband's creditors.

Sarah Hagar's unlucky choice of husbands proved Charity and Sylvia's good fortune when, in 1808, she leased the couple a quarter-acre of land, probably exchanging lifelong residence rights in exchange for a set fee. No deed for this original transaction survives to clarify the exact terms. It is possible that the women kept the matter private out of concern that the town fathers would not approve of women engaging in land deals. Later tax records listed Charity and Sylvia as "owners" of their quarter-acre parcel, rather than "occupants" (or renters).[9] But a deed dating to 1837 describes the women as possessing only the buildings on the property, rather than having "right, title, claim, or demand" to the land itself.[10] Whatever its exact terms, the anomalous arrangement worked well for all three women. Sarah Hagar supplemented her husband's inconsistent support without having to leave the farm that she needed to support herself and her six children. Meanwhile, living on the property of a woman landowner freed Charity and Sylvia from the rumors of sexual misbehavior that might attach to single women living on a man's property.[11] Neither Charity nor Sylvia would be mistaken for an adulterer's mistress.

Living on a woman's property could not protect Charity and Sylvia from rumors of another variety of illicit sexuality, however. The rare households established by pairs of women in early America risked raising community concerns about lesbianism. For example, a pair of Philadelphia women were arrested in 1792 on a charge of "cohabiting," a term typically applied against unmarried opposite-sex couples who set up homes together. The authorities apparently suspected the women of having a sexual relationship.[12] Visitors to Charity and Sylvia's home, viewing the single bedstead in their one-room house, had to confront the same sexual potential within the women's relationship.[13] Although bed-sharing was common on the nineteenth-century frontier, medical and moral authorities expressed concerns about the sexual dangers of the practice, warning that bed-sharing might lead to the "fondling of young persons of the same sex" and train youth in the habits of sodomy.[14] By building a home together and sharing the same bed, Charity and Sylvia created strong cause for concern in Weybridge. To maintain their domestic arrangement, the women would have to counter potential anxieties about their lesbianism.

Some female couples before Charity and Sylvia had found acceptance in their communities by projecting a Christian reputation and contributing to the public welfare. Hannah Catherall and Rebecca Jones, who lived together in Philadelphia from the 1760s to the 1780s, gained the respect of the town's Quaker elders despite their reputation as "yoke fellows," a common metaphor for spouses. The women's piety and good works protected them from questions about their sexuality.[15] Alternatively, the Ladies of Llangollen, Eleanor Butler and Sarah Ponsonby, relied on their elite social class to maintain the open secret of their sexuality. Satirical accounts of the women's mannish appearance suggest that people considered them to be lesbians, but their gentility allowed the women's reputation to weather these suspicions.[16] The same held true for the mannish Anne Lister and her partner Ann Walker, who lived together in Yorkshire. Suspicions about Lister's sexuality in particular were quashed by her aristocratic social power.[17] Charity's evident masculinity made her and Sylvia's unusual household equally vulnerable to sexual suspicion, but she possessed neither the money nor the elite status that insulated Butler, Ponsonby, Lister, and Walker from assault. Instead, Charity and Sylvia, like Catherall and Jones, would have to build reputations for piety and good works to secure communal toleration. It took time to acquire this social capital, and at the outset of their lives together many in the community treated the new house with suspicion.

Adding to the challenge, the house proved too inviting to other women in the community who were looking for female intimacy. Soon after Charity and Sylvia took possession of the structure they invited a visit from the minister's nineteen-year-old-sister, Mary Hovey, who was working as a schoolteacher nearby. The visit seemed designed to demonstrate the respectability of the household, but it had unexpected consequences. Mary became enamored with not only the house but one of its inhabitants. In a thank-you letter sent soon after the visit, Mary gushed about the women's delightful home and confessed that her mind kept traveling back to their door: "O my dear girls, how often do my roving thoughts visit you in your little habitation." Mary understood that the women's shared home signaled their inseparability; on that account, she wrote, "you will not take it amiss that I addressed you both in one letter."[18] But in the months that followed, the young teacher began directing increasing attention toward Charity alone.

Mary's first letter initiated a flurry of pages to follow. Of the seventeen letters (at a minimum) that she sent to the house before the end of the year, only four of the most brief came addressed to Sylvia. Two more arrived addressed to both women, a common practice for married correspondents.[19] The rest bore Charity's name alone. Mary's letters to Charity showed all the hallmarks of the romantic correspondence that Charity had received in her twenties. Mary filled her letters with praise for Charity's "refined" taste, "noble mind," and the "propriety, ease, and elegance" of her writing.[20] She humbled herself before "such a person" as her new friend.[21] She differentiated the "real friendship" they shared from the false friendships between most women.[22] She gave the impression of being thoroughly taken with her new friend.

Charity may have courted Mary's affections at first, as she had courted other women teachers in the past, but when Sylvia expressed reservations about the friendship by treating Mary with coldness, Charity changed course.[23] First she sought to reassure Sylvia of her commitment to their union. At the end of July, after receiving a solicitous letter from Mary, Charity composed a romantic poem for Sylvia that pledged her lifelong fidelity: "For Heaven my witness can prove / That from thee I ne'er wish to part; / That as ever I sincerely love, / And own thee, the friend of my heart."[24] Mary's attentions had not changed her feelings, Charity promised; she loved Sylvia as truly "as ever." But Charity's reassurances could not resolve the problem of Mary's increasingly fervent letters. The final straw came in August, when Mary seems to have sent Charity a romantic token: a little paper heart inscribed to her friend with her initials and Charity's framed inside delicately inked loops, and on the rear side more hearts set within leafy and fruiting vines.[25]

Mary Hovey may not have known how her gesture took part in a tradition of landscape imagery that women used to express their desires for other women, but Charity recognized the heart's meaning. She had once given a very similar object to Lydia Richards. The heart compelled a firm response. Rather than bring Charity closer, the token forced Charity to sever her intimacy with Mary by rejecting the gift. Although Charity's words are lost, Mary's apology for overstepping the boundaries of their relationship survives. "If my dear, I have given you any occasion of offence, or have been the cause of one disagreeable feeling I, in a most serious and humble manner ask your forgiveness," Mary wrote with a heavy heart. Once she had "been so happy as to call [Charity] my FRIEND." Mary did not realize how this name, inscribed on the valentine, would overstep the limits of their acquaintance. "I vainly tho't [the name] without offence—But alas! I fear I have been too hasty, not feeling my inferiority to yourself, I have been too presuming, I have flattered myself too much happiness to have it granted me—but my dearest! (friend I had almost said) I hope you will put the most charitable constructions on what is pass'd and forgive."[26] Mary's attempts at intimacy had been repelled at the cottage gates.[27] This aborted relationship was Charity's last romantic friendship. She never again entered into such a heated correspondence with another woman.

There was only room for one soul besides Charity beneath the fruited vine, and that was Sylvia. In the prophetic imagery of Micah and Isaiah, the vine and fig tree represent household happiness.[28] The women frequently called upon this imagery in representing their household together. Sylvia referred to their house as "our own vine."[29] They planted vining roses around the house as a symbol of their love, and one of the women worked the symbol into the braided hair framing the twinned silhouettes cut for them by a traveling portrait artist (see the frontispiece).[30]

Charity's relations best appreciated the house's symbolic function as a representation of Charity and Sylvia's commitment. Soon after moving in, the women sent news of the house back to the Bryant family. Charity's close cousin Vesta, who had been abandoned by her disreputable husband and forced to live in her younger brother's home, celebrated news of the house. She wrote to Charity that "your new method of living with your agreeable companion must I am confident add greatly to your happiness." Without a home to call her own, Vesta recognized her cousin's good fortune. She imagined it was "a great satisfaction to a thinking mind to retire into some peaceful and sequestered spot from the busy scenes of life and there enjoy the pleasures of reflection." Vesta also felt sympathy for Sarah Hagar as the fellow victim of a poor marriage choice, writing to Charity that "the description which you give of your Landlady is truly elegant; Oh! how does Virtue shine even in the most distress'd circumstances."[31] To a woman like Vesta, who had experienced the worst aspects of traditional marriage, having been abused and abandoned by an alcoholic husband, it appeared that Charity and Sylvia's unusual living situation had a lot to recommend it.

Both Sylvia and Charity wrote to Anna Kingman to tell her about the house, and Charity's sister wrote back to each in kind. Acknowledging Sylvia's role as the goodwife within the household, Anna congratulated Sylvia on the "little dwelling which you have so prettily described." It would fall to Sylvia to keep the home clean and pleasing to the eye.[32] A surging tide of domestic ideology sweeping North America in the early 1800s stressed the need for even frontier farmwives to keep attractive homes.[33] To fulfill this mandate, Sylvia not only busied her days with washing, sweeping, cleaning, and keeping general order in the little house, she hung pictures on the walls.[34] By contrast, in her letter to Charity, Anna applauded the house as a "neat little cell." This turn of phrase cast her sister in the role of a holy woman rather than a wife, and implied that the new house served a higher spiritual purpose, uniting the women in service to God.[35] The fact that Anna knew of the more earthy dimensions to the women's relationship (she once closed a letter to Charity with the instructions "do kiss Sylvia, for me once," suggesting that Charity kissed Sylvia quite often for herself) reveals how she endeavored to cast her youngest sister's iconoclasms in the most acceptable light.[36]

Peter Bryant acknowledged the announcement of his sister's new home in his typical laughing way. "I am…very glad to hear that you have derived benefit from plastering," he wrote to Charity in March 1809, making a medical pun that suited his profession. Despite his gentle teasing, Peter recognized the magnitude of Charity's accomplishment in constructing a space to spend her future with Sylvia. "I hope, however necessary it may be found to plaster, or even to white wash, [it] will sustain the rude shocks of time and the elements for many years yet to come!"[37] The house's sturdiness represented the solidity of the women's connection.

Peter's good wishes, as close to a benediction of her marriage as Charity could hope to receive from her jocular older brother, bore out. The following year, when spring greened the vines that grew around their house, Charity and Sylvia enjoyed the annual rebirth, finally reassured that it did not herald a looming separation as they so feared in years past. Spring had lost its cruel sting. In a pair of twinned poems from March 1810, Charity heralded the change of seasons as presaging the women's long future together. "May the beautiful season so lately commenc'd / Pass unclouded by disorder and strife," Charity addressed Sylvia in the first poem. "And may we be gratefull for favor dispens'd / thus may we pass our whole life." The flowering of spring, Charity wrote with great optimism, symbolized the bright outlooks for their future. When troubles did intrude upon their lives, Charity promised in the second poem, then "O might we still unite / And spend our days in Peace and calm of delight."[38] With a common dwelling to shelter them, any difficulties the women encountered could be resolved together.

In conventional marriages, the husband's ownership of the marital house represented his place at the head of the family. In contrast, Charity and Sylvia always emphasized their joint ownership of the cottage. They used the expression "our own dwelling," or a variation on these words, as their most common term to describe the house.[39] These three words captured the essence of the matter: Charity and Sylvia had a home together that they could call their own. The act of joint possession made the house beloved to the women. Sometimes the women referred with affection to its

diminutive size. Acknowledging the small dimensions of the house only emphasized the magnitude of their accomplishment in building a home together. Charity
wrote to her brother of the great satisfaction she took in hosting relatives and friends
"at our own little dwelling."[40] The house might have been just a "mite," in the words
of more than one guest, but as in the parable of the poor widow from the Gospel of
Mark, who by throwing her "mite" into the temple treasury made a contribution of
all that she had (Mark 12:41–44), the symbolic significance of Charity and Sylvia's
hospitality exceeded their material offerings.[41]

Gradually, over the years, as Charity and Sylvia earned money through their tailoring business, they built onto he original structure to make it more hospitable. In
1812 they built a second small room, presumably a separate chamber for sleeping, as
well as closets and a clothespress, or wardrobe, for storing their work. Before that
time, the women's spare clothing probably hung on pegs attached to the walls. The
1812 expansion began the process of separating the public and private aspects of the
house, creating spaces suitable for guests where the question of Charity and Sylvia's
sexual relationship would not intrude so blatantly.

Soon after the expansion, Sylvia wrote to implore her mother to make an extended
visit to the house. The Drake family's reception of the women's new home had been
more frosty than the Bryants', who had been relieved of the burden of policing the
women's sexuality by the imposition of such a great distance. Sylvia's mother and
several of her brothers felt no such relief, and their response to the house's symbolic
representation of the women's commitment was consequently less approving. Sylvia,
who as the youngest daughter had grown up very close to her mother, hoped that the
expansion of the house could help heal the breach. "Do visit here my dear Mother as
soon as the roads are settled," Sylvia wrote to Mary in April 1813. "If your life + health
+ ours should be spar'd, I shall see you but a few times more according to our former
practice of visiting if we should both live these twenty years."[42]

At first, Mary resisted her youngest daughter's invitations. The following
Christmas, a holiday traditionally spent with family, Sylvia wrote to her mother
bemoaning that it had been more than a year since they had seen each other. Charity
and Sylvia had built yet another room onto the house that year, and they now had
sufficient space for long-term visitors. Charity's friend Lydia was staying for the
winter. Sylvia hoped Mary would soon take similar advantage of their hospitality.
She accepted blame for the long separation between her mother and herself, acknowledging that she led a "wicked and abandoned life." But still she begged her mother's
acceptance for the new household she had established. Assuring Mary of Charity's
"strongest affection to you," Sylvia implored "May you my dear Mother let her share
with me your parental love she well deserves it she is everything I could wish."[43]
Finally, in the early spring of 1815, Mary came for a short call at her daughter's "little

dwelling." Afterward, Sylvia thanked her mother for the visit, which "endears this little spot to me." Mary's stay marked a new acceptance within the Drake family of the permanency of Charity and Sylvia's union.[44]

Over the next several years, the women continued to expand the house. They filled in the space between the main house and the woodhouse, adding another functional room. In 1819, ten years after first moving into the twelve-by-twelve-foot structure, Charity and Sylvia finally had "a large chamber bedroom" built, as well as a cistern room for water storage and bathing. The previous sleeping space could now be repurposed as a separate dining room, making it easier to entertain large parties.[45] Sylvia and Charity began to host holiday meals, cooking turkeys to share with family and friends.[46] After a decade, the women's household was achieving integration within the family circle.

On December 21, 1821, Charity and Sylvia hosted a grand Christmas dinner to welcome Sylvia's mother Mary, aged seventy-nine, who had arrived the day before to spend the winter with her youngest daughter. The gathering was so large that the women had to move the stove to make room for all the guests before Sylvia began cooking a turkey large enough to feed the family.[47] Polly and Asaph Hayward came, along with sister Rhoda and her husband, Chauncey Ellsworth, and numerous nieces and nephews. One of the women's apprentices, whom they regarded almost as daughters, also joined the gathering, along with a friend. The meal represented a social triumph for Sylvia. She seemed to have secured her mother's acceptance for her household, but after the dinner ended and the guests went home, she discovered that the tensions between them lingered.

Too often during that first long visit, mother and daughter passed their evenings in front of the fire in uncomfortable silence. Sylvia could not find the path back to her mother's good graces. By accepting her youngest daughter's invitation to spend the winter in her home, Mary had ceded her toleration to Sylvia's unusual household, but still she withheld her approval. Several chilly months later, after Mary had left to rejoin her sons in Bristol, Sylvia wrote morosely in her diary, "All nature looks dreary, And silent." The view outside represented the feelings in her heart. The long-dreamt-of reunion with her mother had not brought the restoration of affections Sylvia so passionately desired. "Has my mother been gone so soon," Sylvia questioned in her diary. "Alas! I dream, our life is nothing more."[48] Their lives, Sylvia feared, would slip away without a true reconciliation.

Sylvia found it impossible to broach the reserve between herself and her mother because she could not speak forthrightly about its source. Her mother had avoided the house because of the union it symbolized, and to speak honestly about her sexual concerns would make it less, not more, possible for Mary to spend time there as a guest. Sylvia faced an impossible task clearing the air without naming the source of the trouble. She tried, nonetheless, sending a letter to Bristol shortly after Mary's departure begging forgiveness for their long silent evenings. "My Mother, I have not anything to write, which I might not have said, When you was pleasd to bless me with your presence," Sylvia wrote. "But as I neglected to say anything which I ought to have said, + am incapable of writing that which I wish to convey and on this account, the great object for which we meet, + [illeg.] in the same world has + I fear ever will remain unaccomplished."[49] Even in a moment of great candor, Sylvia could not name the "mute sin" that silenced her mother and herself. She felt crippled by the sense that "on this account," she would never be saved, but terror of the after-world could not move her tongue to speak the problem to her mother and lose any future hope for reconciliation. The open secret of her sexuality had to remain silenced.

Despite the tensions between them, the next spring Mary came for a second extended stay. Her visit coincided with a thorough renovation that filled the house with enough noise and activity to cover any long silences. Charity and Sylvia had a cellar dug. They built new chambers over the shop-room for the apprentices to live in. They refinished the rough board exterior with clapboard, shingles, and bricks. They installed glass windows and interior doors between the rooms.[50] After living in a construction site for over a month, Sylvia complained that the house was "an heap of confusion."[51] Working frantically at her sewing to pay for the ongoing construction, Sylvia muttered over the "continued scene of dirt + confusion" that surrounded her.[52] In the third week of May, Sylvia began painting the house herself, starting with the chamber, then proceeding to the kitchen, the buttery, the working room, and even the clothespress.[53] She put the finishing touches on the house on May 24. Charity whitewashed.[54] The construction was complete. Although the house remained a cottage, Charity and Sylvia had finally achieved a standard of refinement that matched their respectable station in life.

Many prominent residents of Weybridge either helped with the renovations or came to check on their progress. It took seven men to raise the roof and four to frame the house.[55] Local doctor Zenas Shaw helped to dig the cellar.[56] The respect-fully titled "Captain Wales" made the "pavements" (possibly the exterior path).[57] Asaph Hayward stoned the cellar and did brick work.[58] Members of the Lathrop, Wilson, Marshall, Ayers, Foster, Kellogg, Sturdivant, and Brewster families all par-ticipated in the renovations.[59] Nephews Edwin and Azel Hayward, and Isaac and Lauren Drake worked on the house as well. Charity and Sylvia paid some of the workers in clothing and others with cash, but the overwhelming community involve-ment in the renovations suggests that many helped primarily out of respect. As the renovations reached their conclusion, Sylvia and Charity hosted visits from many estimable local women as well as their husbands.[60]

After the renovations were completed, Sarah Hagar's sons came to inspect the improvements to the property. Although Charity and Sylvia leased the property from Sarah, since she held it in trust the approval of her three oldest sons was essential to the women's comfort. Charity and Sylvia had a long acquaintance with the men, who were still boys when the women first moved to the property. The oldest, Benjamin, had attended Middlebury College and studied medicine; the second, Luther, was a successful storekeeper; the third, Jonathan, was also a merchant, and a man of faith.[61] Sharing Charity and Sylvia's middle-class principles of frugality, piety, and learning, the Hagar brothers respected the women and felt grateful to Charity and Sylvia for taking care of their increasingly enfeebled mother. After Jonathan and his wife came for a visit, Sylvia recorded with relief that Jonathan "assures us of his friendship."[62] Sarah's younger son Henry, born after Luther Martin deeded her the property, also came to inspect. He had no say in the property's disposition, but his feelings still had consequence. Sylvia reported that she served him a drink and he left on good terms.[63]

Some of Sylvia's relations, however, still did not share the community's general enthusiasm. Her brother Asaph Drake, who had once been a great friend to Charity and Sylvia, came to the new house on May 15, 1823, to pay the women interest on a debt he owed to them, but Sylvia noted ruefully that he "refuse[d] to eat" at their table.[64] This slight crushed Sylvia's feelings, leading her to bitter recriminations. The next morning, Sylvia wrote Asaph a letter retracting "what I said the other day in the warmth of my wicked feelings" and begging him to forgive anything she had done "to make you shun my society."[65] That night she could not sleep from anxiety that the letter, meant as an apology, would offend her beloved brother. She wished that she could claw the words back. When Asaph wrote back the next day, assuring Sylvia of his continued love, his sister felt even more wretched. "Writing in half broken sentences," with "eyes bathed in tears," she expressed her regrets for making "mole hills into mountains." Her reaction to Asaph's perceived slight had been overblown. She confessed to having a "jealous disposition" and a "corrupt + depravd heart" that could not tolerate a slight. But Sylvia did not take the blame for the misunderstanding entirely on herself. She also attributed her over-sensitivity to the rejection she had suffered from her brothers Isaac and Oliver. "They have <u>said</u> they did not wish to come here because there was no man for them to visit," she explained to Asaph. So when he had hurried away from her house the day before, she suspected that he had joined their boycott.[66]

Unfortunately, Sylvia may have been more correct than Asaph could admit. Four years later, he continued to be an infrequent visitor at the women's house. His absence became the source of "so much suffering" and "affliction" to Sylvia, that it was "more <u>bitter</u> than words can tell or language can express." One Sunday in

October 1827, when Sylvia left the house to attend meeting, Charity picked up her pen to try and set things right. She took the blame on herself for driving Asaph away. If "the dwelling of your <u>sister</u> has become <u>almost</u> forsaken by you," she observed, the cause must be in "some imperfection which you have (by acquaintance) discover'd in me." She begged Asaph to resume his visits to their home, reminding him of the hospitality she had once found at his door. When Charity first arrived in Weybridge, she met "a friendly welcome at your hospitable dwelling." She was a "stranger in a strange Land," and Asaph had taken her in like the Midianites had accepted Moses after he fled Egypt. Then, like Moses, Charity had married into her host's family. Because of "the connection which has since take place between your sister and myself" Charity wrote, using a common nineteenth-century synonym for marriage, she had come to consider Asaph in a "fraternal relation" as a brother. Little could she imagine that one day he would "shun this dwelling And keep far from its inmates in your <u>affections</u>, and forget that they are <u>related</u> to you, either by the <u>bonds</u> of <u>Nature</u> or <u>Friendship</u>."[67] Now she sought to remind him of that bond and of his duty to his sisters. She begged him to renew his visits to their home.

The claims of kinship had great power in rural New England. The Drakes, always a close-knit family, would not abandon Sylvia altogether. Their youngest sister's choice to spend her life in "connection" with another woman discomfited her mother and her brothers, a feeling they expressed by avoiding visits to her house. But on the rare occasions that Sylvia and Charity spoke out against this mistreatment, the family compromised its embargo to preserve family amity. Sylvia recorded these encounters with enthusiasm—for example, "Brother Solomon + wife + Miriam comes. Quite overjoyd to have a Brother + sister come to make us a visit."[68] On another occasion, Sylvia recorded a large family gathering at her table, "three of my Brothers + their wives call + stay about 2 hours. Brother Isaac + wife Br Oliver wife + Brother Asaphs wife stay to tea + sister Hayward."[69] But many years passed between the sporadic visits. An 1835 visit from Solomon, who lived in the neighboring town of Bristol, produced the reflection that "6 years has elapsd since he made me a visit all was laid willingly aside to entertain so strange a guest."[70] Even Asaph, who visited his sister the most frequently, could be cold in his affections. A note of relief pervaded Sylvia's diary when she recorded that during a visit to Asaph's house he "appears like a Br indeed."[71] Their friendly reception could never be taken for granted.

The absence of a man in Sylvia's house did not trouble her sister Polly as it did their brothers. Polly, who lived close by, paid weekly visits to her little sister despite her own obligations caring for a large family at home. "Sister Hd here," Sylvia recorded in her diary again and again over the years. Polly often stayed for tea or a meal. On several occasions she spent the night. She came to help out with sewing or housework, to mix a batch of currant wine, dip candles, or to cook a meal. Around the table, the sisters mulled over the sermons they heard at the meetinghouse.[72] In the sex-segregated culture of early New England, a wife like Polly Hayward could feel at ease in the feminine space of Charity and Sylvia's cottage. Sylvia felt grateful for Polly's constancy of affection over the years. "My Sister. Ah! much has she done," Sylvia reflected in her diary in June 1821, before leaving on a trip for Massachusetts.[73] She owed a debt of gratitude to the sister who not only introduced her to Charity, but also gave her blessing to their household.

Polly's frequent transit back and forth from Sylvia's door beat a path for her husband to follow as well. Asaph Hayward remained resolutely friendly to both Sylvia and Charity throughout the years, visiting their house with his wife and children or on his own.[74] To Asaph Hayward, the women's lack of a man at home gave more reason to visit, not less, as he took it upon himself to help with conventionally male household chores. He sharpened their axes. He set up their bedstead. He repaired things around the house, fixing the sink, building a shelf in the woodhouse, cutting wood chips for the stove. He hooped barrels for their use. He brought the women fresh fish from Otter Creek. He butchered their hog. The women repaid him with occasional gifts of clothes, sewed free of charge. But the relationship was not strictly mercenary. Sylvia noted that Asaph Hayward called on occasion just to take tea with herself and her companion. Familial affection motivated Asaph's attentions as much as material reward.[75]

Over time, the tensions between Sylvia and her mother abated. Mary Drake lived to the very old age of eighty-seven, requiring years of care from her children, many of whom faced troubles in their own lives. Brother Isaac, for example, who died a bankrupt, was unable to house his mother and could only make promises to pay Asaph Drake to cover his share of their mother's support at some future point.[76] In the final eight years of her life, Mary spent more than thirty-six months living with Charity and Sylvia at their expense, joining her daughter and her companion in sewing, cooking, and common prayer.[77] Throughout this time, she continued to feel troubled by her daughter's sexual connection to another woman. After an extended visit in 1824, Sylvia admitted in a letter that she had frequently left her mother alone because the air in the room was too thick to breathe. Sylvia never felt able to discuss the situation openly, confessing "such were my feelings, such the guilt + magnitude of my own crimes, that I was unable to open the doors of my lips to you when you were here last, as it respected your own feelings on this momentous subject." But Sylvia assured her "best of Mothers" that she loved her and was trying her best to follow God's righteous path.[78]

All things considered, Sylvia felt proud that she and Charity had established a comfortable house where her mother could reside. "How thankfull I ought to be for having a Mother so long spar'd and for the means to make her as comfortable as we do," she reflected in her diary.[79] Whatever her mother might think of the relationship, Sylvia proved more useful to the aging woman by binding herself to Charity, who helped her to build a comfortable home, than she would have been had she remained single and dependent on her family's support.

13

Wild Affections

1811

CHARITY'S MIND WAS far away when she stepped through the cottage door after arriving home from a prayer meeting one April evening in 1811. At the end of worship she had raised her voice in song with her spiritual brothers and sisters, and now two lines of the final hymn echoed repeatedly through her head. "Where will those wild affections roll / which let a Saviour go?" She had listened to the poetry of Isaac Watts all her life, learning much of her sense of rhyme and meter from his devotional lines. But tonight his words took on new meaning, and she felt impressed with the gravity of her own fallen state. For years, she acknowledged, she had let "wild affections" possess her, and she had "abus'd the mercy of God." Deep in the contemplation of her own transgressions, Charity was taken by surprise to discover, when she came in the house, that Sylvia, who had stayed at home that evening, was in a terrible state of distress over her own fallen state. Charity hurried over to her beloved, and together the women raised their voices in prayer. The blood of their savior, Charity assured Sylvia, could wash away even the worst iniquities. Jesus had promised "whatever are thy crimes, my Goodness can exceed them." United in faith, the women repented for their sins.[1]

Several days later, Charity approached the doors of Weybridge's meetinghouse with a firm sense of purpose. For the first time, Charity felt awakened to the depth of her fallen state. She rejoiced that "whereas I was blind, I now see!" Possessed by this powerful religious conviction, Charity decided to offer herself as a candidate for full admission to the village's Congregational church. Charity and Sylvia had joined the church together soon after they began their marriage, but the orthodox congregation, which kept true to the Puritan traditions of New England's early settlers, administered communion only to members who testified to their spiritual rebirth.[2] Ironically, Charity's new sensitivity to her own depravity made her a suitable candidate for the privilege of communion. The orthodox creed preached the depravity of all humanity and regarded sin as mankind's common inheritance; an individual's true conviction of his own fallen state was the necessary first step in spiritual rebirth, rather than a rationale for exclusion.

Charity voiced her desire to unite with the church even though she did "not judge myself worthy of that honor, Nor do I think that of myself I can walk agreeably to the proffession." Her rebirth had brought knowledge of her fallen state, but no sense of surety that she would not sin in the future. The title of the Isaac Watts hymn that had catalyzed Charity's rebirth, "Backslidings and Returns," spoke to the common lapses into sin that afflicted even the most faithful. Both Charity and her spiritual brethren acknowledged the powerful possibility that as a lowly sinner she might succumb to her wild affections in the future as she had in the past.[3] Curled up at night in bed with her beloved, the temptation was sometimes too strong to resist.[4]

The Puritan author John Milton used the phrase "wild affections" to describe sexual expression outside of marriage.[5] Charity adapted the term for her own unsanctioned physical relationship. St. Paul warned his church about the "vile affections" by which "women did change the natural use into that which is against nature" (Romans 1:26). This passage was the most common biblical verse used to condemn lesbianism in early America. The legal code of New Haven Colony quoted Romans 1:26 to justify imposing the death penalty on women discovered having sex with other women.[6] The penalty was never enforced, and the last executions for male sodomy in North America took place during the mid-eighteenth century, but the Christian sentiment against such vile affections remained powerful in the early nineteenth century.[7]

Charity and Sylvia's struggle to find grace and overcome their sinfulness provides some of the best textual evidence of their erotic relationship. The language that they used to describe their sins often suggested that they considered themselves to be guilty of committing specific sexual transgressions. Since women of their generation and social class rarely wrote explicitly about sex (especially illicit sex), Charity and Sylvia's religious reflections open a critical window onto their erotic lives.[8] But these textual fragments are not the only or even the best evidence that Charity and Sylvia were lovers.

The clearest evidence that the women were lovers is the fact that they regarded each other as spouses and shared a bed for their entire lives. If the women were a cross-sex couple, those facts alone would be enough to establish the pair as sexual partners. The presumption of heterosexuality stands in the place of written evidence. Certainly, the children who result from most traditional marriages offer their own evidence of a couple's sexual relationship, but the sexuality of childless couples is rarely questioned, nor do historians often pose the question of paternity (that a couple's children might not result from their own sexual relationship). There is a corollary presumption: that in the past there were women who had sexual relations, and historical subjects who lived in same-sex unions can be presumed to be lovers.[9] Although the evidence will never permit total certainty, and it is possible to imagine that Charity and Sylvia shared a celibate intimacy throughout their lives, the women's confessional writings corroborate the presumption of a sexual bond between them.

The circumstantial evidence of Charity and Sylvia's sexual relationship not only bolsters the fragmentary confessional evidence, but also provides an important counterpoint to the bias inherent in the latter source. While the women's religious writings capture their feelings of sexual guilt, their lifetime of bed-sharing suggests the positive attachment they felt toward physical intimacy. The history of same-sex sexuality has been overdetermined by the selective evidence available for its study. Reliant on religious doctrines, court records, and psychological theories, the history of same-sex sexuality is often framed around the poles of oppression and resistance. The missing evidence of pleasure must be supplied by the imagination. Enjoyment of each other was the daily glue that bound Charity and Sylvia despite their intermittent episodes of self-recrimination.

Charity's guilty feeling about her sexual connections with women long predated her relationship with Sylvia. In 1798, after she first became a target of sexual gossip, her guilt inspired her to copy out passages from "The Suicide," a dramatic dialogue about a youth driven to despair over his sexual sins.[10] In 1806, following the exposure of her relationship with Mercy Ford, Charity "felt the weight of my transgressions to be more than I could bear," according to her confession before the Weybridge church. She "felt 'to abhor myself and repent in dust and ashes.' My iniquities appear'd so great that I thought the justice of God could not pardon them."[11] The wording of her confession is telling. *Iniquity* was associated with a catalog of sexual misdeeds in Leviticus 18:25, and in Ezekiel 18:49–50 the word was used to describe the misdeeds of the women of Sodom in particular. The word also connoted repetition or a pattern of wrong behavior. Charity's confession of guilt suggested she had not committed one sexual misdeed, but many.

Charity's spiritual crisis in 1806 did not lead to her spiritual rebirth, probably because it coincided with the renewal of her relationship with Lydia Richards. After her arrival in Cummington, she confessed, "I kept my feelings chiefly to myself till in the <u>Vortex</u> of <u>Worldly</u> cares they were mostly swallow'd up." Over the next several years, as Charity traveled to Vermont, joined in a marriage with Sylvia, and built a home, she kept her feelings of guilt suppressed. She "abus'd the mercy of God" and returned to her old ways.[12] She did not become irreligious at this time; the poems she wrote during her early years with Sylvia were suffused with pious sentiment.[13] But she returned to those transgressions and iniquities that had haunted her twenties. The same early poems that invoked God's blessings on Sylvia also depicted a relationship between the two women that was passionate and physical, involving mutual caresses.

Charity remained blind to her iniquities until 1810, when Mercy, who had experienced a spiritual rebirth, wrote to Charity encouraging her former lover to repent. Mercy's letter instructed Charity that God's love was more satisfying than any sensual pleasures to be taken from the earthly world. You cannot imagine, she wrote to Charity, the joys that redemption would bring: "You may form a faint idea by what you have felt in the enjoyment of the dearest friend you ever had in your happiest moment but you know I have also tasted that sweet and permit me upon experience to tell you that it has but a faint resemblance."[14] Mercy's language contrasted their history of shared fleshly pleasures with the promise of future spiritual joys. To make her case, she quoted from a Watts hymn that renounced the sensual world for religion: "Where can such sweetness be / As I have tasted in thy love / As I have found in thee?"[15] Mercy's testimony that she had "tasted that sweet" clearly referred to Watts's hymn. But her choice of words also echoed colonial America's most popular midwifery manual, *Aristotle's Masterpiece*, which used the words "sweetness of love" as a term for orgasm.[16] When Mercy claimed that she had experienced the sweet of a friend's enjoyment in the happiest moment, but now knew that God's love was even better, she suggested that redemption surpassed the sensual pleasures that she and Charity had once enjoyed together. Charity could take it from someone who knew: God's love was the best love of all.

The arrival of Mercy's letter coincided with a spiritual revival taking place in Weybridge. Mercy even quoted the same Watts hymn that had so moved Charity on the evening she returned home to find Sylvia in distress. The combined influence of her old lover's testimony and the charismatic preaching of her minister in Weybridge overcame Charity's defenses and resurrected her long-suppressed guilt over the wild affections that possessed her soul. The sight of Sylvia's sorrow sealed her conviction, persuading Charity that she was the "chiefest of sinners." Repentance could wait no longer. At long last Charity accepted her savior's love and renounced the sinful carnality that had plagued her throughout her adult life.[17]

Rejecting her sinful past could not preserve her from the danger of backsliding in the future, however. Sylvia's presence beside her every evening in bed over the next forty years presented temptations that were too powerful to overcome. Like many sinners who had been reborn, Charity struggled with her besetting sins for the rest of her days. In the final decade of her life, Charity wrote Sylvia a poem that described this private challenge. A person, she wrote, must fight:

> ...the secret cherishd sin
> The poison serpents tooth
> The treacherous clam that lurks within
> Destroying age + youth.[18]

Charity's sexual proclivities haunted her throughout both "age + youth." They were the "treacherous clam" (so obvious a sexual innuendo that Charity abandoned the language in a later draft of the poem) and the "secret cherishd sin."

The secret sin, in the language of the time, was a common euphemism for masturbation. Martin Luther himself had once called masturbation the secret sin. In the early nineteenth century, this corrupt practice or secret vice became an obsession within the American medical establishment. Leading doctors argued that masturbation was the primary cause of disease among American youth, leading to consumption, blindness, insanity, and even death. Notably, a close reading of anti-masturbation texts reveals that what early nineteenth-century doctors called masturbation among girls, we might call lesbian sex today. The secret vice, according to the authorities, was a sin that girls taught to each other and frequently practiced together for maximum titillation.[19]

The fact that Charity was still writing poems about the dangers of the secret sin during the last decade of her life suggests she never escaped her sexual feelings for Sylvia. As their relationship matured, and the women grew older and suffered from increasing episodes of ill health, the sexual dynamic between them likely cooled, but there is no evidence that the erotic dimension in their relationship ever disappeared. Instead, Charity seems to have settled into a state of resignation. She acknowledged that her wild affections made her a sinner, and she prayed that God's grace was sufficient to redeem even the chiefest sinner like herself.

Sylvia's diary reveals the same evidence of an unresolved struggle to overcome her physical desires. Like Charity, she perceived herself to be a sinner of the very worst variety. A decade after the religious crisis that awakened them to the magnitude of their sins, Sylvia continued to be afflicted by backslidings into temptation. Pouring out her misery onto the pages of her diary, Sylvia berated herself: "Oh! had my life been less stain'd with sins of the first magnitude Sins which embitter all the sweets of life."[20] For Sylvia, the phrase "sins of the first magnitude" was not vague hyperbole. These were sins clearly enumerated within Congregationalist theology as those most heinous in the eyes of God. They included murder, sodomy, incest, adultery, and theft.[21] There is only one sin in the list that Sylvia had the chance to repeat regularly, as her diary entry suggests. Murder can be crossed off the list. As a single woman, Sylvia could not commit adultery (if she had sex with a married man, the crime would have been regarded as fornication, not adultery). Living as she did in a subsistence economy, making rare visits to stores and in possession of few personal goods, it seems unlikely that Sylvia had much opportunity for theft. Incest cannot be excluded from possibility, but as she lived apart from her relatives it again seems unlikely to have been a regular habit. Atheism or blasphemy might also be considered as sins of the first magnitude, but Sylvia's constant prayers and contributions to her church reveal the force of her faith. That leaves sodomy, defined at the time as extending to sexual relations between women, as the only sin of the first magnitude possible for Sylvia.[22]

At another place in her diary, Sylvia suggested that she considered herself a Sodomite. On April 1, 1821, two weeks after berating herself for committing sins of the first magnitude, Sylvia attended a sermon preached by her friend, the Reverend Eli Moody, an ultra-orthodox Congregationalist who rejected any leavening of the sacred truths.[23] During the sermon, Moody berated his congregants for their religious torpor. The sermon, Sylvia wrote, "reminds me of Lot preaching to the sodomites."[24] It was an interesting choice of words. At one level, she probably meant to say that she and the other villagers of Weybridge, like the Sodomites, were turning a deaf ear to a godly man. But the Sodomites were not infamous for their deafness. They were known to early New Englanders for their willingness to countenance sex between men (or, more accurately, homosexual rape).[25] Sylvia's imagining herself as one of the Sodomites cannot be divorced from the imputation of same-sex sexuality.

Elsewhere in her diary, Sylvia described herself as guilty of "unclean" sins, another common descriptor for homosexual sex. Early Americans often used the language of uncleanness to describe sexual sins.[26] They applied this language to sex between men or between women in particular since, in the book of Genesis, God destroyed the city of Sodom because its people were "unclean."[27] In keeping with her identification as a Sodomite, Sylvia repeatedly berated herself for being unclean and prayed for Christ to purify her. She confessed in the pages of her diary that she was "a person of unclean lips," using a phrase often assigned to people who cursed or blasphemed, but which also had sexual overtones.[28]

If sex between women was considered an unclean sin, then sexual practices involving either the face or genitals or both could produce unclean lips. *Aristotle's Masterpiece* described the labia majora as "lips," and later editions also promised that the morphology of a person's facial lips revealed a great deal about her true character.[29]

There are multiple places in the diary where Sylvia seems to connect her sinfulness directly to her lips, tongue, or mouth. She certainly saw herself as too liable to speak angrily. But she may also have seen her mouth as unclean because of how she used it in her physical relationship with Charity. In one particularly recriminating diary entry she attacked herself as "proud arrogant contentious deceitfull jealous envious unkind given to fleshly appetites covetous given to anger."[30] This long list of flaws mixed temperamental weaknesses such as irritability with physical besettings such as "fleshly appetites," or sexual lusts, making no distinction between the two expressions of uncleanness. Elsewhere, she rebuked herself for possessing "an unnatural appetite," a phrase that echoed common descriptions of homosexual sex as an "unnatural" connection or offense.[31]

In another particularly suggestive passage Sylvia rebuked herself with the words "the tongue is a little member + boasteth great things."[32] This phrase, taken from James 3:5, warned against false teachers. Sylvia, who taught Bible classes to village youth but doubted her own salvation, had reason to worry that she was a hypocrite as well as a bad role model. At the same time, Sylvia's choice of language indicated another concern. The word *member* served as a common synonym for penis in early America. To call her tongue a little member acknowledged the phallic potential of the organ. The fact that Sylvia wrote this entry on a rare day when she and Charity had been at home alone suggests that opportunities for intimacy during the free afternoon, rather than time spent in religious instruction, gave Sylvia cause for later repentance about her unclean mouth.[33]

There is no question that Sylvia connected her relationship to Charity with feelings of great sinfulness. On the thirty-first anniversary of the commencement of her marriage, Sylvia noted the day in her diary with a mixture of love and regret:

> 31 years since I left my mother's house and commenc'd serving in company with Dear Miss B. Sin mars all earthly bliss, and no common sinner have I been, but God has spared my life, given me every thing I would enjoy and now I have a space, if I improve it, to exercise true penitence.[34]

The notion that marriage brought an earthly bliss tainted by sin was familiar to Christian theology. It originated in the story of Adam and Eve. In the beginning, Adam and Eve lived in a state of pure earthly bliss in the Garden of Eden. But after Eve and Adam ate from the tree of knowledge, they gained awareness of their sexuality and were cast out of paradise. Ever since, men and women's earthly bliss has been stained by sin. In the Augustinian tradition that Sylvia's faith emerged from, sexuality was by nature defiling, which is why Augustine advocated celibacy for the priesthood. Protestants, who were persuaded that celibacy was impossible, recommended marriage as an alternative framework to contain humanity's sinful carnality. But even within this pro-marital theology, sexuality retained its sinful stain. Sylvia's diary entry on her thirty-first anniversary implied that she viewed her union with Charity as a site for earthly bliss, like other marriages, but she believed that the sin tainting her earthly bliss was worse than ordinary. Sylvia's relationship to Charity made her "no common sinner."

Three decades after meeting her beloved, Sylvia still struggled with the temptation to succumb to wild affections. With great relief, shortly after her thirty-first anniversary Sylvia noted that she had attended a sermon where the minister announced that people often took thirty or forty years to master their besettings or sins. Sylvia commented that she was "never more interested" by a sermon, and she seemed to take hope that the time had finally come for her to move beyond her own besettings and "exercise true penitence."[35] The day that Sylvia had come to live with Charity she embarked on a career of sin; at long last she hoped to find a more righteous path.

Despite her best hopes, another decade passed without Sylvia mastering her besettings. A poem that she wrote for Charity in 1848 showed Sylvia in the same mixed mind about her marriage as ever. She was grateful for spending her life with Charity and yet was persuaded that their relationship was stained by sin. "Life's thread is quickly spun / All earthly bliss is marr'd," Sylvia wrote in the poem's opening lines. For forty-one years the women had "clung" to their love, but all that time their earthly bliss was tainted. Only in Heaven, Sylvia wrote, would she and Charity find the pure love denied to them in the sublunary world. There "Rivers of love in heaven, perpetual flow, / Yes, such as finite mortal cannot know. / And when <u>thy</u> throbbing pulse shall cease to beat / No disappointment be then thy bliss complete." These closing lines are remarkable for their sexualized imagery of salvation and their insistence on Charity's salvation regardless of the sin that marked her life. Sylvia painted Heaven as an ecstatic, even orgasmic, place, where rivers of love perpetual flow and where Charity's bliss would not be marred by disappointment. If the women's physical intimacy was a sin of the first magnitude, Sylvia prayed that Jesus would forgive them and reward them with a more holy intimacy in heaven.[36]

14

Miss Bryant Was the Man

1820

IN AUGUST 1820, census takers fanned out across the state of Vermont to execute the decennial record of the nation's population. An appointed recorder visited roughly 130 households in Weybridge, noting the race, sex, age, and occupation of the inhabitants within each. The only names he took were the heads of household. A great many Benjamins, Samuels, and Williams filled his rolls. About halfway through his record, after knocking at the doors of Asaph Hayward and Benjamin Hagar, the visitor inscribed the first woman's name into the record. Occupying a small house near the Hagar farm, he found two women, in the age group 26–44 years, who operated a commercial business. In careful penmanship, he recorded the proper spelling of the head of the household: "Charity Bryant."[1]

The census taker ten years later had fine handwriting, but poor spelling. Between the Hayward and Hagar farms, he enumerated a household headed by "Carity Briand," including two women, one aged 40–50 and the other 20–30.[2] Sylvia was actually thirty-five at the time, but compared to most Weybridge women her age, who bore the physical strain of multiple pregnancies, Sylvia likely appeared quite young. In 1840, the census taker got both Charity's name and Sylvia's age right. He also recorded a third woman aged 30–40 living in the household, one of the couple's sewing assistants.[3] The 1840 census included many more women as heads of household than had been the case twenty years before, but Sylvia remained unnamed within the federal population count until 1850, the year that dependents' names finally entered the rolls. In that Seventh Census of the United States, Sylvia Drake appeared for the first time in the official records of the American population. She was sixty-six years old.[4]

By 1850, the legal doctrine of "coverture" that had long subsumed married women's civic identities under the identities of their husbands was beginning to weaken. The passage of married women's property acts in many states entitled wives to own property separately from their husbands; an emergent women's rights movement called for women's prerogative to make their own decisions about childbearing; and wives and other dependent members of households finally had their names entered into the census. But the dismantling of coverture was a slow-moving process. Wives living with their husbands did not become coequal heads of household in 1850; they retained their subordinate position beneath their husbands. Accordingly, when Sylvia Drake was counted in the seventh decennial U.S. census, her name fell below Charity Bryant's.[5]

From the July day in 1807 that Sylvia came to live with Charity until the October day in 1851 that death divided them, Charity headed the women's household in their own eyes, as well as in the eyes of their family, their friends, and their community. William Cullen Bryant likened Charity to a "husband," and Sylvia to her "fond wife."[6] Charity used the term "my help-meet" to describe Sylvia, adopting a common synonym for wife, given to Eve in the book of Genesis. By extension, Charity figured herself as the Adam-like patriarch within the household.[7] With less eloquence but great clarity, Hiram Hurlburt defined Charity's role in simple terms: "Miss Bryant was the man."[8]

Charity's role as head of household, husband, or the man, however definitive, never overwrote her female identity as Miss Bryant. Charity did not pass as male-bodied. Rather short, probably as a consequence of her sickly childhood, she wore traditional women's garments.[9] At work she wrapped her hair in a turban to keep it from her eyes, and she wore a plain dress made from woolen circassian and a calico apron. She went without adornment, but on special occasions she might don plaited ruffles, displaying her skill as a tailor.[10] Her appearance projected a certain masculinity. She carried herself like a man and bore a strong resemblance to her brother Peter.[11] Charity's mixture of characteristics presented some confusion to a traditional rural community like Weybridge, where men and women performed very different social roles, but the division of Charity and Sylvia's marriage along the conventional lines of husband and wife made the union more comprehensible to the community, not less. It made them recognizable as a couple rather than as two independent single women.

It helped that Charity's combination of masculine and feminine qualities recalled the well-known archetype of the female husband, a popular antihero in

Anglo-American culture. The term "female husband" first appeared in a late seventeenth-century humorous ballad about a hermaphrodite, raised as a woman, who impregnated a woman and then married her.[12] The character of the female husband was popularized a century later in British novelist Henry Fielding's true-crime pamphlet *The Female Husband* (1746), which related the picaresque adventures of female-bodied George/Mary Hamilton, who dressed as a man and married several women before his true identity was revealed.[13] Fielding's work launched a century of humorous writings about female-bodied cross-dressers who married women.

Female husbands were not merely figments of the imagination, dreamed up by satirists and pornographers. The term described a real, if incongruous, variety of gender and sexual expression familiar in North America as well as Great Britain.[14] American newspapers in the late 1700s and early 1800s carried so many stories of female husbands that they became repetitious.[15] In 1829 a Maine newspaper published a humorous anecdote in which a woman who sought a summons against her husband was asked by the judge, "What, another female husband?" Actually, she reassured the judge, her husband was just a bigamist.[16] In general, the stories about female husbands, though sensational, did not treat their subjects as villains. The female husband's escapades were disreputable but impressive. She personified admirable masculine qualities including mastery, courage, and initiative.

Charity shared these personality characteristics with the archetypal female husband, which made her appear appropriate to head the household. William Cullen Bryant wrote that his aunt was "more enterprising and spirited in her temper" than her companion, and thus naturally "represent[ed] the male head of the family."[17] Hiram Hurlburt remembered how the first time that he entered the women's shop, as a boy, Charity had pointed a finger at him and commanded "you will wait." She then put Hiram in his place by naming his family lineage, before permitting him to approach the cutting table. Charity's demonstration of mastery led Hiram to conclude that it was "perfectly proper" for her to be "the man."[18] Since her youth, Charity had expressed a superior temperament that led her family to teasingly address her as "your ladyship."[19] After the move to Vermont, her dominating personality enabled her to transition from a lady to a female husband.

As a female husband, Charity did not claim all the legal privileges of coverture that were due to a male husband. The state recognized her as the quasi-head of household, but Sylvia maintained her own independent identity as a *feme sole*, the official legal status for an unmarried woman. For example, Weybridge village tax records listed Charity's name before Sylvia's in accountings of their common property, but the secondary appearance of Drake's name in the records indicates a compromise between the strict application of coverture, which would have erased Drake's name altogether, and the treatment of the two women as individual femes sole, which should have separated and divided ownership of their property between them. The local government recognized the financial integrity of their joint assets, which included the lease on a quarter-acre of land, a variety of buildings on that land, and financial instruments of fluctuating value.[20] Considering that Sylvia's male relatives served in many key civic positions in the town—including as tithing man, town clerk, treasurer, and collector of taxes—it can be concluded that the Drakes recognized Charity's status as a female husband and Sylvia's role as her help-meet.[21]

Charity's name also came first in the Weybridge land records, with Sylvia's name appearing afterward, whereas a conventional wife would not be listed in the records at all. When the women's longtime landlord Sarah Hagar grew feeble in the 1830s, she established an indenture with Charity and Sylvia protecting their rights to the property they occupied after her death, while guaranteeing that after their own deaths the land would pass to the next generation of Hagars. The contract guaranteed Charity and Sylvia's claim to "peacefully possess, occupy, and enjoy all the buildings heretofore erected by the said Charity and Sylvia…during the natural lives of the said Charity Bryant and Sylvia Drake."[22] In 1843, after Sarah died, her son and inheritor Henry W. Hagar entered into a new indenture with Charity and Sylvia, again promising "the said Charity Bryant and Sylvia Drake" the right to continue occupying their property for their "natural lives."[23] Four decades before, Charity and Sylvia had moved onto Sarah Hagar's property because she was one of Weybridge's only female landlords, and the arrangement protected the women from gossip. By 1843, no one was going to raise questions about Aunt Charity and Aunt Sylvia living on Henry's farm. Not only were the women old and venerable, by that time female-headed households had become far more common in Weybridge. Still, deeds cosigned by two *femes sole* in a joint capacity remained highly unusual.

Charity assumed even more authority in the couple's private business dealings than she did in their dealings with civic authorities. Charity and Sylvia kept detailed records of the tailoring work they performed for clients, and the payments they received in exchange, during the forty years they ran their business. In a cash-poor farming economy like Weybridge's, where businesses depended on the exchange of goods and credit more than direct payment, businesses needed to keep careful track. While each day Sylvia recorded in her diary the sewing that the women and their assistants performed, Charity maintained the accounts for their clients. Her name alone appeared on these records.

A typical account, detailing work done for Mr. Jehiel Wright during 1827 and 1828, listed each of the items sewed for the client, the price for each item, the goods received in payment (for example, a portion of wheat valued at $3), and closed with a final reckoning of the obligation. At the bottom, the record read "due to Miss Briant $3.83," which was followed by Charity's signature next to the words "Rec'd payment."[24] The debt was formally recorded as being owed to Charity, and Charity alone made formal acknowledgment of its payment. Almost the only exception to the rule of Charity's name appearing alone on the business dealings was in the case of exchanges the women made with Sylvia's brother Asaph Drake. When Charity and Sylvia did work for Asaph, or received food and services from him, they recorded the transactions in both their names. Still, even in those accounts, Charity's name came first. When Asaph lent the women $50 in December 1818, the note was made "jointly to Charity Bryant & Sylvia Drake."[25] In 1834, when Asaph rented his horses to the women for a journey to Massachusetts, both Charity's and Sylvia's names appeared on the record, but only Charity signed off on the repayment of their debt.[26]

Taking responsibility for settling debts with clients required more from Charity than simple accounting skills and the ability to sign her name. The early nineteenth century was a period of great economic instability. Currency fluctuations, financial panics, and crop failures all resulted in frequent bankruptcies.[27] Charity's brothers Peter and Bezaliel, as well as her sister Silence's husband, Ichabod, and her nephews Oliver and Daniel, all endured bankruptcies. The same plague of failures hit the families of Weybridge. It made collecting debts tricky. Charity and Sylvia avoided some of the worst financial crises by maintaining accounts for years, leaving time for debtors to acquire the resources to repay them. But sometimes Charity had to collect on debtors who could not easily satisfy their obligations. Sylvia made note in her diary one evening in 1822, a few years after the Panic of 1819, that Charity was writing "dunning letters."[28] Reminding the importunate of debts they owed was not a task for the faint-hearted. It required fortitude, a willingness to brave resistance and rejection, and a heart steeled to misfortune. But it had to be done for Charity and Sylvia to remain afloat.

Charity and Sylvia's union depended on the preservation of their independent household, and that required Charity to assume a husband's social role in collecting debts. Charity also took on debts for the women's business in her name alone.[29] Being a tailor necessitated frequent outlays for the purchase of fabric and notions such as thread and buttons. Charity bought these items in Middlebury, the nearest market town to Weybridge. Sylvia rarely if ever accompanied Charity on her shopping trips, although her state of health made her more fit than Charity for the long walk or ride to Middlebury. Even in the dead of winter, after days of feeling ill, Charity went into town to buy necessaries, leaving Sylvia at home.[30] If Charity gained status by asserting herself as head of household in the women's business dealings, Sylvia flexed the prerogative of domestic femininity to remain at home on a cold Vermont winter day.

To be clear, Sylvia did not defer to Charity in public financial matters because she lacked a feeling of ownership over their work. She saw their business as belonging to both of them, and she asserted her claim to an equal share in the marital property. When the women made gifts to Weybridge's Female Benevolent Society, which Charity led, they put both their names down for a single contribution. When the Society reimbursed the women for purchases they had made on behalf of the organization, Charity and Sylvia exempted $4 from the total as "their own tax."[31]

Sylvia valued her claim to their joint property for more than material reasons; she derived self-worth from her financial independence. One wintry evening, in a gloomy mood, Sylvia sat down to write out an informal will for the eventual disposition of her property. She described the small wealth that she had accumulated as the result of her own hard work, ably supported by Charity:

> Should the sudden stroke of death lay my frail body cold in the grave perhaps some friend might like to know my wish respecting my little that I leave, Hard work + close calculation will not accumulate properties unless you have confidence + a disposition to demand something for your labour. To the beloved Miss Bryant I am indebted for all the confidence I possess + generally for making a demand for my just due. We have toiled day + night almost, And now it is my wish she should enjoy peaceable + quiet by and during her natural life my share of the house we have built together, all the household furniture with some little exceptions which I shall name. The interest of my share of the notes held by Brother Asaph Drake, + Anna Bell esq + all the book, accounts.[32]

Sylvia's will makes clear that she saw herself as an equal partner in the tailoring business, an equal possessor of the house, and an equal holder of the accounts Charity signed. Charity's name on the financial documents did not signify that she was the boss and Sylvia was the assistant, but that she was the head of household and Sylvia her help-meet. Charity signed the accounts in Sylvia's name as well as her own. In this way, their union followed the logic of coverture, which subsumed a wife's identity under her husband's. But Sylvia preserved a feme sole's independent claim to the property she helped the household to acquire.

Sylvia's role as a wife in the marriage also involved exerting control over the private realm that fell to ordinary nineteenth-century wives. Sylvia took charge of feeding the family and keeping the house. She kept records of the foods brought to the house by neighbors, family, and friends: "Laura brings us calves feet," "Emma brings us bread milk + watermelon," "Edwin calls brings us apple sauce venison + sausages."[33] The deliveries might appear simple gifts, but Sylvia kept careful track of every calf's foot and watermelon she received. In return for these deliveries, Sylvia made presents of food or work herself.

In the rural nineteenth-century economy, one person's surplus supplied another person's need. In one diary entry, Sylvia recorded a complicated chain of food exchanges between herself, her landlord, her doctor, and her sister: "Mrs Hr bring us load Apples. I bake ginger bread. give Mrs Hr salt pork + fresh Dr P send us fresh pork send him salt pork send sister a little piece. She send us samp Mrs Hr bring us samp."[34] A surviving food-exchange record, which Sylvia kept for the year 1846–47, noted names, dates, and amounts with precision. Each tablespoon of sugar was counted in future obligations. The record is a rare testimony to the complexity of the food-exchange economy, which contributed as significantly to a family's upkeep as the monetary economy of the business world.[35]

Sylvia also prepared all the food for the couple, assisted by the apprentices who lived with them. Sylvia's diary is filled with accounts of baking bread, biscuits, cakes, "pyes," and "cookeys."[36] Although cooking could be a chore, the women approached food as a pleasure and were glad to serve tasty meals to their guests. "Bake sparerib boil onions + Mrs Hr dine with us + Miss W with Henry," Sylvia recorded after a shared dinner.[37] She was equally happy to enjoy the good cooking of others. "Laura gave me some pancakes, which I found very comfortably warm," she noted on a sick day when an apprentice cooked.[38] Charity almost never prepared food for the family, preferring to avoid such domestic labor.

Sylvia also did all the housekeeping, which she resented for its tedium. Maintaining even a small house in the age before running water or electricity took an enormous outlay of time and effort. "Making fires sweeping washing dishes + cooking as usual occupy most of the day," Sylvia grumbled in a January 1822 diary entry.[39] By working long into the night, Sylvia managed to combine these responsibilities with her sewing work. Another diary entry captures this fatiguing double load:

I spend Monday in taking care of meat baking sew the sleevelings + pockets + one seam on Mr Fs tunic And make the buttonholes on one side make the button holes on Mr Lees pts + on Edwins sew down + stick the lapells to Mr Pratts box o + make the button holes. Make Edwins vest + Mr Bacons Bake twice in the oven + wash + iron a little.[40]

Charity worked as hard as Sylvia, but she spent nearly all her time working on clothes.[41] She did perform some of the simple home repairs and furniture maintenance that typically fell to a husband. On a warm summer afternoon (the quiet season for their business), Sylvia noted that while Charity "mends the table + c + c Miss P + I knead bread + biscuit."[42] But at other times, Charity enjoyed her husbandly freedom from domestic responsibilities. On a summer day that Sylvia spent occupied by "a great washing" and mopping, Charity rode to Middlebury to attend the college commencement ceremonies and dine with a Mr. Merril. As Charity and her host sat down to a dinner prepared by women, and discussed the Latin and English orations of the young men who matriculated that day, Charity performed her role as husband before the community.[43]

In their social relations, as in their civic and business dealings, Charity positioned herself as the head of household. The couple maintained a busy correspondence over the years with friends, relatives, and ministers. Almost always the letters came addressed to Charity on the outside, although the greetings inside might extend to both women. Charity presented the couple's public face. Even Sylvia's own relations often observed this rule. When Sylvia's nephew Azel Hayward wrote to the women in 1825, giving an account of his legal studies in Massachusetts, he addressed the letter to Charity, then began with the words "Dear Aunts."[44] The rule for letter-writing put the husband's name on the outside of the envelope.

In polite conversation and writing, married women often went unnamed except by their status as a man's relation. When Jonathan Hovey, a former Weybridge minister, wrote a letter to Sylvia's brother Asaph in 1820, he observed this rule for Charity and Sylvia, bidding hello to all his former Weybridge friends including "Brother Southworth + his family—to Miss Bryant + yr sister—to Esq. Wright + his family—to Esq. Kellog + his family—to the Mr. Bills and their families—to Mr. Hagar + his family—Mr. Brewster + his family etc. etc. etc. etc."[45] Hovey named only the husbands and left their dependents unspecified, interweaving Charity and the unnamed Sylvia seamlessly into the mix. Just as at the dinner table, Charity joined the ranks of the esquires, misters, and brethren, while Sylvia took her place among the family.

However, if Charity was the husband and Sylvia the wife within their marriage, they were a different sort of husband and wife than most married couples of their day. At one level, their union reinforced the era's unequal model of marriage by demonstrating the naturalness of pairing a dominant husband and submissive wife, even in a relationship between two women. But Charity's role as husband also undermined the conventional justification for husbands' authority over wives as an expression of men's supposed physical and spiritual superiority. Charity's example opened the question of what made a husband's dominance and a wife's submission natural, or whether the division between roles had to be hierarchical at all.[46]

In addition, the women's conformity to the traditional roles of husband and wife, both in public and in private, had important limits. Each combined her married role with an identity as a spinster, which, in some ways, acted as a precursor for twentieth-century lesbian identity.[47] Somehow the incongruous parts fit together into a redefined vision of marriage. At twenty-three, Charity had declared her desire never to be married: "thousands in the world may call me a *fool* but I do not feel that their different opinions would add to my internal felicity."[48] When, on meeting Sylvia, Charity chose to marry after all, she did not entirely forswear her earlier objections. This may be one reason that in their private addresses to each other Charity and Sylvia used synonyms for spouse that connoted their equal standing within the relationship, rather than the ranked titles of husband and wife.

Sylvia often used *companion* to describe Charity, a word that operated as a common synonym for husband or wife. The word frequently appeared in obituaries to describe both widowers and widows.[49] As in those death notices, Sylvia used the word "companion" to convey the longevity of her and Charity's union. A diary entry from 1835 described Charity as "her who has been my companion ever since 1807."[50] In a loving flourish, Sylvia once referred to Charity as the "companion of my way."[51] This use of the word connected Charity and Sylvia to the tradition of romantic friendship by echoing lines from an elegy written by Philadelphia poet Hannah Griffits for a deceased friend, the "dear belov'd companion of my way / Friend of my youth, and partner of my heart."[52] Sylvia seemed to know this poem, echoing it elsewhere in her writings.[53] When Sylvia labeled Charity the "companion of my way," she represented her as both a romantic friend and as a spouse, two overlapping categories in her mind.

That overlap is even more obvious in both women's frequent naming of each other as friend, again a common synonym for spouse.[54] Sylvia stressed the women's mutual devotion by referring to Charity as her "beloved friend," coincidentally the same term of address that self-assertive wife Abigail Adams used for her husband, President John Adams.[55] Charity reciprocated, describing herself as Sylvia's friend in most of her poems.[56] Like Sylvia, she sometimes embellished the word, calling Sylvia the "friend of my heart" or her "faithfull friend."[57] The word *friend* implied no diminution of feelings to either Charity and Sylvia. Charity swore to the tremendous value she placed on the word friend, as "from the dearest of Titles I would not be free / For what millions of treasure could buy."[58] The word testified to their love and to the reciprocity of their relationship. *Friend* put the women's union on equal footing. They merged the unity of traditional marriage with the egalitarianism of romantic friendship.

Those who knew the women well also described their union in language that alluded to the roles they shared equally. Many people described the women as companions, echoing Sylvia. Minister Jonathan Hovey addressed the women as "Miss Charity Bryant & her beloved Companion," capturing the intense emotions that could be associated with the word.[59] Charity's cousin Roland Howard sent greetings to Sylvia, bidding Charity to "tender my respects to your companion."[60] Lydia

Richards described the women as partners, another word that served as a vernacular for spouse in the eighteenth and nineteenth centuries and that captured Charity and Sylvia's balanced footing within their union.[61] Charity's closest cousin, Vesta Guild, described Sylvia in a letter to Charity as "your other self," capturing both the marital oneness linking Charity and Sylvia and the symmetry of the women's positions within their marriage.[62]

Charity and Sylvia's union challenged traditional marriage by reimagining the roles of husband and wife, and in so doing it troubled the sexual order with the suggestion that they share an erotic bond. Early Americans understood the relationship between husband and wife as sexual by definition. The marriage ceremony included in the Book of Common Prayer, for example, stated that marriage had two main purposes: to encourage procreation and to offer a legitimate outlet for sexual passions. Ministers advised marrying couples that marriage was ordained as "a remedy against sin, and to prevent fornication."[63] The appropriate release of sexual passions within marriage extended to people who could not have children, which is why elderly widowers and widows got remarried long after the close of their childbearing years. The belief that marriage existed to impose order on people's sexual passions extended to women as well as to men. Early New Englanders acknowledged that women had a right to sexual satisfaction, and even some women past menopause sued for divorce on the grounds that their husbands were incapable or unwilling to provide sex.[64]

The association between marriage and sex applied to relationships involving female husbands. Charity's masculinity brought questions about her sexual relationship with Sylvia to the foreground because it was a running assumption that the desire for sexual intimacy with their own sex was a main reason that women became husbands.[65] Readers enjoyed speculating about the sexual lives of female husbands; it made their stories thrilling.[66] Restrictions on sexual speech led writers to introduce this possibility in an allusive fashion, raising the possibility in order to reject it, which planted the seed in a reader's mind while still protecting the author against charges of obscenity.[67] Writers also used euphemisms to depict female husbands as sexual offenders. For example, an 1842 New Hampshire newspaper reported the arrest of a female husband who was charged with committing "enormities," a word used in prosecutions of eighteenth- and nineteenth-century sodomites.[68]

The traditional silencing of same-sex sexuality through the use of euphemisms like "enormities" became a saving grace for Charity and Sylvia. Public recognition of their union depended on the community's willingness to avoid professing knowledge of its sexual implications. Their family, friends, and neighbors had to understand the possibility that Charity and Sylvia performed the sexual aspect of their roles as husband and wife, but they did not have to say as much. They could let silence preserve the open secret of the women's lesbianism.[69] This concession placed Charity and Sylvia in a vulnerable position. At any moment, the community had the power to withdraw their sanction for the women's relationship by breaking the silence. Weybridge could not tolerate public lesbianism. The community held a power over Charity and Sylvia that regulated the women's behavior. By adopting traditional marital roles and by devoting themselves to the health of the village's church, youth, and economy, Charity and Sylvia enlisted the support of their neighbors. They secured toleration not by keeping their marriage a secret but by making their relationship as public-minded as possible.

15

Dear Aunts

1823

ON A COLD and stormy Saturday in mid-February, Sylvia set the table in her newly expanded dining room. The wind outside blew something fierce, but the mood around the table was warm and convivial. Brother Asaph's children Polly and Isaac Drake took their seats alongside brother Oliver's children Nathan and Almira Drake, sister Rhoda's children Walter and Moriah Ellsworth, sister Polly's son Edwin Hayward, sister Desire's daughter Amerett Soper, and brother Solomon's daughter Arzina Drake. Altogether, Sylvia crowed in her diary, she served tea that afternoon to fourteen people "almost all Nephews + Nieces." Five of the children spent the night with Charity and Sylvia. The next day they had pancakes.[1]

None of the children, all born in the first two decades of the nineteenth century, could remember a time before Charity and Sylvia lived together in their hospitable little cottage on the Hagar farm. Since their earliest recollections, their aunts' house had been a sure place to find a good meal and a brief refuge from their own overcrowded homes. Visits from the second generation of the Drake family went a long way to make up for the absences of their often chilly parents. Some member of the Drake family visited Charity and Sylvia's house on average at least every other day.[2]

They came to enjoy Aunt Charity's wise company as much as Aunt Sylvia's pies and cookies. The Drake children rarely acknowledged any difference in their relationships to the two women. When away from Weybridge, the nieces and nephews addressed letters jointly to their "dear aunts."[3] They viewed the women as one kindly unit. Writing to her "dear aunts" from Moira, New York, in 1845, Polly's daughter Emma expressed gratitude to both women together for the "unveried kindness you have always shown from my birth untill now…my dear friends."[4]

Although nieces and nephews descended from the Bryant family did not grow up next door to Charity and Sylvia, they treated Sylvia with the same affection that the Drakes extended to Charity. Oliver Bryant assured his "dear aunts" in 1844, "I do not know of a nephew or a niece in our family there is none but entertain the most tender regard for yourself."[5] The two women paid frequent visits to Massachusetts, typically every other year, when the second generation of the family was growing up. Sylvia, who was more approachable than Charity, found many friends among the children. Peter's sons may have jokingly called Sylvia "Uncle Drake" in her absence, but she was always Aunt Sylvia in their hearts.[6] Peter's youngest, John Howard Bryant, born in July 1807 just days after Charity and Sylvia moved in together, addressed his letters to his "dear aunts" just as the Drake children did. So did Anna Kingman's son Freeman, Silence Bryant's son Oliver, and Cyrus Bryant's son Daniel.[7] "Please give a great deal of love to Aunt Sylvia," Silence Bryant's granddaughter Emme wrote to Charity in 1844.[8] It requires a family tree to distinguish Emme from Emma and discern the bonds of biology that tied which woman to which aunt.

Making matters more confusing, several children on the Drake side bore the Bryant name. Sylvia's brother Asaph named his fifth son Cyrus Bryant Drake for Charity's deceased brother. Sylvia's brother Oliver named one of his sons Cyrus and one of his daughters Charity in Charity's honor.[9] Sylvia's nephew William Ellsworth, the son of her sister Rhoda, named his son Charles Bryant. In a letter to Asaph Drake, William Ellsworth explained that "I did not name my oldest Charity Bryant but came as near to as I could," adding a loving message to the person in question, "aunt charity I have not forgotten you I send my best respects to you and aunt Sylvia I hope you have not forgotten me."[10] The Bryant name even continued to circulate through the fourth generation of the Drake family. Asaph Drake's son Elijah's daughter Sarah named her son Willis Bryant Child shortly after Charity's death. Sarah, who knew her great-aunt Charity from birth, chose the name to memorialize her venerable relative.[11]

The majority of Drake children named for Charity were sons, not daughters, and Charity's surname made a more lasting impact on the family than did her first name. Their daughters, the Drakes named for Sylvia. Asaph named a daughter Sylvia Louisa. Sylvia's sister Desire named a daughter Sylvia Ann. Sylvia's brother Oliver twice named a daughter Selvina.[12] But there were no male adaptations— no Sylvans—among all the Sylvias. Only Charity broke the naming pattern that typically predominated in New England families—daughters named for mothers and sisters, sons for fathers and brothers.

Charity and Sylvia singled out their namesakes on both sides for special generosity, which probably explains why the prolific Oliver named four of his eighteen children for the women. Altogether, Charity and Sylvia's nieces, nephews, grandnieces, and grandnephews numbered in the hundreds. If the women could not dote equally on all these young people, they formed close connections to a remarkable number. From the 1820s onward, the women received regular correspondence and visits from more than twenty nieces, nephews, grandnieces, and grandnephews. They were especially close to Asaph Drake's and Polly Hayward's children in Vermont and to Silence Bryant's children in Massachusetts. Silence, who suffered many family losses over the years, welcomed Sylvia as her "second sister."[13] It is little wonder that these siblings' children, above all, looked to both Charity and Sylvia as beloved aunts.

A few of their relationships stand out in particular. Polly's oldest daughter, Achsah, who had been the first person to tell Sylvia about Charity's special charms, shared a particular intimacy with both women. Sadly, not long after Charity moved to Weybridge, Achsah began showing signs of the tubercular infection that killed so many New Englanders of the era. The women did their best to care for their witty young niece. Charity wrote to her brother Peter seeking remedies; he recommended alcornoque bark and bleeding.[14] In 1817, Sylvia and Charity took Achsah on a visit to Massachusetts, at her request. Travel was often prescribed to victims of consumption, although more so for men than women.[15] Charity and Sylvia had great hopes that the trip would be restorative.[16] Once arrived, Achsah took pleasure in meeting Charity's sisters and brothers and nieces and nephews, who fussed over her.[17] She returned feeling better than when she left, but the trip did little to improve her health. Achsah died the following spring at the age of twenty-five. Her aunts mourned her loss to the end of their days. Charity described Achsah's death in her brief 1844 memoir. Achsah, she wrote, had "gradually sunk under the power of that fatal Disease, Consumption, untill May 1818 when much lamented she bid her Friends a final farewell!" Charity used more words to describe Achsah's end than the deaths of her sister Anna Kingman in 1811 (from tuberculosis), her father, Philip, in 1816 (from old age), or her brother Peter Bryant in 1820 (also from tuberculosis). Achsah's death was the only loss on Sylvia's side of the family that she noted at all; it still carried a sting thirty years after the fact.[18]

The women also had a special relationship with Charity's godson Cyrus Bryant Drake. When his father Asaph Drake asked Charity, as godmother, to name his newborn son, Charity chose the name of her middle brother who had died in 1798. From the day of his naming, Charity contributed to the boy's upbringing. The small gifts of clothes or treats that she made to Cyrus during his youth helped bind his affection to her, but they were really only pledges toward a more important responsibility to come. "From the first moment that it was known that I had nam'd your son to the present time," Charity wrote to Asaph in the summer of 1829, it has often been said to me "you are going to send <u>him</u> to College, are you not?"

After receiving permission from his father, Charity arranged to pay for Cyrus to attend Middlebury. The cost was significant. Charity and Sylvia paid his tuition, bought his books, and sewed his clothes during his years in preparatory school prior to college, then gave him $24 a year toward college support, and continued to give him gifts of clothes and books throughout his post-collegiate studies at Andover Seminary, where he trained for the ministry.[19] Cyrus was one of the only children in his generation of Drakes to attend college. Few sons on the Bryant side had this opportunity either. Even Peter's "genius" son Cullen could not afford to attend Yale, the school of his choice, but went to lesser-priced Williams College before withdrawing early to train for a legal career.[20]

Cyrus never forgot his aunts' largesse. He remained a faithful nephew, repaying the women in visits and affection. Even while he studied at Andover, he made trips back to Weybridge to spend time with his aunts, drinking tea in their parlor and reading aloud from religious books.[21] He became so much his aunts' son that Asaph renounced his own claim to paternal authority:

you must know if you have not learnt it before that I have not a son of that Name I had one once on whome my hart doted and on whome I depended on to perform manuel labor on my farme and likewise to take the care of my secular concerns that I in my infirm state of boddy and decline of life might be releived in some measure of the burden. But [I don't say allas] I have no such son now. I hope he is not dead absconded or become Lunitic—neither have I disinherited him But by hard struggle not with Inclination nor Duty but with pecunary embarisments I have given him to A Valued friend of mine and my fileys who richly deserves Him and much more from me.

Asaph's renunciation of Cyrus was bittersweet. He felt Cyrus's attachment to Charity and Sylvia as a loss, yet he refused to regret that loss. His own relationship to Charity, although tense at times, had given enormous meaning to his life. He described the early years of their friendship as "not only the Happyest but the most rich and blest moments of my Life." Now, as a result of this friendship, Cyrus received a college education and became a well-respected and wealthy minister. Asaph, who had little faith in his own salvation, credited that good fortune entirely to his adopted "sister."[22]

Remarkably, Cyrus was not the only Drake whom Charity and Sylvia considered sending to college. Charity inquired about sending one of their nieces to America's first women's college, Mount Holyoke Academy, in 1837, the year that it was founded. They probably had in mind Sylvia Louisa, Cyrus Bryant Drake's younger sister, as the prospective pupil. Charity and Sylvia were especially close to Sylvia Louisa. The women saw Sylvia Louisa, a smart and independent girl, as the Drake niece who bore the closest resemblance to themselves. In her 1821 will Sylvia left clothes to the four other girls named after herself, but she promised to give Sylvia Louisa fees at "some Academy or school for the purpose of instructing young ladys."[23] When Mount Holyoke opened, Sylvia Louisa was twenty-seven and single, a good candidate for college. Charity wrote to their friend the Reverend Eli Moody, who lived in a town near Mount Holyoke, asking for information about the school. The minister judged it an excellent institution and described the requisites for entering: "an acquaintance with the general principles of English grammar, a good knowledge of modern geography, History of the United States, Watts on the Mind, Colburn's first lessons, + the whole of Adams' New Arithmetic." He also promised to act as a guardian to their niece while she was away from home.[24]

None of the young Miss Drakes did end up attending Mount Holyoke. Whether that was a result of expense, inadequate preparation, or the unfamiliarity of a college for women is unclear. Although Charity and Sylvia did not send Sylvia Louisa to college, they still earned her loyalty. Sylvia Louisa never married or left Weybridge. After Charity's death, she proved a faithful friend to her aging aunt, accompanying her on visits to relatives, sending letters for her, and treating her with love and compassion.[25] "I am glad you have such good Children," Sylvia wrote to her brother Asaph, after Sylvia Louisa had taken her on an important errand.[26] More than anyone else, Sylvia Louisa guaranteed that her aunt was comfortable in her old age.

Charity and Sylvia could not offer to send all their nieces and nephews to college, but they made many smaller gifts over the years that went a long way to securing their affections. Edwin Bryant, son of Charity's sister Silence, wrote to his aunts recalling the joy he felt as a little boy when they gave him a new set of clothes: "Oh! how proud I was! How I exulted when permitted to wear them. The great mogul himself had not half of the genuine coxcombing that I then felt. Alas! The joy and pleasures of childhood! How they have all passed away, and made room for the sterner scenes of manhood." Edwin closed this nostalgic letter with a request for Charity to "remember me particularly to Aunt Sylvia."[27]

Perhaps Edwin, who never married but "died a bachelor," felt an unspoken connection to his spinster aunts.[28] Certainly their affections created some of the rare happy memories in a difficult childhood. The 1809 bankruptcy of his father, Ichabod Bryant, forced Edwin to leave school at age fifteen. Charity and Sylvia tried to help the family by lining up a job for Ichabod at Middlebury College, but the position fell through, and Edwin, as the oldest son, was forced to go to work to protect the interests of his six younger siblings.[29] He had a peripatetic youth, working for a spell with his Uncle Bezaliel in New York State, trying his hand at business in Boston, moving to Kentucky to edit newspapers in Lexington and Louisville, and traveling before the Gold Rush to California, where he bought San Francisco real estate that later earned him a fortune.

To this quintessential modern self-made man, his aunts represented a honeyed lost world of tradition, stability, and family.[30] Writing from a wearied perspective later in life, Edwin acknowledged that his aunt Sylvia was perhaps not a true aunt in the eyes of the world, but he regretted the loss of his innocence on this count. "Give my love to 'Aunt Sylvia' as I was wont to call her when a boy," Edwin wrote to Charity. "I shall never forget her and your kindnesses at that period of my life."[31] Thankfully, both his aunts had already passed away when Edwin threw himself from the window of a hotel in Louisville, Kentucky, in 1869. An obituary writer opined, "he was perhaps too sensitive for this world; the cords of his soul may have been too finely attuned for the rough fingers of the demons of the storms of human life."[32] A more pithy observer commented that Edwin's "wealth did not bring happiness"—at least not the happiness of a little boy receiving a new suit of clothes from his tailor aunts.[33]

Charity and Sylvia made similar gestures of generosity to many of their nieces and nephews. They brought gifts to distribute on their trips to Massachusetts. The Weybridge relations frequently received small gifts from their aunts, as did Sylvia's brothers' children in Bristol. In the summer of 1823, Sylvia and Charity brought "Brothers sisters Nephews + friends" in Bristol gifts amounting to nearly $7 in value. In return, the Bristol relatives treated Charity and Sylvia to "good cherry whiskey" as well as "good fish + potatoes biscuit pye + c."[34] Sylvia, who kept notes, enjoyed the meal, but in general the women did not expect to earn back the value of their gifts.

Charity and Sylvia's reputation for generosity encouraged several nephews to apply to them for significant financial help at critical points. Polly's son Azel, a longtime favorite whom the women had once brought with them on a visit to Massachusetts, asked for a loan of $100 in 1826 to buy a law library and enter the legal business.[35] Asaph's oldest son, Elijah, received help establishing a brick kiln from his aunts, who contributed funds they earned from the industry of their own "assiduous hands."[36] Cyrus Bryant's orphaned spendthrift son Daniel more than once sought the support of his indulgent aunts.

The women offered advice on the matters of faith, work, and love in even greater quantities than cash. Anna Kingman's son Freeman fondly remembered their solicitude for his spiritual welfare during his youth. "It has always been a source of pleasure," he wrote to his "dear aunts," to "recollect the warmth of your attachment the gentle pressing of my hand with a look of anxious solicitude for my future welfare which was generally conducive to my present pleasures."[37] Since his own mother died when he was young, and his father could be hostile to religion, Freeman appreciated having someone in the family express care about his spiritual well-being. Charity's concerns for the children extended beyond their spiritual welfare. She often inquired into the marital prospects of nieces and nephews, expressing a longstanding interest in the world of conventional courtship that Sylvia did not always share. Charity's nephew Oliver Bryant even accepted his aunts' help in finding him a wife after a prolonged bachelorhood.[38]

Charity had the most advice to offer on the subject of her nephews' economic futures. The women's consistent success at earning a living through skilled labor during an era of intense economic instability provided a useful example. The scarcity of available arable land in New England, as well as the expansion of the commercial economy in the early nineteenth century, drove many in the second generation of Bryants and Drakes to seek a career in business rather than on the farm. Aunt Charity in particular seemed able to help steer them along this path. Oliver wrote to Charity asking her advice about whether he should borrow money to buy into a store.[39] Charity tried to line up a job for Peter's son John with one of her Middlebury customers. When that opportunity failed, she gave John advice on his plan to further his education at Colby College.[40] She sent her niece's husband Abiel Rankin a notice of masonry work taking place at Middlebury College to help him find steady employment.[41] She also tried to line up jobs for numerous Drake nephews, working her family networks in Massachusetts to identify opportunities.[42]

Charity tried many times, without luck, to help the orphaned Daniel Bryant, who was raised by his grandparents. Rather than provide Daniel with an education, Philip and Hannah began to hire him out as a laborer when he was in his early teens. He complained that his step-grandmother worked him "worse than a negro had ought to been used."[43] Perhaps to make up for this misuse, Philip left Daniel half his sizeable real estate following his death in 1816.[44] But loosed from the tyrannical oversight of his grandfather and grandmother, Daniel rapidly spent all his inheritance. For the rest of his life, he struggled to earn a living. Charity was diligent about keeping in touch over the years, even after other family members wrote Daniel off as a profligate. When Daniel lost title to his grandfather's house, Charity invited him to come settle in Weybridge, but her nephew's young wife, Lucy, had a "presentiment against the place," so the couple remained in temporary lodgings in Massachusetts. If Charity could not help Daniel in the way she wished, she at least let him know that she loved him and worried on his account. Daniel took comfort from this knowledge, keeping up his end of the correspondence with Charity despite his general flightiness, and he never forgot in his letters to send his love to Aunt Sylvia.[45]

Charity and Sylvia also tried to help their nieces by training them for the tailoring trade. Wage opportunities for rural girls were expanding during the antebellum era thanks to outwork industries such as hat-making and the growth of mill towns such as Lowell. Neither hat-making nor the mills offered as much financial independence as skilled tailoring, however.[46] Charity offered instruction not only in how to sew, a common skill among nineteenth-century women, but in cutting cloth, a specialized trade that distinguished tailors from less-skilled seamstresses. She sought to give these girls a means to support themselves throughout their lives.[47] Edwin Hayward's twin sister, Emma, lived with and worked for the women for much of 1821. Afterward they helped pay for her school fees.[48] Asaph's daughter Sylvia Louisa and Isaac Drake's daughter Emmeline also both learned to sew from their aunts.[49] Silence's daughter Elizabeth came to Weybridge for a season, but homesickness cut her apprenticeship short.[50]

Charity tried to persuade her father to allow Daniel's sister Zibby to live in Weybridge and learn the trade, but Philip refused to permit Zibby to leave the family home because he insisted that the young girl owed him her service in exchange for his care during her infancy. If she left, Philip and Hannah would have to hire a girl to take care of them. Zibby and Charity were both disappointed by Philip's unfeeling refusal.[51] After Philip died, Zibby refused to remain in the house and take care of her step-grandmother. Instead she hired herself out to another family.[52] By the time Hannah died, ten months later, Zibby had found a different path to independence by marrying and starting a household of her own.[53] She was in such a hurry to leave the Byrant homestead that many in the family believed she married down. As her uncle Peter crudely put it, "Zibbeah I hear has thrown herself away upon a DICKERMAN!"[54] Charity's cousin Vesta remarked more kindly that she hoped Zibby had made "a good bargain."[55] Unfortunately, Peter's prejudice bore out. Zibby's husband Benjamin Dickerman found it difficult to earn enough to support the family, giving his wife good cause to regret not learning a trade of her own as a young woman.

Of course, some nephews and nieces resented Charity and Sylvia's interfering ways. The women were not shy from offering their opinions on the states of the children's souls. During one trip to Massachusetts, Anna's son Lysander Kingman stayed out in the fields while Charity and Sylvia visited the family. His cousin Elizabeth later explained to her aunts that Lysander "thought you would say something upon a subject that he did not like to hear about."[56] The matter may have been religion or it may have been work. Either way, he chose to absent himself from the routine questioning that Charity and Sylvia's visits entailed. Though Lysander blamed his absence on work, claiming that he had to be haying during their visit, his aunts saw through the ruse.[57]

When Charity and Sylvia felt neglected or slighted by their nieces and nephews, they said as much. A leavening of guilt alongside their generosity helped bind the second generation close. Charity was probably overly sensitive about family rejection, which was only natural considering her difficult relationship with her father and stepmother. Up to his death in 1816, Philip sought to punish his youngest daughter for her nonconformity, even leaving her less in his will than many in the family thought she deserved.[58] Rather than leave her valuable property, his main bequest was title to a chamber in his house, a slap in the face to Charity, who for almost a decade had made her own home in Vermont with Sylvia.[59]

A Bridgewater friend, Nabby Snell, wrote to Charity trying to put a positive spin on the will, declaring "I, should be pleas'd if it was agreeable to you, and could be for your benefit that you would take possession of your chamber and occupy it yourself with Sylvia."[60] But the notion that Charity and Sylvia would leave their beloved cottage and move back into the house with Charity's decrepit and detested stepmother was unthinkable. Later that year when Hannah Richards Bryant lay on her own deathbed she followed her husband's precedent and made a final gesture of rejection toward her stepdaughter by giving away the household furniture Charity had inherited.[61] In the years that followed, Charity's west chamber became more of a burden than an asset. She sought to extract a yearly rent from the unwilling family who bought the property excluding Charity's room, but they resisted paying their absentee landlord. For years, Charity's agents in North Bridgewater wrote letters of complaint about the difficulty of collecting the meager sum.[62] Charity's father's disapproval haunted her for decades.

Charity never overcame the anxiety that her family did not love her. While her brother Peter was alive, she worried about his affections.[63] After Peter died, Charity expressed doubt about the affections of his widow, Sally.[64] And when Peter's children grew up, she worried about their love too.[65] When they and their mother moved together to Illinois in the 1830s, Charity seemed to take it personally. Despite her anxieties, Peter's children expressed their continued affection for their sensitive aunt by writing her detailed letters from Illinois and preserving her name into the next generation. Charity's nephew Cyrus Bryant named his daughter, born in Illinois in 1848, after her great-aunt.[66]

Although Charity's choice to spend her life in the company of another woman set her apart from the family, her facility with the pen established her as an exemplar of the family tradition in the minds of the younger generations. As William Cullen Bryant increased in literary fame during the antebellum era, his many cousins and their children staked claim to a family tradition of poetic accomplishment. They admired Charity's poetry for what it revealed about the whole family's worth. Many of the Bryant nephews and nieces asked Charity for acrostics on their names, which they might save and pass down to descendants. Anna Kingman's granddaughter Jane begged her aunt to write acrostics on the names of her sisters, Martha and Ellen, after their untimely deaths.[67] Silence's daughter Elizabeth sought an acrostic not only for herself, but for her husband Hiram Tavener.[68]

The Drakes found the prestige of the Bryant family name almost as alluring as the Bryants themselves did. Being connected to the Bryant family through Charity helped solidify the Drakes' claims to gentility, which they had started to rebuild by becoming landowners in Vermont. It is little wonder then that the Drake nieces and nephews sought the gift of Charity's verses with the same avidity as their Bryant cousins. Charity wrote acrostics for all of Polly's children. She also wrote an epitaph for Polly's granddaughter Semantha. Charity's name appeared beneath the lines on Semantha's gravestone, intermixing the Hayward and Bryant family names for the centuries to come.[69]

Both Charity and Sylvia wrote poems for Polly's son Edwin Hayward, who was a special favorite. Sylvia wrote an acrostic on his name, which Polly had asked Charity to pick after his birth in Bridgewater in 1803. Sylvia's lines encouraged the young man to be serious about his faith and seek salvation.[70] At the time Sylvia crafted the poem, Edwin was a frequent visitor to his aunts' home, helping out with household chores as his father once had and accepting small gifts of clothing in return.[71] That his interest in the household extended beyond his aunts became clear when he married their sewing assistant, Lucy Ann Warner. Charity and Sylvia were delighted by the union and may even have engineered it. May "peace and love & every Christian grace / Adorn your lives And ever bless your Home," Charity wrote in a poem for the couple after they married.[72] A third poem, which Charity wrote for Edwin's forty-fourth birthday, expressed more personal sentiments.

The poem began with Charity's recollection of first holding him as a babe:

Dear Edwin forty years & four the day
Have took their flight swiftly and rolld away
Since to this world of mingld joys and strife
You & your mate were usher'd into Life
And yet it seems but yesterday or less
Since first I saw you in your infant dress
And when I first your little form caress'd
And in my arms you took your just nights rest

The opening lines conveyed the depth of the love Charity felt for Edwin as a surrogate son. When Polly placed her baby in Charity's arms and allowed Charity the privilege of choosing his name, she gave her future sister-in-law an invaluable gift: a share in the experience of motherhood that she missed by deciding not to marry a husband.[73]

Motherhood defined women's status in the early national period. A cult of motherhood emerged following the Revolution, which ascribed enormous responsibility to women as parents of the new republican generation. Mothering literature proliferated in the early nineteenth century, and in the 1820s, women began to assemble in "maternalist associations" throughout the northeast, coming together in a common cause and helping to lay the basis for a future women's rights movement.[74] Charity and Sylvia were invited to join the maternalist association in Weybridge, but on at least one occasion, they declined to attend the meeting.[75] Whether this was because of work, or because they felt uneasy grouping themselves with the town's mothers, they did not make clear.

Either way, Charity and Sylvia expressed no regrets that their life together did not provide the opportunity for motherhood. Witnessing the incredible burden that motherhood placed on their older sisters and almost every other woman they knew, Charity and Sylvia had reason to prefer the status of aunts. Bearing children could be disastrous to their friends' and sisters' health, causing tooth loss, fistulas, and even death. After giving birth to her first child, one friend of Charity's developed such a terrible infection in her breasts that one ruptured and the other had to be lanced.[76] Other friends and relatives suffered terribly from experiencing stillbirths or bearing sickly infants who soon died. Even when both mothers and their infants had the fortune of good health, raising children placed an enormous burden on women.

Seeking to avoid this burden, Charity's friend Lydia waited until she was past the age of childbearing before she accepted a marriage proposal from a widowed local minister. When she reached her forties, with her parents growing old, Lydia had to be sensible about her future. She had good reason to hope that accepting a marriage proposal would add to her security without extracting the cost of bearing children. She even wrote to Charity shortly before the marriage promising that the "new connexion will [never] exclude you from this bosom!"[77] But the work of caring for her stepchildren and later her step-grandchildren proved more onerous, and demoralizing, than she could ever have imagined.[78] Following the marriage, her correspondence declined at once from a letter every couple of months to a letter only once or twice a year. Between December 1828 and May 1832, Lydia wrote no letters at all. When she did resume the pen, Lydia apologized that "other things so imperiously demand every moment of my time."[79] Her domestic labors were so intense that at times Lydia sank into bitter tears over her "want of power and authority, or ability, to order, or control any event or arrangement for my own pleasure." Despite her affection for her husband, Lydia mourned over the change in her circumstances, "it is more agreeable to nature to feel a little more independent."[80]

By comparison, Charity and Sylvia lived a privileged life. Their freedom from motherhood allowed them to engage in voluntary relations, rather than act as "servants" to their children (as Lydia put it). The hundreds of letters they wrote to nieces and nephews testified to the control they exercised over their own hours. Their independence elevated their roles within the family, permitting them to act as conduits of information, rather than isolating them from relations.[81] To some of their young nieces, this model of family affection appeared far more appealing than conventional motherhood. If Charity had once been inspired by her own Aunt Charity's single life, so several of her own independent-minded nieces saw a valuable lesson in her and Sylvia's example. Grandniece Emma Rankin, for example, pledged herself never to marry, but like her aunts derive her affection from the legions of nephews and nieces that her siblings provided.

Voluntary bonds of affection also united Charity and Sylvia to many young people who were not biological relations at all, most importantly, their sewing assistants. After Charity and Sylvia expanded their house in 1819, they had the space to invite their assistants to live with them. In the course of three decades, a large number of young women resided in the house, including Lucy Ann Warner, Philomela Wood, Laura Hagar, Lucy Hurlbut, Fidelia Southard, and Belinda Brownwell. Correspondents referred to the young women who lived with Charity and Sylvia as "your girls."[82] Sylvia described these young women in her diary as family. For example, after a long sickness in the summer of 1823, she rejoiced to "take breakfast with the Family."[83] At other times, she referred to Charity leading their family in prayer, fulfilling a traditional patriarchal role.[84] As head of household, Charity assumed a parental role with her apprentices that had long fallen to masters.

Some young apprentices welcomed the role of foster daughter. Philomela Wood in particular embraced Charity and Sylvia as family. She lived with the women for almost a decade, coming to join them in 1827, when she was only twenty-one, and remaining until after she married, in 1836.[85] During this time, Charity and Sylvia not only taught Philomela the sewing trade, but also supported her study for several terms as a student at a school in nearby Jericho. Although she enjoyed the opportunity, Philomela felt homesick for the shop and longed for "Miss D and Miss B standing with her shears in her hands happy in each others society and in the cause of your master."[86] After school, she returned to live with the women for many years, before she married Edwon Wilcox and moved away to Bridport. Philomela addressed her first letter back to the women who had so long given her a home, "Dear Mothers." Happy to have married, she nonetheless missed the house "where I have spent so many years of happiness, where those reside that I love." She thanked Charity and Sylvia for all their "motherly care."[87]

Several of Philomela's fellow apprentices regarded the women with the same affection. Philena Wheelock, who came to work in 1835, wrote after her departure that "happier hours than those I have spent with you, I never expect to enjoy in this life."[88]

Philena also thanked Charity and Sylvia for treating her with the "tenderness of a mother."[89] And again, like Philomela, Philena did not leave the household for good until she got married.[90] Even after these surrogate daughters left their house, Charity and Sylvia continued to care for them. They wrote poems for their former assistants, sent them presents, and welcomed them back for visits.[91] Motherly affection outlasted the bonds of service.

Philomela's and Philena's terms of maternal endearment, however, were exceptional. Most of the youth of Weybridge, whether Drakes or not, regarded Charity and Sylvia as aunts. Mothers to none, they became aunts to all the young people in the town. When a boy from Weybridge moved to North Bridgewater, a friend of Charity and Sylvia's named Sally Field reported back that all "the boys in the shop laugh, he tells so much about Aunt Charity." But, Sally reported, "he don't care he has (it seemed he did not know how to express) he has a great wish for them two Lady's…he tells how kind you are. He wants to hear from you verry much."[92] Despite having hundreds of nieces and nephews to call on their attentions, Charity and Sylvia had kindness enough to share among generations of unrelated village children.

Several village youth even named their own children for the women despite having no familial relationship to either. Constant Southworth, a minister who grew up in Weybridge, wrote to Charity and Sylvia soon after a daughter was born in 1834, to announce that he and his wife had chosen the name "Charity Jane" for the little girl.[93] The name was inspired by the memory of "my frequent calls at your door in my childhood" and "the reality of your holy benevolence."[94] Charity wrote back with a better suggestion. Two months later Constant told Charity that "I can vouch for the acceptableness of your name + c in behalf of wife + all our children."[95] The girl's new name was Charity Sylvia. Later on, Constant reported that people often told him "I think more of CSS than all my other children." He could not deny the charge. When Constant brought his children to Charity and Sylvia's house for a visit in 1835, they must have been deeply interested to meet the little girl who bore both their names.[96] Excluded from the legal form of marriage, Charity and Sylvia never had the opportunity to adopt the same name or to give that name to their children. How gratifying then to see their names united and passed on to a future generation.

16

Stand Fast in One Spirit

1828

THIRTY-FIVE WOMEN CROWDED into the old meeting house on top of Weybridge Hill on a chilly November day in 1828. Many of the women were cousins whose parents, the first generation of Drake siblings, had helped to build the church a quarter century before. Now come of age, the young women pledged to make their own contribution to the congregation's well-being. In a firm hand, Charity took notes as Rebekah Drake, Louisa Drake, Harriet Drake, their sisters, and their friends from the Hagar, Brewster, Shaw, Jewett, and Bell families, promised to give "a portion of the good things which the lord has given them" to the formation of the Weybridge Female Benevolent Society. Charity signed her name at the bottom of the page, then handed over the pen. Immediately below her companion, and above her many nieces, Sylvia Drake added her signature with a satisfied flourish.[1]

The organization of the Weybridge Female Benevolent Society elevated the Drake nieces' bonds of consanguinity to a new spiritual dimension. It united the women of the family, along with other pious young women of the village, into a common Christian family, at the head of which Sylvia and Charity assumed the place of spiritual mothers. At the same time, Christian service reconfigured the relationship between Charity and Sylvia, conferring a religious sanction on their unsanctified union. By joining in service to Weybridge's spiritual welfare, Charity and Sylvia came to be acknowledged by ministers and congregants in Weybridge as united "sisters in Christ."[2]

From the outset, Charity and Sylvia cast their relationship as being devoted to the service of God. In early summer 1807, when Charity wrote imploring Sylvia to come live with her in Weybridge, she insisted that her own desires should be subordinated to God's will. Though I "wish it present when you shall be with me," Charity explained, "I am constrain'd to say Thy Will, O! God! be done. Thou knowest best what is best for me, and O may resignation to Thy will ever predominate in my feelings."[3] Sylvia's arrival seemed to confirm that God intended the women to be together. Months later, in December 1807, they went together to join Weybridge's First Ecclesiastical Society.[4] Soon, according to Charity, the relationship led her to a spiritual rebirth. Sylvia's spiritual despair in the spring of 1811 opened Charity's heart to the truth of God's saving grace, spurring her to a conversion experience that she may never have arrived at on her own. Witnessing her lover's distress wrenched Charity's soul in a way that ministerial sermons and biblical readings never had accomplished.[5]

The passionate romantic bond between Charity and Sylvia laid the basis for the development of a spiritual bond as they spent their lives together. Eventually, Sylvia took to referring to Charity in her diary as "Sister CB."[6] This surprising intertwining of Charity's and Sylvia's identities as lovers and sisters reveals the complexity of female relationships in the nineteenth century, when middle-class women's relative social segregation from men and confinement to the domestic sphere caused the intensification of a diverse range of same-sex interactions. Not only romantic friendships but also sisterly bonds became imbued with a passionate intimacy. Many romantic friends referred to each other as "sisters," and many biological sisters regarded each other as romantic friends.[7]

Of course, for many centuries spiritual sisterhood had its own distinct, if whispered, erotic reputation. Prior to the modern era, religious communities were some of the main sites where unrelated women lived together.[8] Sensationalist and pornographic anti-Catholic literature frequently depicted the convent as a site of sexual encounters between women. The Marquis de Sade's *Juliette* and Denis Diderot's *La Religieuse* popularized the image of the lesbian nun in the eighteenth century. In New England, rabid anti-Catholicism inspired the belief that many nuns were Sapphic monsters. The American gothic narratives *Six Months Residence in a Convent* (1835) and *Awful Disclosures of the Hotel Dieu Convent of Montreal* (1836), which became runaway bestsellers during the nineteenth century, described corrupt sexual practices.[9]

Charity and Sylvia read *Six Months Residence*, the story of Rebecca Reed, a young woman from a poor Protestant family in Massachusetts who converted to Catholicism and joined an Ursuline convent outside Boston in 1831. She soon ran away because of the abuses she encountered, including being forced by the mother superior to make the sign of the cross on the floor with her tongue. The stories Reed told inspired anti-Catholic mobs to burn the convent down in 1834; afterward she published *Six Months Residence* to justify her role in the affair.[10] When Sylvia read the book, she commented in her diary that "lying + deceit + every kind of fraud is practicd upon these poor deluded females when once within the iron fangs of these unfeeling wretches."[11] She found the subject of nuns' perversities to be compelling reading.

It is unlikely that Sylvia identified her own spiritual sisterhood with the goings-on at Reed's convent. Religious communities of Protestant women provided a more identifiable model for Charity and Sylvia. The first half of the nineteenth century witnessed an outbreak of intense Protestant revivalism and sectarian proliferation, known as the Second Great Awakening, which gave rise to a wide range of communitarian living experiments in the North. Several of these communities, including the Rappites, the Society of the Universal Friend, and the Shakers, embraced celibacy and housed members in sex-segregated dormitories.[12] Charity and Sylvia, who kept subscriptions to evangelical magazines like *The Christian Union* and *The Home Missionary*, had opportunities to read about these communities. Sylvia commented favorably on Shaker practice in her diary, observing the depth of their religiosity: "They say we must not only honor God with our lips but with our head + hands + feet + every part of the body. They profess to forsake all + allow Christ their Husband + wives + c."[13] Unlike the Ursulines, the Shakers earned no derogatory remarks from Sylvia. The notion that Protestant women could live together as sister-wives to Christ had a strong appeal.

Although Charity and Sylvia belonged to a traditional Trinitarian Congregational society, Sylvia's diary suggests she felt an unusual inclination toward a woman-oriented religious practice. She sought out memoirs of spiritual women like Susannah Anthony, a fellow New Englander who rejected marriage for a lifetime of regular prayer and fasting and supported herself by sewing work.[14] Anthony met and prayed in a women's devotional circle every week. Sylvia also took special satisfaction from gathering in a "female circle of friends devoted to prayer."[15] An interest in women spiritual figures even led Sylvia to an almost Catholic devotion to the Virgin Mary. She observed Candlemas, a traditional Catholic holiday celebrating the purification of the blessed Virgin Mary.[16] Most Puritans rejected Candlemas, along with other Catholic holidays. (Eventually it reappeared on the American calendar as the secular Groundhog's Day.) But Sylvia may have been attracted to Candlemas's imagery of female holiness. She included references to Mary elsewhere in her writing. For example, in an acrostic for Charity, Sylvia prayed that "In Mary's place is hope, + joy, and rest."[17] During an era when Protestant culture preached masculine authority, Sylvia directed her prayers toward a feminine spirit.[18]

Through her relationship with Charity, Sylvia sought to incarnate her Marian religious ideals. The women placed devotion to Christ at the center of their relationship for four decades. They served as pillars of Weybridge's First Ecclesiastical Society, sustaining the church as it came into competition with new religious societies that formed in the village during the Second Great Awakening, most prominently the Methodists.[19] Sylvia recorded her disappointment when congregants sought certificates of "dismission" from the church, allowing them to join a dissenting sect.[20] She and Charity devoted themselves to strengthening the church of their ancestors. The women befriended the many ministers who served terms in the village. Charity organized the church women's charitable society. Sylvia taught Sunday school. They contributed their time and money to cleaning and furnishing the meetinghouse. They counseled the deacons, participated in church governance, and acted as spiritual guardians to the town's youth. It is no wonder that when listening to a sermon on the text "she hath done what she could," Sylvia commented that she was "never more interested."[21] These words, with their combination of female service and modesty, captured the women's relation to the church.

Finding power in a feminine spiritual orientation grounded Charity and Sylvia to form unusual friendships with the town's male ministers. The social segregation of middle-class women and men in the nineteenth century led many ministers to distance themselves from their female congregants. A frosty hierarchy of dominance and submission shaped the relation between holy men and pious women.[22] But Sylvia and Charity's embrace of female religious authority, and their social situation outside the conventional domestic sphere, bridged the distance between themselves and their ministers. Charity in particular was able to establish the sort of egalitarian bonds with the town's ministers that defined friendship at the time. Her role as a female husband made it easier rather than harder for her to form intimacies with men. Her distinctive female masculinity linked the male world of authority and intellect to the female world of submission and piety.

When Sylvia and Charity first settled in Weybridge, Jonathan Hovey led the church. He was an impassioned minister who inspired a revival in the congregation soon after his installation in 1806. Sixty-eight people, including Sylvia and Charity, joined the church during 1806 and 1807, revitalizing the town's religious community.[23] But few of these converts claimed as close a friendship to the minister as Charity and Sylvia did. After Hovey moved to a different ministry in 1816, he and his wife Clarissa maintained a correspondence with them for the rest of their lives.[24] In his letters, Jonathan addressed Charity and Sylvia as his "sisters in Christ."[25] Jonathan and Clarissa viewed the couple as religious exemplars.[26]

Jonathan Hovey's early acceptance of Sylvia and Charity helped to secure their acceptance within the respectable ranks of Weybridge society. His esteem for the women cannot be ascribed to ignorance about the romantic nature of their relationship. He, of all people, confronted the intensity of their passion for each other when his younger sister Mary Hovey tried to initiate a romantic friendship with Charity and was rebuked by Charity for her presumption. Mary's distress gave her brother good reason to understand that Charity and Sylvia's relationship was romantic, exclusive, and devoted, but this knowledge did not prevent him from judging Sylvia and Charity to be ideals of Christian sisterhood.

The ministers who followed Hovey in the pulpit seconded his judgment. Eli Moody, who became minister of the Weybridge church shortly after Hovey, developed an even closer friendship with the women than his predecessor had. In one of their first acts of organized fundraising for the church, Charity and Sylvia collected $10 in 1820 to subscribe Moody as a member for life of the American Education Society, a charity that supported poor young men studying for the ministry. Notice of the contribution appeared in a short-lived Middlebury journal, *The Religious Reporter*, under the headline "She hath wrought a good work." The conclusion to the article also stressed the feminine devotion behind the contribution, expressing the hope that "frequent occasion be presented, to say of this Society, 'the *daughters* saw her and blessed her.'" Sylvia should have felt pleased.[27] Three years later, the women made a similar gift, contributing their own funds to have Moody named a life member in the American Tract Society.[28]

Too soon, Moody asked to be released from the Weybridge congregation on account of his poor health. He would struggle with invalidism for the rest of his life. Sylvia both attended the church meeting where Moody's request was announced and voted for the council that would arrange the practical terms of the separation. This simple act of voting, denied to women in the American civic sphere for another century, reveals the extent of Sylvia's authority within her religious community. Casting her vote saddened her; "Gods ways is not as ours," she commented briefly in her diary.[29] Despite her disappointment at losing Moody's service, she and Charity affirmed their friendship for the minister by representing his interests in a multiyear battle to retrieve wages that the congregation withheld from him in anger over his departure. To fulfill this commission, the women had to repeatedly approach the church deacons to collect the disputed money and then carry it to Massachusetts, where Moody had relocated. The fact that Charity and Sylvia were able to perform this unpleasant task without fracturing the church reveals the remarkable authority that they held within their community of faith.[30]

Despite moving away, Eli Moody and his wife (also named Clarissa) remained Charity and Sylvia's most faithful correspondents for the rest of their lives. Hardly a year passed without multiple letters from Eli and Clarissa to Sylvia and Charity. In some years, the couples exchanged as many as seven long letters, a remarkable number considering the busyness and intermittent poor health of all the parties.[31] Eli and Clarissa were Charity and Sylvia's only correspondents who addressed letters to both women. They followed a simple alternating basis, one letter mailed to Charity, the next to Sylvia. Who sent the letter did not affect the pattern of address. Eli wrote most of the letters, and Clarissa filled in when he was too sick or busy. On occasion, the Moodys became forgetful and addressed a run of letters to Charity, who as husband represented the household's public face. But Eli and Clarissa made an effort to distribute their correspondence evenly between the women. Like Jonathan Hovey, Eli Moody sanctioned Sylvia and Charity's union. He advised the women to "stand fast in one spirit, with one mind striving together for the faith of the gospel." This eloquent testimony to his belief in Charity and Sylvia's spiritual sisterhood is derived from St. Paul's letters to the church of Philippi. The phrase suggested that the women, like the Philippians, were unified in one holy body. They were one flesh, united in a spiritual marriage.[32]

After Moody left the church, bad feelings divided the congregation, and Weybridge suffered through a long spell of temporary preachers. It took several years for the breach to heal enough that the members were able to agree on a new candidate they could invite to the pulpit. Eventually Moody was replaced by the Reverend Harvey Smith, who, like both his predecessors, became friends with Charity and Sylvia. By that point, the women had reached middle age and were powerful members of the community. If Charity and Sylvia had needed Reverend Hovey's approval at the beginning of their relationship, it was Reverend Smith who needed their approval two decades later.

Again the women formed an affectionate relationship with their minister. When Harvey Smith left Weybridge after three years in the pulpit—owing to arguments over money—he stayed in correspondence with Sylvia and Charity. Harvey cared about the women's opinion of him. "Do not Miss B. give me up as an apostate," he wrote to Charity in the spring of 1828, announcing the end of his ministry in the town.[33] Harvey and his wife, Diann, a schoolteacher, relocated to the town of Jericho, Vermont, forty miles north where he invited the women to visit. Later they helped their apprentice Philomela Wood to enroll in Diann's school.[34] The Smiths' letters showed the same respect for the women's union expressed by the town's prior ministers and their families. Diann acknowledged Sylvia and Charity as a family, treating them as surrogate parents to Philomela and advising them of her progress.[35] Meanwhile, when letters between the couples slacked off, Harvey wrote to Charity regretting the lagging communication "of our families." His comparison of his own conventional family to the unusual combination made by Charity, Sylvia, and their apprentices is astounding.[36]

Following Harvey Smith's departure, a new series of temporary ministers filled the Weybridge pulpit. The town installed another minister in 1833, Jonathan Lee, who became friendly with the women before his own premature removal from the congregation in 1837. More short-termers followed. Charity and Sylvia maintained their spiritual standing throughout these ceaseless changes in the ministry. Many temporary preachers became just as enamored of the women as their longer-serving counterparts. D. D. Cook, who preached in the town during the early 1830s, afterward wrote letters addressing Sylvia and Charity as "sisters in Christ." He corresponded with the women for two decades and was the rare friend, along with Reverend Moody, who kept writing to Sylvia after Charity died.[37] D. D. Cook, like Harvey Smith, recognized Charity and Sylvia's significant spiritual authority. Cook wanted their approval as much as they wanted his. After one preachy letter Cook apologized "it rather looks to me as though I was writing to inferiors, than to those to whom I have ever been accustomed to feel as my superiors."[38] By the mid-1830s, Sylvia and Charity had more spiritual authority in the town than any newcomer could hope to possess. A minister who failed to recognize this fact had little chance of success with the villagers.

Charity and Sylvia's elevated position within the town's Congregationalist community is mostly attributable to the seriousness of their religious devotion, but the women's contributions to the physical upkeep of the church and its ministers also helped. The women donated their skilled labor to providing for both. In 1822, Sylvia recorded that she and Charity presented Eli Moody with a vest and coat. The fabric's cost was borne by Mr. James, but Sylvia recorded with pride that "the Making + trimming [were] presented by us."[39] The couple also sewed clothes for subsequent ministers, including Jonathan Lee and Edwin Hall.[40] Years after he left the congregation, Lee informed Charity and Sylvia that he still enjoyed wearing the well-constructed clothes they had made for him.[41] The women also sewed covers for the Sunday school books and stitched the "dressing of the sacred desk," or altar cloth.[42] Nor were they reluctant to contribute more menial labor, sweeping before church meetings, repairing the lamps, and cleaning their house to host prayer circles.[43]

Charity and Sylvia also donated generously to religious causes. The early nineteenth century has often been described as an age of reform. Inspired by the Second Great Awakening, Americans gathered together in voluntary organizations to raise money for foreign missions, the distribution of religious tracts, seminary scholarships, and other righteous endeavors. Women played a leading role in this benevolent empire, and their leadership in charitable organizations contributed directly to the formation of the women's rights movement, which coalesced in the 1848 convention at Seneca Falls.[44]

Charity and Sylvia exemplified this trend. In 1822, the women helped to establish the Weybridge Female Education Society, led by their sister-in-law Louisa Drake.[45] The next year, they contributed to the Auxiliary Tract Society.[46] Five years later, they took the lead in organizing and running the town's female benevolent society. Charity served as secretary to the organization for the first four years while Sylvia served as treasurer. In 1832, both women took on the role of "directresses." The constitution to the Weybridge Female Benevolent Society, written by Charity, reveals the link between American women's participation in movements for reform and their growing sense of independence. The constitution's preamble stated that its members would contribute to the society what they had gained "by labouring with their hands." The pledge reveals how a prideful sense of self-sufficiency empowered Charity and Sylvia to lay claim to positions of authority as directresses within the charitable organization, and moral leaders within the town. Each year, the women contributed more to the society than any of the other women.[47]

Sylvia and Charity also directed their charitable efforts outside the community. Charity's old lover Mercy Ford enlisted the women in 1848 to gather funds and clothing to help a group of refugee Portuguese Protestants who had been driven from Madeira.[48] (The group eventually settled in Illinois.) Mercy, who never married and lived her later years with another woman, became a fervent Christian in her thirties. She regarded Charity and Sylvia as her spiritual "sisters," both because of their commitment to the church and because of their commitment to each other.[49] Alerted by Mercy to the "destitute condition of the *persecuted Portuguese*," Sylvia and Charity turned to the members of their extended spiritual family for contributions. Polly Hayward and her daughter-in-law Lucy Ann Hayward, Sylvia Louisa Drake and her sister Polly A. Shaw, and their cousins Harriet E. Drake, Louisa Drake, and Mary B. Drake, all gave money, as did Charity and Sylvia's apprentices Belinda Brownwell and Emmeline E. Hagar, and Eli Moody's foster daughter, Chrissa Moody.[50] Charity and Sylvia's names led the list of contributors, Charity's on top, of course.

The women matched their cash contributions to the cause of religion with the equally valuable, if less tangible, work of spiritual leadership. They provided mentorship to village youth who were seeking redemption. Sylvia taught Sunday school for years. She kept records of her students, noting who learned their lessons, who joined the church, who was pious, and who seemed "sensible" about the state of their souls.[51] The women also engaged in less formal mentorship, especially of the girls who worked for them. When Philena Wheelock approached Charity and Sylvia about becoming their apprentice, she made clear that their Christian reputation played a large role in her request. "Oh! my friends, could I number myself among your household I should be highly gratified; to receive the instruction…from the pious conversation, and faithfulness, of those whom I esteem as friends."[52] One father who wrote to the women seeking an apprenticeship for his daughter in 1843 expressed his "fullest confidence in you to instruct the mind, as well as the fingers."[53] Several apprentices underwent conversions during their residence in the household. Weybridge's former minister Harvey Smith wrote to Charity and Sylvia in 1830 celebrating the conversion of his niece, who had been living with them.[54]

Despite the public success of their religious profession, both Charity and Sylvia struggled with a private sense of spiritual failing. Sylvia often agonized about being a poor model for the village youth. How many were there, she wondered, "which my wicked example has ruined."[55] Children warmed to Sylvia because of her generous spirit and willingness to speak at their own level, but she feared that her foolish talk might lead them away from God.[56] Considering herself to be guilty of sins of the first magnitude, Sylvia worried both that she was a false teacher and that her own soul would never be saved. She pursued a desperate search for redemption, day after day, not limiting her devotions to Sunday morning church meetings and Sunday after-noon prayer conferences. She used the discipline of writing in her diary and studying religious texts to keep a perpetual focus on the spiritual world. And yet no matter how many missionary magazines she read or how many self-reflections she penned, Sylvia considered her own efforts to be insufficient. She felt that her soul was a dry stone, she was "not in earnest" about her faith, she was troubled with the "enui," and had a "decietfull wayward heart prone to wander."[57] Temptation led her into sin. She lived contrary to her beliefs.[58] By her own lights, Sylvia was a failed Christian.

Charity's religious practice also betrayed tensions. Despite her friendships with the town's ministers, Charity often missed Sunday meetings. Sometimes, Sylvia ascribed the cause to Charity's poor health. Unwell for most of March 1823, Sylvia noted on the last Sunday of the month: "My dear C again + again denied a privilege so much abus'd."[59] Charity tried to substitute private devotions for public prayer when she could. On March 2, 1823, Sylvia went off to church alone, but when she returned the women read a Christian magazine together. A month later, the community of the faithful observed the yearly fast day (a traditional counterpoint to the Thanksgiving day that is still celebrated). Charity could not attend the service. This time when Sylvia returned she found her "beloved C almost sick from fast-ing."[60] Sylvia's worry echoes from the page.

Yet Charity's pattern of private rather than public devotions cannot be explained entirely by ill health. The pattern was too longstanding and various. Sundays that Charity spent sick were often followed by Mondays when she felt sufficiently recuper-ated to go about her business. On Sunday she would stay home from meeting, but on Monday she would walk into neighboring Middlebury to make purchases. Nor can her erratic church attendance be ascribed to disagreements with one particular pastor or discomfort in one particular congregation. Even when they were traveling, Charity sometimes hung back from services.[61] Her health, while never strong, was good enough to support long days of travel by foot and horse cart over poor roads in trying weather. But on Sundays Charity felt too unwell to go to church. Incapacitated by sickness one Sunday in July 1817, while traveling through Massachusetts, Charity felt well enough the next day to travel ten miles. "Dear Miss B. much better," Sylvia reported in her diary.[62]

Falling ill on Sundays was a problem that afflicted many Americans in the nineteenth century. The ailment even had its own name: "Sabbath Sickness." An 1847 article in the *Evangelical Repository* noted sarcastically that "the disease is far more prevalent than is generally imagined, and it is thought to be contagious."[63] On at least one occasion, Sylvia worried that she had caught it. "All in this house + Mrs Hr detain at home by Sabbath sickness," she bemoaned in her diary. Sylvia felt so ill she took to bed; Charity on the other hand felt well enough to wait on her and make tea.[64]

Charity never admitted to malingering, but she may have projected her guilt onto Sylvia's brother, Asaph Drake. In the fall of 1829, the Weybridge church was in crisis. Their most recent minister, Harvey Smith, had left the church on acrimonious terms the prior year. The congregation was at odds. In the midst of these troubles, Charity attended a meeting with six of the church brethren to plan for hiring a new minister. That night Charity had a dream that haunted her for days. She saw Asaph standing in a small group of people, his upper body almost naked except for a few tattered rags. Consumed with worry about the state of the church, Charity approached Asaph to ask his help reuniting the congregation. In the dream, Charity and Asaph had a long and spirited discussion about the dangerous situation of their community, but Charity could not persuade Asaph to help. When she asked him if he planned to attend the next meeting, Charity recounted to him later, "You reply'd you thought not for you had some medicine to take and you must stay at home and attend to that (tho' you then appeard to be in usual health and spirit)." Asaph's answer filled Charity with distress; he seemed able to take care of his physical body but was forsaking his spiritual well-being. "I can make no comment upon this dream," Charity wrote to Asaph. "I know not the interpritation thereof."[65] One possible interpretation that Charity did not explore might identify the dream-figure of Asaph with Charity herself. She too seemed more capable of fellowship than her spotty church attendance indicated. Healthy or not, she always kept at work, standing at her cutting table all day no matter how she felt.[66] Only on Sundays could poor health keep her from her duties.

The concerns about malingering that Charity expressed in her dream about Asaph represented only one aspect of her spiritual distress. Deeper tensions contributed to her absence from meetings. Unlike Sylvia, Charity did not leave behind a diary that recorded her feelings of sinfulness and self-recrimination, but these feelings plagued her nonetheless, even after her rebirth in 1811. Charity gave the appearance of spiritual self-confidence; she attended religious meetings with the male leaders of the church, she carried on correspondence with ministers, she counseled youth on the state of their souls, but her feelings inside did not match her exterior. "Did you know me as I am you would no more wish to be remember'd in my affection or esteem," Charity wrote in an 1816 letter to her former lover Lydia, offering a rare moment of self-disclosure.[67] She felt as deeply convicted of her spiritual unworthiness as Sylvia did. Charity once advised Asaph, who shared his sisters' feelings of spiritual unworthiness, that "Our Bible tells us if we have done <u>Iniquity to do so no more</u>, And that all sins shall be forgiven."[68] She found this wisdom hard to apply to herself.

Both Charity and Sylvia, united by their shared belief in Christ and salvation, faced the challenge of living in a manner contrary to their beliefs. As sisters in Christ they loved each other deeply, but as lovers they violated their faith. They lived with this paradox for decades. They joined the church together and departed from church teachings together. As Sylvia pithily put it on their thirty-first anniversary, "Sin mars all earthly bliss, and no common sinner have I been, but God has spared my life, given me everything I would enjoy."[69] God's greatest gift to Sylvia had been the source of her greatest sin.

The feelings of spiritual failing that both Sylvia and Charity experienced led to a great deal of suffering in their lives. They shared those feelings with each other, which gave each woman comfort. But they rarely revealed the depths of their distress to others in the community. Charity and Sylvia's Christian maternal authority within the family of faith made their unorthodox relationship acceptable to the community. Confessing their sins would undermine that toleration. Moreover, their spiritual daughters and sisters had no interest in hearing the women's confession. The community could not risk losing the women's contributions to the community of faith. The instability in Weybridge's ministry made Charity and Sylvia's constant devotion to the church necessary to the village. No pastor remained long enough to guide the town's children from baptism through first Sabbath School toward an adult conversion experience. Sylvia and Charity nurtured the souls of children in their community for over forty years. Those who grew up in the village, including the ministers Cyrus Bryant Drake and Constant Southworth, celebrated the women's role in their spiritual development. And despite the distraught state of their souls, Charity and Sylvia took enormous pleasure in attending both men's sermons.[70] If they could not save their own souls, at least they had helped to save others.

17

Diligent in Business

1835

SYLVIA WATCHED WITH resignation as the front gate swung open once again. Mr. Lyman bustled through with a bundle in his arms. That sight could only mean one thing: more work. His visit capped a long and trying day. Waking with the remains of a sick headache, Sylvia had dragged herself from bed and set to work, but after half a day's sewing, ill health forced her to put down the needle and find some other task to do. There was never a shortage of work in reserve. Turning her attention to the washing, the most urgent chore, Sylvia looked on guiltily as Charity struggled through the day's sewing despite her own aching head and sore stomach. Their young assistant, Martha Flanagan, was not much help. When Mr. Storrs walked in the gate at 3:00 to have a pair of pants made, Sylvia insisted on offering him some supper. Soon after he departed, the gate swung back open, admitting Lyman. Lyman wanted a coat mended, but the fabric was too worn down to be made decent. He would need a new coat made, as soon as Sylvia and Charity finished the orders that were overdue to customers in the neighboring towns of Addison and Cornwall. When Lyman departed, Sylvia felt deep relief. Still, as the gate swung shut behind his retreating figure, Sylvia must have recognized that without such custom there would be no gate to close, no window to watch from, and no bed to retreat to at the end of a long day.[1]

For more than forty years, Sylvia and Charity worked without rest. Sacrificing sleep and health, the women labored eighteen-hour days sewing clothes for men, women, and children in the area. Their marriage spanned a period of rapid economic expansion and transformation in the United States. Improved transportation and communication networks facilitated the commercialization of agriculture and the development of new industries, including America's first textile mills.

These changes reached everywhere, reshaping the economy even of frontier farming communities like Weybridge, where a craze for breeding Merino sheep, which produced a fine wool valued for clothing manufacture, led many landowners to convert their wheat fields to pasture. At the height of the craze, sheep outnumbered people in Weybridge by six to one. Meanwhile, the town's women found new opportunities to earn cash in outwork industries. The expanding availability and declining cost of milled fabric, combined with the increasing circulation of cash and credit, drove business to Charity and Sylvia's door.[2] The steady demand for their services made it possible for the two women to support themselves without the earnings of a man, but only through nonstop labor. Sylvia celebrated in her diary the odd day when the thermometer dipped so low that no customers came to the front gate, but opposite the Scylla of overwork lay the Charybdis of dependence, and with it the probable loss of the life they built together.[3]

During the women's first decades together, Charity's spinster aunt, Charity Howard, presented a sad example of the economic vulnerability of single women. Although Aunt Charity was a very talented seamstress, she never earned a living from her needle. Her college-educated father may have disapproved of such a common occupation, or she may have been unwilling to be at other people's service. Either way, Aunt Charity entered middle age unmarried and without a source of income. When she outlived her parents and siblings, her care fell to her nephews and nieces, who themselves were struggling to remain afloat in the vicissitudes of the transforming economy. By 1810, Aunt Charity was reduced to living as an unwelcome guest at her nephew Roland Howard's house in Easton.[4] As she lingered for the next twenty years, she drained the resources of her frustrated relations, especially Roland and his sister Vesta Guild, who had been deserted by her husband and could not support herself. The siblings had to board their aunt out in a series of homes, paying thirty to sixty dollars a year for her upkeep.[5] Later, Vesta and Roland could not afford even this care.[6] In 1821, they were forced to turn to the town for public support.[7] Aunt Charity died in the poorhouse eight years later at the advanced age of eighty-two.[8]

Watching the slow decline of Aunt Charity's circumstances kept Charity and Sylvia hard at work. Better to labor without cease than to end their days divided by poverty, living as poor relations with their natal families, or even worse farmed out to village families who took in indigents. During their early years together, Charity and Sylvia started sewing every day before dawn and continued by candlelight long after the sun went down. In an 1814 letter to Sally Bryant, Charity complained, "I know well what it is to be overwhelm'd in business, to be hurried and perplex'd."[9] If Sally thought her childless sister-in-law enjoyed more leisure time than herself, she was mistaken. "When I take a retrospective view of the first 15 years which I spent in this town," Charity recalled in 1833, I am "rather surpriz'd that I am still alive."[10] As late as 1822, Sylvia's diary captured both women staying awake until two in the morning to fill their orders, then rising to start their days at five or six.

Always in fragile health, Charity could hardly stand the strain. It was not much easier for Sylvia. Both women endured sickness from overwork.[11] Charity's back and feet often ached from standing all day to cut fabric.[12] During the winter she kept a warming box, filled on one side with coal, by her cutting table. Charity would perch on the empty half as she worked her well-worn scissors for hours.[13] During the summer, she suffered from the oppressive heat in the little shop.[14]

Sylvia's wrists, hands, and head suffered most from the long days she spent plying the needle. The repetitive stress gave her a "lame" wrist, but even when her wrist was aching, she kept at work until past one in the morning, not allowing the injury time to heal.[15] As painful as her wrist may have gotten, the headaches brought on by endless stitching in weak light were even worse. During the winter, when the sun set at 4:00 or 5:00 in the afternoon, Sylvia sometimes sewed for eight hours or more by candlelight or the dim glow of the hearth. When she could, Sylvia worked through the pain. "With an aching head finish with Miss B assistance a vest for Mr S Wilson," Sylvia recorded in a typical diary entry.[16]

Despite its physical toll, Charity and Sylvia took great pride in their work. Their outlook challenged the common opinion of the time that women were dishonored by paid labor, and by sewing work especially. Emma Willard, the pioneer of women's education who opened her first school in Middlebury in 1807, wrote that among Americans "there is something degrading in a woman's doing any thing to earn money." As late as the 1830s, Willard decried the absurdity that "in families with us, where the father employs his hands from morning till night…his daughters would consider it a shocking degradation to employ theirs to earn money, by making caps, or hats, or dresses for others." Charity and Sylvia, who read Willard's book with great interest, must have cheered for their former neighbor when she declared that American women should be more independent in earning and possessing property.[17]

The satisfaction Charity and Sylvia derived from their work shines through their letters and diary. Charity had a high regard for her own skill with the scissors, which secured the women's constant flow of customers. Prior to the late nineteenth century, there were no printed clothing patterns available. Although many women were able to sew shirts or other simple items, clothing that required more complex geometry, like coats and pants, had to be prepared by a skilled artisan. Cutting fabric was a specialized trade that required study. A tailor had to learn how to transform a two-dimensional material into a three-dimensional form that both fit the wearer and allowed for a full range of movement.[18] Charity arrived in Weybridge skilled at cutting many items, including men's coats, suits, vests, and pantaloons and women's gowns, bonnets, spencers, and cloaks. The ability to cut men's clothes positioned Charity at the top of the trade, in a position usually occupied by men, and enabled her to earn higher wages than most female seamstresses. After leaving North Bridgewater, she continued to send clothes in the mail to her father, who complained that nobody else could make pants that fit as well.[19]

Sylvia shared Charity's belief in the quality of their clothes. When a young man of the village showed up at the shop one fall afternoon with some clothes another tailor had made for him, all of which were incorrectly cut, Sylvia's clucking insistence on resizing the work conveyed her satisfaction in making clothes the right way.[20] But the best evidence of the pride that Sylvia felt in her work is the will she drafted in 1821, which called attention to the property that she and Charity had accumulated together. "Hard work + close calculation will not accumulate properties unless you have confidence + a disposition to demand something for your labour," Sylvia wrote. With Charity's help, Sylvia had found the confidence and disposition to demand her just dues. And at age thirty-six, she had enough to her name to worry over its distribution should she die unexpectedly. "We have toiled day + night almost," Sylvia wrote, and now she wanted to be certain that in the case of her sudden demise, the money would support all the people she loved.[21]

Sylvia and Charity never became rich, but their hard work indeed paid off. An inventory of the women's moveable property made in summer 1822 compared favorably to an inventory of Charity's father's property taken in 1816. Charity and Sylvia owned bedding worth more than $135; Philip Bryant's beds and bedding, and library and medicine, altogether were valued at $150. The women's kitchen items were worth around $85, Philip's around $95. The main difference in the value of their estates lay in land wealth. Philip owned nearly $3,000 in property (including his home). Charity and Sylvia never became landowners. Yet by the ends of their lives they had accumulated a significant amount of property in other forms. The tax records of Weybridge from the 1840s show Charity and Sylvia in possession of a personal estate worth about $800, not including the value of their house, which was approximately $200. Some of their personal estate took the form of cash and notes, or, in other words, investments. While this property did not put Charity and Sylvia among the wealthiest villagers (Sylvia's brother-in-law Asaph Hayward owned land valued at $6,460), it stood them fairly well. The average tax burden in 1842 per Weybridge family was $13.50. Charity and Sylvia paid $9.70. Their tax obligation placed them

far above the most needy residents of the town, like the landless families and illit-
erate French Canadians who performed manual labor for the town's landowners.[22]

The relative comfort that the women secured through their hard work is especially remarkable considering the difficulty of the times in which they lived. Two
financial panics during the prime decades of their business, one in the late 1810s and
one in the late 1830s, drove many of their neighbors and relatives into bankruptcy.
The contraction of credit and recall of loans touched every person who had taken
part in the expanding market economy. Three-quarters of Philadelphia's workingmen
went unemployed during the 1819 panic. One-third of New York workingmen lost
their jobs at the outset of the 1837 panic, but the collapse of the wheat crop that year,
which precipitated the crisis, guaranteed that farming communities suffered in kind.
The price of Merino wool also sank, devastating the Weybridge economy, despite its
turn away from wheat farming.[23]

Charity's brother Peter Bryant fell into deep debt during the first period of
economic instability. Charity tried to comfort her brother about his losses. "I am
extremely sorry to hear of your misfortune respecting pecuniary affairs," she wrote,
adding for comfort, "I hope however that your strength will be equal to your day."[24]
A year later, Peter's circumstances were still no better. Charity wrote again that she
was "extremely sorry for your misfortune, and have no doubt but what it is a great
imbarrasment to you, and a great disturber of your calculations and of your peace."
Peter's outlook was poor, but Charity expressed her "hope you will not suffer your
mind to sink under the trials of this transitory state of things." Many people in
Middlebury were having just as hard a time. The jail had filled with debtors unable
to make good on their obligations. Even such a well-regarded community figure as
old "General Cook" the bondsman was imprisoned for debts amounting to $500.[25]
Despite his sister's hopes, Peter's circumstances never improved, and when he died
in 1820 he left his widow and children in straitened circumstances.

The women's business accounts from the 1810s have not been preserved, but it
appears they weathered the nineteenth century's first economic crisis fairly well. In
her letters to Peter, Charity did not complain of hardship.[26] In 1818 the women had
to borrow $50 from Asaph Drake and their neighbor Silas Wright, but they paid off
the debt.[27] The money might have gone to the additions they made to the house in
1819, surely a sign that their business was still thriving. By 1821 Sylvia's diary itemized
work that should have earned the women several hundred dollars a year in income.
Some of their income came as goods rather than cash. Customers paid in cords of
wood, since Sylvia and Charity had neither a woodlot nor the time and strength to
cut wood.[28] Customers paid in work on the house, by fixing the cistern, digging the
garden, and repairing the fence. The women accepted bushels of potatoes, pounds of
butter, and barrels of meat in payment.[29]

Charity and Sylvia weathered the second financial panic as well. They kept their house, their personal property, and their business intact, which is much more than many Americans could say. In fact, between 1822 and 1842, Charity and Sylvia's total property seems to have more than doubled from roughly $400 to nearly $1,000 (though some of that increase may be attributed to inflation). In 1837 their business took a blow. Judging from the accounts, their income dipped by at least half that year. But they muddled through, picking up the work they could, accepting payment in ham, onions, and apples.[30]

Once again, relatives near and dear to the women were hit hard by the crisis. Their nephew Oliver Bryant, who owned a dry goods shop in Enfield, Massachusetts, suffered a total collapse of his business in 1837. His creditors sent constables to search his home for anything of value. In Oliver's words, they were trying "to see if I had not more <u>pork</u> + potatoes than the law would allow." Although his words paint a picture of the situation's absurdity, the outcome was far from funny. Oliver spent thirty days in jail in Northampton while one creditor tried to get hold of a piece of jewelry that Oliver's wife had brought into the marriage. The humiliation of imprisonment and the threat to his wife afflicted Oliver.[31] Three years later, the continuing recession still pinched at him. Struggling to keep afloat in 1840, Oliver expressed his gratitude that his aunts were not hit by the widespread difficulties. "I suppose," he wrote, "that it has not reached your business as you say you have a multitude of business." He worried that the women's client base of farmers might still feel the pinch in the future. But overall Charity and Sylvia were enduring the crisis better than he.[32]

The stability of Charity and Sylvia's business amid the time's economic uncertainty helps explain why the women were in such demand as employers. Throughout the decades that they operated their shop, a constant flow of girls and women sought the opportunity to work for them. A job in the shop promised not only cash wages, but training in a skill that could support them through the hardest times. A long parade of women march through the pages of Sylvia's diary.

Some came for only a short spell. Young Martha Flanagan arrived to help the women in summer 1835, but ill health and homesickness cut her service short. The women sent her home after three weeks, with eight yards of fabric and a pair of linen stockings in payment.[33] Many of Sylvia's and Charity's nieces also worked brief spells for the women. Sarah Harriet Drake, Emma Hayward, Laura Hayward, and Emmeline Drake all sewed for their aunts. The girls sometimes spent weeks lodging while they worked, and sometimes they came only for a day. Laura Hayward came to live with Sylvia and Charity in January 1821. She stayed for a spell, went home because of ill health, but frequently returned to work a day for her aunts. The work brought her a little cash, but she may have been motivated more by the desire to spend time with her aunts than by the promise of recompense.[34]

In addition to the short-termers, Charity and Sylvia played host over the years to a number of more permanent apprentices with whom they built deep bonds of affection. Philomela Wood in particular lived with the women off and on for close to a decade. Her friend, Philena Wheelock, first asked the women for a job in 1825.[35] She stayed for several years before leaving in 1830 to marry. When her husband died the next year, Philena picked up the needle to support herself.[36] She worked some seasons in Bridport, her native town. But she also returned to Charity and Sylvia's house to work once more for them. She saw her stays with the women as an opportunity "for my own improvement."[37] Writing in the fall of 1839, to make arrangements to spend the next season at Charity and Sylvia's, Philena praised her employer's home as a "winter paradise."[38] Before she traveled to their heavenly dwelling, however, a proposal of marriage changed her plans. In February 1840, Philena remarried a widower named Freeman Field, and together they moved across Lake Champlain to Peru, New York. Charity and Sylvia had helped Philena to survive many uncertain years, and she remained forever grateful to them on this account.[39]

For the women Charity and Sylvia employed long-term, the work represented not just a source of wages but also an apprenticeship into a profession. Former assistants frequently acted as go-betweens for young women seeking instruction from Charity and Sylvia. Philena recommended Abigail Grandy from her town as another likely young woman who wished "to learn the trade."[40] Lucy Hurlbut, who lived with Charity and Sylvia for years, wrote after her departure to recommend a new assistant:

> A young lady of this town has solicited me to inform you that she would like to reside with you for the purpose of learning your occupation—She is a steady respectable girl and a member of our church She has no home and has generally spun and done house work and has not been accustomed to sewing upon fulled cloth. She is very anxious to learn the trade. She is a _very_ healthy person and I know nothing but would answer your purpose. Her name is Marisa Ramsdell.[41]

For most of the assistants, like Grandy and Ramsdell, learning the trade meant learning fine needle skills like sewing button holes.[42] Occasionally, Charity offered the added valuable instruction in cutting. Lucy Hurlbut was one of the lucky young women who learned this skill from Charity.[43]

The value of the training that Charity and Sylvia offered, however, could not mitigate the difficulty of a future working in the sewing trade. When Lucy returned home from her initial apprenticeship, she set herself up as a seamstress in her hometown. The immediate demand on her hours was so great that she barely found a moment to breathe. "I have been sewing on fulled cloth about two months—have had scarcely a moments leisure," Lucy reported to her former employers. "The people all seem to think they have a claim upon me and they all want me <u>this minute</u> where their work is ready."[44] The demand was so unrelenting that Lucy actually had to turn away business—despite hiring a number of younger women to work as assistants for her. There was too much to do.

Charity felt the same way when she first started sewing for a living while living with her father in 1801. "'Tis a slavish life, to be at every ones call," Charity had complained.[45] But her determination not to get married, and her need for an independent means of support, drove her to continue her profession. Decades later, her work continued to be just as demanding. In 1822, she and Sylvia tried to put an end to sewing past midnight. But there is no evidence that the pace of their labor ever slackened. Charity's cousin Vesta Guild begged the women to stop sitting up all night to work in 1816.[46] But when she came to visit Weybridge in 1839, she was distraught to find her ailing sixty-two-year-old cousin still working at the same frenetic pace.[47] The women's former minister Eli Moody, whose own health problems forced him to give up the pulpit, wrote to the women that they should follow his example—if not for the sake of their bodies, than for their souls. "You are yet hurrying thro' the world. It is well to be diligent in business, but we should be careful to be, at the same time, fervent in spirit."[48] The minister, a dear friend, tried to couch his concerns in a language that Sylvia and Charity would heed. Perhaps duty to God could force the women to scale back, where calls to self-care had failed.

Moody's suggestion that profession might be displacing religion in Sylvia and Charity's life was not wholly fantastical. The tension between God and Mammon troubled many Americans at a time when both evangelical Protestantism and capitalism were booming.[49] The rapid growth of the economy had great benefits, but the accelerating pace of business, as Americans transitioned from the traditional rhythms of the agricultural economy to the scheduled hours of the industrial economy, took a toll on individuals and communities. Not only did bankruptcies reduce families to states of extreme physical need, the disruption of traditional life placed people in spiritual distress. The sacred in the everyday seemed to get lost in the ruthless rational calculations that drove the new economy. This loss in turn energized the period's Protestant revivalism.[50] For Charity and Sylvia, the furious pace of their workdays, which may have distracted their attention to spiritual matters, heightened their desire to seek refuge in the church.

The pace of the women's work life was so grueling that no one would choose to follow their example except from necessity. Philomela, Philena, and Lucy each underwent long years of apprenticeship to learn the trade but left the business for marriage when the opportunity presented itself. It seems likely that some of the

short-term assistants who ended their apprenticeships because of ill health or homesickness, including their niece Laura Hayward, may have really been running away
from the hours they were expected to work. By working days with her aunts, then
returning home at night, Laura escaped the call to sew by candlelight until the wee
hours. For most women, the price of independence was too high to pay if marriage
was a possible alternative. Charity and Sylvia's dedication to their business reveals
the depths of their commitment to each other.

Even if one of the women's apprentices felt as passionately opposed to marrying a
man as her mentors did, she might not have been able to follow their path after all.
The new economy that overloaded Charity and Sylvia with business soon made their
business obsolete. The invention of the sewing machine and the development of
printed sewing patterns led to the transformation of the tailoring trade in the
1850s. Home sewers could now construct fine items themselves. The business of
clothing manufacture became a large-scale industry run on the industrial model.
Capitalists bought raw materials and distributed them to workers, either at home or
in factories, who assembled clothing in return for wages. After the Civil War, sewing
remained a primary means by which women could earn a living, but the business
rarely afforded them the independence that Charity and Sylvia had been able to
achieve. This transformation took place even in rural Vermont. Around the time
that Charity and Sylvia retired from work, a local newspaper ran an advertisement
for "12 tailoress girls; also 6 apprentices, to whom will be given weekly pay for their
services."[51] The language of apprenticeship and trade remained in place, but the
future for this group of eighteen waged employees looked very different from the
future that Philena, Philomela, or Lucy anticipated when they sought positions with
Charity and Sylvia.

18

The Cure of Her I Love

1839

THE PAIN BEGAN in her solar plexus: a sharp stab that knocked the wind out of her. After the first savage thrust, the pain radiated up her spine, between her shoulders, out along her arms, into her neck and lower jaw, and finally across both cheeks to her forehead. The terrible assault transformed each breath into an agonizing groan. Charity sat immobilized and suffocated, drawing just enough air to keep from losing consciousness.[1]

When the attack passed, the words came flooding back. Charity put pen to paper, sending off a slew of letters to seek a diagnosis and cure for this new affliction. Her friends wrote back with the information she sought. The doctors they consulted called the pain by various names: spasmodic neuralgia, walking breast pang, angina pectoris, and simply heart disease.[2] All agreed that the condition would prove fatal, but perhaps not straight away. Sally Field reported that her own mother had suffered from chest pains similar to Charity's for several years. During her long sickness, she derived great comfort from being bled. By the end, scars covered her arms from wrist to elbow, but Sally felt certain the treatment had prolonged her life.[3] Charity, who had been bled many times before, up to a pint of blood at a time, was bound to agree.[4]

Charity had deep familiarity with sickness and its treatment by the summer of 1839, when she endured her first episode of heart disease. She was likely afflicted from birth by the endemic tuberculosis that killed her mother, her sisters Ruth and Anna, and her brothers Cyrus and Peter. Charity described herself as a "great sufferer

175

by Asthma," a reference to her frequent shortness of breath, which suggests the diminished lung capacity associated with tuberculosis.[5] She also repeatedly fell sick from the epidemic diseases that ravaged the nation. The great yellow fever epidemic of 1802, which spread as far north as Boston, may have been the cause of one severe illness. In a letter to her sister-in-law Sally, Charity described feeling "intense pain in my head, with successive fits of heat + cold."[6] On the other hand, the symptoms may have been caused by typhoid fever, which some in Massachusetts referred to as "fall fever" because of its regularity during that season.[7] Charity hoped that the move to Vermont in 1807 would situate her in a healthier environment—a common rationale behind nineteenth-century migrations.[8] But from the beginning of her life with Sylvia, "sickness made long and frequent visits to their dwelling."[9]

In fall 1824, Charity had a health crisis that began with a "nirvous pain in the left-side of my head and ear." After three days the pain spread throughout the left side of Charity's face, which became "completely paralized, no motion remain'd in any part of it." For six weeks, pain, paralysis, and fever left her unable to read or write a word. She had to bind her left eye shut to protect it from the light. The doctor diagnosed a "liver complaint" and recommended bleeding. (It was more likely Bell's palsy, which is sometimes caused by a virus).[10] After eight weeks, Charity felt mostly recovered, although her face still felt "greatly different from the former state."[11]

Sylvia's health was little better than Charity's. She was a lifelong victim of headaches. Entries recording "severe pain in my head" filled the pages of her diary.[12] All sorts of irritations catalyzed Sylvia's headaches, and even a superficial affliction could be a trigger. "Discover a pimple on my nose," Sylvia noted in her diary one spring day; two days later she noted ruefully, "the pimple on my nose causes some pain in my head."[13] Her headaches often produced insomnia.[14] At times, nausea, light sensitivity, and noise sensitivity accompanied the pain, suggesting that Sylvia was prone to migraines.[15] Once she complained she was "almost blind" with "strong symptoms of severe headache."[16] Many of Sylvia's correspondents noted her susceptibility to "sick headaches."[17] She also experienced frequent disorders related to her mouth such as toothaches, gum biles, sore throat, "ague in [the] face," and "swollen" face.[18]

As the women grew older, both faced the onset of menopause and the increasing debility of old age. When Charity went through the "change in nature" during the mid-1820s, she struggled with frequent headaches.[19] The prescription of her nephew Dr. Samuel Shaw (husband to William Cullen Bryant's sister Sarah) was the same as the recommendations for treating her heart disease and Bell's palsy: bleeding. In particular, her nephew recommended using leeches to let blood from the side of Charity's head, on the theory that menopause had produced "too great a congestion, there was too great a flow, or pressure of <u>blood</u> in the <u>head</u>." If Charity was not willing to have her head leeched, she could try having the blood taken from her arm. This treatment, Shaw advised, should be followed by taking four grains of "blue mercurial pill" every night until salivation occurred, as well as a moderate dose of Epsom salts in the mornings. Charity should not fear if the treatment produced a "<u>purging</u> of blood" from her uterus. Lastly, the doctor recommended a prescription for "<u>Balsam</u> of <u>Pine</u>," including spirit of turpentine, gum Arabic, oil of cloves, and sugar to sweeten the mix. "Take a table spoonful for a dose before eating, three times a day." Charity left no record of whether she followed these directions.[20]

Shaw's abundant prescriptions for treating Charity's menopause were perfectly in keeping with the medical logic of the age of "heroic medicine." The virulent endemic and epidemic diseases that produced startlingly high mortality rates throughout the nineteenth century demanded equally powerful treatments with visible effects. Bleeding, which often caused the temperatures of feverish patients to break, was used to treat an endless list of ailments, including malaria, fractures, consumption, burns, puerperal fever, and menopause. Bleeding exemplified the logic of heroic medicine. The treatments available to medical practitioners were few in number and blunt instruments, but doctors felt the need to offer some intervention beyond passive acceptance and prayers for salvation.[21]

At least Samuel Shaw recommended only small bleedings for Charity's menopause. Many contemporary doctors advocated letting blood until the patient fell into unconsciousness. Shaw was also cautious in his prescription of mercury, one of the most common, and fatal, medicines of the nineteenth century. During the 1793 yellow fever epidemic, Philadelphia physician Benjamin Rush prescribed patients ten grains a day of mercury. Many doctors recommended that patients take mercury past salivation, after which point patients' teeth and sometimes their tongues, palates, and even jawbones could fall from their mouths. On the other hand, irregular compounding and lack of standard dosages made it possible that Shaw's recommended dosage differed little from Rush's.[22]

To remedy the range of ailments they suffered over their lifetimes, Sylvia and Charity made use of both the surgeries and chemicals prescribed by male practitioners of heroic medicine, like Samuel Shaw, as well as the wide range of herbal remedies that constituted a female vernacular healing tradition in North America.[23] Willing to try anything that worked, the women mixed doses of mercury with cabbage poultices, brisk walks with bleedings. They cultivated a garden where they grew medicinal herbs such as hyssop, used as an expectorant for pulmonary disease; cayenne, a treatment for Sylvia's sore mouth; thoroughwort, an emetic; catmint, used topically for respiratory complaints and to promote menstruation; rhubarb, a cathartic; and mustard seed, another topical remedy.[24] They also collected medicinal wild plants, like sweet fern, which could be used as an expectorant or an astringent; burdock leaves, applied topically to remove pain; sweet flag root, to soothe the stomach; hemlock leaves, for rheumatism; prickly ash, for toothaches and external pain; and ginseng, for colds.[25] And they purchased foreign herbs from the apothecary in Middlebury, including ipecacuanha, another emetic (and the derivative for ipecac); red and black pepper, used as stimulants; spikenard, to make poultices; and elecampane for asthma.[26]

The apothecary also supplied the women with the most popular chemical emetic of the age, mercury-based calomel. Since heroic medicine favored drugs that produced dramatic results, calomel was designed to cause patients to throw up with great force. As one doctor recalled, the vomit "did not come up in gentle puffs and gusts, but the action was cyclonic. If, perchance, the stomach was passed the expulsion would be by the rectum and anus, and this would be equal to a regular oil-well gusher."[27] Sylvia embraced this medical logic; when she took emetics she aimed to remove all matter from her digestive tract, and she felt disappointed with any halfway measures. "Take an emetic just before sunset," she recorded during one sick spell; it "operates 9 times, but the load from my stomach not removd" she concluded with disappointment.[28] On another occasion she noted with great satisfaction that a dose of emetic wine caused her to vomit fifteen times.[29] Following their doctors' recommendations, Charity and Sylvia often dosed with emetics over an extended period. After a week of heavy dosing in 1822, Sylvia found herself so unwell she was "unable to set up." Still she continued the dosing, recording with grim determination that she had "puke[d] much in consequence of using solution of tartar."[30] On occasion, Sylvia felt distressed at having an emetic take "a different course" than intended.[31] But she was not averse to taking cathartics with the intention of producing rectal expulsions. When really ill, both women combined cathartics and emetics to empty everything at once.[32]

The women also sampled many of the patent medicines of the age, which were advertised by their inventors as gentler remedies since they typically did not contain mercury.[33] Charity took doses of Stoughton's Elixir, designed to soothe rather than purge the gut.[34] Lydia recommended Hungarian Balsam of Life for Charity's asthma.[35] The women used Kittredge grease to treat sprains.[36] They tried Vienna pills, Blue pills, and Coits pills, an emetic manufactured by local Vermont practitioner Dr. Daniel Coit.[37] Coit promised that his pills could treat "Yellow Fever, Bilious Fevers, Ague and Fever, Cholic pains, Flatulencies, Indigestion, Costiveness, Hypocondriacal and Hysteric complaints, Stranguary, Gravel, Rheumatism, and Gout." Sylvia may also have been persuaded by Dr. Coit's promise that the drug was "peculiarly serviceable in female disorders."[38]

The women judged treatments as effective if they produced results, rarely differentiating between positive and negative outcomes. Sylvia favored emetics and cathartics despite the weight loss they caused. The frequent vomiting and fasting made it a struggle for Sylvia to reach even one hundred pounds in weight.[39] "One fortnight since I have dine the least thing," she recorded after a long spell of dosing. Fearing Sylvia would waste away, her brother brought over fresh fish and dried apples to lure her back to the table.[40]

The opium, laudanum, and morphine that Charity and Sylvia took on occasion also caused distress as well as relief.[41] The women knew that opium and its derivatives disordered the mind. After she observed Charity taking opium during an 1838 visit to Massachusetts, Charity's sister Silence wrote an admonitory letter to the women describing the ill effects the medicine had on a neighborhood woman. Silence's neighbor Mrs. Packard, who "was in the habit of using opium," had "become an idiot for she took so much that many times she did not appear to know what she was about."[42] Silence hoped that her sister, who vested so much identity in her intellect, would treat the drug with greater caution.

Alcohol, a common ingredient in their medical recipes, could be a killer as well as a curative. The women frequently bathed their aching limbs in brandy, and Sylvia attributed the healing of her lame wrist to "British ale."[43] But they also witnessed friends and neighbors abuse alcohol to the point of death, not only via alcoholism but through accidental poisonings. "Hear of the death of Harriet Hagar 2nd daughter of Luther H and Mr Burgers by intoxication. Since I have heard [I'm] refraining from it," Sylvia recorded after one tragic episode.[44] When a young man who worked for the women informed Sylvia that he was going to remove his name from the temperance pledge, she warned "if he becomes a drunkard, as I assurd him he would in 10 years, that he would take a pistol + blow out his brains."[45] Judgmental in the extreme, Sylvia looked down on friends who overindulged in alcohol during social calls. When Mrs. Farmer became intoxicated on a visit to the women's house and spilled her glass of brandy, Charity served the unfortunate woman camphor and water to sober her up.[46] The women witnessed the deleterious effects of alcohol on the health of tipplers in the community, but they continued to rely on it as a medicine throughout their lives.[47]

Ultimately, the women took a catholic approach to medicine, best illustrated through the range of treatments that Charity endured during a prolonged and severe episode of arm pain, which she diagnosed as rheumatism. On the morning of Charity's forty-fifth birthday, both women awoke with pain in their arms. At first Sylvia seemed the worse sufferer; Charity applied a poultice of burdock leaves and brandy to Sylvia's right arm.[48] Sylvia's pain soon resolved. Charity's arm, however, continued to distress her for months, during which time the women tried every treatment from native herbs to traditional drugs to surgeries.

To begin, Charity tried bathing—not her arm, but her feet.[49] This gentle nostrum represented an innovative approach. For centuries Anglo-Americans had avoided bathing as dangerous, but in the early nineteenth century localized bathing, and later full immersion, came to be seen as a promising treatment for disease.[50] Unfortunately, the water did not resolve Charity's rheumatism. A couple months later the pain returned with more severity.[51] Next, Sylvia tried bathing Charity's arm directly with hot cloths.[52] She followed that treatment with massage, still without success.[53]

Two months after the first flare-up, the women began experimenting with medicines. They began by trying "wickup," an Algonquian name for fireweed, an herb often used to treat skin wounds.[54] Like the bathing, Sylvia reported, this medicine had "no effect on Miss Bs arm."[55] A few days later, Charity and Sylvia tried wickup again, this time mixed with "spirits of wine burdock leaves + vinegar mullen leaves + red + black pepper + ginger, rum brandy salt + c + c a strengthening plaister." The list combined native plants (burdock), nonnative plants (mullein), imported spices (red pepper), and alcohol, as well as a surgical approach, blistering. Again, all the treatments were "to no good effect."[56] The next day, Charity turned to a stronger surgical measure, inviting the local doctor to come and bleed her. She followed that heroic measure with a dose of calomel and jalup. Sylvia returned home to find Charity "much distressd." The stress of the situation, perhaps, prompted Sylvia to feel a "severe pain in my head," and both women went early to bed.[57] After this treatment, Charity felt moderately recovered for a few days.

But in less than a week the pain returned. Sylvia tried a range of new remedies, including topical applications of mustard seed, cold water, and hemlock.[58] A good friend brought over special spa water to treat the arm.[59] Finally Charity sought out a second opinion from Dr. J. A. Allen, who prescribed "salts of ammonia gumguacum," "swathing the arm," and "electricity."[60] Dr. Allen was one of many antebellum doctors experimenting with the use of electricity as a cure for ailments including "gravel, dysentery, agues in the breast, local inflammations, tumors, cramps, fevers, hystericks, cholic, palsy, dropsy, lock-jaw, ocular diseases" and "any complaints, to which females only are subject."[61] Allen even taught classes on the medical applications of electricity in nearby Brattleboro.[62] Sylvia did not record whether Charity submitted to electric treatment, but her diary in the following months listed an ever-expanding catalog of topical applications, including prickly ash, cider brandy, flax seed, scabish leaves, wheat bread, catmint leaves, sweet oil, brimstone, castile soap, horseradish leaves (placed on the soles of Charity's feet), and salmon oil.[63] Sylvia recorded with grim disappointment that the last treatment, recommended by their neighbor Mrs. Hagar, "fails like every other medicine."[64] A game patient, Charity showed willingness to try just about any treatment available.

Perhaps the women's most unusual healing practice was their habit of rocking each other in an adult-sized cradle constructed for them by brother-in-law Asaph

Hayward. Made of pine boards painted olive green, narrow at the base and wider at the lip, with a backboard to rest one's head, the wooden cradle stretched over five feet long, sufficiently large for many adults of the village. They kept the cradle in the main room of the house, before the hearth. Sylvia used rests in the cradle to treat her toothaches and headaches. Sometimes she even worked in the cradle while Charity rocked her.[65]

Charity and Sylvia also approved some rather unusual aspects of heroic medicine. When a doctor trepanned Sylvia's sickly nephew, drilling a hole into his skull, she enthusiastically recorded the consequences: "Sister E's…little boy able to walk about who has been trepand and eleven pieces of bone taken out of his head. How great are the mercies of Him, who spares our lives."[66] Charity expressed similar support for another practice on the outer reaches of medicine, autopsy. Most Americans disapproved of human dissection as desecrating and atheistic.[67] Sylvia shared this opinion, complaining of one doctor that he spoke "very thoughtlessly on cutting up the dead."[68] But Charity wrote to her brother Peter with fascination about an autopsy conducted in Weybridge in 1820. When a young woman took sick and died suddenly, the doctor "not being fully satisfied with respect to her disorder open'd her head and found a small bladder of water in the center of the brain and pronounc'd it to be the dropsy."[69] Eager to share this medical knowledge with her doctor brother, Charity seemed unworried about the ethics of defacing the young woman's corpse.

The women's support for heroic medicine did have limits. Their frequent encounters with the era's doctors were bound to produce occasional negative reactions. Sylvia complained about cavalier doctors who ended up "killing their patients" rather than curing them.[70] This was a common refrain of the time. Vesta Guild disparaged the "strolling quacks" who came through town dispensing patent medicines.[71] After suffering through calomel treatment for a tubercular carbuncle that developed on her neck, Lydia Richards expressed grave doubt about treatments that "might perhaps be thought to be as bad as the disease."[72] Her later letters to Charity took a more passive approach to sickness, focusing on the afterlife rather than the possibility of a terrestrial cure. "If your body is destin'd to decay and soon drop into the grave," Lydia wrote to Charity a few years after her calomel treatment, "may you be enabled by faith to look beyond this dreary prison to a glorious immortality in the mansion of eternal day."[73]

Critiques of heroic medicine gave rise to a range of health reform movements in the mid-nineteenth century, including hydropathy and homeopathy. Reformers looked to diet, cold water, and fresh air as substitutes for mercury and bleeding.[74] Charity's nephew Cyrus Bryant, descended from three generations of medical practitioners (Abiel Howard, Philip Bryant, and Peter Bryant), and at least two generations of consumptives (Silence Howard Bryant, Peter Bryant), became a subscriber to homeopathy in his later years. "As I grow older," he confessed in a letter to his aunt, "I must say I have less confidence in the efficacy of drugs than I formerly had— if people could or would study more into the nature + peculiarities of their own constitutions, be more cautious in their diet + make a free use of the bath, I think health might be preserved & life might be sustained" better than through "allopathy."[75]

Sylvia and Charity sampled the new regimes as they had the old. "[I] think Spare diet better than medium," Sylvia commented in her diary in 1835, a statement undercut by her appreciative account of the cream, sausage, and mince pie she ate for dinner the following week.[76] On a trip to Massachusetts in 1838, a Mitchell cousin offered the women graham loaf, the new whole meal bread invented by health reformer Sylvester Graham.[77] They tried bathing, herbal treatments, and abstinence from alcohol. Late in life, they even gave up drinking tea, which William Cullen Bryant complained they had formerly "indulged immoderately."[78] On a visit to the women in 1843, Cullen brought them homeopathic medicines, which he believed proved healing for Sylvia.[79]

Since many of Charity and Sylvia's healing practices necessitated mutual care-taking, episodes of sickness served as a context in which the women expressed physical love and mutual devotion. Charity wrote one of her earliest love poems for Sylvia when the younger woman fell ill from a fever, "Oh! might my bosom prove / thy pillow and the cure of her I love," the poem entreated.[80] Sylvia's most affectionate diary entries about Charity followed accounts of being nursed by her. "How much I owe to my beloved friend which spares no pains when I am sick," Sylvia recorded gratefully after Charity helped her through the effects of an emetic. Charity's care led Sylvia to recommit to the relationship, "O may we live in such a manner here that our affection for each other may increase thro' the boundless ages of Eternity."[81] The women's lifelong battles with ill health tested the integrity of their mutual devotion. From the chalice of sickness their bond emerged burnished and bright.

The women demonstrated their love through actions as well as words. Charity plastered, bathed, soothed, and dosed Sylvia.[82] She rose before dawn to do Sylvia's housework before the latter awoke, then returned to the bedroom and treated her sick friend with herbs.[83] Despite her distaste for the kitchen, Charity even cooked Sylvia chicken soup.[84] For her part, Sylvia bathed Charity, massaged her aching limbs, made her tea, and prepared her meals. For nearly a year when Charity's rheumatic arm was at its worst, Sylvia dressed Charity every single morning. On April 1, 1821, Charity came downstairs in clothes and joked that she had "made an April fool" of Sylvia.[85]

In truth, the women's mutual physical care was no laughing matter. Charity wrote to her brother Peter that she attributed her very survival to Sylvia's nursing. Her "kind attentions have doubtless under <u>Providence</u> prolong'd my thread of existence," Charity testified, still searching perhaps for Peter's approval.[86] Over the decades, the healing touch formed an intimate bond between Charity and Sylvia. It may even have possessed an erotic dimension. Sometimes treatments led directly to the women taking "rest" together.[87] Sylvia differentiated these lie-downs from their evenings' sleep, perhaps leaving a cryptic reference to erotic encounters.[88]

Sickness licensed bodily expressions of love between Charity and Sylvia, shifting touch from the realm of the sexual to the realm of nurture. There was an irony to this sanction, since according to the medical thought of the day the women's unusual attachment to each other was a likely cause of their ill health. Nineteenth-century doctors, both traditionalists and reformers, warned emphatically of the dangers posed by masturbation—a term they extended to the mutual manual stimulation between women that constituted a common element of lesbian erotic practice.[89] Anti-masturbation activists, among them Sylvester Graham, believed that the excessive expression of sexual energies resulted in debilitating enervation. Even married couples, they recommended should avoid having intercourse more than once a month or so. Masturbation, often indulged in immoderately by youths, was a cause of epilepsy, consumption, idiocy, and death.[90]

According to the medical logic of the time, Charity and Sylvia's relationship also caused ill health by taking the place of the normal sexual relations that, in moderation, were necessary for health. Popular home health guides like William Buchan's *Domestic Medicine*, consulted by the women, pronounced that "old maids" incurred grievous physical harm from lack of sex with men. *Domestic Medicine* identified female "celibacy" as a leading cause of cancer, especially among women who were prone to excessive "religious melancholy," such as nuns.[91] While Buchan was correct to note the increased rate of breast cancers (one of the most easily diagnosed cancers in the nineteenth century) within convents, contrary to contemporary medical theories these cancers were correlated with nuns' increased incidence of menstruation compared to sexually active women who experienced multiple pregnancies, rather than their unsexed nature or "suppressed evacuations."[92]

William Whitty Hall, author of another home health guide, expanded the list of dangers that lack of intercourse posed to women: "Two-thirds of the suicides among women are unmarried, two-thirds of the inmates of lunatics are single women," Hall warned. "There is a multitude of human ailments peculiar to women which originate in celibacy; the universally observed eccentricities of old maids are a direct result of their celibate condition."[93] The message was clear, whether a lack of sex with men or a surfeit of sex with each other was most to blame, Charity and Sylvia's ill health owed much to their choice of each other as partners.

The women's concern that their relationship was a cause of their ill health, which Sylvia expressed in her diary, was buttressed by their religious belief that God punished the wicked through physical sufferings. Charity and Sylvia took the providential view that illness was a holy instrument used to chastise and direct believers along the righteous path. Sylvia berated herself when she failed to acknowledge God's direction behind her ill health. "Feel sick + have no realizing sense of the spiritual meaning of this holy ordinance," she wrote with deep remorse.[94] "We give ourselves the wounds we feel, we drink the poisonous gall," she acknowledged.[95] Sylvia connected her physical symptoms directly to her sinfulness. "I am sick with Hd a-h [headache] on account of sin," she berated herself in the pages of her diary.[96] Her frequent cranial and oral distress connected to her guilty mind and mouth. In her diary, Sylvia berated herself for thinking evil thoughts, as well as for being sharp-tongued and prone to mislead youth with pious speech that disguised a barren heart.[97] She might also have associated her mouth, a potent instrument of physical intimacy, with sexual sinfulness. "Woe is me for I am a person of unclean lips," Sylvia confessed on a day when she felt "sick with a cold."[98] Likewise, a powerful sermon that brought Sylvia to a new awareness of her fallen state plunged her into physical distress, "retire early with a severe pain in my head find no rest untill after Midnight. With awfull reflections of meeting those at the bar of Christ which my wicked example has ruined."[99]

More consumed with guilt than Charity, Sylvia even assumed spiritual responsibility for Charity's health woes. When Charity awoke ill one morning, Sylvia confessed to her diary "Miss Bryant most sick, sick of so perfidious a friend." She attributed Charity's sufferings to her own fallen state, admitting "not a day passes but I in tho't word or deed commit sins of the deepest dye."[100] The religious logic structuring this odd claim originated in Puritan covenant theory. According to New England's founders, God entered into contracts with a community, whom he rewarded and punished as a whole for their observation or abrogation of his laws.[101] Thus God might visit his wrath on the household, which included Charity, for the "sins of the deepest dye" committed by another of its members.

Sylvia's fear that her sins had brought sickness on the household would hardly have surprised Charity, who also subscribed to a covenant theory of disease. When outbreaks of measles and diphtheria swept Weybridge in the spring of 1813, Charity identified God's agency behind the epidemics, writing to her brother Peter that "when the destroying Anger will sheath His sword is known only to Him who has given Him his commission."[102] God had sent death among the people of Weybridge to punish them for falling off the path of righteousness. By the same logic, he sent sickness to Charity and Sylvia's home to express his displeasure with the sins committed there.

Yet God was not without mercy. Despite the frequent sickness that he visited on Charity and Sylvia, over and again he restored the women to health. He was the true physician capable of healing all woes. "There is balm in Gilead," Sylvia reflected, "turn our backs [and] apply [to] some other Physician + we perish."[103] God's mercies on her household, Sylvia believed, were undeserved. She remained a dreadful sinner to the end, never able to overcome her besettings. She could not even express proper thanks to God for his healing grace.[104] But God in his great goodness forgave her and Charity, and permitted the women to continue on together in their own little dwelling for many long decades. "Oh! how thankfull ought I to be to that kind Providence who has preservd the Life of my friend," Sylvia reflected in the pages of her diary. "Many a time when I almost despaird [He] has returned her to me in safety."[105] The sufferings they experienced over many decades of ill health brought the women closer to God; they were a gift as well as a punishment.

Charity and Sylvia's long familiarity with ill health prepared the women to serve as healers to family, friends, and neighbors. Their knowledge of medicine acquired renown. The women developed their own recipes for common ailments, to complement the many recipes they adopted from medical manuals and doctor friends.[106] Nephews and nieces in Vermont came to the women for treatment and to borrow from their medical stores. They bought pearlash (potassium carbonate) and tamarind to treat nephew Cyrus Bryant Drake's frequent bronchial infections.[107] They treated niece Emmeline Drake with peppercorns, hops, and vinegar when she came down with a headache during a visit. She spent the night and woke the next morning still under the weather. Determined to restore her to good health, the women applied "burdock leaves to her bowels + the soles of her feet," and administered "eppicack + mustardseed balm + Hyson tea gruel rice" and "blue pills." The next day, Sylvia recorded with satisfaction, Emmeline felt "a little better."[108] When Edwin Hayward came down with the mumps, the women dispensed tartar.[109] Later, after a piece of timber fell on Edwin, Charity helped a doctor to bind the wound and then applied plasters herself in the days that followed.[110] The women also went to tremendous lengths to heal their favorite niece Achsah Drake when she developed consumption during her early twenties, although neither medicines nor travel could save her.

Charity and Sylvia likewise volunteered their medical knowledge and care for many in the community. They dispensed prescriptions and medicines in person as well as through the mail.[111] Caring for their apprentices' health fell within the women's maternal duties. When their assistant Martha grew sick, Charity and Sylvia called in the doctor to have her bled, then rocked her to sleep in the cradle.[112] When their assistant Lucy Warner felt ill, Sylvia clucked affectionately "Miss B + I quite busy taking care of our invalid."[113] They were similarly solicitous to their neighbors.

Their shop doubled as a medical office for landlord Sarah Hagar. "Mrs Hagar comes into the shop I give her a puke," Sylvia recorded on a summer day, a decade after they moved into their house.[114] When Sarah Hagar's sister Miss Martin lay dying, Charity and Sylvia paid frequent visits to nurse her and comb her hair.[115] After Martin's death, Sylvia made a shroud and helped prepare her body for the grave.[116]

Charity and Sylvia also nursed their Bryant kin on visits to Massachusetts. After brother Peter died from consumption, Charity and Sylvia visited the family in Cummington and were distressed to find his daughter Sarah wasting away from the same disease. "Spend much time with Sarah endeavoring to remove her pain by outward application," Sylvia recorded in her travel journal. When that did not work, the women tried an ingestible remedy. Sylvia recorded with gratitude a day later that "Sarah is better after the operation of an emetic." This temporary relief, however, did not deceive Sylvia into feeling hopeful for her niece's future. Sarah was "a lovely girl," but Sylvia acknowledged, "a victim to disease + I fear death."[117] Sarah followed her father to the grave a few years later. Beloved by her siblings, she inspired her brother Cullen's oft-anthologized elegy "The Death of the Flowers."[118]

As much as Charity and Sylvia liked to dispense medical advice, they rarely listened to the admonitions of all who cared about them to stop working so hard. Despite their health woes, they could never afford to relax the regimen of labor that preserved their independence. To keep and maintain their own little dwelling, the women had to work both day and night at the expense of their well-being. "My Dear Cy tho fatigud sits up + cuts clothes untill 2 in the morning," Sylvia commented tersely in her diary during the winter of 1822. The work made Charity sick, but still she toiled on.[119] A month later, it was Sylvia who sat up until two in the morning working, making herself sick. "Bake sew + c active [until] two in the morning," she recorded on February 11. A day later, her diary entry consisted of only four words: "cold + blustering most sick."[120] The women knew that overwork contributed to their ill health. "Sew too much feel most sick," Sylvia wrote ruefully in her diary on a typical day.[121] She made the same observation about Charity, "My Dear C most sick in consequence of too much application to business."[122] In addition, overwork made it more difficult for the women to recover from their bouts of illness. After a week of headaches, Charity seemed to be feeling a little better when a relentless day in the shop—eighteen customers placed orders for clothes—caused her to "almost sink under the pressure of business."[123] Still they toiled on.

From necessity, the women could accomplish great feats of industry even when sick. After an evening in which headache kept her awake for hours, Sylvia arose the next day feeling "very unwell," but managed to "clean the buttery, cupboard, bed chamber, dining room + kitchen, make crackers + bake them," as well as do the laundering, an onerous task that many early American women despised above all other housework.[124] The women did not always succeed at working through ill health, but the economy of their lives demanded that they make the effort. "A severe pain in my head, try in vain to work," Sylvia wrote with regret one Sunday. Neither ill health nor her knowledge that the day "ought to be kept holy" could keep Sylvia from trying to tackle the mountain of work that awaited. Still, unable to make the progress she wished, Sylvia noted that the next day she woke "at 3 in the morning" to make up for lost time.[125]

Frequent visits to family in Massachusetts also took their toll on the women's health. From early on, Charity and Sylvia found the six-hundred-mile roundtrip from Weybridge to southern Massachusetts, much of which they traveled by foot, to be exhausting. Their 1811 journey left the two women so fatigued that Charity still felt unwell months later.[126] The trips did not get any easier with age. Setting off in the summer of 1836, Sylvia remarked that "disease seems preparing our bodies for a different journey from what we have ever taken."[127] No wonder, then, that the women required an arsenal of medication to endure their final trip in 1838. On the first day the women left Weybridge, Charity came down with "a severe cold." Day two Charity began dosing with thoroughwort and rhubarb. Day three she swallowed half a pill of opium. By day four she was restocking her opium supply at a village apothecary. At stores and in fields along the road south, the women collected camphor, Macaboy snuff, Richardson's medicine, tamarind, sassafras, and wintergreen to medicate their ailing bodies.[128] The 1838 journey exacted a great toll on sixty-one-year-old Charity and fifty-four-year-old Sylvia. Understanding that this trip might be their last, Charity and Sylvia paid careful visits to the graves of Sylvia's father, Charity's mother and father, and her beloved sister Anna. It had come time to say goodbye.[129]

Months after the women's return to Vermont they received a letter bearing awful news. Charity's cousin Vesta Guild had passed away. Her death came at the same moment that Charity suffered her first episode of heart disease. In fact, news of her death arrived in a letter from Roland Howard, Vesta's brother, responding to a letter Charity had mailed Vesta seeking advice about her new symptoms. Roland wrote back, bemoaning the fact that Vesta's hands "no longer possessed the power to break the seal" on Charity's letter. On a recent visit to their relations the Mitchells, Vesta had been overcome by stomach pain and fever. Soon she grew delirious. Confined to the Mitchells' house, she spent her final weeks "deranged." Vesta died on September 13, 1839, severing Charity's strongest tie to the region where she had been raised. Born eleven days apart, Vesta and Charity had moved through life in tandem. Both endured difficult youths, both lived as single women, both taught school and earned money by the needle, both gave their service to faith and family, and now, it seemed, both were bound for the grave.[130]

Many friends and relations passed away in the years that followed. Each letter from Massachusetts carried some new account of a cousin or acquaintance whose life had reached its end.[131] Roland Howard followed his sister to the grave in 1844.[132] In 1846, Lydia Richards (Snell) succumbed to the consumption that had haunted her for years, making her unable to stop from "losing my appetite, losing strength & losing flesh! notwithstanding all the medicine which I was taking."[133] Sister-in-law Sally Snell Bryant followed Lydia a year later. She had always been a hale and healthy woman, weathering the move to northern Illinois at age sixty-six without ill effect and even coming back east to make a visit when she was seventy-four. She was capable of riding well into old age, but her vitality proved her undoing when she took a fall from a horse at age seventy-eight and broke the neck of her hip socket. She died a few months later.[134]

The Revolutionary generation was passing into the dust. On a visit to her daughter's lodgings in Boston in 1843, Charity's oldest sister Silence, born in 1774, watched from the windows as a parade marched by to commemorate the erection of one of the first Revolutionary War monuments in the United States, an obelisk dedicated to the Battle of Bunker Hill.[135] "A hundred and seven Revolutionary soldiers twelve of whom fought in the Battle of Bunker-Hill and three in the Battle of Lexington" joined the procession, Silence wrote in amazement to her younger sister, "the oldest was ninety seven." Her own age weighed heavily on her shoulders, as she contemplated whether she might ever see her younger sister in this world again.[136]

The passing years and the women's increasing debility seemed to render that desire a pipe dream, but the construction of a rail line to Vermont created an unexpected opportunity for seventy-seven-year-old Silence to visit in the late summer of 1851, accompanied by her daughter Carry. They found both Charity and Sylvia to be in "delicate health," but Carry was pleased to discover that Charity's faculties remained "uncommonly bright." She expressed great curiosity "in everything that was going on."[137] True to form, Charity continued on with her work of cutting clothes. She kept up with the world by reading issues of *The American and Foreign Christian Union*, and by writing weekly letters to friends and family, who sent her news of the Swedish nightingale Jenny Lind's American tour, of nephew Edwin Bryant's fantastic success in the California real estate market, and of nephew Cullen's most recent books of poetry and letters.[138]

Despite Charity's frailty, Silence and Carry felt "cheerful" about her prospects as she stood waving in the cottage door on their parting day. Traveling along Weybridge's main road, the women passed the town's burying ground at the junction with the road to Middlebury. Carry took notice of its location, thinking "it might contain at some period the mortal remains of those who were dear to me." But she busied herself with thoughts of buying gifts in Boston to send to her aging aunts, perhaps the music box Charity longed for and some brightly colored fabric for Sylvia to sew.[139]

Three weeks later, after the presents were bought but before they had been sent, a "telegraphic dispatch" arrived in Boston bearing news. The day before, on October 6, 1851, Aunt Charity had died in her chair from a paroxysm of the heart.[140]

19

Sylvia Drake | W

1851

SIXTY-SIX YEARS OLD when her companion died, Sylvia Drake may never before have spent an evening on her own. She grew up as the youngest daughter in a family of eight children, driven by her father's bankruptcy into the homes of others during her childhood, and raised in the rude cottages of frontier Vermont. It is possible that Sylvia had never slept in a bed by herself before meeting Charity at age twenty-two. After Sylvia joined Charity in her Weybridge lodgings, there is no evidence that they spent a further night apart.[1] Acquiring their own twelve-by-twelve-foot home on the first day of 1809, the two women lived the next forty-two years in the closest proximity. Such intimacy imbued the women's home with more emptiness, following Charity's death, than any little dwelling could possibly possess.

No one who knew the women could imagine Sylvia occupying the small cottage on her own. "We think of your habitation…and are ready to exclaim, how desolate must that habitation now appear to our friend who survives," wrote the women's longtime correspondent the Reverend Eli Moody, after receiving news of Charity's death. Charity's niece Caroline Rankin felt the same way. "I know you must feel nothing but utter desolation and loneliness in every step you take in your home there will be so many little things to remind you of her and that she has left it for-ever." Grandniece Emma Rankin asked if her great-aunt would "remain in your house" since it would be "so lonely to live all alone." Of course, Sylvia had done more than share a house with Charity. For years she had devoted herself to answering

Charity's "every want and ministering to her every necessity," in Caroline's words. A day spent apart from her beloved friend was almost as alien to Sylvia as a night.[2]

The magnitude of Sylvia's loss could hardly be expressed. This poverty of language prevented some from writing immediately. Even William Cullen Bryant's ever-busy pen paused before the task. A telegram to New York City informed the poet of his aunt's death straight away. Later that fall he visited with his cousin Caroline, who described her final trip to Weybridge and recounted Charity's last days. Sensible to his family responsibilities, Cullen wrote an informative letter to his brother Cyrus, sharing the details of Aunt Charity's passing with their Illinois relations. Of course, he knew that his responsibilities did not end there. Long a favorite of both Charity and Sylvia, Cullen told Cyrus that he had "been thinking of writing to Miss Drake," but he confessed "I have not yet done it." Rarely at a loss for words, Cullen found this ending hard to write.[3]

One word came easily to every friend and relative who wrote to Sylvia following Charity's death: *loneliness*. Days after Charity's death, Cyrus Bryant Drake, trained for the pulpit thanks to his aunts' beneficence, wrote to Sylvia, "your loneliness must be very marked." The now-middle-aged minister consoled his elderly aunt that "you are not <u>alone</u> but have the presence of Him who can give light in darkness + joy in sorrow." As spiritual emissaries, the many ministers Sylvia knew could reach beyond their own limited capacities to offer solace. Eli Moody frankly acknowledged in his consolation letter to Sylvia that he could not "fully realize what must be your <u>lonely state</u>," but he assured his old friend that she would find "support and comfort" in the spiritual realm. A third minister, the Reverend D. D. Cook, wrote with perhaps the most welcome religious counsel. Cook's letter advised his "lonely & afflicted friend" that Charity remained watching over her: "who is more likely to be commissioned as your ministering spirit than she, who more likely to be sent to watch around your bed in the still and lonesome hours of night, and guard and protect you." This domestic vision may have helped lighten the gloom that shadowed the cottage.[4]

In contrast to their male counterparts, the women who wrote letters of condolence generally expressed their sympathies in less flowery language, perhaps reflecting their more limited educations. Sylvia's niece Polly Drake, who had migrated to western New York, wrote in plainspoken terms, "I feel sad on your account dear Aunt knowing that you must be very lonely." Clarissa Moody added her voice to her husband's in a to-the-point postscript at the bottom of his letter: "you must have learned the meaning of the word alone." Unable to find a better word to describe Sylvia's loss, her women friends used *lonely* to convey a deeper meaning than it typically expressed. Charity's death had taken away part of Sylvia, like a tree trunk split by lightning, one half left standing.[5]

What all Sylvia's correspondents stumbled was over how to describe the nature of her loss, since the most adequate words, *widow* and *husband*, were problematic. Charity and Sylvia were generally known as a married couple, and Charity was regarded as Sylvia's husband, but their sex precluded most friends and relatives from naming them as spouses, especially in writing. Communal acceptance of their union rested on its silencing. The women's old friend Diann Smith, a schoolteacher and the widow of their former minister Harvey Smith, identified the problem in a condolence letter that it took her more than a year to send, a fact for which she apologized. Diann reminded Sylvia that God took care of "the widow," although "you do not as literally represent that class as I do, yet you must feel the same loneliness, which enters into the core of the heart." Her words simultaneously included and excluded Sylvia in the category of widowhood, recognizing her emotional state as equivalent while denying her the formal name.

Correspondents also found themselves in a linguistic bind when they sought to name Charity's relation to Sylvia. Denied the term *husband*, friends and family had to write their way around the women's connection. Nephew Cyrus Bryant Drake called Charity by the descriptive but awkward phrase: "one with whom you have lived so many years." D. D. Cook also described Charity as Sylvia's longtime cohabitant, and he stressed the emotional dimension of their relationship, calling Charity "her whose society and intercourse you have so long and so happily enjoyed." Despite their deep feelings for Sylvia, the language problem gave the condolences of old friends a stilted tone.[6]

Sylvia lost more than a word in her exclusion from the category of widowhood. Early American women assumed the name of widow as a powerful identity following the deaths of their husbands; it conferred qualities of holiness, authority, and piteousness that commanded a certain respect, or at least compassion, from others. The word served as a title in nineteenth-century New England. After the death of her husband, a surviving wife became *the Widow So-and-So*. The parable of the widow's mite, which was well known at the time, depicted the widow as a worthy figure who deserved consideration. To be a widow might be the "most Forlorn and Dismal of all states," as Abigail Adams put it, but that very extremity made the status meaningful. Without the title of widow, Sylvia lacked recognition of both the honor and the suffering it imputed.[7]

The one person willing to name Sylvia as *widow* was Charity. Her last acrostic for Sylvia appended a line beginning with W at the end. The theme of the acrostic, the women's inevitable separation through death, suggests that the *W* stood for widow. The inspiration for the poem may have been Sylvia's worries, which she confided to her diary one evening around the time Charity wrote her verses, about a newly widowed woman in their community. "Could think of nothing else for a long time after retiring but the loss sustaind by the afflictd widow," Sylvia recorded. "Mans days is determind." Voicing her concerns to Charity in their shared bed likely influenced the latter to put pen to paper.[8]

"Swiftly our moment pass away / Yes! And how swiftly all our years," read the acrostic's opening lines. The phrase "all our years" evoked a line from Psalm 90, often read at funerals: "for all our days are passed away in thy wrath: we spend our years as a tale that is told." In Charity's telling, her own death would make Sylvia a widow. Like the funereal psalm, Charity's acrostic dwelt on the fleeting quality of life and the need for wisdom to guide men toward the righteous path, away from iniquities and "secret sins." Despite people's wishes to the contrary, their days soon passed "down to the Shades of endless night." Finally, under the penultimate line starting with *E*, Charity drew a short line. The last sentence admonished Sylvia to "Wait on the Lord, & strength renew." In total, the first letters of the poem's first lines spelled out "Sylvia Drake | W." During the years that Sylvia had to wait before their reunion in the afterlife, Charity's poetic testimony to her widowhood offered a source of comfort.[9]

As it turned out, Sylvia had a long time to wait. She survived Charity by sixteen and a half years. During the final decade and a half of her life, Sylvia followed the widow's convention of wearing only black. She spent the first half of her widowhood living in the cottage, which had been Charity's wish. In an 1847 birthday poem for Sylvia, Charity foretold her approaching death and voiced her desire that Sylvia's property rights be secured:

> As more than seven years
> Your senior I am found;
> I may be first to leave
> This little spot of Ground
> On which so many years
> Our dwelling place has been
> …
> While you sojourn Here
> May no rude Changes come
> To cross your daily path,
> And mar your peaceful Home.[10]

In another act of writing, more important than verses, Charity left a will that sought to guarantee Sylvia's claim on her home. The will named Sylvia executrix and indicated that Charity's real estate was "owned by the deceasd in common with Drake." Charity did not neglect her Bryant relations in the will. She distributed articles of clothing and other valuable keepsakes to her beloved nephews and nieces. Sylvia worried about their reactions to the will, but two of Silence's children wrote to promise her their lasting friendship. Oliver Bryant assured Sylvia she need not worry about "offending any of our family by any disposition of matters and things relating to yourself and Aunt C," and he expressed his desire to continue their correspondence. Grandniece Emma Rankin also professed her love and insisted, "we shall always be glad to hear from you whenever you feel as if you could write." Without objections from Charity's relatives, the probate court approved Sylvia's handling of the will, and the year after Charity's death she appeared in the village's tax records as the sole owner of the women's residence.[11]

Handling the details of the estate and running the tailoring business on her own kept Sylvia very busy in the years immediately following Charity's death. In fact, despite the concerns of well-intentioned relations and friends, Sylvia had little time alone in the cottage at first.[12] But without Charity by her side, as age magnified her own infirmities, the business began to fail. By the mid-1850s, Sylvia had to turn to her well-off brother Asaph for financial support. She stopped sewing for her living, although she kept making clothes for the family, and the village stopped taxing her personal property after 1855. Still she continued to live in the cottage until the summer of 1859, when she abandoned the old dwelling to join her brother Asaph, and his unmarried daughter Sylvia Louisa, in his elegant brick house.[13]

Although Sylvia enjoyed "the stillness + quiet + all the conveniences + comforts" that Asaph's fine house afforded, she made the move not only for her own benefit but also to care for her elderly widowed brother. In 1859, Asaph had developed a putrefying infection in his right hand that caused him debilitating pain. Sylvia, long practiced in nursing from her years of caring for Charity, took responsibility for dressing the wound, a regimen that tortured the old man. Although Asaph sought to have the diseased portion removed by a doctor in Boston, he never recovered the use of the hand. Asaph's difficulties, and Sylvia's responsibilities, were compounded in 1863 when he went blind. At some point, his daughter Polly Angelina Shaw and her husband, Fordyce, returned from living in Massachusetts and also moved into the house. Increasingly irritable with old age, Sylvia reportedly "made it very hard" for Fordyce Shaw. Still, she continued to contribute to the community, hosting prayer meetings at Asaph's brick house and mentoring the village youth.[14]

Orpha Jewett, born nine months after Charity's death (on July 3, 1852, Sylvia and Charity's forty-fifth anniversary), was one of the village youth who attended prayer meetings at Asaph Drake's house during Sylvia's final years. She kept note of the occasions in a diary she started at the beginning of 1868. On the evening of January 31, the fifteen-year-old recorded a full house at Old Deacon Drake's. Sylvia must have been pleased by this showing of religious spirit in Weybridge. If she had been alive to see it, she would have been equally pleased by the spirited gathering that followed her funeral not three weeks later. Sylvia Drake passed away on February 13, 1868, at the advanced age of eighty-three. Five days later, Orpha noted in her diary, "Aunt Silvy was buried." The Reverend Cozzens preached. Afterward, the villagers held a "very good meeting" at the church.[15]

Tucked inside the back-cover flap of Orpha's little red diary are a series of newspaper clippings from the year of Sylvia's death, including a humorous bit on the subject of old women. "There are three classes into which all the women past seventy that ever I knew were to be divided:—1, That dear old soul; 2, That old woman; 3, That old witch." Orpha's account of the funeral suggests that most people in Weybridge regarded Sylvia as a specimen of the first kind. She had outlived almost everybody who knew her before she met Charity, and few people remained who might see the two women's connection as outside the town's natural order. The many nieces and nephews—biological and acquired—who mourned her passing had grown up to venerate their aunts' Christian household.[16]

Even Fordyce Shaw, who had lived uneasily with Sylvia during her final years, agreed to set aside any personal irritation to commemorate his aunt as she deserved. In the summer of 1868 he approved the request of W. N. Oliver, owner of the Rutland Marble Works, to inscribe Sylvia and Charity's headstone with raised letters instead of carved, a decision that increased the price for the monument. Oliver explained, "I propose this as I think [you] desire a fine job and do not care to stand about 10 or 15 dollars if the money is well earned as in this case it will be." Fordyce agreed, and the temporary marker that Sylvia had purchased after Charity's death was replaced by a single headstone marking both their bodies.[17] The combined memorial ensured that the town's recognition of the women's union would last long beyond the living memories of those who had known them. In death, Charity and Sylvia realized a fantasy of eternal union expressed by many women lovers both before and after, yet seldom achieved.[18] Their joint gravestone is a rare monument to the women's perseverance in spending their lives and deaths together.

Sylvia's will also preserved evidence of the connection with Charity that had defined her life. The first instruction in the will set aside half of her property, both personal and real, for Mary B. Rankin and Oliver Bryant, the children of Charity's sister Silence Bryant. Charity and Sylvia had earned their property through joint effort, and each possessed just title to half the accumulated wealth. In traditional Anglo-American law, when a husband died his wife inherited a life interest in one-third of the property, to be distributed among the children following her death. Charity, on the other hand, left all her real property to Sylvia, with the understanding that following Sylvia's death the property would be evenly divided between the two women's respective families.

Charity and Sylvia's unusual arrangement reflected an egalitarian approach to marital property, which had once set them apart from nearly every other couple, but by the late 1860s was becoming a central principle of the first women's rights movement.[19] In 1805, two years before Charity and Sylvia established their union, the Supreme Judicial Court of Massachusetts issued a decision in the case of *Martin v. Massachusetts* confirming that the Revolution's disruption of traditional political hierarchies would not extend to patriarchal control over property. *Martin v. Massachusetts* reinscribed coverture into American law for generations to come. Charity and Sylvia's household, in which both women contributed labor to build wealth that they shared equally, represented a radical innovation.[20]

The women were decades ahead of their time. Sixty-three years later, when Sylvia passed away, American law was just beginning to catch up. The principles enumerated in the Declaration of Sentiments, signed at Seneca Falls in 1848, included the demand for married women to gain control over their own wages and their share of the joint marital property. Over the following two decades, feminists pursued the passage of "married women's property acts" by state legislatures. As of 1865, twenty-nine states had passed such laws. And in 1868, the year of Sylvia's death, passage of the Fourteenth Amendment guaranteeing due process of law for all American citizens inspired feminists to launch a new campaign against the strictures of coverture (though sadly, they were not successful).[21]

Sylvia's will further confirmed her commitment to women's property rights by distributing the half of her property reserved for her Drake kin to her nieces rather than her nephews. She gave $10 each to the daughters of her sister Desire. She left $25 to her grandniece Harriet Emily Bowdish, who had been abandoned by her ne'er-do-well husband and gotten divorced in the year before Sylvia's death. She left another $25 bequest to a blind grandniece, Ann L. Drake. The remainder of her property, if there was any, was to be divided into three parts and split between the church, her grandnieces Harriet Emily Bowdish and Sarah S. Child (who had named her son after Charity), and lastly her nephew Lauren—a miserable "sponge" who was unable to care for himself.

At the time of her death, Sylvia had $75 cash in hand, and notes for debts due to her totaling $750, which her executors might or might not be able to collect. Since she had distributed her furnishings to her nieces prior to her death, during the years she spent living with Asaph, she left behind personal property valued at only $10.75. These were items she kept in her chamber at Asaph's house and used for daily living. They included a stove, kettle, warming pan, bedstead, a few chairs and tables, and the *Encyclopedia of Religious Knowledge*. Even these tokens she willed to grandniece Emmeline Drake.[22] Sylvia's preference for female heirs over male heirs, and her desire to use her share of the marital property to support indigent nieces, echoed the 1816 will of another better-known early American proto-feminist, Abigail Adams. One wonders whether Sylvia, whose hometown was not far from where Adams lived, had her example in mind.[23]

In contrast, when Sylvia's brother Asaph died three years later, at age ninety-six, the division of his sizable property, valued at $14,334.11, adopted the usual pattern of preferring males to females. Although the heirs received shares based not on gender but on their degree of relation to Asaph—one-ninth for children or their surviving spouses, one-eighteenth for nearby grandchildren, and one-fifty-fourth for distant grandchildren—in the practical matter of dividing his several hundreds of acres, the will directed that lines were to be drawn in a way that benefited males over their female relations.[24] Another of Sylvia's brothers who died before her gave similar preference to male heirs. Oliver Drake left his widow, Ruth Drake, a fourth of his estate and the right to remain in their home "so long as she shall remain my widow and no longer." He left cash legacies to only two of his sons, splitting the rest of his limited property among those of his eighteen children who outlived him.[25]

The Drakes had been a remarkably prolific family, and the villages surrounding Weybridge were crowded with the children and grandchildren of Sylvia's brothers and sisters. Many of her nephews became substantial landowners, ministers, and industrialists. They restored the legacy of the Drake family, whose fortune had fallen so low during the Revolution. Asaph's son Cyrus Bryant Drake served as secretary of the Vermont Domestic Missionary Society and invested his money wisely, dying a rich man. His brother Isaac Drake became the richest man in Weybridge, with a farm stretching over hundreds of acres. Sylvia's brother Solomon, who lived in neighboring Bristol, also possessed a farm of several hundred acres, and he held numerous civic offices in the town. His son Thomas S. Drake, one of ten children, became president of the National Bank of Vergennes, managed an electrical plant, and invested in real estate.

Like many New England families, the Drakes traveled west in the nineteenth century. Thomas's brother Ransom became a pharmacist in the Midwest, and his son Nelson Asaph Drake became surgeon to the Chicago, Rock Island, and Pacific Railways. Other cousins became respectable citizens in New York State, Canada, Ohio, Iowa, Wisconsin, and California.[26]

Unfortunately, the primary beneficiary of Sylvia's will, Harriet Emily Bowdish, sank into a disabling paranoia in the years following Sylvia's death. Her marriage fell apart when she became persuaded that her husband was conspiring with the hired girl to poison her. After their separation she moved in with her sister Sarah, who had two children, one named Willis Bryant Child. Eventually, Harriet Emily moved into the next-door homestead of her widowed, childless uncle Isaac. Her paranoia worsened over time. She became mortally afraid of burglars and was subject to "violent gusts of ill temper over seemingly small provocation," which led her to say "the most intemperate and unreasonable things." Her frequent self-medication from mysterious bottles may have contributed to her off-balance personality. After Cyrus Bryant Drake's death in 1878, his unstable, unmarried daughter, Louisa Bryant Drake, moved in with Harriet Emily. She also had a "nervous sanguine temperament" and followed her aunt around the house like a shadow. When uncle Isaac died, unscrupulous male family members and neighbors sought to take advantage of the two single women. A hired man named Rollin Shaw isolated Harriet Emily and Louisa from the family, acquiring power of attorney and enriching himself from their property.[27]

The failure of her niece and grandniece to carve out satisfactory lives suggests that the world Sylvia left behind, although less restrictive than the world she had been born into, remained far from hospitable for single women. After Harriet Emily separated from her philandering husband, her sympathetic niece recalled, "male relatives chose to remain very quiet and neutral" rather than to offer any support. Louisa's life seemed equally blighted. Despite being a "fine scholar fond of intellectual pursuits," she lived a life of confinement that bore little resemblance to the illustrious achievements of her father, a Doctor of Divinity who served a term in the Vermont legislature. After Louisa's death, her father's wealth was bequeathed to his alma mater, Middlebury College, which his daughter never had the opportunity to attend.[28]

Yet the experience of another niece, who lived far from rural Weybridge, reveals that other new opportunities did open for women like Charity and Sylvia after their deaths. Julia Sands Bryant was William Cullen Bryant's daughter. Born in 1831, the younger of his two children, she received the sort of privileged attention that her great-aunt, the youngest of ten, never had. She was, in her mother's words, "the pet of the house," and by age two her parents judged her "quite smart." Her parents brought her to Europe for the first time at age three. Over the years she matured into a sophisticated and attractive young woman. Rumor had it that she turned down an offer of marriage from Samuel J. Tilden, future governor of New York State and Democratic candidate for the presidency in 1876.

But instead of becoming a political wife, like her mother and her sister, Julia formed a connection to "chum" Anna Rebecca Fairchild, a cousin who moved into the household at age eighteen. When William Cullen Bryant died in 1878, Julia and Anna moved to Paris, where they lived together for the next thirty years. At the time, Paris was home to a uniquely open lesbian subculture, depicted in Émile Zola's novel *Nana* (1880). In Paris, Julia and Anna collected rare needlework. Julia left half her sizable wealth, around $250,000, to Anna on her death in 1907. All of her personal property, including her furniture and jewels, also went to Anna. The real estate was put into trust, with the interest going to Anna's support and the principal to revert to Julia's nieces and nephews after Anna's death. Anna devoted her final years to preserving the Bryant family legacy.[29]

A significant degree of wealth differentiated the lives of Julia and Anna from their great-aunts. Charity and Sylvia sewed for a living; Julia and Anna collected exquisite lace. Still, the temporal and geographic distance between early national Vermont and fin-de-siècle Paris differentiated the women's experiences to an even greater degree than their economic standing. Between the beginning of the nineteenth century and its closing decades, a cultural revolution had taken place. Charity and Sylvia were among a pioneer generation of women at the beginning of the century who sought to shape independent lives as neither wives nor mothers. By the end of the century, women like Julia and Anna, who loved and desired other women, could participate in a lesbian subculture with its own meeting places, literary culture, and lingo.[30]

In the twentieth century, lesbian subcultures spread throughout cities in the United States as well. Eventually, lesbianism would go mainstream, finding representation on network television and the pages of mass-market magazines, as well as within the language of nondiscrimination statutes. But this shift to the mainstream caused a curious amnesia. The self-congratulatory certitude that modern times represented an apogee of tolerance compared to the benighted wasteland of the past has made it hard to fit women like Charity and Sylvia into the historical memory. How could two women have forged a marriage in a traditional New England village, governed by the old faith, and been accepted by their family and friends despite every evidence that they were lovers? Our shock at this tale indicates a failure of imagination. The history of sexual nonconformity is not only a saga of oppression and suffering; it is also a tale of creative ingenuity and accommodation. It is a story of beloved aunts and winking nephews, of cruel gossip and endurance, of erotic touch and spiritual unease, of guarded reputations and public-mindedness, of private pleasures and willful ignorance. The historical record is littered with Charities and Sylvias; we need only open our eyes and see.

We spend our years as a tale that is told!

—ELI MOODY to SYLVIA DRAKE, April 12, 1855

Afterword

CHARITY AND SYLVIA'S story has been told before, in snippets and bits, if never at length. In the century and a half that followed their deaths, the two women were never entirely forgotten.

A few circumstances ensured the preservation of the women's memories. By the time of Sylvia's death, as New Englanders confronted waves of new immigrants from alien regions of Europe, they felt anxious to preserve evidence of the region's original settler families. Thus local history collector Henry Sheldon was happy to accept a trunk of the women's papers from Angelina Shaw, Asaph Drake's daughter, who wished to clear the old woman's effects from the brick house she had inherited from her father. To Sheldon, Charity and Sylvia represented the town's founding era. In addition, their connection to America's most-beloved nineteenth-century poet endowed their writings with more than local value. Since the nineteenth century, Charity's correspondence has enriched the works of scholars of William Cullen Bryant's poetry, and she has appeared as a footnote in several of the great man's biographies.[1] But Charity and Sylvia's story has also survived as more than an adjunct to their nephew's memory. Their relationship has always held a romantic appeal of its own.

William Cullen Bryant's son-in-law Parke Godwin selected the poet's letter describing Charity and Sylvia's marriage, from thousands of others he discarded, to be included in a two-volume biography of the poet published in 1883 soon after Bryant's death. In fact, he expanded on his father-in-law's account by identifying both women by their full names and supplying background context. Godwin explained to readers that Charity and Sylvia had met

> when they were about twenty years of age each, and forming the attachment spoken of in the extract, they removed to Waybridge [*sic*], where they set up the romantic mode of life which was continued for more than fifty years. Miss Charity died at the age of seventy-three, and the other did not long survive her loss.

Godwin's story if anything romanticized Charity and Sylvia's relationship to an even greater extent than the original source. His slight errors had the result of exaggerating, not mitigating, the intimacy of the connection. By taking a decade from Charity's age when the relationship began, he erased the unhappy history of her early adulthood and the series of failed relationships she had with women before Sylvia. By truncating Sylvia's widowhood, he likewise erased the younger woman's sixteen years of living independently of her companion. Because Godwin's account reduced both Charity and Sylvia to the bounds of their relationship, he highlighted rather than deflected attention from their union.[2]

A decade later, when Hiram Harvey Hurlburt Jr. penned his memoirs for his children and grandchildren to read, he likewise called attention toward Charity and Sylvia's relationship, which was accepted "as if Miss Bryant and Miss Drake were married to each other." Rather than erase this evidence of marital nonconformity from New England's past, Hurlburt selected the women's story as especially worthy of interest for his descendants by nature of its unusual quality. His sympathetic description cast same-sex marriage as a benign variation on the ordinary. The women "got along pleasantly together," he wrote, and contributed to the town church.[3]

At the beginning of the next century, the memory of another old-timer, recorded by a local historian, contributed an additional account to the repertoire of Charity and Sylvia stories. Laura Hagar, who had delivered milk to the women when she was a little girl, remembered how Sylvia would reward her with a cookie when she behaved well. According to Hagar, both Sylvia and Charity placed a high premium on proper behavior. On one occasion, Laura and her friend Lucy Ann Hayward, Sylvia's grandniece, spent a sunny afternoon rolling down the grassy hill in front of the women's cottage "laughing and shouting in their glee." That night, Aunt Charity handed Laura a note to give to her mother, which gave "a report of the rude and unladylike manner in which her daughter had played that afternoon." Laura remembered the lesson long into her old age. This story, although focused on a little girl's experience of being scolded, added to the popular memory of Charity and Sylvia's household as a bastion of respectability—a reputation that they cultivated.[4]

The positive memory of Charity and Sylvia's marital connection circulated within Weybridge even a century after Charity's death. When high school teacher and amateur historian Frank Heys Jr. researched Charity and Sylvia's story for a 1953 article in *Vermont Quarterly*, he interviewed villagers who still recalled the women's story. According to local tradition, Heys explained in his essay, the "two women, strongly attracted to each other, swore never to marry but instead to live as companions for the rest of their lives."[5] A few family members who were unaware of this tradition expressed happy surprise to make the discovery. Merritt P. Allen, a Drake descendant who had a career as a children's book author, learned Sylvia and Charity's story from reading Heys. Afterward, he wrote a letter to his cousin Hattie Painter, then visiting Weybridge from her home in Ohio, to share his discovery. "You may not have heard this story. At least, I never heard it before," he confessed. Rather than secret the knowledge away, Allen felt inspired to share his discovery with his cousin.[6]

Family members, genealogists, and local chroniclers preserved the memory of Charity and Sylvia's romantic relationship for more than a century, during a time when most professional historians deliberately excluded any reference to same-sex sexuality within their accounts of the past. Only in the 1970s, as the gay rights movement gathered steam, did professional historians begin to battle against the historical erasure of same-sex sexuality.[7] As late as 1988, the pioneering LGBT historian Martin Duberman considered the scholarly study of the gay and lesbian past to be in its infancy.[8] Yet popular memory managed to preserve evidence of the gay past where History with a capital H had failed because amateurs felt able to frame their stories with the same ambiguous gesture of the open secret that had made Charity and Sylvia's relationship tolerable during its own time. Popular texts incorporated allusions to same-sex sexuality that were intended to provoke smiles and maybe a little titillation. Without naming Charity and Sylvia as lesbians, Godwin, Hurlburt, and Heys offered up the evidence of their romance.

After the gay rights movement licensed newly explicit modes of speech about lesbianism, Vermonters resurrected the memory of Charity and Sylvia for the overt purpose of supporting same-sex marriage. Same-sex marriage, they insisted, did not represent an imposition by recent progressive settlers in the state, as opponents claimed. The practice traced back to the original generations of settlers.[9] When I spoke to local Weybridge historian Ida H. Washington in 2006, as I began researching this book, the eighty-two-year-old spoke with great excitement about recognizing Charity and Sylvia as lesbian founding mothers of the town. Today, local historians at the Henry Sheldon Museum in Vermont celebrate Charity and Sylvia as "'married' in their love if not in their rights."[10] And a recent genealogy by a Drake descendant lists Sylvia Drake as having been in a "marriage" with Charity Bryant.[11]

Even so, popular memory about Charity and Sylvia has largely skirted the question of their sexuality, seeking neither to confirm nor deny whether the women were lovers. Drawing on the tradition of the open secret, family historians and local chroniclers now acknowledge the romantic and marital quality of the women's relationship while allowing readers to draw their own conclusions about the sexual implications. Some readers have likely dismissed the possibility of the women's sexual relationship on the grounds that proper women back then would not do such a thing. More worldly readers might assume that two women in love would not share a pillow for forty-four years without also sharing erotic moments.

The only previous writer to explicitly consider the sexual implications of Charity and Sylvia's relationship is Lillian Faderman, one of the founders of the field of lesbian history. While her account treats the question with the openness one would expect from a practitioner of lesbian history, her conclusions might surprise readers. Faderman uses William Cullen Bryant's letter about Charity and Sylvia to demonstrate the unimaginability of lesbian sexuality within pre-twentieth-century American culture. Faderman positions Charity and Sylvia's story on the opening page of her history of modern lesbianism, as a point of contrast against what follows. She argues that before the end of the nineteenth century, stories like Sylvia and Charity's could be told without raising any sexual suspicion. Indeed, Faderman claims, many women like Charity and Sylvia "cultivated their own asexuality, and while they may have kissed and hugged on the same pillow, their intimate relationships never crossed the boundary to the genitally sexual." Only during the twentieth century did the rise of sexology and the naming of homosexuality as a perversion destroy everyone's innocence. Had William Cullen Bryant published his account of Charity and Sylvia in the next century, Faderman hypothesizes, his aunts would have sued him for defamation.[12]

Faderman's analysis misses the ambiguities that governed how the story of Charity and Sylvia was told both in their own time and in the century and a half that followed. Toleration for Charity and Sylvia's unusual marriage did not depend on their era's total innocence of the possibility that two women might engage in sexual acts together. It depended on a strategic silencing of that possibility and the choice to focus attention on their positive contributions to their family, faith, and community.

It remains possible today to write about Charity and Sylvia without addressing the question of whether they had sex.[13] But more importantly, thanks to the work of scholars and activists like Lillian Faderman and Martin Duberman, it has also become possible to ask the question. The tale of Charity and Sylvia as lovers can be told.

Two centuries ago there lived two women who chose to marry each other rather than any man. For more than forty years they shared a purse, common relations, and a bed, where when the spirit moved them they shared their bodies as well. When they died, they were buried under the same gravestone. And there you can find them still.

In the interest of space, the names of the following archives and collections have been abbreviated in the notes.

ACAL American Congregational Association Library, Boston, Massachusetts
ACPR Addison County Probate Records, Addison County Probate Court, Middlebury, Vermont
BBFP Bryant Family Papers, Bureau County Historical Society, Princeton, Illinois
BCPFP Bristol County Probate File Papers, 1690–1881, MJA
BCPR Bristol County Probate Records, MJA
BDP Charity Bryant–Sylvia Drake Papers, HSM
BFF Bryant Family Folder, HSM
BGP Bryant-Godwin Papers, New York Public Library, New York, New York
CCC Cummington Community House, Cummington, Massachusetts
DFP Drake Family Papers, HSM
GWR Georgia Willis Read Papers, HL
HBFP Bryant Family Papers, Long Island Studies Institute, Hofstra University, Hempstead, New York
HL Huntington Library, San Marino, California
HOU Peter Bryant Papers, bMS Am 1438, Houghton Library, Harvard University, Cambridge, Massachusetts
HSM Henry Sheldon Museum of Vermont History, Middlebury, Vermont
MBFP Bryant Family Papers, MHS

MHS	Massachusetts Historical Society, Boston, Massachusetts
MJA	Massachusetts Supreme Court Judicial Archive, Boston, Massachusetts
OCHS	Old Colony Historical Society, Taunton, Massachusetts
PCPR	Plymouth County Probate Records, MJA
SDD	Sylvia Drake Diary, BDP
SDP	Fordyce Shaw–Polly Drake Papers, HSM
SSBD	Sarah Snell Bryant diary, HOU
WCBH	William Cullen Bryant Letters & MSS, HL
WCCR	Weybridge Congregational Church Records, WTH
WLR	Weybridge Land Records, WTH
WTH	Weybridge Town Hall, Weybridge, Vermont
WTMR	Weybridge Town Meeting Records, WTH
WTR	Weybridge Tax Records, WTH

NOTES

PREFACE

1. Double silhouette of Charity Bryant and Sylvia Drake. Accession #1979.325. HSM. The silhouettes are undated. They may have been cut in 1830, when a traveling silhouette artist came to Weybridge; see Helen Britell Huntley Memories, December 25, 1911. HSM.

2. Account of her Travels by Charity Bryant, April 9, 1844. BDP.

3. W. N. Oliver, The Rutland Marble Works, to F. M. Shaw, July 14, 1868. SDP.

4. Diary of Hiram Harvey Hurlburt Jr., 1897, chapter 6. Privately held manuscript, courtesy of Samuel Minter.

5. William Cullen Bryant, Letters of a Traveller, or Notes of Things Seen in Europe and America (New York: George G. Putnam, 1850), 136.

6. Diary of Hiram Harvey Hurlburt Jr.; William Cullen Bryant, Letters of a Traveller.

7. Account of her Travels by Charity Bryant, April 9, 1844; signature scrap. BDP.

8. Hendrik Hartog, Man and Wife in America: A History (Cambridge, Mass.: Harvard University Press, 2000), 103–15.

9. Charity Bryant, Untitled [Amen, I can verily say], March 1810. BDP.

10. Hector Davis Morgan, The Doctrine and Law of Marriage, Adultery and Divorce (Oxford, 1826), 1:38.

11. Sarah Snell Bryant to Charity Bryant and Sylvia Drake, August 3, 1843. Charity's brother Bezaliel echoed this comment, "I consider you and Sylvia as one," Bezaliel Bryant to Charity Bryant, June 24, 1818. BDP.

12. Asaph Drake to Charity Bryant, June 10, 1833. BDP.

13. Lydia Richards to Charity Bryant, July 31, 1821. BDP.

14. Anna Hayden to Charity Bryant, August 18, 1822; October 10, 1831; September 25, 1844. BDP.

15. SDD, February 3, 1821. Charity Bryant Administration Account, ACPR 25:78.

16. The nature of the closet as an open secret is explored in Eve Kosofsky Sedgwick, *Epistemology of the Closet* (Berkeley: University of California Press, 2008); D. A. Miller, "Secret Subjects, Open Secrets," in *The Novel and the Police* (Berkeley: University of California Press, 1988). The word "queer" has been reclaimed by critics and historians to signify the constructed quality of lesbian and gay identities, as well as the existence of a broad community based on "shared dissent from the dominant organization of sex and gender." Lisa Duggan, "Making It Perfectly Queer," *Socialist Review* 22, no. 1 (1992): 20.

17. Lisa L. Moore, *Sister Arts: The Erotics of Lesbian Landscapes* (Minneapolis: University of Minnesota Press, 2011), 141. Recent works of rural gay history include John Howard, *Men Like That: A Southern Queer History* (Chicago: University of Chicago Press, 2001); E. Patrick Johnson, *Sweet Tea: Black Gay Men of the South* (Chapel Hill: University of North Carolina Press, 2008); Brock Thompson, *The Un-Natural State: Arkansas and the Queer South* (Fayetteville: University of Arkansas Press, 2010). Examples of traditional works focused on the city include Elizabeth Kennedy and Madeline Davis, *Boots of Leather, Slippers of Gold: The History of a Lesbian Community* (New York: Penguin, 1994); George Chauncey, *Gay New York: Gender, Urban Culture, and the Making of the Gay World, 1890–1940* (New York: Basic Books, 1995).

18. Autobiography of Asaph Drake, 1846. DFP.

19. SDD, January 1, 1835; George Herbert, *The Works of George Herbert. In Prose and Verse*, vol. 2 (London: Pickering, 1836).

20. Lucy Burnap Wood to Charity Bryant, November 28, 1821. BDP.

21. Lillian Faderman, *Odd Girls and Twilight Lovers: A History of Lesbian Life in Twentieth-Century America* (New York: Penguin, 1991); William Cullen Bryant, *Letters of a Traveller*.

22. See, for example, Charity Bryant's copy of William Cullen Bryant, "On the Last Judgment," WCBH; also Charity Bryant's copy of William Cullen Bryant's paraphrase of Job, written when the poet was ten years old. HBFP.

23. William Cullen Bryant, *Letters of a Traveller*.

24. Will of Sylvia Drake, dated February 17, 1864, Weybridge. BDP.

25. "Letter Record, 1838–1851." BDP.

26. The majority of these letters were directed to Charity's sister-in-law Sarah Snell Bryant. They are located at the Bureau County Historical Society, in Princeton, Illinois, which was presumably too far away for Charity to enforce her typical directive to have her writings burned. Charity's nieces and nephews in the town may also have chosen to save these letters because they wanted to preserve the legacy of the increasingly famous Bryant family.

27. S. R. Mack to Charity Bryant, December 9, 1846. BDP.

28. Silence Bryant to Charity Bryant, February 5, 1812; Parthenia Brainard to Charity Bryant, February 23, 1813. BDP.

29. Sylvia records that she and Charity "look over our journals," SDD, April 13, 1822. The entry includes recollections from both 1808 and 1815, neither of which years remains extant.

30. See, for example, Brian Loftus, "Speaking Silence: The Strategies and Structures of Queer Autobiography," *College Literature* 24, no. 1 (1997): 28–44; John D. Wrathall, "Provenance as Text: Reading the Silences around Sexuality in Manuscript Collections," *Journal of American History* 79, no. 1 (1992): 165–78; Estelle B. Freedman, "'The Burning of Letters Continues':

Elusive Identities and the Historical Construction of Sexuality," *Journal of Women's History* 9, no. 4 (1998): 181–200.

31. Vern L. Bullough and Martha Voght, "Homosexuality and Its Confusion with the 'Secret Sin' in Pre-Freudian America," *Journal of the History of Medicine and Allied Sciences* 28, no. 2 (1973): 144.

32. Chris White, ed., *Nineteenth-Century Writings on Homosexuality: A Sourcebook* (New York: Routledge, 1999), 56.

33. Martha Vicinus, "Lesbian History: All Theory and No Facts or All Facts and No Theory?," *Radical History Review* 60 (1994): 57–75. See also Terry Castle on the "ghosting" effect, Terry Castle, *The Apparitional Lesbian: Female Homosexuality and Modern Culture* (New York: Columbia University Press, 1993), 5.

34. Jonathan Ned Katz, *Gay American History: Lesbians and Gay Men in the U.S.A., a Documentary* (New York: Avon Books, 1976); Caroll Smith-Rosenberg, "The Female World of Love and Ritual: Relations between Women in Nineteenth-Century America," *Signs* 1, no. 1 (1975): 1–29; Lisa Moore, " 'Something More Tender Still Than Friendship': Romantic Friendship in Early Nineteenth-Century England," *Feminist Studies* 18, no. 3 (1992): 499–520.

35. Michael Warner, *The Trouble with Normal: Sex, Politics, and the Ethics of Queer Life* (Cambridge, Mass.: Harvard University Press, 1999); Nicola Barker, *Not the Marrying Kind: A Feminist Critique of Same-Sex Marriage* (London: Palgrave Macmillan, 2012). For marriage as an instrument of gender order see Nancy F. Cott, "Giving Character to Our Whole Civil Polity: Marriage and the Public Order in the Late Nineteenth Century," in *U.S. History as Women's History: New Feminist Essays*, ed. Linda K. Kerber, Alice Kessler-Harris, and Kathryn Kish Sklar (Chapel Hill: University of North Carolina Press, 1995), 107–24.

CHAPTER 1

1. Bradford Kingman, *History of North Bridgewater, Plymouth County, Massachusetts, from Its First Settlement to the Present Time, with Family Registers* (Boston, 1866), 449.

2. Robert Middlekauff, *The Glorious Cause: The American Revolution, 1763–1789* (New York: Oxford University Press, 1982), 428.

3. Robert E. Cray, "Commemorating the Prison Ship Dead: Revolutionary Memory and the Politics of Sepulture in the Early Republic, 1776–1808," *William and Mary Quarterly* 56, no. 3 (1999): 565–90.

4. "Died," *The Massachusetts Spy*, June 12, 1777. For context see Elizabeth A. Fenn, *Pox Americana: The Great Smallpox Epidemic of 1775–82* (New York: Hill & Wang, 2002).

5. Kingman, *History of North Bridgewater*, 233.

6. Hezekiah Packard, *Memoir of Rev. Hezekiah Packard, D. D.; Chiefly Autobiographical* (Brunswick, Mass.: J. Griffin, 1850).

7. William Cooper Nell, *The Colored Patriots of the American Revolution, with Sketches of Several Distinguished Colored Persons: To Which Is Added a Brief Survey of the Condition and Prospects of Colored Americans* (Boston: Robert F. Wallcut, 1855), 33–34.

8. Charity Bryant to John Bryant, April 5, 1827. BBFP. This date is also recorded in the Bryant Family Bible, "Family Record, Being a Genealogy of the Bryant Family from the time they settled in America," BBFP. Several of the dates recorded in this letter appear to be incorrect, including sister Anna's birth year, which was 1771, not 1772.

9. D. Alden Smith, "Descendants of Stephen Bryant of Plymouth, and of His Son-in-Law Lt. John Bryant of Plympton," *New England Genealogical Register* 155, April (2001): 196.

10. For Oliver's service record see *Massachusetts Soldiers and Sailors of the Revolutionary War*, 17 vols. (Boston: Wright & Potter Printing Co., 1896), 2:735. For the presence of Col. Cary's regiment at the Battle of Long Island, see David Smith and Graham Turner, *New York 1776: The Continentals' First Battle* (New York: Osprey Publishing Ltd., 2008), 26.

11. Oliver Bryant gravestone, Snell Cemetery, Brockton, Massachusetts. For confirmation of the August 24 date see also Kingman, *History of North Bridgewater*, 449. This date is concurred by Smith, "Descendants of Stephen Bryant."

12. For the marriage date see *Vital Records of Bridgewater, Massachusetts, to the Year 1850*, vol. 2—Marriages and Deaths (Boston: New England Historic Genealogical Society, 1916), 66. For Oliver's birth date see *Vital Records of Bridgewater, Massachusetts, to the Year 1850*, vol. 1—Births (Boston: New England Historic Genealogical Society, 1916), 60. For rates of premarital pregnancy among eighteenth-century women see Daniel Scott Smith and Michael S. Hindus, "Premarital Pregnancy in America, 1640–1971: An Overview and Interpretation," *Journal of Interdisciplinary History* 5 (1975): 535–70. There are discrepancies in the sources over the spelling of Charity's father's name, Philip. I have settled on a single-p and single-l as the most common spelling, which appears on his gravestone.

13. Accounts of Silence's children are included in genealogical histories such as *Vital Records of Bridgewater, Massachusetts, to the Year 1850*, 1:57–60, as well as in an April 5, 1827, letter from Charity Bryant to her nephew John Bryant. BBFP. There are some discrepancies between sources. Charity mentions Ruth's twin but gives no name. *Vital Records* includes an entry for "Philip" born on May 18, 1761, but states that this entry was crossed out, probably signifying that the infant died soon after birth, hence his exclusion from other family accounts. A 1761 birth helps explain why there was a three-year gap between Ruth (b. 1760) and her next youngest sibling Daniel (b. 1763), when the other children were typically spaced two years apart.

14. For Abiel Howard's work as a teacher see Joshua E. Crane, "History of Bridgewater," in *History of Plymouth County, Massachusetts, with Biographical Sketches of Many of Its Pioneers and Prominent Men*, ed. D. Hamilton Hurd (Philadelphia: J. W. Lewis & Co., 1884), 814. For his epitaph see Williams Latham, *Epitaphs in Old Bridgewater, Massachusetts* (Bridgewater, Mass.: Henry T. Pratt, 1882), 48.

15. PCPR, 23:121.

16. Ruth Staples Bryant grave, Snell Cemetery, Brockton, Massachusetts.

17. Charity Bryant, "A Child of Melancholy" [November 1800]. BDP.

18. Anna Kingman, "A Sister's Farewell." BDP.

19. Silence Howard, Charity's grandmother, at least received an epitaph written by her poet-husband on her gravestone; Latham, *Epitaphs in Old Bridgewater, Massachusetts*, 46.

20. Silence could have named her last daughter after her married sister Jane Ames. She had named her two previous daughters, Anna and Silence, for another married sister and for herself; *Vital Records of Bridgewater*, 1:57–60.

21. Michigan Historical Museum, Catalog #88.138.77; Henry Art Gallery, University of Washington, Blanche Payne Collection, TC 66.50–366. The drapes are mentioned in Laurel Thatcher Ulrich, "'Independence Herself': A New Spin on Old Stories about Household Production in Early New England," in *Exploring Women's Studies: Looking Forward, Looking Back*, ed. Carol Berkin (Boston: Pearson Prentice Hall, 2006), 150. There is confusion in the

label on the Washington textile, which names the seamstress as William Cullen Bryant's great-aunt Charity Bryant and dates the textile to circa 1750. William Cullen Bryant's great-aunt seamstress was Charity Howard, but a later relative probably mistook her last name. In addition, Howard is unlikely to have produced the textile before the mid-1760s, when she was in her twenties.

22. *Vital Records of Bridgewater,* 2:137; the date of Charity Howard's death is recorded in Heman Howard, *The Howard Genealogy; Descendants of John Howard of Bridgewater, Massachusetts from 1643 to 1903* (Brockton, Mass.: Standard Printing Co., 1903), 15–16.

23. Hayward is described as a "spinster" in her probate record. PCPR, 38:131.

24. Kingman, "A Sister's Farewell."

25. Charity Bryant to Grace Hayward, June 6, 1800. BDP; Account of her Travels by Charity Bryant (1844). BDP.

26. The standard guide to infant care at the time was William Buchan, *Domestic Medicine; or, the Family Physician* (Boston: John Trumbull, 1778).

27. Charity Bryant celebrated Grace Hayward in an acrostic poem, "A Good Name is Better than Riches." For Grace Hayward's presence in the household after 1779, see Anna Kingman to Charity Bryant, August 26, 1799. BDP. Grace Hayward was probably a distant relative of Charity's. The name Hayward was an alternative spelling for Howard, Charity's mother's family name.

28. Sheila Rothman, *Living in the Shadow of Death: Tuberculosis and the Social Experience of Illness in American History* (Baltimore: Johns Hopkins University Press, 1995).

29. For a full account of Ruth Bryant's poetry see Rachel Hope Cleves, "'Heedless Youth': The Revolutionary War Poetry of Ruth Bryant, (1760–83)," *William and Mary Quarterly* (2010): 519–48.

30. SDD, July 17, 1838.

31. Anna Kingman to Charity Bryant, May 25, 1797. BDP.

32. Anna Kingman to Charity Bryant, August 26, 1799. BDP.

33. Kingman, "A Sister's Farewell."

34. Charity Bryant, "Anna Bryant," November 1800. BDP.

35. For the individualism of the Revolutionary generation see Joyce Appleby, *Inheriting the Revolution: The First Generation of Americans* (Cambridge, Mass.: The Belknap Press of Harvard University Press, 2000), chapter 1. For the Revolution as a family drama see Edwin G. Burrows and Michael Wallace, "The American Revolution: The Ideology and Psychology of National Liberation," *Perspectives in American History* 6 (1972): 167–306; Jay Fliegelman, *Prodigals and Pilgrims: The American Revolution against Patriarchal Authority, 1750–1800* (New York: Cambridge University Press, 1982).

36. Diary of Hiram Harvey Hurlburt Jr.

37. Charity Bryant to John H. Bryant, April 5, 1827. BBFP.

CHAPTER 2

1. An account of the weather in eastern Massachusetts that fall can be found in Mary Smith Cranch to Abigail Adams, November 6, 1784; *Founding Families: Digital Editions of the Papers of the Winthrops and the Adamses,* ed. C. James Taylor (Boston: Massachusetts Historical Society, 2007).

2. William L. Chaffin, *History of the Town of Easton, Massachusetts* (Cambridge, Mass.: John Wilson and Son, 1886), 241.

3. *Massachusetts Soldiers and Sailors of the Revolutionary War*, 4:954; Chaffin, *History of the Town of Easton, Massachusetts*, 206–57.

4. Woody Holton, *Unruly Americans and the Origins of the American Revolution* (New York: Hill & Wang, 2007). Goods listed are from advertisements in *The Continental Journal*, January 2, 1785; *The Massachusetts Centinel*, January 1, 1785; *Essex Journal*, February 2, 1785; *The Massachusetts Centinel*, March 5, 1785; *The Independent Ledger*, May 9, 1785; *The American Herald*, July 18, 1785; *The Massachusetts Spy*, September 15, 1785; and *The Massachusetts Spy*, December 8, 1785.

5. Holton, *Unruly Americans*, 29.

6. Chaffin, *History of the Town of Easton, Massachusetts*, chapter 25.

7. 1756 Map of Easton and 1825 Map of Easton, Easton Historical Society, Easton, Massachusetts.

8. Historians argue whether the middle class emerged in the eighteenth or nineteenth century. An argument for the significance of this category in the Revolutionary era is C. Dallett Hemphill, "Middle Class Rising in Revolutionary America: The Evidence from Manners," *Journal of Social History* 30, no. 2 (1996): 317–44. The standard argument for a later antebellum development is Stuart M. Blumin, *The Emergence of the Middle Class: Social Experience in the American City, 1776–1900* (New York: Cambridge University Press, 1989). Also Mary P. Ryan, *Cradle of the Middle Class: The Family in Oneida County, New York, 1790–1865* (New York: Cambridge University Press, 1981).

9. Bettye Hobbs Pruitt, ed., *The Massachusetts Tax Valuation List of 1771* (Boston: G. K. Hall & Co., 1978). For Thomas Drake II see 570–71; for Philip Bryant see 636–37; for Abiel Howard see 622–23.

10. Chaffin, *History of the Town of Easton, Massachusetts*, 39.

11. John W. Adams and Alice Bee Kasakoff, "Migration and the Family in Colonial New England: The View from Genealogies," *Journal of Family History* 9, no. 24 (1984): 24–43.

12. *Bristol County Docket Book, Court of Common Pleas, 1783 December–1785 September*. MJA. Also *Suffolk County Supreme Judicial Court Docket Books*, Reel 3. MJA.

13. BPCFP, Series 2, Box #105. MJA. There were numerous Thomas Drakes resident in Easton during this period, and this probate record may refer to a relative other than Sylvia Drake's paternal grandfather.

14. For an interesting comparison, see the experiences of the Patch family who became landless in the 1790s and went to work in the Rhode Island mills; Paul E. Johnson, *Sam Patch: The Famous Jumper* (New York: Hill & Wang, 2003).

15. Autobiography of Asaph Drake. DFP. For Roland Howard's cotton mill, see Howard, *The Howard Genealogy*, 66.

16. Sylvia Drake, "Acrostic for Sister Polly Hayward" [undated, ca. 1820s–1830s]. BDP.

17. Autobiography of Asaph Drake (1846). DFP.

18. Appleby, *Inheriting the Revolution*, 3.

19. W. J. Rorabaugh, *The Craft Apprentice: From Franklin to the Machine Age in America* (New York: Oxford University Press, 1986), 32–56, 135.

20. 1st Federal Census, reel 4, sheet 209.

21. Chaffin, *History of the Town of Easton, Massachusetts*, chapter 25.

22. Autobiography of Asaph Drake. DFP.

23. Autobiography of Asaph Drake. DFP.

24. Ida Washington, *History of Weybridge, Vermont* (Weybridge: Weybridge Bicentennial Commission, 1991).

25. Autobiography of Asaph Drake. DFP.

26. For marriage and birth dates, see the Drake Family genealogy. DFP. For David Belding's and Asaph Drake's positions in the town see "Records of the Proprietors of Weybridge, Vermont" (online database: NewEnglandAncestors.org, New England Historic Genealogical Society, 2004) (unpublished typescript compiled by Benjamin M. Hayward. "Weybridge, Vermont Proprietors Records," 1942).

27. "Easton March 5th, 1789 Rec'd of Thomas Drake Constable for AD 1784," inside Elijah Howard's Farm Account Book, November 1790–September 10, 1820. OCHS.

28. Polly Hayward to Sylvia Drake, October 1, 1801; this letter mentions Sylvia last being in Massachusetts two years before. BDP.

29. Easton's industries are described in Chaffin, *History of the Town of Easton, Massachusetts*, chapter 30. Description of Weybridge from Timothy Dwight, *Travels in New-England and New-York* (New Haven, Conn.: S. Converse, 1821), 2:421–22.

CHAPTER 3

1. Parish Records, May 31, 1738–March 22, 1852. Brockton, Mass. Christ Congregational Church, UCC Records, 1783–1980. ACAL.

2. Eli Forbes, *The Importance of the Rising Generation. A Sermon, Preached at the Desire of the Selectmen, and the Committee for Inspecting the Town Schools: Occasioned by the Dedication of a New and Very Commodious Grammar School House, Lately Erected in the First Parish of the Town of Gloucester, on the 5th of March, 1795* (Newburyport, Mass.: Blunt and March, 1795); Rachel Hope Cleves, *The Reign of Terror in America: Visions of Violence from Anti-Jacobinism to Antislavery* (New York: Cambridge University Press, 2009), chapter 5; James Block, *The Crucible of Consent: American Child Rearing and the Forging of Liberal Society* (Cambridge, Mass.: Harvard University Press, 2012).

3. Joseph Kett, *Rites of Passage: Adolescence in America, 1790 to the Present* (New York: Basic Books, 1977); Appleby, *Inheriting the Revolution*.

4. C. Dallett Hemphill, *Siblings: Brothers and Sisters in American History* (New York: Oxford University Press, 2011), chapter 4.

5. For Daniel Bryant's service record see *Massachusetts Soldiers and Sailors of the Revolutionary War*, 726. He is the last of the "Daniel Bryants" listed, identifiable by his age and the name of his commanding officer, Abram Washburn, a Bridgewater native. For an account of the beef squad, see Crane, "History of Bridgewater," 800.

6. Anne Lombard, *Making Manhood: Growing Up Male in Colonial New England* (Cambridge, Mass.: Harvard University Press, 2003).

7. G. J. Barker-Benfield, *The Culture of Sensibility: Sex and Society in Eighteenth-Century Britain* (Chicago: University of Chicago Press, 1992); Hemphill, *Siblings*, chapter 4; Caleb Crain, *American Sympathy: Men, Friendship, and Literature in the New Nation* (New Haven, Conn.: Yale University Press, 2001); Johann Neem, *Creating a Nation of Joiners: Democracy and Civil Society in Early National Massachusetts* (Cambridge, Mass.: Harvard University Press, 2008); Richard Godbeer, *The Overflowing of Friendship: Love between Men and the Creation of the American Republic* (Baltimore: Johns Hopkins University Press, 2009).

8. Daniel Bryant to Gideon Howard, Nov. 4, 1786. MBFP.

9. Godbeer, *Overflowing of Friendship*; Lillian Faderman, *Surpassing the Love of Men: Romantic Friendship and Love between Women from the Renaissance to the Present* (New York:

William Morrow, 1981). For works that acknowledge friendship's risks see Bryan Waterman, "Coquetry and Correspondence in Revolutionary-Era Connecticut: Reading Elizabeth Whitman's Letters," *Early American Literature* 46, no. 3 (2011): 541–63; Crain, *American Sympathy*.

10. Daniel Bryant to Gideon Howard, May 15, 1787. MBFP.

11. Cassandra Good, "Friendly Relations: Situating Friendships between Men and Women in the Early American Republic, 1780–1830," *Gender & History* 24, no. 1 (2012): 18–34.

12. Daniel Bryant to Gideon Howard, May 15, 1787. MBFP. On gossip see Edith Gelles, "Gossip: An Eighteenth-Century Case," *Journal of Social History* 22, no. 4 (1989): 667–83; Karen V. Hansen, *A Very Social Time: Crafting Community in Antebellum New England* (Berkeley: University of California Press, 1994), chapter 5; Cynthia A. Kierner, *Scandal at Bizarre: Rumor and Reputation in Jefferson's America* (Charlottesville: University of Virginia Press, 2006).

13. Daniel Bryant to Gideon Howard, May 15, 1787. MBFP.

14. Charity Bryant to John H. Bryant, April 5, 1827. BBFP.

15. William Cullen Bryant II, "The Genesis of 'Thanatopsis,'" *New England Quarterly* 21, no. 2 (1948): 169. For Edwin Bryant see Georgia Willis Read Papers, Box 2, Folder 4. HL.

16. "On the Effects of Love Upon a Mind Fraught with Sensibility," *City Gazette and Daily Advertiser* [Charleston, S.C.], February 7, 1788.

17. Hannah Webster Foster and William Hill Brown, *The Power of Sympathy and the Coquette*, ed. Carla Mulford (New York: Penguin, 1996); Susanna Rowson, *Charlotte Temple* (New York: Penguin, 1991); Charles Brockden Brown, *Ormond; or the Secret Witness* (New York: G. Forman, 1985); Charles Brockden Brown, *Wieland, or, the Transformation: An American Tale and Other Stories* (New York: Modern Library, 2002).

18. Peter Bryant to Gideon Howard, April 8, 1787. HBFP.

19. William Scott, *Lessons in Elocution; or Miscellaneous Pieces in Prose and Verse, Selected from the Best Authors for the Perusal of Persons of Taste* (Dublin: C. Talbot, 1781), 123–26; *Poor Richard Improved: Being an Almanack and Ephemeris…For the Year of Our Lord 1764* (Philadelphia: B. Franklin and D. Hall, 1763); James Fordyce, *Addresses to Young Men* (Boston: William Green, 1782), 2:224. Also Godbeer, *Overflowing of Friendship*, 8. For an argument that Damon and Pythias were in fact "potent symbols and archetypes of homosexuality" during the English Renaissance see Claude J. Summers, "Homosexuality and Renaissance Literature, or the Anxieties of Anachronism," *South Central Review* 9, no. 1 (1992): 8, 13.

20. Peter Bryant to Gideon Howard, February 11, 1787. HOU.

21. Stanley N. Katz, "Republicanism and the Law of Inheritance in the American Revolutionary Era," *Michigan Law Review* 76, no. 1 (1977): 1–29.

22. Peter Bryant to Gideon Howard, February 11, 1787. HOU. For a brief account of Peter Bryant's love of learning and political career see Kingman, *History of North Bridgewater*, 179.

23. "Mr Gideon Howard Bridgwater Honoured by a friend to Literature" by Peter Bryant. HOU. Virgil, *The Eclogues*, trans. Guy Lee (New York: Penguin Classics, 1984). Virgil's characters were recycled by many eighteenth-century poets, including Richard Sheridan. Charity had a copy of Sheridan's poem "Delia to Damon" in her possession later in life. BDP. For an analysis of Peter Bryant's poetry, see Donald M. Murray, "Dr. Peter Bryant: Preceptor in Poetry to William Cullen Bryant," *New England Quarterly* 33, no. 4 (1960): 513–22.

24. Peter Bryant to Philip Bryant, May 23, 1804. BBFP.

25. Thomas G. Voss and William Cullen Bryant II, *The Letters of William Cullen Bryant* (New York: Fordham University Press, 1975–92), 1:9, 60fn3. William Cullen Bryant II's author biography identifies himself as a "collateral descendant" of Peter's son, William Cullen Bryant.

26. Peter Bryant to Philip Bryant, May 29, 1803; Peter Bryant to Philip Bryant, May 23, 1804; Peter Bryant to Philip Bryant, June 25, 1810. BBFP.

27. Philip Bryant to Charity Bryant, January 9 and 17, 1812; Sarah Snell Bryant to Charity Bryant, February 21, 1814. BDP.

28. Charity Bryant to Peter Bryant, May 25, 1817. BBFP.

29. Linda K. Kerber, *Women of the Republic: Intellect and Ideology in Revolutionary America* (Chapel Hill: University of North Carolina Press, 1980); Kathryn Kish Sklar, "The Schooling of Girls and Changing Community Values in Massachusetts Towns, 1750–1820," *History of Educational Quarterly* 33, no. 4 (1993): 511–42; Sheila Skemp, *Judith Sargent Murray: A Brief Biography with Documents*, (New York: Bedford Books, 1998); Mary Kelley, *Learning to Stand and Speak: Women, Education and Public Life in America's Republic* (Chapel Hill: University of North Carolina Press, 2006).

30. Waterman, "Coquetry and Correspondence"; Foster and Brown, *Power of Sympathy and the Coquette*; Cathy Davidson, *Revolution and the Word: The Rise of the Novel in America* (New York: Oxford University Press, 1986).

31. Parish Records, May 31, 1738–March 22, 1852, Brockton, MA, Christ Congregational Church. ACAL.

32. Anna Kingman to Charity Bryant, December 1809. BDP.

33. Charity Bryant to Sarah Snell Bryant, November 9, 1800. BBFP.

34. Charity Bryant to Sarah Snell Bryant, November 9, 1800. BBFP.

35. Anna Kingman to Charity Bryant, June 10, 1799, BDP.

36. Charity's aversion to domestic work is evident from Sylvia Drake's diary. See further discussion below, in chapter 14.

37. Gloria L. Main, "An Inquiry into When and Why Women Learned to Write in Colonial New England," *Journal of Social History* 24, no. 3 (1991): 579–89. One note from Hannah Richards Bryant to Charity is included within a letter from Charity's father; Philip Bryant to Charity Bryant, January 9 and 17, 1812. BDP.

38. Edward Young, *The Complaint: Or, Night-Thoughts on Life, Death, and Immorality.* (Philadelphia: Prichard & Hall, 1787). Mercy discusses reading Young with Charity in Mercy Ford to Charity Bryant, June 24, 1804. Lydia Richards calls Edward Young "our favorite poet" in a letter to Charity Bryant, March 24, 1811. BDP. Charity quotes Young in a letter to her sister-in-law as late as 1825; Charity Bryant to Sarah Snell Bryant, January 9, 1825. BBFP.

39. Kingman, *History of North Bridgewater*, 179.

40. Anna Kingman to Charity Bryant, December 1809. BDP.

41. Charity Bryant, "A Child of Melancholy" (1800). BDP.

42. Anna Kingman to Charity Bryant, August 26, 1799. BDP. Anna wrote this letter following a slightly later argument between Charity and her father.

43. Charity Bryant, "Oh I reflect how hard my fate" (December 1800). BDP.

CHAPTER 4

1. Charity's words are quoted in Lydia Richards to Charity Bryant, August 24, 1799. Lydia Richards refers to Charity's habit of writing in the schoolhouse in Lydia Richards to Charity Bryant, August 6, 1800. BDP.

2. For Bryant's book sales, see "Philip Briante, 1756–1760" account in James Dean Account Book, 1747 onward. OCHS. For Abiel Howard's library, and Philip Bryant's service on the school committee, see Kingman, *History of North Bridgewater*, 115, 79.

3. Other literary women of the late eighteenth century, such as Mercy Otis Warren, acquired their educations through their brothers. Judith Sargent Murray resented her older brother's superior education and educated herself from the family library. Kate Davies, *Catharine Macaulay and Mercy Otis Warren: The Revolutionary Atlantic and the Politics of Gender* (Oxford: Oxford University Press, 2005); Skemp, *Judith Sargent Murray*.

4. P. P. Kingman to Charity Bryant, June 6, 1849. BDP.

5. Katharine Guild, *The Ancestors and Dependents of Josiah Snell Copeland and Katharine Guild of Easton, Massachusetts* (Chariton, Iowa: Office of the Chariton Herald, 1907), 8.

6. *Vital Records of Brockton, Massachusetts: To the Year 1850* (Boston: New England Historic Genealogical Society, 1911), 316.

7. Peter Bryant to Philip Bryant, September 7, 1799. BBFP; Charity Bryant to Grace Hayward, June 6, 1800. BFF; Charity Bryant to Sally Bryant, September 16, 1801. BBFP. Financial transactions still routinely took place in shillings and pence at the turn of the century. Charity did not keep a record of all the schools where she taught, but as late as 1806 a friend went looking for news of Charity "at the schoolhouse," Rhoda Ayres to Charity Bryant, August 1806. BDP.

8. Charity Bryant to Grace Hayward, June 6, 1800. BFF.

9. Gloria L. Main, "Gender, Work, and Wages in Colonial New England," *William and Mary Quarterly* 51, no. 1 (1994): 39–66; Dorothy A. Mays, "Domestic Labor," in *Women in Early America: Struggle, Survival, and Freedom in a New World* (Santa Barbara, Calif.: ABC-CLIO, 2004); Karin Wulf, *Not All Wives: Women of Colonial Philadelphia* (Ithaca, N.Y.: Cornell University Press, 2000), 102–6.

10. Richard M. Bernard and Maris A. Vinovskis, "The Female School Teacher in Ante-Bellum Massachusetts," *Journal of Social History* 10, no. 3 (1977): 332–45; Thomas Dublin, *Transforming Women's Work: New England Lives in the Industrial Revolution* (Ithaca, N.Y.: Cornell University Press, 1994); E. Jennifer Monaghan, *Learning to Read and Write in Colonial America* (Amherst: University of Massachusetts Press, 2005), 29–30, 43; Hiram Carleton, *Genealogical and Family History of the State of Vermont* (New York: Lewis Publishing Company, 1903).

11. Massachusetts Board of Education, *First Annual Report of the Board of Education, Together with the First Annual Report of the Secretary of the Board* (Boston, 1838), 28.

12. Wulf, *Not All Wives*, 106–10.

13. Charity Bryant to Grace Hayward, June 6, 1800. BFF.

14. Jo Anne Preston, "Domestic Ideology, School Reformers, and Female Teachers: School-Teaching Becomes Women's Work in Nineteenth-Century New England," *New England Quarterly* 66, no. 4 (1993): 531–51.

15. Nancy Warner to Charity Bryant, May 20, 1800. BDP.

16. Lydia Richards to Charity Bryant, August 6, 1800. Lydia lists her domestic duties in Lydia Richards to Charity Bryant, October 21, 1804. Lydia repeats her complaints about teaching in letters to Charity on September 17, 1803, and January 25, 1806. BDP.

17. William Merrill Decker, *Epistolary Practices: Letter Writing in America before Telecommunications* (Chapel Hill: University of North Carolina Press, 1998).

18. Mary Hovey to Charity Bryant, August 2, 1809. BDP.

19. Maria Clark to Charity Bryant, August 16, 1799. See also Nancy Warner to Charity Bryant, December 3, 1799. BDP.

20. Lydia Richards to Charity Bryant, October 26, 1799. BDP.

21. Lydia Richards to Charity Bryant, August 15, 1799. BDP.

22. Charity Bryant to Sarah Snell Bryant, September 13, 1800. BBFP.

23. Samuel Richardson, "Pamela, or Virtue Rewarded," *The Novelist's Magazine* (London, 1786), 20:551. This line comes immediately before the lines of poetry Charity quoted in her letter to Sally Bryant. The line varies in different editions of the novel.

24. Lydia Richards to Charity Bryant, November 1, 1800. BDP.

25. On the culture of early American women's writing see Pattie Cowell, *Women Poets in Pre-Revolutionary America 1650–1775: An Anthology* (Troy, N.Y.: The Whitson Publishing Company, 1981); Catherine La Courreye Blecki and Karin A. Wulf, eds., *Milcah Martha Moore's Book: A Commonplace Book from Revolutionary America* (Philadelphia: Pennsylvania State University Press, 1997); Hugh Amory and David D. Hall, *A History of the Book in America: The Colonial Book in the Atlantic World* (New York: Cambridge University Press, 2000), 1:148; Shira Wolosky, "Modest Claims," in *The Cambridge History of American Literature*, Vol. 4: *Nineteenth-Century Poetry*, 1800–1910, ed. Sacvan Bercovitch (New York: Cambridge University Press, 2004), 155–99; Angela Vietto, *Women and Authorship in Revolutionary America* (Burlington: Ashgate, 2006). Strictures on women's publication loosened in the nineteenth century, but Nathaniel Hawthorne's infamous slander against "scribbling women" revealed the persistence of negative attitudes toward women writers.

26. Lavinia Brainerd to Charity Bryant, June 5, 1814. BDP. For Lavinia's biography see David Dudley Field, *The Genealogy of the Brainerd Family in the United States: With Numerous Sketches of Individuals* (New York: John F. Trow, 1857), 197–98.

27. Charity Bryant, "Love, Youth, Death." BDP.

28. Charity Bryant, "Dartmouth, February 26, 1798." BDP.

29. Charity Bryant, "Bridgewater November 1800"; Charity Bryant, "Oh I reflect how hard my fate. December 1800." BDP. Charity's older sister Ruth adapted hymn meter even before her sister. See Cleves, "'Heedless Youth.'" Several of Charity's relatives settled in Amherst, Massachusetts, where Dickinson was raised. Charity's grandnieces knew Dickinson; Mabel Loomis Todd, ed., *Letters of Emily Dickinson* (New York: Dover Press, 2003), 83.

30. "'Queen Mary's Lamentation' to Miss Charity Bryant from her friend M. A. B."

31. M. A. B., "Where now are all my flattering dreams." BDP.

32. Mary Hovey to Charity Bryant, August 22, 1809. BDP.

33. "To Sensibility." BDP.

34. Mary Hovey to Charity Bryant, August 22, 1809. BDP.

35. Maria Clark to Charity Bryant, August 16, 1799. BDP.

36. Maria Clark to Charity Bryant, August 16, 1799; Sarah Fielding, *The Governess, or the Little Female Academy*, (Teddington: The Echo Library, 2008), 70. Although the poem praises virtue, its speaker is later revealed to be a trickster, leaving open the question of whether the poem's message should be trusted. Maria's choice of the lines may have expressed a certain ambivalence about the lip service given to virtue in genteel women's culture.

37. Lydia Richards to Charity Bryant, January 5, 1800. BDP.

38. Lydia Richards to Charity Bryant, "No 2d" [note written on envelope]. Lydia's second letter to Charity is dated August 21, 1799. This envelope probably accompanied the letter. BDP.

39. Lydia Richards, "Acrostic for Charity Bryant," September 4, 1806. BDP.

40. Charity Bryant, "Acrostic to Patty Fling," January 1, 1801; Charity Bryant, "Acrostic for Rhoda Ayres," October 31, 1806; Charity Bryant, "Anna Hayden" [undated]; Charity Bryant, "Peggy Fling" [undated]; Charity Bryant, Susannah Shaw acrostic, undated; Charity Bryant, Polly Hayward Acrostic, undated [ca. 1805]. BDP.

41. "What's Fickle." BDP; Robert K. Dodge, ed. *A Topical Index of Early U.S. Almanacs, 1776–1800* (Westport, Conn.: Greenwood Press, 1997), 90.

CHAPTER 5

1. Charity described this gathering in a poem to Lydia Richards written in 1846; Charity Bryant, "I have been young" (April 24, 1846). The encounter is also recalled by Lydia's sister; Sarah Mack to Charity Bryant, June 27, 1846. BDP. There were three guests invited to Lydia Richards's house. The identification of the other two guests as Maria Clark and Nancy Warner is an educated guess; all four young women taught schools locally and became friends that summer.

2. Maria Clark to Charity Bryant, June 15, 1800. BDP.

3. Bernard and Vinovskis, "Female School Teacher in Ante-Bellum Massachusetts," 332–45. Nonetheless, more than one of Charity's married friends and relatives took teaching jobs out of economic necessity. Charity's older sister Anna Kingman worked as a teacher in the 1790s even after marrying; Anna Kingman to Charity Bryant, May 25, 1797. BDP.

4. Moore, *Sister Arts*. See also Clare Lyons, *Sex Among the Rabble: An Intimate History of Gender and Power in the Age of Revolution, Philadelphia, 1730–1830* (Chapel Hill: University of North Carolina Press, 2006); Richard Godbeer, *The Sexual Revolution in Early America* (Baltimore: Johns Hopkins University Press, 2002). Mark E. Kann discusses attempts to police this new spirit of sexual experimentation in Mark E. Kann, *Taming Passions for the Public Good: Policing Sex in the Early Republic* (New York: New York University Press, 2013). Even earlier, in colonial Philadelphia, unmarried women teachers established an exciting intellectual milieu; Wulf, *Not All Wives*, 45–50.

5. For histories that note this trope see Elizabeth Susan Wahl, *Invisible Relations: Representations of Female Intimacy in the Age of Enlightenment* (Stanford: Stanford University Press, 1999); Emma Donoghue, *Passions between Women: British Lesbian Culture, 1668–1801* (New York: Harper Perennial, 1993). For sample primary sources that warn against, or indulge in fantasies of, schoolgirl lesbianism see Francis Grose, *A Classical Dictionary of the Vulgar Tongue* (London: S. Hooper, 1785), 52; Henry Thomas Kitchener, *Letters on Marriage, on the Causes of Matrimonial Infidelity, and on the Reciprocal Relations of the Sex* (London: C. Chapple, 1812); "Masturbation," *Boston Medical and Surgical Journal* 27 (1843).

6. For example, Patricia Cline Cohen, *The Murder of Helen Jewett: The Life and Death of a Prostitute in Nineteenth-Century New York* (New York: Vintage, 1998), chapter 3.

7. Patricia Cline Cohen, Timothy J. Gilfoyle, and Helen Lefkowitz Horowitz, eds., *The Flash Press: Sporting Male Weeklies in 1840s New York* (Chicago: University of Chicago Press, 2008), 22.

8. Vicinus, "Lesbian History"; Karen V. Hansen, "'No *Kisses* Is Like Youres': An Erotic Friendship between Two African-American Women during the Mid-Nineteenth Century," in *Lesbian Subjects: A Feminist Studies Reader*, ed. Martha Vicinus (Bloomington: Indiana University Press, 1996), 178–207; Moore, *Sister Arts*, 145–52.

9. Guild, *Ancestors and Descendants of Josiah Snell Copeland and Katharine Guild*, 21. Sampson married Benjamin Gannett, whose brother Josiah married a Howard, from Charity's mother's family. Gannett was also connected to Bryant through the Snell family.

10. Herman Mann, *The Female Review: Or, Memoirs of an American Young Lady; Whose Life and Character Are Peculiarly Distinguished—Being a Continental Soldier, for Nearly Three Years, in the Late American War* (Dedham, 1797); Alfred F. Young, *Masquerade: The Life and Times of Deborah Sampson, Continental Soldier* (New York: Vintage, 2004).

11. Anna Kingman to Charity Bryant, August 20, 1797. BDP.

12. Eliza [Hull?] to Charity Bryant, January 15, 1798. BDP.

13. Maria Clark to Charity Bryant, August 16, 1799. BDP.

14. Maria Clark to Charity Bryant, December 9, 1799. BDP.

15. Maria Clark to Charity Bryant, July 30, 1799. BDP. Dorinda Catesby, *Ermina; or the Fair Recluse* (W. Payne, 1789). The name also appeared in a sentimental passage from a popular letter-writing manual of the time; *The Complete Letter-Writer. Containing Familiar Letters on the Most Common Occasions in Life* (Boston: John W. Folsom, 1794), 179–83.

16. Maria Clark to Charity Bryant, August 16, 1799. BDP.

17. Maria Clark to Charity Bryant, September 2, 1799. BDP.

18. Maria Clark to Charity Bryant, August 25, 1799. BDP.

19. Charity Bryant, "I have been young."

20. Lydia Richards to Charity Bryant, August 15, 1799. BDP.

21. Lydia Richards to Charity Bryant, November 23, 1799. BDP.

22. Lydia Richards to Charity Bryant, October 18, 1799; Lydia Richards to Charity Bryant, September 28, 1799. BDP.

23. Charity Bryant, "Lovely in Person" [ca. 1801]. BDP.

24. Moore, *Sister Arts*, chapter 3. For a few examples of Seward's poems appearing in newspapers see "Epitaph on Hannah," *The Independent Journal*, May 18, 1785; "The Country Maid. A Pastoral," *The Diary of Loudon's Register*, September 26, 1792; "The Muses," *Farmer's Weekly Museum*, May 3, 1803. For examples of her poetry in period collections see the 1802, 1803, 1804, and 1807 editions of *The Poetical Register, and Repository of Fugitive Poetry* (London). The New York *Commercial Advertiser* listed her book of *Sonnets* for sale in 1801. Catalogues from the Library Company of Philadelphia in the early nineteenth century include Anna Seward.

25. Lydia Richards to Charity Bryant, September 28, 1799. BDP.

26. Eliza to Charity Bryant, January 1798. BDP.

27. Eliza to Charity Bryant, January 15, 1798. BDP.

28. Eliza to Charity Bryant, January 1798. BDP.

29. Eliza to Charity Bryant, May 14, 1798. BDP.

30. Eliza to Charity Bryant, January 1798. BDP.

31. [Mercy Ford] to Charity Bryant, February 3, 1799. The letter is unsigned, but handwriting and context strongly indicate Ford as the author. Mercy expressed a similar sentiment in Mercy Ford to Charity Bryant, August 23, 1801. BDP.

32. Eliza to Charity Bryant, May 14, 1798. BDP.

33. Eliza to Charity Bryant, January 27, 1799. BDP.

34. Maria Clark to Charity Bryant, December 9, 1799. BDP.

35. Maria Clark to Charity Bryant, July 30, 1799. In the letter Maria describes her views on friendship as in agreement with the views Charity expressed in a previous letter. BDP.

36. Moore, "'Something More Tender Still Than Friendship,'" 499–520; Liz Stanley, "Romantic Friendship? Some Issues in Researching Lesbian History and Biography," *Women's History Review* 1, no. 2 (1992): 193–216; Sharon Marcus, *Between Women: Friendship, Desire, and Marriage in Victorian England* (Princeton, N.J.: Princeton University Press, 2007); Leila Rupp, *Sapphistries: A Global History of Love between Women* (New York: New York University Press, 2009); Moore, *Sister Arts*.

37. Catesby, *Ermina; or the Fair Recluse*. For additional examples of the role played by friends in (failed) courtship novels see Foster, *The Coquette*; Rowson, *Charlotte Temple*.

38. Marcus, *Between Women*.

39. Helena Whitbread, ed., *I Know My Own Heart: The Diaries of Anne Lister 1791–1840* (New York: New York University Press, 1992). Also Hansen, "No *Kisses* Is Like Youres." Older scholarship was more doubtful about whether romantic friends ever became sexual partners: Faderman, *Surpassing the Love of Men*; Smith-Rosenberg, "Female World of Love and Ritual."

40. John Mannock, *The Poor Man's Catechism; or, the Christian Doctrine Explained*, first American ed. (Baltimore: Bernard Dornin, 1815), 149, 298–99.

41. Wahl, *Invisible Relations*; Donoghue, *Passions between Women*; Kristin M. Comment, "Charles Brockden Brown's *Ormond* and Lesbian Possibility in the Early Republic," *Early American Literature* 40, no. 1 (2005): 57–78; Clare Lyons, "Mapping an Atlantic Sexual Culture: Homoeroticism in Eighteenth-Century Philadelphia," *William and Mary Quarterly* 60 (2003): 119–54; Thomas A. Foster, *Sex and the Eighteenth-Century Man: Massachusetts and the History of Sexuality in America* (Boston: Beacon Press, 2006).

42. Martha Tomhave Blauvelt, *The Work of the Heart: Young Women and Emotion, 1780–1830* (Charlottesville: University of Virginia Press, 2007), chapter 5.

43. Emma Donoghue, *Inseparable: Desire between Women in Literature* (New York: Alfred A. Knopf, 2010); Whitbread, *I Know My Own Heart*, 24–25.

44. On honor culture, see Joanne B. Freeman, *Affairs of Honor: National Politics in the New Republic* (New Haven, Conn.: Yale University Press, 2001).

45. Maria comments on Charity's modest dress; Maria Clark to Charity Bryant, September 2, 1799. BDP.

46. Lydia Richards to Charity Bryant, October 12, 1807. See also Lydia Richards to Charity Bryant, September 18, 1811. BDP.

47. "A Society of Patriotic Ladies at Edenton, North Carolina" (London, 1775).

48. "Letter to D'Israeli," *The Lady's Magazine or Evening Companion for the Fair Sex* (London, 1795), 452–53. See also Susan Branson, *These Fiery, Frenchified Dames: Women and Political Culture in Early National Philadelphia* (Philadelphia: University of Pennsylvania Press, 2001).

49. The quotation is included within Robert Christy, *Proverbs, Maxims, and Phrases of All Ages* (New York, 1887), 482. Although the quotation comes from one of Shakespeare's less popular plays, *Troilus and Cressida*, it circulated within readers and periodicals such as *The Lady's Magazine; or Evening Companion for the Fair Sex* (London, 1790), 629.

50. Donoghue, *Passions between Women*.

51. The peak of this trend came for New England women born during the Civil War, more than 20 percent of whom remained unmarried for life; Lee Virginia Chambers-Schiller, *Liberty, a Better Husband: Single Women in America: The Generations of 1780–1840* (New Haven, Conn.:

Yale University Press, 1984). Some disagree with viewing antebellum spinsterhood as an anti-marital choice; Zsuzsa Berend, " 'The Best or None!' Spinsterhood in Nineteenth-Century New England," *Journal of Social History* 33, no. 4 (2000): 935–57. Charity's consciousness of negative attitudes toward single women in Massachusetts is discussed in Peter Bryant to Charity Bryant, February 13, 1819. HBFP. Historians have debated whether "spinsters" constituted a proto-lesbian identity category. For a recent reflection on the lesbian quality of the "spinster aesthetic," see Heather Love, "Gyn/Apology: Sarah Orne Jewett's Spinster Aesthetics," *ESQ: A Journal of the American Renaissance* 55, no. 3–4 (2009): 305–34.

52. Freeman, *Affairs of Honor*, 69, 162. Young women and men in Charity's generation penned instructive poems and aphorisms on the dangers of gossip into their copybooks. See, for example, the entry "slander" in the Guernsey Letters collection. CCC.

53. Bullough and Voght, "Homosexuality and Its Confusion with the 'Secret Sin,' " 144.

54. Vicinus, "Lesbian History."

55. Anna Kingman to Charity Bryant, June 1798. BDP.

56. Eliza to Charity Bryant, May 14, 1798. BDP.

57. Eliza to Charity Bryant, June 21, 1798. BDP.

58. Eliza to Charity Bryant, August 15, 1798. BDP.

59. Eliza to Charity Bryant, June 16, 1799; Eliza to Charity, December 21, 1800. BDP.

60. Charity Bryant, "Long Before Adam or his Eve" [Dartmouth]. The original version of this poem was published in Charles Hutton, *The Diarian Miscellany: Consisting of All the Useful and Entertaining Parts, Both Mathematical and Poetical, Extracted from the Ladies' Diary, from the Beginning of That Work in the Year 1704, Down to the End of Year 1773* (London: G. Robinson, 1775), 291.

61. Charity Bryant, "A Poem to a Friend" (February 26, 1798). BDP.

62. "The Suicide," BDP. The original was published in 1797. Thomas Day, *The Suicide. A Dialogue Exhibited on the Stage at the Public Commencement of Yale-College, Sept 13th. M.Dcc. Xcvii* (Litchfield, Conn.: T. Collier, 1797).

63. Maria Clark to Charity Bryant, August 16, 1799. BDP.

64. Lydia Richards to Charity Bryant, September 10, 1801. BDP.

65. Nancy Warner to Charity Bryant, No. 2; Nancy Warner to Charity Bryant, No. 3. BDP. For the account of Nancy's later life see Theron Baldwin, *Historical Address Delivered in Monticello, Illinois, June 27, 1855, at the Seventeenth Anniversary of Monticello Female Seminary* (New York: J. F. Trow, 1855), 18–19. For young women's participation in the Second Great Awakening see Nancy Cott, "Young Women in the Second Great Awakening in New England," *Feminist Studies* 3, no. 1/2 (1975): 15–29.

66. Nancy Warner to Charity Bryant, December 5, 1799. BDP.

67. Nancy Warner to Charity Bryant, December 24, 1799. BDP.

68. Nancy Warner to Charity Bryant, January 18, 1800. BDP.

69. Nancy Warner to Charity Bryant, December 5, 1799. BDP.

70. Charity Bryant to Sally Bryant, September 13, 1801. BBFP.

71. Charity Bryant, "Winter" (December 1800). BDP.

72. Lydia Richards to Charity Bryant, November 1, 1800. BDP.

73. Charity Bryant, "Spring" (May 1801). BDP.

74. Charity Bryant, "Now sinks my soul," BDP. Charity wrote a fourth acrostic on Nancy Warner's name before the dissolution of the friendship. Not included with the winter–spring

cycle, the earlier acrostic praised Nancy's religious fidelity; Charity Bryant, "A suppos'd Voice from the Grave!" BDP.

75. Charity Bryant, "Dear N---y." BDP.

76. *Brief Biographies of the figurines on display in the Illinois state historical library* (Springfield, Illinois, 1932), 44; Baldwin, *Historical Address Delivered at Monticello*, 18–19.

77. Charity Bryant to Sally Bryant, September 13, 1801. Charity complained of this again the following year, Charity Bryant to Sally Bryant, October 19, 1802. BBFP.

78. Lydia Richards to Charity Bryant, January 6, 1801; Lydia Richards to Charity Bryant, November 1, 1800. BDP.

79. Charity Bryant to Sarah Snell Bryant, September 13, 1800. BBFP.

CHAPTER 6

1. Sylvia's attendance at school in winter 1800–1801 is noted by Asaph Hayward to Sylvia Drake, Weybridge, February 14, 1801. BDP. The presence of coal-burning stoves in Vermont classrooms at the turn of the nineteenth century is from "I find from recent accounts," *Spooner's Vermont Journal*, February 1, 1803.

2. E. Jennifer Monaghan, *Learning to Read and Write in Colonial America* (Amherst: University of Massachusetts Press, 2005).

3. Chaffin, *History of the Town of Easton, Massachusetts*, 380–91.

4. "Heads of Acts Passed during the Last Session of the Legislature of Massachusetts," *The Medley, or Newbedford Marine Journal*, March 15, 1799; "Bridgewater Academy," *Columbian Centinel*, July 23, 1800; "Exhibition; Senior Class; Bridgewater Academy," *The Democrat*, August 27, 1806.

5. "In the days of yore," *Spooner's Vermont Journal*, July 9, 1805.

6. Kelley, *Learning to Stand and Speak*; Sklar, "The Schooling of Girls."

7. Washington, *History of Weybridge*.

8. H. P. Smith, ed., *History of Addison County, Vermont* (Syracuse: D. Mason & Co., 1886), 411.

9. One old-timer recorded in Samuel Swift's 1859 history of Middlebury recalled receiving instruction from Idea Strong in 1800; Samuel Swift, *History of the Town of Middlebury, in the County of Addison, Vermont* (Middlebury: A. H. Copeland, 1859), 208. The first mention of Strong's Academy in the *Middlebury Mercury* appears on March 3, 1802.

10. "Young Ladies' Academy," *Middlebury Mercury*, November 3, 1802.

11. "Died," *Middlebury Mercury*, October 3, 1804.

12. Emma Willard, *Journal and Letters: From France and Great-Britain* (Troy, N.Y.: N. Tuttle, 1833); Kelley, *Learning to Stand and Speak*, 86–89. Pierce's Litchfield Academy also taught these subjects by 1814, and most other female academies followed suit in the 1820s.

13. SDD, April 6, 1836.

14. Kelley, *Learning to Stand and Speak*, 32.

15. Asaph Hayward to Sylvia Drake, February 14, 1801. BDP.

16. "Advertisement Extra!!" *Middlebury Mercury*, September 10, 1806.

17. "Autobiography of Asaph Drake." DFP.

18. Stephen West, *Sketches of the Life of the Late Rev. Samuel Hopkins, D.D. Pastor of the First Congregational Church in Newport, Written by Himself* (Hartford: Hudson and Goodwin, 1805),

24–25; Joseph Conforti, "Samuel Hopkins and the New Divinity: Theology, Ethics, and Social Reform in Eighteenth-Century New England," *William and Mary Quarterly* 34, no. 4 (1977): 572–89.

19. Chaffin, *History of the Town of Easton, Massachusetts*, 264.

20. Asaph Hayward to Sylvia Drake, February 14, 1801. BDP.

21. 1st Federal Census, reel 51, sheets 50, 120.

22. Swift, *History of the Town of Middlebury*, 333.

23. "Mrs. Lovina Wainwright," *Woodstock Observer*, May 8, 1821.

24. SDD, April 11, 1821.

25. Polly Hayward to Sylvia Drake, June 29, 1801. BDP. It is unclear where Polly learned to write as well as she did. She was more literate than her brother Asaph, suggesting that she did not gain her learning within the family.

26. Samuel Danforth, *The Cry of Sodom Enquired into; Upon Occasion of the Arraignment and Condemnation of Benjamin Goad, for His Prodigious Villany* (Cambridge, Mass.: Marmaduke Johnson, 1674), 3.

27. Polly Hayward to Sylvia Drake, October 31, 1804. BDP.

28. "Autobiography of Asaph Drake." DFP.

29. Achsah Hayward to Sylvia Drake, May 1, 1803; Achsah Hayward to Sylvia Drake, November 13, 1803; Achsah Hayward to Sylvia Drake, November 14, 1804; Achsah Hayward to Sylvia Drake, June 4, 1805; Achsah Hayward to Sylvia Drake, February 3, 1805. BDP.

30. Achsah Hayward to Sylvia Drake, May 1, 1803; Achsah Hayward to Sylvia Drake, November 13, 1803. BDP.

31. Achsah Hayward to Sylvia Drake, November 13, 1803. BDP.

32. Polly Hayward to Sylvia Drake, June 10, 1804. BDP.

33. Sylvia Drake to Mary Drake, May 9, 1813. DFP.

34. Solomon Drake, "Copy Book" (1833). DFP. The famous pedagogue Noah Webster included Pope's quotation in his early national "reader," widely circulated in New England; Noah Webster, *An American Selection of Lessons in Reading and Speaking. Calculated to Improve the Minds and Refine the Taste of Youth. And Also, to Instruct Them in the Geography, History, and Politics of the United States* (Boston: Thomas and Andrews, 1790), 219.

35. Appleby, *Inheriting the Revolution*, 3.

CHAPTER 7

1. Charity Bryant to Sarah Snell Bryant, September 13, 1800. BBFP. Charity's sister Silence Bryant's marriage date and the dates of her children's births can be found in Smith, "Descendants of Stephen Bryant of Plymouth."

2. For the profile, see SSBD, May 8, 1799. For the receipt of Charity's letter, see SSBD, November 18, 1800.

3. Charity Bryant to Sarah Snell Bryant, September 13, 1800. BBFP.

4. "The New Recruit, or the Gallant Volunteer, a New Song," *Pennsylvania Packet or the General Advertiser*, April 8, 1778.

5. For the celebration of marriage and motherhood see Kerber, *Women of the Republic*; January Lewis, "The Republican Wife: Virtue and Seduction in the Early Republic," *William and Mary Quarterly* 44, no. 4 (1987): 689–721. For the rise of ideals of romantic love see Karen

Lystra, *Searching the Heart: Women, Men, and Romantic Love in Nineteenth-Century America* (New York: Oxford University Press, 1989).

6. In addition to Sarah Snell Bryant's letter asking Charity if she was to marry soon, see Peter Bryant's similar question in Peter Bryant to Charity Bryant, November 13, 1804. BDP. Peter's remarks at this subsequent date indicate that the family was not entirely willing to believe Charity's 1800 announcement.

7. Vesta Guild to Charity Bryant, February 23, 1814. BDP.

8. Terri L. Premo, *Winter Friends: Women Growing Old in the New Republic, 1785–1835* (Urbana: University of Illinois Press, 1990), 38–47; Foster, *Sex and the Eighteenth-Century Man.*

9. Solomon Drake copybook, December 22, 1833. DFP.

10. Wulf, *Not All Wives*; Chambers-Schiller, *Liberty, a Better Husband.*

11. Charity Bryant, "Blest be this Mansion," June 1801. BDP.

12. Zsuzsa Berend has argued that many nineteenth-century women remained single because their romantic ideal of marriage caused them to refuse a compromise match; Berend, "'The Best or None!'".

13. Maria Clark to Charity Bryant, December 17, 1799; Maria Clark to Charity Bryant, June 15, 1800. BDP.

14. Herman Mann, *The Female Review* (Bedford, Mass.: Applewood Books, 2009), 174–75. Despite Mann's allusion to an erotic component within the relationship, he assured readers that since Deborah did not possess a penis she was unequipped to penetrate Fatima, and no true harm resulted ("incapacity . . . must render her in this respect unimpeachable").

15. Eliza to Charity Bryant, May 29, 1798; Eliza to Charity Bryant, January 27, 1799. BDP.

16. Anna Kingman to Charity Bryant, August 26, 1799. BDP. Anna just records receiving the letter from Mr. Fobes; she's not specific if it is Philander Fobes.

17. Charity Bryant to Sally Snell, November 9, 1800; Charity Bryant to Sally Snell, September 13, 1801. BBDP.

18. Charity Bryant to Sally Bryant, September 13, 1800. BBDP.

19. Gelles, "Gossip: An Eighteenth-Century Case."

20. Smith and Hindus, "Premarital Pregnancy in America"; John D'Emilio and Estelle B. Freedman, *Intimate Matters: A History of Sexuality in America*, 2nd ed. (Chicago: University of Chicago Press, 1997), 43.

21. Cyrus and Polly's marriage date and Zibby's birth date are recorded in *Vital Records of Bridgewater*, 1:60, 2:64.

22. Brockton, Mass. Christ Congregational Church, UCC Records, 1738–1980. ACAL.

23. Brockton, Mass. Christ Congregational Church, UCC Records, 1738–1980. ACAL.

24. Bristol County Court of Common Pleas Court of General Sessions of the Peace. MJA.

25. Gelles, "Gossip: An Eighteenth-Century Case."

26. Peter Bryant to Charity Bryant, November 13, 1804. BDP.

27. Anna Kingman to Charity Bryant, December 1809. BDP.

28. Silence Bryant to Charity Bryant, 1807; Silence Bryant to Charity Bryant, July 2, 1809; Anna Kingman to Charity Bryant, July 12, 1809. BDP.

29. Whitbread, *I Know My Own Heart*, xxv.

30. Anna Hayden to Charity Bryant, June 1, 1806. BDP.

31. Anna Kingman apologized profusely when Henry opened a letter and "put a name in it" against her permission. Anna Kingman to Charity Bryant, October 13, 1802. BDP.

32. Charity Bryant, "A good name is better than riches" (1800). BDP.

33. PCPR, 38:131.

CHAPTER 8

1. Mercy Ford to Charity Bryant, May 5, 1805. BDP.

2. Charity Bryant to Sally Bryant, September 16, 1801. BBFP.

3. Charity Bryant to Sally Bryant, November 9, 1800; Charity Bryant to Sally Bryant, September 16, 1801. BBFP; Lydia Richards to Charity Bryant, May 24, 1801. BDP.

4. *Vital Records of Pembroke Massachusetts to the Year 1850* (Boston: New England Historic Genealogical Society, 1911), 84–85. Mercy Ford's name had several alternate spellings: her first name was sometimes written Marcy, and her last name sometimes was spelled Foord. In the signature on her letters she seems to have preferred Mercy Ford. Mercy Ford [?] to Charity Bryant, February 3, 1799, records that sister Thankful Ford had been sent to work at Mr. Silas Snow's.

5. [?] Bridgewater, to Charity Bryant, February 3, 1799. The author of this letter isn't labeled, but clues within the text including the reference to Thankful Ford as "Thanky," and the signature "Adieu," indicate that Mercy Ford was its author. Also Mercy Ford to Charity Bryant, April 22, 1803. BDP.

6. Mercy Ford to Charity Bryant, April 22, 1803. BDP. Sadly, Mercy had little more power at work than she had at home. Her subordination to her employers sometimes put her at risk. In one household, Mercy seems to have suffered the unwanted attentions of her master. "My situation is truly dangerous," she confided to Charity. "I determine to leave it at least for a while and seek a more agreeable one." Returning home, she escaped from danger but came once again under the heavy hand of her mother. Mercy Ford to Charity Bryant, November 13, 1803; Mercy Ford to Charity Bryant, October 20, 1804. BDP.

7. Charity Bryant, "Accept dear. . . . from a heart sincere." BDP. The poem is undated, but it echoes a June 1801 poem for Anna Kingman and was likely written during the same period. The use of five dashes for the recipient in the opening and closing lines leaves open the question of its intended recipient. Mercy was Charity's most proximate friend at the time and likely the poem's recipient. See also Charity Bryant, "In Prosperous Gales," June 1801, BDP.

8. Charity Bryant to Sally Bryant, September 13, 1801; Charity Bryant to Sally Bryant, November 9, 1800. BBFP.

9. Charity Bryant, "Accept dear. . . . From a heart sincere." BDP.

10. Peter Bryant to Charity Bryant, November 13, 1804. BDP.

11. Mercy Ford to Charity Bryant, July 1804. BDP.

12. Mercy Ford to Charity Bryant, August 23, 1801. This letter, numbered 28, comes from the sequence of correspondence that has gone missing. BDP.

13. Patricia Anderson, *When Passion Reigned: Sex and the Victorians* (New York: Basic Books, 1995), 8.

14. R. J. Brodie, *The Secret Companion, a Medical Work on Onanism or Self-Pollution* (London, 1845), 12.

15. Anderson, *When Passion Reigned.*

16. Mercy Ford to Charity Bryant, November 20, 1804. BDP.

17. Whitbread, *I Know My Own Heart*; Judith Halberstam, *Female Masculinity* (Durham: Duke University Press, 1998), 70–71; Helena Whitbread, ed., *No Priest but Love: The Journals of Anne Lister from 1824–1826* (New York: New York University Press, 1988).

18. Mercy Ford to Charity Bryant, June 4, 1808. BDP.

19. Mercy Ford to Charity Bryant, September 10, 1804. Mercy also used French in her letters to Charity by signing them "adieu." BDP.

20. Mercy Ford to Charity Bryant, April 23, 1805. BDP.

21. Mercy Ford to Charity Bryant, May 1805. BDP.

22. Mercy Ford to Charity Bryant, May 1805. BDP.

23. Lydia Richards to Charity Bryant, May 24, 1805. BDP.

24. Mercy Ford to Charity Bryant, September 5, 1805. BDP.

25. Account of her Travels by Charity Bryant, April 9, 1844. BDP.

26. Peter Bryant to Charity Bryant, November 13, 1804. BDP.

27. Anna Kingman to Charity Bryant, February 12, 1805. BDP.

CHAPTER 9

1. She rejected suitors in 1802 and 1808; Lydia Richards to Charity Bryant, February 21, 1802; Lydia Richards to Charity Bryant, January 3, 1808. BDP.

2. Lydia describes her happiness at teaching and her lack of time for writing while at home in Lydia Richards to Charity Bryant, August 6, 1800. See further references to her teaching experiences in Lydia Richards to Charity Brant, September 10, 1801; Lydia Richards to Charity Bryant, October 9, 1802; Lydia Richards to Charity Bryant, September 17, 1803; Lydia Richards to Charity Bryant, May 24, 1805; Lydia Richards to Charity Bryant, January 25, 1806; Lydia Richards to Charity Bryant, June 14, 1807. BDP.

3. Lydia Richards to Charity Bryant, November 22, 1806. BDP.

4. Charity Bryant, "Recollections and Reflections Occasion'd by the following sentence written in a Letter from a Friend, April 24, 1846: 'I have been young but now I am Old'" (1846). BDP.

5. Lydia Richards, "My Charity," included in Lydia Richards to Charity Bryant, May 24, 1801. BDP.

6. Charity Bryant to Sally Bryant, November 24, 1804. BBFP.

7. Lydia Richards to Charity Bryant, October 26, 1799. BDP.

8. S. R. Mack to Charity Bryant, December 9, 1846. This letter from Lydia's sister describes how Lydia used to read "parts" of the letters aloud when Charity and Lydia first became acquainted. BDP.

9. Lydia Richards to Charity Bryant, September 17, 1803. BDP.

10. Lydia Richards to Charity Bryant, February 21, 1802. BDP.

11. Lydia Richards to Charity Bryant, September 17, 1803. BDP.

12. "Forbidden love" is equated with prostitution and adultery in *Sermons and other Practical Works of the Late Reverend and Learned Mr. Ralph Erskine* (Falkirk, 1796), 10:496. For a reference to sodomy as forbidden love see the observation that soldiers in a standing army "acquired a taste for the pleasures of forbidden love, [and] they would either not marry at all or marry later than their ancestors," in John Pinkerton, *General Collection of the Best and Most Interesting Voyages and Travels in All Parts of the World* (London, 1809), 6:115.

13. Lydia Richards to Charity Bryant, October 21, 1804. BDP.

14. Lydia Richards to Charity Bryant, May 24, 1805. BDP.

15. Lydia Richards to Charity Bryant, January 25, 1806. BDP.

16. Account of her Travels by Charity Bryant, April 9, 1844. BDP.

17. Vesta Guild to Charity Bryant, July 18, 1806. BDP.

18. Vesta Guild to Charity Bryant, December 28, 1806. BDP.

19. Peter Bryant to Charity Bryant, August 4, 1806. HBFP.

20. Lydia Richards to Charity Bryant, July 5, 1806. BDP. It is unclear whom Lydia is quoting with the phrase "in prospect smiles," perhaps a missing poem by Charity. Notably, William Cullen Bryant later used this phrase in his 1815 poem "On Death"; Parke Godwin, *A Biography of William Cullen Bryant, with Extracts from His Private Correspondence* (New York: D. Appleton and Company, 1883), 132.

21. SSBD, August 14, 1806.

22. Hansen, "No *Kisses* Is Like Youres." It is unclear from the letter whether Brown meant a particular breast by the phrase "favorite one" or whether the term was possibly a euphemism for her genitals.

23. Lystra, *Searching the Heart*, 62–64.

24. Donoghue, *Passions between Women*; Wahl, *Invisible Relations*; John Cleland, *Memoirs of a Woman of Pleasure* (New York: Oxford University Press, 1985); Halberstam, *Female Masculinity*. As Judith Butler puts it, "The phallus can be symbolized by an arm, a tongue, a hand (or two), a knee, a thigh, a pelvic bone, an array of purposefully instrumentalized body-like things." Judith Butler, *Bodies That Matter: On the Discursive Limits Of "Sex"* (New York: Routledge, 1993), 55.

25. Lydia Richards to Charity Bryant, December 3, 1806. BDP.

26. Lydia Richards to Charity Bryant, September 4, 1806. BDP.

27. Lydia Richards to Charity Bryant, September 4, 1806. BDP.

28. Lydia Richards to Charity Bryant, September 5, 1806. BDP.

29. Lydia Richards to Charity Bryant, September 17, 1806. BDP.

30. Lydia Richards to Charity Bryant, October 27, 1806. BDP.

31. Lydia Richards to Charity Bryant, October 30, 1806. BDP.

32. SSBD, November 13, 1806.

33. After his in-laws' deaths in 1813, Peter Bryant wrote to Charity "you may now be assured none are *now* covered by my roof who would not rejoice to see you," Peter Bryant to Charity Bryant, June 9, 1814. HBFP. William Cullen Bryant describes Ebenezer Snell in his autobiography, included in Godwin, *Biography of William Cullen Bryant*.

34. Peter Bryant to Charity Bryant, October 14, 1807. HBFP.

35. Among the tasks Sally listed performing in the fall of 1806, without Charity's help, were washing, mending, ironing, picking wool, baking, cheese-making, and brewing; SSBD, September–December 1806.

36. Lydia Richards to Charity Bryant, November 22, 1806. BDP.

37. Lydia Richards to Charity Bryant, May 24, 1801. BDP.

38. Lydia Richards to Charity Bryant, November 22, 1806. BDP.

39. Lydia Richards to Charity Bryant, September 29, 1806. BDP.

40. Elizabeth Mavor, *The Ladies of Llangollen: A Study in Romantic Friendship* (London: Michael Joseph, 1971).

41. Anna Seward, *Llangollen Vale and Other Poems* (London: G. Sael, 1796); *The Poetical Register, and Repository of Fugitive Poetry, for 1802* (London, 1803), 84–87; Terry Castle, ed., *The Literature of Lesbianism: A Historical Anthology from Aristo to Stonewall* (New York: Columbia University Press, 2003), 339–43.

42. Lisa L. Moore, "The Swan of Litchfield: Sarah Pierce and the Lesbian Landscape Poem," in *Long before Stonewall: Histories of Same-Sex Sexuality in Early America*, ed. Thomas A. Foster (New York: New York University Press, 2007), 263.

43. Letters where Lydia uses the word include Lydia Richards to Charity Bryant, January 21, 1800; Lydia Richards to Charity Bryant, May 24, 1805; Lydia Richards to Charity Bryant, September 29, 1806. BDP. On Seward's use of the word "vale," see Moore, "Long before Stonewall"; Lisa L. Moore, "Queer Gardens: Mary Delaney's Flowers and Friendships," *Eighteenth-Century Studies* 39, no. 1 (2005): 49–70.

44. She used the word twice in her Monody on Major Andre, published in at least six American editions; *The Monody on Major Andre* was advertised for sale in the United States in the *Pennsylvania Packet*, December 15, 1790; *The General Advertiser and Political, Commercial, Agricultural and Literary Journal*, January 4, 1791; and *The Independent Gazetteer*, October 20, 1792. She used it twice more in her "Three Love Epistles," twice in a farewell poem to Butler and Ponsonby, and twice in a September 1799 sonnet about Llangollen: *The Poetical Register, and Repository of Fugitive Poetry for 1802* (London, 1803), 4, 7, 84, 85; *The Poetical Register, and Repository of Fugitive Poetry for 1804* (London, 1806), 376; "The Country Maid," *The Diary of Loudon's Register*, 26 September 1792. She also used the word frequently in her sonnets to women, including those to Honora Sneyd. "Vale" appears in thirteen of the sonnets in Seward's 1799 collection and in later sonnets devoted to women, like "The Country Maid" and "Song"; Sonnets V, VI, XVIII, XXIII, XXV, XXX, XLIV, LXXXVI, LXXXVIII, XCI, and three of the Horace translations. Anna Seward, *Original Sonnets on Various Subjects: And Odes Paraphrased from Horace* (London, 1799). "The Country Maid," *The Diary of Loudon's Register*, September 26, 1792; "Song," *The Poetical Register, and Repository of Fugitive Poetry for 1804* (London, 1806), 79.

45. "Song," *The Poetical Register, and Repository of Fugitive Poetry for* 1804 (London, 1806), 79.

46. Estelle Anna Lewis, *Records of the Heart* (New York, 1844), 111–17.

47. "Spring" by Lydia Richards, May 1804, copied for Miss Bryant, January 17, 1807. BDP.

48. Lydia Richards to Charity Bryant, November 30, 1806. BDP.

49. Lydia Richards to Charity Bryant, December 3, 1806. BDP.

50. Lydia Richards to Charity Bryant, December 1, 1806. BDP; Thomas Otway, *Venice Preserv'd: Or, a Plot Discover'd. A Tragedy* (London, 1766), 75.

51. Lydia Richards, "Poem for Miss CB, January 1, 1807." BDP.

52. SSBD, January 23, 1807. This was not the women's first trip away from Plainfield since Charity's arrival in early December. Sarah Snell Bryant records that Charity made a visit on December 29, 1807. Whether that visit was in Lydia's company is unclear.

53. Lydia Richards to Charity Bryant, January 26, 1807. BDP.

54. Asaph Hayward to Charity Briant [*sic*], June 22, 1806. BDP.

55. Lydia Richards to Charity Bryant, February 10, 1807. BDP.

56. Lydia Richards to Charity Bryant, July 21, 1807; August 23, 1807; October 12, 1807; November 3, 1807. BDP.

57. Lydia Richards to Charity Bryant, February 13, 1807. BDP.

58. Lydia Richards to Charity Bryant, March 15, 1807. BDP.

59. Lydia Richards to Charity Bryant, March 15, 1807. BDP.

60. Wrathall, "Provenance as Text"; Freedman, "'The Burning of Letters Continues.'"

61. Lydia Richards to Charity Bryant, March 15, 1807. BDP.

62. Daniel Scott Smith, "Parental Power and Marriage Patterns: An Analysis of Historical Trends in Hingham, Massachusetts," *Journal of Marriage and Family* 35, no. 3 (1973): 419–28.

63. Lydia Richards to Charity Bryant, June 14, 1807. BDP.

64. Lydia Richards to Charity Bryant, July 31, 1807. BDP.

65. Lydia Richards to Charity Bryant, November 3, 1807. BDP.

66. Lydia Richards to Charity Bryant, October 12, 1807. BDP.

67. Lydia Richards to Charity Bryant, October 12, 1807. BDP.

68. "Thou Glorious Orb," to Charity Bryant, Weybridge [undated]. BDP; Rowson, *Charlotte Temple*, 78.

69. Lydia may have made some effort to obscure her identity as the sender, since the copied poem is unsigned. The poem is in Lydia's handwriting, and the reverse side is superscribed, "to the care of Rev. Mr. S. Parsons." Lydia wrote earlier to Charity about sending her mail via "Dean Parsons of Goshen who propos'd taking a trip to Vermont" (the Rev. Silas Parsons from neighboring Goshen was a family friend). Lydia Richards to Charity Bryant, November 3, 1807. BDP. Daniel Oliver Morton, *Memoir of Rev. Levi Parsons* (Poultney, 1824), 30; Hiram Barrus, *History of the Town of Goshen, Hampshire County, Massachusetts, from Its First Settlement in 1761 to 1881* (Boston, 1881), 55.

70. Lydia Richards to Charity Bryant, January 8, 1808. BDP.

71. Lydia Richards to Charity Bryant, February 22, 1808. BDP.

72. Lydia Richards to Charity Bryant, March 29, 1808. BDP.

73. Lydia Richards to Charity Bryant, April 10, 1808. BDP.

74. Lydia Richards to Charity Bryant, May 30, 1808 [wrapper]. BDP.

75. Isaac Watts, *The Works of the Rev. Isaac Watts, D.D. in Nine Volumes* (Leeds: Edward Baines, 1813), 9:163.

76. Watts, *Works of the Rev. Isaac Watts, D.D. in Nine Volumes*, 9:132.

77. Watts, *Works of the Rev. Isaac Watts, D.D. in Nine Volumes*, 9:304.

78. James M. Winchell, ed., *An Arrangement of the Psalms, Hymns, and Spiritual Songs of the Rev. Isaac Watts, D.D.* (Boston: Lincoln & Edmands, 1820), cxix.

79. *The Missionary Herald, for the Year 1818* (Boston, 1818), 64.

80. Lydia Richards to Charity Bryant, September 20, 1808. BDP; "The Mourning-Piece," in Watts, *Works of the Rev. Isaac Watts, D.D. in Nine Volumes*, 9:283–90.

CHAPTER 10

1. Account of her Travels by Charity Bryant, April 9, 1844. BDP.

2. Peter Bryant quotes Charity in Peter Bryant to Charity Bryant, February 13, 1819. BDP.

3. Anna Hayden to Charity Bryant, February 15, 1807. BDP.

4. Asaph Hayward to Charity Bryant, January 18, 1807. BDP.

5. Asaph Hayward to Charity Bryant, June 22, 1806, notes that "Mrs. Hayward finds many inconveniences in our house and for the want of many things that we had before we came from Bridgwater." BDP.

6. "Hanover, January 30," *The North Star* [Vermont], February 10, 1807; "Montpelier: Monday, February 9, 1807," *The Precursor* [Vermont], February 9, 1807.

7. "Canandaigua, March 3," *Middlebury Mercury*, March 25, 1807; "Keene, (N.H.) January 24," *The Rutland Herald*, February 14, 1807; "Genesee," *The Rutland Herald*, April 4, 1807.

8. "Montpelier: Monday, March 30, 1807," *The Precursor*, March 30, 1807; "Montpelier: April 6, 1807," *The Precursor*, April 6, 1807.

9. Brockton, Mass. Christ Church Congregational Church, UCC Records, 1738–1980. ACAL.

10. Achsah Hayward to Sylvia Drake, May 1, 1803, reports that Charity has named the twins. David Mallett, *Edwin and Emma* (Edinburgh: Alexander Kincaid, 1760). The poem describes Edwin's father as "a sordid man, / who love nor pity knew."

11. Asaph Hayward to Charity Bryant, January 18, 1807. BDP.

12. Achsah Hayward to Sylvia Drake, May 1, 1803; Achsah Hayward to Sylvia Drake, November 13, 1803. BDP.

13. Achsah Hayward to Sylvia Drake, November 13, 1803. BDP.

14. Evidence of family intersections comes from "Autobiography of Asaph Drake." DFP. Evidence of the connection between Asaph Hayward and Grace Hayward comes from PCPR, 38:146.

15. Charity Bryant, "A Midnight Prayer," August 7, 1809; Charity Bryant, "Acrostic written by firelight on the prospect of a speedy separation," March 1810. BDP.

16. Several feet of snow covered the ground that year into April; "Montpelier: Monday, March 30, 1807," *The Precursor*, March 30, 1807; "Montpelier: April 6, 1807," *The Precursor*, April 6, 1807.

17. Peter Bryant to Charity Bryant, October 14, 1807. HBFP.

18. Lydia Richards to Charity Bryant, October 12, 1807. BDP.

19. Sylvia Drake, "Spring" [n.d.] BDP; S. D., "Ode to Spring," *Middlebury Mercury*, June 10, 1807. Sylvia's undated "Spring" almost certainly dates to before her marriage to Charity. At the base of the poem she drew an embroidery or quilting pattern of leaves and blossoms, indicating time for ornamental work that hardly fit into her busy work life after the marriage.

20. Sylvia Drake, "No matter when or where," May 22, 1848. BDP.

21. T. S. Eliot, *The Waste Land and Other Poems* (New York: Harcourt Brace Jovanovich, 1962).

22. Account of her Travels by Charity Bryant, April 9, 1844. BDP.

23. Lydia Richards to Charity Bryant, March 15, 1807. BDP.

24. Charity informed Lydia of this decision in a letter dated May 22, 1807; see Lydia's acknowledgment of the letter and its news in Lydia Richards to Charity Bryant, June 14, 1807. BDP.

25. William Cullen Bryant, *Letters of a Traveller*, 136.

26. Charity Bryant to Sylvia Drake, June 7, 1807. BDP.

27. 2 Corinthians 1:21. King James Version.

28. The location of Charity's first independent Weybridge residence is unrecorded. The women moved into their permanent home on the Hagar farm on December 31, 1808, which is discussed in Chapter 12.

29. Charity Bryant to Sylvia Drake, June 28, 1807. BDP.

30. Charity Bryant to Sylvia Drake, July 2, 1807. BDP.

31. SDD, July 3, 1838. BDP. The entry acknowledges the thirty-first anniversary of the women's union. Sylvia's diary from 1807 no longer remains.

CHAPTER 11

1. Account of her Travels by Charity Bryant, April 9, 1844. BDP.

2. R. B. Outhwaite, *Clandestine Marriage in England, 1500–1850* (London: Hambledon Press, 1995), 2.

3. Hartog, *Man and Wife in America*; Martha Hodes, *White Women, Black Men: Illicit Sex in the Nineteenth-Century South* (New Haven, Conn.: Yale University Press, 1999); Ariela R. Dubler, "Governing through Contract: Common Law Marriage in the Nineteenth Century," *Yale Law Journal* 107, no. 6 (1998): 1885–1920.

4. Alexander M. Burrill, *A New Law Dictionary and Glossary* (New York: John S. Vorhees, 1850), 707, quoted in Hartog, *Man and Wife in America*, 1.

5. For examples of "help-meet" used as a word for wife, see "Matrimony," *The Philadelphia Minerva*, March 12, 1796; "The Bachelor's Will," *The Political Repository*, March 4, 1800; "The Matrimonial Corner," *The Camden Gazette*, May 26, 1817.

6. William Blackstone, *Commentaries on the Laws of England, in Four Books* (London: A. Strahan, 1809), 441.

7. Quoted in Dubler, "Governing through Contract," 1885.

8. Laurel Thatcher Ulrich, *A Midwife's Tale: The Life of Martha Ballard, Based on Her Diary, 1785–1812* (New York: Vintage, 1991), 140–42. On the residential patterns of newly married couples see Smith, "Parental Power and Marriage Patterns"; Phillip Greven Jr., *Four Generations: Population, Land, and Family in Colonial Andover* (Ithaca, N.Y.: Cornell University Press, 1970), 75–82.

9. Lydia Richards to Charity Bryant, September 13, 1807. BDP.

10. "An Acrostic present to Miss S. D. by her friend—C. Bryant, Shoreham, August 17, 1807." BDP. Charity made several visits to Shoreham in the summer of 1807.

11. Godbeer, *Sexual Revolution in Early America*, chapter 2.

12. Peter Bryant to Charity Bryant, October 14, 1807. BDP.

13. Lydia Richards to Charity Bryant, October 12, 1807. BDP.

14. Lydia Richards to Charity Bryant, October 12, 1807. BDP.

15. Anna Kingman to Charity Bryant, October 17, 1807. BDP.

16. Lydia Richards to Charity Bryant, March 29, 1808. Lydia notes that Charity has not written to her or to Pelham relations since November 1807. Mercy Ford to Charity Bryant, January 30, 1808. BDP.

17. Charity Bryant, "On the Prospect of Separation, March 18, 1808." BDP.

18. John Fawcett, "Blessed be the Tie that Binds," *Hymns Adapted to the Circumstances of Public Worship* (1782). The song was widely reprinted in American hymnals during the late eighteenth century.

19. Barbara Penner, *Newlyweds on Tour: Honeymooning in Nineteenth-Century America* (Lebanon: University of New Hampshire Press, 2009).

20. Account of her Travels by Charity Bryant, April 9, 1844. BDP.

21. Charity Bryant to Sally Bryant, June 18, 1808. BBDP.

22. Anna Kingman to Sylvia Drake, 1808. DFP.

23. Sylvia Drake to Mary Drake, undated. This letter is only partial, but context dates it to the 1808 trip. BDP.

24. Anna Kingman to Charity Bryant, 1808. BDP.

25. Lydia Richards to Charity Bryant, June 21, 1807. BDP.

26. Lydia Richards to Charity Bryant, August 23, 1807. BDP.

27. Lydia Richards to Charity Bryant, January 3, 1808. BDP.

28. Lydia Richards to Charity Bryant, May 30, 1808. BDP.

29. Philip Bryant to Charity Bryant, March 13, 1808. BDP.

30. Sylvia Drake to Mary Drake, undated [ca. 1808]. BDP.

31. Mercy Ford to Charity Bryant, June 21, 1810. BDP.

32. Sylvia Drake to Mary Drake, undated [ca. 1808]. BDP.

33. John Demos, *A Little Commonwealth: Family Life in Plymouth Colony* (New York: Oxford University Press, 1970); Greven, *Four Generations*.

34. Mercy Ford to Charity Bryant, June 21, 1810. BDP.

35. SSBD, September 3–7, 1808.

36. SSBD, August 1, 1810.

37. Sarah Snell Bryant to Charity Bryant, February 21, 1814. BDP.

38. Lydia Richards to Charity Bryant, September 20, 1808. BDP.

39. Lydia Richards to Charity Bryant, September 25, 1808. BDP.

40. Lydia Richards to Charity Bryant, October 30, 1808. BDP.

41. Thomas Crawford, ed., *The Correspondence of James Boswell and William Johnson Temple* (New Haven, Conn.: Yale University Press, 1997), 1:269.

42. Lydia Richards to Charity Bryant, November 27, 1808. BDP.

43. Peter Bryant to Charity Bryant, March 6, 1809. HBFP.

44. Grooms' rings were a consumerist innovation of the mid-twentieth century; Vicki Howard, "A 'Real Man's Ring': Gender and the Invention of Tradition," *Journal of Social History* 36, no. 4 (2003): 837–56.

45. "Cash paid for coal," *Middlebury Mercury*, March 2, 1808.

46. Peter Bryant to Charity Bryant, May 15, 1809; Peter Bryant to Charity Bryant, June 25, 1810. HBFP.

47. Account of her Travels by Charity Bryant, April 9, 1844. BDP.

CHAPTER 12

1. Account of her Travels by Charity Bryant, April 9, 1844. BDP; SDD, April 13, 1822.

2. Charity describes the dimensions in Charity Bryant to Sarah Snell Bryant, June 8, 1833. BBFP.

3. Many people, including Sylvia, used this word for the house. SDD, July 19, 1823; Mary Hovey to Sylvia Drake, September 5, 1809; Lydia Richards to Charity Bryant, December 20, 1812; Clarissa Hovey to Sylvia Drake and Charity Bryant, undated. BDP.

4. Lombard, *Making Manhood*.

5. Moore, *Sister Arts*.

6. Donoghue, *Inseparable*, 61.

7. Luther Martin to Sarah Hagar, 1808. WLR, Book 3:502. Weybridge acquired one other female landowner at this time; Bill Solomon to Sarah Parmale. WLR, Book 3:63.

8. SDD, March 19, 1821.

9. WTR, 1842–1866.

10. WLR, Book 7:59.

11. Charity Bryant and Sylvia Drake to Sarah Hagar, November 1837. WLR, Book 7:59. Bryant also specifies in her 1844 record that the house she and Sylvia occupied on December 31, 1808, was the same they lived in for the rest of their lives together; Account of her Travels by Charity Bryant, April 9, 1844. BDP.

12. Lyons, "Mapping an Atlantic Sexual Culture," 148.

13. The sexual implications of bed-sharing has been a topic of debate in nineteenth-century American history, in large part because of its role in the question of Abraham Lincoln's sexuality. Biographer C. A. Tripp, who argued for Lincoln's homosexuality, pointed to the four years he shared a bed with his beloved friend Joshua Speed. Tripp's critics reject the sexual salience of bed-sharing. See C. A. Tripp, *The Intimate World of Abraham Lincoln* (New York: Free Press, 2005); Richard Brookhiser, "Was Lincoln Gay?," *New York Times*, January 9, 2005.

14. Samuel Bayard Woodward, *Hints for the Young in Relation to the Health of Body and Mind* (Boston: George W. Light, 1840), 32. Another doctor warned that "children as they approach adolescence should never be permitted to sleep together," because the privacy and physical intimacy of the bed were likely to result in mutual masturbation; Seth Pancoast, *The Ladies' Medical Guide: A Complete Instructor and Counsellor* (Philadelphia: Hubbard Bros., 1875), 590. Also D'Emilio and Freedman, *Intimate Matters*, 126.

15. Wulf, *Not All Wives*, 47, 113. Wulf turns up evidence of several lesbian-like households in eighteenth-century Philadelphia, including one kept by two Irish merchant women, Ruth Webb and Mary Taggart (145).

16. Martha Vicinus, *Intimate Friends: Women Who Loved Women, 1778–1928* (Chicago: University of Chicago Press, 2006), 9–15.

17. Jill Liddington, "Anne Lister of Shibden Hall, Halifax (1791–1840): Her Diaries and the Historians," *History Workshop* 35, no. 1 (1993): 45–77.

18. Mary Hovey to Charity Bryant, February 1809. BDP.

19. Good, "Friendly Relations."

20. Mary Hovey to Charity Bryant, July 1809; Mary Hovey to Charity Bryant, July 14, 1809; Mary Hovey to Charity Bryant, August 2, 1809; Mary Hovey to Charity Bryant, August 2, 1809. BDP.

21. Mary Hovey to Charity Bryant, July 1809. BDP.

22. Mary Hovey to Charity Bryant, July 14, 1809; Mary Hovey to Charity Bryant, August 4, 1809. BDP.

23. Mary Hovey to Sylvia Drake, August 2, 1809. BDP.

24. "Charity Bryant, to Miss Sylvia Drake, July 29, 1809." BDP.

25. The scrap is undated, but Mary's letter of apology, dated August 22, 1809, seems to make reference to the love token. BDP.

26. Mary Hovey to Charity Bryant, August 22, 1809. BDP.

27. Letters from Mary Hovey continued through 1811. She married Dr. Jabez Spicer, a doctor and minister, around this time, and the pair later moved to the Midwest.

28. Micah 4:4; Isaiah 36:16.

29. SDD, December 7, 1821.

30. The roses are mentioned in William Cullen Bryant, *Letters of a Traveller*, 136.

31. Vesta Guild to Charity Bryant, January 13, 1810. Vesta wrote the letter in response to a May 1809 letter from Charity. BDP.

32. Anna Kingman to Sylvia Drake, May 8, 1809. BDP.

33. Richard Lyman Bushman, *The Refinement of America: Persons, Houses, Cities* (New York: Vintage, 1993).

34. Sylvia records her constant housekeeping duties in SDD, 1821–1823 and 1835–1836. Lydia Richards to Charity Bryant, April 14, 1811, refers to the fact that her "profile" hung in the house. BDP.

35. Anna Kingman to Charity Bryant, May 8, 1809. BDP.

36. Anna Kingman to Charity Bryant, October 1808. BDP.

37. Peter Bryant to Charity Bryant, March 6, 1809. HBFP.

38. Charity Bryant, "Untitled [Amen, I can verily say]," March 1810. Charity repeats her wish to remain united to Sylvia in "Acrostic Written by Firelight on the Prospect of a Speedy Separation," March 1810. BDP.

39. For example, SDD, December 29, 1821; Charity Bryant, "This Little Spot of Ground" (1847). BDP.

40. Charity Bryant to Peter Bryant, August 31, 1814. HBFP. See also Sylvia's affectionate reference to the small house as a "cottage most dear," SDD, February 28, 1823.

41. SDD, April 28, 1823; May 16, 1823.

42. Sylvia Drake to Mary Drake, April 4, 1813. DFP.

43. Sylvia Drake to Mary Drake, December 25, 1814. DFP.

44. Sylvia Drake to Mary Drake, March 19, 1815. DFP.

45. The complete list of rooms and construction dates is from "Buildings of C Bryant & S Drake." DFP.

46. For example, SDD, January 5, 1821; February 1, 1821; January 28, 1822.

47. SDD, December 21, 1821; "Record of Mary Drake's visits in the 1820s." DFP.

48. SDD, April 4, 1822.

49. Sylvia Drake to Mary Drake, April 14, 1822. DFP.

50. Sylvia records progress on the 1823 renovations in SDD, April 1–May 24, 1823.

51. SDD, May 9, 1823.

52. SDD, May 13, 1823.

53. SDD, May 23, 1823.

54. SDD, May 24, 1823.

55. SDD, April 4, 1823.

56. SDD, March 31, 1823; April 1, 1823; May 8, 1823; May 10, 1823.

57. SDD, April 15, 1823; April 16, 1823.

58. SDD, April 7, 1823; April 8, 1823.

59. SDD, April 1, 1823; April 2, 1823; April 3, 1823; April 8, 1823; April 16, 1823; April 21, 1823.

60. SDD, April 26, 1823; April 27, 1823; April 28, 1823.

61. Elias Child, *Geneaology of the Child, Childs, and Childe Families* (Utica, N.Y.: Curtis & Childs, 1881), 561–62.

62. SDD, April 28, 1823.

63. SDD, April 24, 1823.

64. SDD, May 15, 1823.

65. SDD, May 16, 1823; Sylvia Drake to Asaph Drake [May 15, 1823]. DFP.

66. Sylvia Drake to Asaph Drake, May 16, 1823. DFP. The letter bears the date May 16, 1823, but in Sylvia's diary she records receiving Asaph's letter and writing her reply on May 17. SDD, May 17, 1823.

67. Charity Bryant to Asaph Drake, October 14, 1827. DFP.

68. SDD, March 20, 1823.

69. SDD, February 19, 1823. Oliver and his wife also visited on October 1, 1823.

70. SDD, September 3, 1835.

71. SDD, September 5, 1835.

72. For example, SDD, February 13, 1821; May 11, 1821; September 23, 1821; February 6, 1822; April 28, 1822; May 2, 1822; July 29, 1822; October 2, 1822; January 16, 1823.

73. SDD, June 18, 1821.

74. For example, SDD, March 24, 1821; April 6, 1821; July 29, 1821; September 6, 1822; March 17, 1823; February 14, 1835.

75. SDD, August 8, 1821; April 20, 1822; August 2, 1822; December 20, 1822; June 17, 1823; November 7, 1823; December 13, 1823; January 1, 1835; January 17, 1835; March 28, 1835; May 16, 1835; June 11, 1835.

76. Asaph Drake and Isaac Drake contract, June 22, 1827. DFP.

77. Record of Mary Drake's visits. DFP. SDD, January 15, 1821; January 21, 1821; January 27, 1821; February 25, 1821.

78. Sylvia Drake to Mary Drake, August 8, 1824. DFP.

79. SDD, March 8, 1821.

CHAPTER 13

1. Charity Bryant, "My Christian Friends," April 26, 1811; Weybridge First Ecclesiastical Society. HSM. The quotation comes from "Hymn XX, Backslidings and returns," in Watts, *Works of the Rev. Isaac Watts, D.D. in Nine Volumes*, 9:156.

2. For the dates they joined the church see WCCR. For a classic account of rules for communion under the Puritans see Edmund S. Morgan, *Visible Saints: The History of a Puritan Idea* (Ithaca, N.Y.: Cornell University Press, 1963). See also Horton Davies, "The Lord's Supper in the Congregational Christian Tradition," *Prism: A Theological Forum for the United Church of Christ* 1, no. 2 (1998): 28–36.

3. Charity Bryant, "My Christian Friends."

4. The assertion that Charity and Sylvia held each other in bed at night is supported by SDD, August 14, 1838.

5. John Milton, *The Doctrine and Discipline of Divorce* (London, 1643), 6.

6. New Haven Colony Law, quoted in Katz, *Gay American History*, 23. For another example of a colonial text that associated Romans 1:26 with lesbianism see *Aristotle's Masterpiece* (New York, 1793), 76.

7. Jonathan Ned Katz, *Love Stories: Sex between Men before Homosexuality* (Chicago: University of Chicago Press, 2003), 63.

8. Helen Lefkowitz Horowitz, *Rereading Sex: Battles over Sexual Knowledge and Suppression in Nineteenth-Century America* (New York: Vintage, 2002).

9. The term "presumption of heterosexuality" originates from B. W. Cook, "Female Support Networks and Political Activism: Lillian Wald, Crystal Eastman, Emma Goldman," *Chrysalis* 3 (1977): 43–61.

10. Charity Bryant, "The Suicide." BDP. The original is Day, *The Suicide.*

11. Charity Bryant, "My Christian Friends."

12. Charity Bryant, "My Christian Friends."

13. For example, Charity Bryant, "A Midnight Prayer," August 7, 1809. BDP.

14. Mercy Ford to Charity Bryant, April 15, 1811. BDP.

15. Watts, *Works of the Rev. Isaac Watts, D.D. in Nine Volumes*, 9:165.

16. *Aristotle's Compleat Masterpiece* (London, 1755), 24.

17. Charity Bryant, "My Christian Friends."

18. Charity Bryant, "Fear Not the Whirlwinds" [ca. 1842]; and "Fear not dear S." [ca. 1850]. BDP.

19. Bullough and Voght, "Homosexuality and Its Confusion with the 'Secret Sin,'" 143–55; Thomas W. Laqueur, *Solitary Sex: A Cultural History of Masturbation* (New York: Zone Books, 2003).

20. SDD, March 14, 1821.

21. Thomas Watson, *A Body of Practical Divinity, Consisting of above One Hundred and Seventy Six Sermons on the Lesser Catechism* (Glasgow, 1761), 523.

22. Early American ministers debated the definition of sodomy. According to Puritan minister Samuel Danforth, the sin involved "filthiness conducted between parties of the same Sex: when Males with Males, and Females with Females work wickedness"; Danforth, *Cry of Sodom*, 3.

23. Charles C. P. Moody, *Biographical Sketches of the Moody Family Embracing Notices of Ten Ministers and Several Laymen from 1633 to 1842* (Boston: Samuel G. Drake, 1847).

24. SDD, April 1, 1821.

25. Foster, *Sex and the Eighteenth-Century Man*, 161.

26. Kathleen Brown, *Foul Bodies: Cleanliness in Early America* (New Haven, Conn.: Yale University Press, 2009), 80–84.

27. Foster, *Sex and the Eighteenth-Century Man*, 161–62.

28. SDD, March 17, 1822; April 18, 1821. Also January 27, 1822; May 24, 1836.

29. *Aristotle's Complete Master-Piece* (New York, 1796), 16–17, 127–31.

30. SDD, December 31, 1822.

31. SDD, July 5, 1838; Foster, *Sex and the Eighteenth-Century Man*, 164.

32. SDD, September 12, 1821.

33. Butler, *Bodies That Matter*, 35–36.

34. SDD, July 3, 1838.

35. SDD, July 22, 1838.

36. Sylvia Drake, Charity Bryant Acrostic, 1848. BDP.

CHAPTER 14

1. 4th Federal Census, reel 126, sheet 23a. Charity and Sylvia did not appear in the 1810 census. The women visited Massachusetts in summer 1810, so they may have been away when the census taker knocked, or they may have been counted within a male relative's household.

2. 5th Federal Census, reel 184, sheet 160.

3. 6th Federal Census, reel 538, sheet 175.

4. 7th Federal Census, reel 920, sheet 430.

5. Norma Basch, *In the Eyes of the Law: Women, Marriage, and Property in Nineteenth-Century New York* (Ithaca, N.Y.: Cornell University Press, 1982); Hartog, *Man and Wife in America*, 187–89; Nancy Cott, *Public Vows: A History of Marriage and the Nation* (Cambridge, Mass.: Harvard University Press, 2002), 49–55, 64–68.

6. William Cullen Bryant, *Letters of a Traveller*.

7. Account of her Travels by Charity Bryant, April 9, 1844. BDP.

8. Diary of Hiram Harvey Hurlburt Jr.

9. Charity's diminutive stature is noted in Sarah Snell Bryant to Charity Bryant, February 21, 1814. BDP. Also Diary of Hiram Harvey Hurlburt Jr.

10. SDD, August 19, 1823; December 12, 1835; June 16, 1836; February 6, 1836.

11. Lydia Richards to Charity Bryant, October 12, 1807. See also Lydia Richards to Charity Bryant, September 18, 1811. BDP.

12. "The Male and Female Husband" (West-Smithfield, 1672–1696?).

13. Henry Fielding, *The Female Husband: Or, the Surprising History of Mrs. Mary, Alias Mr George Hamilton* (London, 1746). For evidence of the text's familiarity in North America see Gwenda Morgan and Peter Rushton, "Fraud and Freedom: Gender, Identity, and Narratives of Deception among the Female Convicts in Colonial America," *Journal for Eighteenth-Century Studies* 34, no. 3 (2011): 335–55.

14. Although the term "female husband" appears paradoxical, female husbands were as "real" as male husbands. This point is parallel to Halberstam's assertion about the realness of female masculinity, despite its seeming contradictoriness, in Judith Halberstam, *Female Masculinity* (Durham, N.C.: Duke University Press, 1998).

15. "The Female Husband," *The New-York Gazette*, October 20, 1766; *The Boston Post-Boy*, November 17, 1766; *The New-London Gazette*, December 5, 1766; *The Baltimore Patriot*, March 14, 1829; *New-Hampshire Gazette*, March 31, 1829; *Vermont Gazette*, April 7, 1829; *The Village Register and Norfolk County Advertiser*, March 19, 1829; "Extraordinary Case of a Female Husband," *The Floridian*, September 17, 1836; *The Farmer's Cabinet* [New Hampshire], August 26, 1836; *The Essex Gazette* [Massachusetts], August 26, 1836; *The Ithaca Herald*, August 31, 1836.

16. "Evil of Speaking in One's Sleep," *Eastern Argus*, May 15, 1829.

17. William Cullen Bryant, *Letters of a Traveller*.

18. Diary of Hiram Harvey Hurlburt Jr.

19. Anna Kingman to Charity Bryant, June 10, 1799. BDP; Peter Bryant to Charity Bryant, August 4, 1806. HBFP. The term "your ladyship" appeared in British period letter-writing guides, but it was notably absent from American adaptations like *The American Letter-Writer: Containing, a Variety of Letters on the most common Occasions in Life, Viz. Friendship, Duty, Advice, Business, Amusement, Love, Marriage, Courtship, &c. With Forms of Message Cards* (Philadelphia: John M'Culloch, 1793).

20. WTR, 1842–1866. There are no surviving tax records in Weybridge predating 1842. Sylvia died in 1866 and disappeared from the tax rolls by 1868.

21. WTMR.

22. WLR, Book 7:59.

23. WLR, Book 7:296.

24. Jehiel Wright Account. BDP.

25. Asaph Drake Note, December 7, 1818. BDP.

26. Charity and Sylvia's business books are a rare window onto the financial life of early national women artisans. Gloria Main has commented on the absence of women's account books, quoted in Marla R. Miller, *The Needle's Eye: Women and Work in the Age of Revolution* (Amherst: University of Massachusetts Press, 2006), 9. Karin Wulf argues that women's labor is hidden in the sources; Wulf, *Not All Wives*, 131.

27. Scott Sandage, *Born Losers: A History of Failure in America* (Cambridge, Mass.: Harvard University Press, 2006).

28. SDD, July 20, 1822.

29. "Bills, Receipts 1813–1816." Jonathan Hagar Family Papers, Box 2. HSM.

30. SDD, January 13, 1821.

31. "Weybridge Female Benevolent Society." BDP.

32. SDD, February 3, 1821.

33. SDD, May 22, 1821; August 28, 1821; January 23, 1835.

34. SDD, November 4, 1836.

35. Sylvia Drake food record. DFP. Other business owners in Weybridge accepted food stuffs in payment for goods; see "The Subscriber will continue the Clothiers business," *The Vermont Mirror*, October 27, 1813; "Cloth Dressing," *The Vermont Mirror*, August 17, 1814; "New Clothing Works," *Columbian Patriot*, October 12, 1814.

36. SDD, June 8, 1821; March 28, 1822; September 24, 1822; November 4, 1822; November 9, 1822; January 1, 1835.

37. SDD, January 26, 1835.

38. SDD, March 29, 1835.

39. SDD, January 18, 1822.

40. SDD, January 31, 1835.

41. On the rare occasion that Charity did contribute to the domestic labor, Sylvia made a point of it in her diary. See, for example, SDD, March 28, 1835.

42. SDD, July 29, 1822.

43. SDD, August 19, 1836.

44. Azel Hayward to Charity Bryant, April 30, 1825. BDP.

45. Jonathan Hovey to Asaph Drake, May 15, 1820. DFP.

46. The perceived relationship between gender and sex has shifted over time. Thomas Laqueur argues that gender rather than sex appeared the stable category before the eighteenth century emergence of a binary sex model. Although popular understandings today differentiate sex as biological and gender as cultural, theorist Judith Butler argues that the two categories remain inseparable and mutually constitutive. Thomas Laqueur, *Making Sex: Body and Gender from the Greeks to Freud* (Cambridge, Mass.: Harvard University Press, 1990); Judith Butler, *Gender Trouble: Feminism and the Subversion of Identity* (New York: Routledge Classics, 2007).

47. Kathryn K. Kent, *Making Girls into Women: American Women's Writing and the Rise of Lesbian Identity* (Durham, N.C.: Duke University Press, 2003), chapter 1; Love, "Gyn/Apology."

48. Charity Bryant to Sarah Snell Bryant, September 13, 1800. BBFP.

49. For example, "Died," *The Middlebury Mercury*, October 16, 1805. See also "Died," *The New Hampshire Gazette*, July 18, 1797; "Died," *Rhode-Island American, and General Advertiser*, August 13, 1819; "Obituary," *Eastern Argus*, September 30, 1828.

50. SDD, February 27, 1835.

51. SDD, March 5, 1821.

52. Hannah Griffits, "To the Memory of Hannah Morris," *The Evening Fire-Side, or Weekly Intelligence* (Philadelphia, 1805), 1:274. Griffits's poems originally circulated in manuscript form among friends and were published later; see Blecki and Wulf, *Milcah Martha Moore's Book*.

53. SDD, July 13, 1823. The phrase also appeared in other poems about friendship; Cleora, "On the Anniversary of the late amiable Miss W-----'s Birth Day," *Boston Evening Post and the General Advertiser*, November 17, 1781. See also William Davis Gallagher, ed., *The Hesperian* (Cincinnati, 1839), 3:100.

54. SDD, September 26, 1821; February 28, 1823; August 27, 1823.

55. SDD, June 3, 1821; November 25, 1821; March 10, 1822; April 10, 1822; July 21, 1822. Abigail Adams and John Adams, *My Dearest Friend: Letters of Abigail and John Adams*, ed. Margaret A. Hogan and C. James Taylor (Cambridge, Mass.: Belknap Press of Harvard University Press, 2010).

56. "An Acrostic Present to Miss S.D. by her friend—C. Bryant" (1807); "Charity Bryant to Miss Sylvia Drake, July 29, 1809"; "Amen, I can verily say from my heart" (March 1810); "To a Friend on her Birth Day. October 31, 1847." BDP.

57. Charity Bryant, "Charity Bryant to Miss Sylvia Drake, July 29, 1809." BDP. Charity Bryant to Peter Bryant, January 30, 1820. HBFP.

58. "Amen, I can verily say from my heart" (March 1810). BDP.

59. Jonathan and Clarissa Hovey to Charity Bryant, April 24, 1818; Jonathan Hovey to Charity Bryant, May 26, 1818. BDP.

60. Roland Howard to Charity Bryant, April 12, 1822. BDP.

61. Lydia Richards to Charity Bryant, May 28, 1810. BDP.

62. Vesta Guild to Charity Bryant, June 18, 1824; Vesta Guild to Charity Bryant, October 11, 1826. BDP.

63. *The Book of Common-Prayer, and Administration of Sacraments. And Other Rites and Ceremonies of the Church According to the Use of the Church of England* (New York: William Bradford, 1710).

64. Godbeer, *Sexual Revolution in Early America*, chapter 2.

65. The connection of female husbands to the category of lesbianism is a source of debate; see Halberstam, *Female Masculinity*, 67; Judith M. Bennett, "'Lesbian-Like' and the Social History of Lesbianisms," *Journal of the History of Sexuality* 9, no. 1–2 (2000): 1–24; Alison Oram, *Her Husband Was a Woman! Women's Gender-Crossing in Modern British Popular Culture* (London: Routledge, 2007); Susan Clayton, "Can Two and a Half Centuries of Female Husbands Inform (Trans)Gender History?," *Journal of Lesbian Studies* 13 (2010): 288–302.

66. See, for example, the following exciting outlaw tale about a female husband caught for stealing and the speculation about whether she had sex with her several brides: "July 25," *The New-York Evening Post*, October 2, 1749.

67. A typical newspaper piece about a female husband whose true sex was revealed after death stated that it would be "uncharitable to repeat the surmises that are insinuated" about why she married a woman: *Baltimore Patriot*, March 28, 1829.

68. "A Female Husband," *The New-Hampshire Patriot and State Gazette*, December 1, 1842. For the word "enormities," see Foster, *Sex and the Eighteenth-Century Man*, 159; Jonathan Ned Katz, "'Coming to Terms': Conceptualizing Men's Erotic and Affectional Relations with Men in the United States, 1820–1892," in *A Queer World: The Center for Lesbian and Gay Studies Reader*, ed. Martin Duberman (New York: New York University Press, 1997), 225. The female husband in the article was arrested in New York, where the sodomy statute at the time contained no provision against sex between women (the law only covered penile penetration of nonvaginal orifices). She had to be charged with a broader offense in order to be prosecuted. William Eskridge, *Dishonorable Passions: Sodomy Laws in America, 1861–2003* (New York: Viking Adult, 2008), 20.

69. Sedgwick, *Epistemology of the Closet*, 164–65. Also Wahl, *Invisible Relations*, 11, 14, 31.

CHAPTER 15

1. SDD, February 15, 1823.

2. Information from the Sylvia Drake Diaries has been tabulated by research assistant Meleisa Ono George.

3. For examples of Drake nieces and nephews addressing Charity and Sylvia as "dear aunts," see Mary W. B. Drake to Charity Bryant and Sylvia Drake [no date]; Azel Hayward to Charity Bryant, April 30, 1825. BDP.

4. Emma J. to Sylvia Drake, June 8, 1845. BDP.

5. Oliver Bryant to Charity Bryant, July 8, 1844. BDP.

6. Voss and Bryant II, *Letters of William Cullen Bryant*, 2:493.

7. John Howard Bryant to Charity Bryant, July 15, 1826; Freeman Kingman to Charity Bryant, October 7, 1828; Oliver Bryant to Charity Bryant, October 26, 1829; Daniel Bryant to Charity Bryant, October 15, 1829. BDP.

8. Emmeline Rankin to Charity Bryant, July 8, 1844. BDP.

9. "Descendants of Joseph Drake." HSM.

10. William Ellsworth to Asaph Drake, October 26, 1847. DFP.

11. "Memoir written by Mrs H. Child Chrysler at the time of the Emily Drake and Rollin Shaw case against the heirs over the Drake Estate" (1929/30). Manuscript held by Pat Fiske, Snake Mt. Rd., Weybridge, Vt.

12. SDD, February 3, 1821. BDP.

13. Silence's son Philip died on the Chesapeake during the War of 1812; Silence Bryant to Charity Bryant, October 15, 1813. One of Philip's sisters died soon after; Silence Bryant to Charity Bryant, June 4, 1815. Silence's husband died prematurely after going bankrupt; Silence Bryant to Charity Bryant, August 20, 1820. For Silence's references to Sylvia as her sister, see Silence Bryant to Charity Bryant, June 4, 1815; Silence Bryant to Charity Bryant, September 29, 1816; Silence Bryant to Charity Bryant, October 21, 1820; Silence Bryant to Charity Bryant, January 20, 1834. BDP.

14. Charity Bryant to Peter Bryant, May 25, 1817. BBFP.

15. Rothman, *Living in the Shadow of Death*, 13–74.

16. SDD fragments [1817]. Asaph Drake to Sylvia Drake, June 2, 1817. BDP.

17. Charity Bryant to Peter Bryant, May 25, 1817. BBFP.

18. Account of her Travels by Charity Bryant, April 9, 1844; for evidence of Charity's relations' concerns about Achsah see Silence Bryant to Charity Bryant, July 23, 1817; Anna Hayden to Charity Bryant, October 21, 1817. BDP.

19. Charity Bryant to Asaph Drake, June 13, 1829. DFP; "Cyrus Bryant Drake," in *Minutes of the Eighty-Third Annual Meeting of the General Convention of Congregational Ministers and Churches of Vermont* (Montpelier: Vermont Chronicle Office, 1878), 59–60.

20. Tremaine McDowell, "William Cullen Bryant and Yale," *New England Quarterly* 3, no. 4 (1930): 706–16.

21. SDD, May 7–12, 1835.

22. Asaph Drake to Charity Bryant, June 10, 1833. Charity reciprocated this sentiment, saying that she considered his "Brotherly kindness" during the early years of their friendship to be one of her "greatest enjoyments" in life; Charity Bryant to Asaph Drake, October 14, 1827. DFP. Asaph referred to Charity as a "sister" whom he "affectionately loved," in Asaph Drake to Sylvia Drake, June 2, 1817. BDP.

23. SDD, February 3, 1821.

24. Eli Moody to Charity Bryant, January 15, 1838. The letter refers to "Miss Drake" attending Mount Holyoke without specifying which Miss Drake. This confused one earlier historian who believed that Charity was expressing interest in the senior Sylvia Drake attending Mount Holyoke.

However, Moody's discussion of the applicant being a young woman, and his promise to act as a guardian to her, makes clear that he could not have had the fifty-four-year-old Sylvia Drake in mind. See Heys, Frank. "The Two Seamstresses of Weybridge, Vermont," *Vermont Quarterly* 21, (1953): 232–37.

25. Louisa and Cyrus Bryant Drake to Polly Shaw, August 9, 1859; Sylvia Louisa Drake to Polly Shaw, January 12, 1868. SDP.

26. Sylvia Drake to Asaph Drake, September 30, 1859. BDP.

27. Edwin Bryant to Charity Bryant, April 12, 1832. BDP.

28. Bayless Hardin to Georgia W. Read, April 8, 1938. GWR.

29. Silence Bryant to Charity Bryant, July 2, 1809; Silence Bryant to Charity Bryant, 1809 [no month or day]; Silence Bryant to Charity Bryant, February 22, 1810; Silence Bryant to Charity Bryant, January 13, 1813; Silence Bryant to Charity Bryant, October 21, 1820; Silence Bryant to Charity Bryant, December 28, 1820. BDP.

30. Edwin Bryant to Charity Bryant, October 11, 1827; Edwin Bryant, ed., *What I Saw in California: By Wagon from Missouri to California in 1847–48* (Omaha: University of Nebraska Press, 1985).

31. Edwin Bryant to Charity Bryant, April 12, 1832. BDP.

32. "Sudden and Terrible Death of Judge Edwin Bryan," *Louisville Courier-Journal*, December 17, 1869.

33. Bayless Hardin to Georgia W. Read, March 18, 1938. GWR.

34. SDD, June 28, 1823.

35. Azel Hayward to Charity Bryant, October 11, 1826. BDP.

36. Elijah Graves Drake to Charity Bryant, February 25, 1828. BDP.

37. Freeman Kingman to Charity Bryant, October 7, 1828. BDP.

38. Oliver Bryant to Charity Bryant, December 1835. BDP.

39. Oliver Bryant to Charity Bryant, January 23, 1827. BDP.

40. John Howard Bryant to Charity Bryant, July 15, 1826. BDP. Charity Bryant to John Howard Bryant, April 5, 1827. BBFP.

41. Abiel Rankin to Charity Bryant, March 3, 1835. BDP.

42. L.N.B. to Charity Bryant, October 21, 1833. BDP.

43. Daniel Bryant to Charity Bryant, January 28, 1817. BDP.

44. Will of Philip Bryant. PCPR, 47:488.

45. Daniel Bryant to Charity Bryant, April 25, 1819; Daniel Bryant to Charity Bryant, January 15, 1821; Daniel Bryant to Charity Bryant, May 1, 1822; Daniel Bryant to Charity Bryant, March 9, 1823; Daniel Bryant to Charity Bryant, July 16, 1826. BDP.

46. Dublin, *Transforming Women's Work*.

47. Lucy Hurlbut to Charity Bryant, December 1, 1832, shows that Charity was training select apprentices to cut clothes. BDP.

48. SDD, June 2, 1821.

49. SDD, December 26, 1835.

50. Silence Bryant to Charity Bryant, June 6, 1830. BDP.

51. Nabby Snell to Charity Bryant, October 23, 1815. BDP.

52. Nabby Snell to Charity Bryant, April 13, 1816. BDP.

53. Daniel Bryant to Charity Bryant, January 28, 1817. BDP.

54. Peter Bryant to Charity Bryant, September 20, 1816. HBFP.

55. Vesta Guild to Charity Bryant, April 11, 1816. BDP.

56. Elizabeth Bryant to Charity Bryant, August 31, 1831. BDP.

57. Ann Maria Kingman to Charity Bryant, January 2, 1832. BDP.

58. Peter Bryant to Charity Bryant, September 20, 1816. HBFP; Silence Bryant to Charity Bryant, January 1817; Nabby Snell to Charity Bryant, October 12, 1816. BDP.

59. Philip Bryant Executors Notice. PCPR 48:69–70.

60. Nabby Snell to Charity Bryant, April 13, 1816. BDP.

61. Nabby Snell to Charity Bryant, January 17, 1817; Daniel Bryant to Charity Bryant, January 28, 1817. BDP.

62. Charity's cousins Vesta Guild and Roland Howard, who lived in Easton, handled the property for her. See their letters complaining about the situation, including Roland Howard to Charity Bryant, January 20, 1821; Roland Howard to Charity Bryant, April 12, 1821; Vesta Guild to Charity Bryant, September 12, 1829; Vesta Guild to Charity Bryant, June 3, 1832. BDP.

63. Lydia Richards to Charity Bryant, December 4, 1811. BDP.

64. Charity Bryant to Sarah Bryant, April 15, 1821. BBFP.

65. Peter R. Bryant to Charity Bryant, June 18, 1822. BDP.

66. Cyrus Bryant to Charity Bryant, January 14, 1851. BDP.

67. Elizabeth Bryant to Charity Bryant, April 28, 1832; Elizabeth Bryant to Charity Bryant, November 22, 1832. Elizabeth reports that her sister Laura also enjoyed her acrostic. Jane Kingman to Charity Bryant, January 28, 1846; Emma Rankin to Charity Bryant, April 19, 1845; Jane P. Kingman to Charity Bryant, December 12, 1851. Jane's request came after Charity's own death, of which Jane had not yet heard. BDP.

68. Charity Bryant, Hiram Tavener Acrostic. Elizabeth Bryant announced her marriage to Tavener in a letter to Charity, March 8, 1833. BDP.

69. Semantha Hayward gravestone, Weybridge Village Cemetery. The lines read: "Could joint affections sigh / And sorrows bitter tear / Eer rescue from the grave / This stone had not been here." Charity also took the responsibility for writing to inform Semantha's parents, who were then homesteading in New York State, of the death; J. Bell to Charity Bryant, June 13, 1830. BDP.

70. The earliest is Sylvia Drake, Edwin Hayward Acrostic [ca. 1832]. BDP. The dating is assigned according to another passage on the same page, copied from the Clay Tazewell debate that took place in the U.S. Congress in 1832.

71. SDD, January 1, 1835; January 9, 1835; January 11, 1835.

72. Charity Bryant, "May strife and discord never find a place," January 1, 1847. BDP.

73. Charity Bryant, "Dear Edwin," March 21, 1847. BDP.

74. Ryan, *Cradle of the Middle Class*, 89–91. See also Kerber, *Women of the Republic*.

75. SDD, January 5, 1836.

76. Lydia Richards to Charity Bryant, October 22, 1809. Lydia describes the suffering of her sister Sally after having her first child.

77. Lydia Richards to Charity Bryant, October 9, 1825. BDP.

78. Lydia Richards to Charity Bryant, May 1, 1832. BDP.

79. Lydia Richards to Charity Bryant, October 8, 1832. BDP.

80. Lydia Richards Snell to Charity Bryant, March 30, 1845. A letter Lydia wrote to Charity earlier, during a visit with her brother's family, suggested that Lydia was not fond of little children; Lydia Richards to Charity Bryant, December 20, 1812. BDP.

81. Silence Bryant to Charity Bryant, February 9, 1822. The letter refers to the way they have been communicating through the children.

82. Philena Field to Charity Bryant, August 1, 1842. BDP.

83. SDD, September 27, 1823.

84. SDD, June 25, 1835.

85. SDD, March 5, 1836.

86. Philomela B. Wood to Charity Bryant, May 1830. She thanks Charity and Sylvia for their support in a letter to Charity Bryant, May 29, 1830. BDP.

87. Philomela Wood Wilcox to Charity Bryant, April 13, 1836. BDP.

88. Philena Wheelock to Charity Bryant, March 18, 1827. BDP.

89. Philena Wheelock to Charity Bryant, July 21, 1828. BDP.

90. Lucy Hurlbut to Charity Bryant, May 12, 1830. Philena, like Philomela, married a man named Wilcox; Philena Wilcox to Charity Bryant, October 17, 1831. He died in 1831.

91. Charity Bryant, "Philomela B. Wood" acrostic; Charity Bryant, "Lucy Hurlbut" acrostic; Charity Bryant, untitled lines to Lucinda Brewster, 1837; Orpha Landon to Charity Bryant, June 12, 1844. BDP.

92. Sally Field to Charity Bryant, March 9, 1845. BDP.

93. Constant Southworth to Charity Bryant, September 19, 1834. BDP.

94. Constant Southworth to Charity Bryant [undated, post-1834]. BDP.

95. Constant Southworth to Charity Bryant and Sylvia Drake, November 9, 1834. BDP.

96. SDD, November 2, 1835. Constant Southworth wanted to bring the little girl to Charity and Sylvia's house for their "blessing"; Constant Southworth to Charity Bryant, January 17, 1836. A couple named Lane and Eleanor Guilder also named a daughter Charity Sylvia for the couple; Lane Guilder to Sylvia Drake, undated. BDP.

CHAPTER 16

1. "Weybridge Female Benevolent Society." BDP.

2. Jonathan Hovey to Charity Bryant, 1819. He also addressed them simply as "sisters": Jonathan Hovey to Charity Bryant, April 24, 1818. BDP.

3. Charity Bryant to Sylvia Drake, June 28, 1807. BDP.

4. WCCR.

5. Charity Bryant, "My Christian Friends," April 26, 1811; Weybridge First Ecclesiastical Society. HSM.

6. SDD, January 1, 1835; April 28, 1835; March 22, 1836.

7. Smith-Rosenberg, "Female World of Love and Ritual"; Carol Lasser, "'Let Us Be Sisters Forever': The Sororal Model of Nineteenth-Century Female Friendship," *Signs* 14, no. 1 (1988): 158–81; William R. Taylor and Christopher Lasch, "Two 'Kindred Spirits': Sorority and Family in New England, 1839–1846," *New England Quarterly* 36, no. 1 (1963): 23–41; Vicinus, *Intimate Friends*, xxvi. For erotic sisterhood in Victorian literature see Marcus, *Between Women*. Curiously, Lynne Cheney, the former chairman of the National Endowment for the Humanities and the wife of former vice-president Dick Cheney, once wrote a novel titled *Sisters* featuring lesbian women on the western frontier: Lynne Cheney, *Sisters* (Toronto: Signet, 1981).

8. As a consequence, medievalist historian Judith M. Bennett has argued that nuns lived "lesbian-like" lives; Bennett, "'Lesbian-Like' and the Social History of Lesbianisms," 1–24. See also Judith C. Brown, *Immodest Acts: The Life of a Lesbian Nun in Renaissance Italy* (New York: Oxford University Press, 1985).

9. Donoghue, *Inseparable*, 108–15. The imagery of convent lesbianism has continued salience in the modern day; see, for example, the genre of films known as "nunsploitation," including the 2010 production "Nude Nuns with Big Guns."

10. Daniel A. Cohen, "The Respectability of Rebecca Reed: Genteel Womanhood and Sectarian Conflict in Antebellum America," *Journal of the Early Republic* 16, no. 3 (1996): 419–61.

11. SDD, May 15, 1835.

12. Lawrence Foster, *Religion and Sexuality: The Shakers, the Mormons, and the Oneida Community* (Urbana: University of Illinois Press, 1981); Stephen Stein, *The Shaker Experience in America: A History of the United Society of Believers* (New Haven, Conn.: Yale University Press, 1992); Susan Juster, "To Slay the Beast: Visionary Women in the Early Republic," in *A Mighty Baptism: Race and Gender in the Creation of American Protestantism*, ed. Susan Juster and Lisa MacFarlane (Ithaca, N.Y.: Cornell University Press, 1996): 19–37.

13. SDD, November 6, 1821.

14. SDD, March 10, 1822.

15. SDD, July 20, 1838. Other examples of Sylvia's diary entries that focus on women's religious practices include SDD, August 18, 1822; May 26, 1835.

16. SDD, February 13, 1836.

17. Sylvia Drake, "Charity Bryant" (1848). BDP.

18. Juster, "To Slay the Beast."

19. H. P. Smith, ed., *History of Addison County, Vermont* (Syracuse: D. Mason & Co., 1886), 722.

20. SDD, March 21, 1823; February 12, 1836.

21. SDD, July 22, 1838.

22. Karin E. Gedge, *Without Benefit of Clergy: Women and the Pastoral Relationship in Nineteenth-Century American Culture* (New York: Oxford University Press, 2003), 113.

23. B. B. Edwards and W. Cogswell, eds., *The American Quarterly Register*, vol. 12 (Boston: American Education Society, 1840).

24. Charity Bryant Letter Record 1838–1851. BDP.

25. Jonathan Hovey to Charity Bryant, 1819. Another correspondent, O. C. Green, also used the phrase "Sisters in Christ" to address a letter to Charity and Sylvia; O. C. Green to Charity Bryant and Sylvia Drake [undated, ca. 1840s]. BDP.

26. Clarissa Hovey to Charity Bryant, March 21, 1812. BDP.

27. "She hath wrought a good work," *Religious Reporter*, September 16, 1820. Charity's and Sylvia's names were not included in the newspaper notice, but Sylvia's diary records making a similar gift three years later (her 1820 diary is missing). Charity and Sylvia are the most likely candidates to have made the contribution. For more on the benevolent empire see Jonathan D. Sassi, *A Republic of Righteousness: The Public Christianity of the Post-Revolutionary New England Clergy* (Oxford: Oxford University Press, 2001).

28. SDD, March 5, 1823.

29. SDD, November 20, 1823.

30. Eli Moody to Sylvia Drake, July 2, 1824; Eli Moody to Charity Bryant, November 4, 1825. BDP.

31. This is true for 1824–26.

32. Eli Moody to Charity Bryant, September 6, 1825. BDP.

33. Harvey Smith to Charity Bryant, April 11, 1828. BDP.

34. Harvey Smith to Charity Bryant, July 4, 1828; Harvey Smith to Charity Bryant, September 16, 1828; Harvey Smith to Charity Bryant, August 8, 1829. BDP.

35. Diann Smith to Charity Bryant, May 12, 1830. See also appendix to letter from Philomela Wood to Charity Bryant, May 1830. BDP.

36. Harvey Smith to Charity Bryant, July 20, 1832. BDP.

37. D. D. Cook to Charity Bryant, January 9, 1848; D. D. Cook to Sylvia Drake, January 27, 1853; D. D. Cook to Sylvia Drake, December 4, 1854. BDP.

38. D. D. Cook to Charity Bryant, November 25, 1833. BDP.

39. SDD, March 22, 1822. BDP.

40. Rev. J. Lee business account, January 1836–May 22, 1837; Edwin Hall to Charity Bryant, July 8, 1829. BDP.

41. Jonathan Lee to Charity Bryant, September 10, 1839. BDP.

42. SDD, April 18, 1835; March 27, 1822.

43. SDD, April 29, 1822. "Weybridge Female Benevolent Society." BDP.

44. Anne M. Boylan, *The Origins of Women's Activism: New York and Boston, 1797–1840* (Chapel Hill: University of North Carolina Press, 2001); Lori D. Ginzberg, *Women and the Work of Benevolence: Morality, Politics, and Class in the Nineteenth-Century United States* (New Haven, Conn.: Yale University Press, 1992); Nancy F. Cott, *The Bonds of Womanhood: "Woman's Sphere" in New England, 1780–1835,* 2nd ed. (New Haven, Conn.: Yale University Press, 1997).

45. SDD, August 30, 1822; February 28, 1823.

46. SDD, March 8, 1823.

47. "Weybridge Female Benevolent Society."

48. Mercy Ford to Charity Bryant, May 6 [undated, ca. 1848]. BDP.

49. Mercy Ford to Charity Bryant, July 8, 1815; Mercy Ford to Charity Bryant, February 9, 1834. BDP.

50. Charity Bryant, "Taking into consideration the distress'd and destitute condition of the persecuted Portuguese," August 4, 1848. Clarissa Moody described Bryant and Drake as Chrissa's "aunts" because, she explained, they were "sisters to me"; Clarissa Moody to Charity Bryant, December 6, 1829. BDP.

51. Sylvia Drake, untitled ephemera. BDP.

52. Philena Wheelock to Charity Bryant, July 2, 1827. BDP.

53. William Samson to Charity Bryant, September 4, 1843. BDP.

54. Harvey Smith to Charity Bryant, March 19, 1830. BDP.

55. SDD, April 7, 1822.

56. Sylvia Drake to Mary Drake, August 8, 1824. BDP.

57. SDD, August 4, 1821; January 5, 1823; August 25, 1822.

58. SDD, April 12, 1836.

59. SDD, March 30, 1823.

60. SDD, April 9, 1823.

61. SDD, Sunday 20 [undated fragment, probably July 1817].

62. SDD, July 15, 1838.

63. "Sabbath Sickness," *Evangelical Repository* (Philadelphia, 1847), 6:443–44.

64. SDD, July 12, 1835.

65. Charity Bryant to Asaph Drake, November 2, 1829. DFP.

66. SDD, December 27, 1823.

67. Quoted in Lydia Richards to Charity Bryant, March 1, 1816. BDP.

68. Charity Bryant to Asaph Drake, October 14, 1827. DFP.

69. SDD, July 3, 1838.

70. SDD, September 2, 1838; July 1, 1838.

CHAPTER 17

1. SDD, August 4, 1835.

2. On the Merino sheep craze see Jan Albers, *Hands on the Land: A History of the Vermont Landscape* (Cambridge, Mass.: MIT Press, 2000), chapter 3. On rural women's work in the transition to capitalism see Dublin, *Transforming Women's Work*, Main, "Gender, Work, and Wages in Colonial New England," 39–66; Naomi Lamoreaux, "Rethinking the Transition to Capitalism in the Early American Northeast," *Journal of American History* 90, no. 2 (2003): 437–61; Cathy Matson, "Women's Economies in North America before 1820: Special Forum Introduction," *Early American Studies* 4, no. 2 (2006): 271–90.

3. SDD, January 7, 1835.

4. Vesta Guild to Charity Bryant, January 13, 1810. BDP.

5. Vesta Guild to Charity Bryant, April 21, 1815. BDP.

6. Roland Howard to Charity Bryant, January 20, 1821. BDP.

7. Roland Howard to Charity Bryant, April 12, 1821. The family first talked of using public support in 1814; Vesta Guild to Charity Bryant, February 23, 1814. BDP.

8. Vesta Guild to Charity Bryant, July 18, 1826; Anna Hayden to Charity Bryant, March 11, 1827; Vesta Guild to Charity Bryant, December 13, 1829. BDP. For age of death see Latham, *Epitaphs in Old Bridgewater*, 46–47.

9. Charity Bryant to Sarah Bryant, May 2, 1814. BBFP.

10. Charity Bryant to Sarah Bryant, June 8, 1833. BBFP.

11. SDD, January 6, 1822; February 1822.

12. SDD, November 5, 1823; December 27, 1823.

13. Diary of Hiram Harvey Hurlburt Jr.

14. Mary Hovey to Charity Bryant, May 1, 1809, mentions that Charity found the advance of the warm weather to be "irksom."

15. SDD, October 30, 1823; November 5, 1823.

16. SDD, February 18, 1821. See also May 24, 1821; June 13, 1821; September 18, 1821.

17. Emma Willard, *Journal and Letters: From France and Great-Britain* (Troy, N.Y.: N. Tuttle, 1833), 237. Sylvia records reading the book, SDD, April 6, 1836.

18. Miller, *Needle's Eye*. Charity's high level of expertise and professionalism is also evident from the fact that she kept good business accounts and maintained a shop; many seamstresses worked out of their parlors and reckoned their accounts more informally, according to Miller.

19. Philip Bryant to Charity Bryant, January 9, 1812. BDP.

20. SDD, October 24, 1836.

21. SDD, February 3, 1836.

22. Philip Bryant Inventory. PCPR, 48:69–70. SDD, Inventory, August 22, 1822. WTR 1842–1860.

23. John Larson, *The Market Revolution in America: Liberty, Ambition, and the Eclipse of the Common Good* (New York: Cambridge University Press, 2009).

24. Charity Bryant to Peter Bryant, May 25, 1817. BBFP.

25. Charity Bryant to Peter Bryant, August 26, 1818. BBFP.

26. Charity Bryant to Peter Bryant, January 30, 1820. BBFP.

27. Silas Wright Notes. BDP.

28. Mahlon Crane Account, June 1829. BDP. See also SDD, May 3, 1821; March 5, 1822; November 27, 1822.

29. Thomas D. H. Lake Account, October 1834. BDP.

30. Asaph Drake Account; Rev. J Lee Account. Analysis of Charity and Sylvia's work and income between 1817 and 1851 has been facilitated by charts and graphs prepared by research assistant Meleisa Ono George.

31. Oliver Bryant to Charity Bryant, July 16, 1839. BDP.

32. Seth Bryant to Charity Bryant, February 25, 1840. BDP.

33. SDD, August 3–24, 1835.

34. SDD, January 9, 1821; April 14, 1821; April 30, 1821; November 19, 1821; March 26, 1822.

35. Philena Wheelock to Charity Bryant, August 20, 1825. BDP.

36. Philena Wilcox to Charity Bryant, October 17, 1831. Philena Wheelock married a Wilcox from Bridport, probably a brother or cousin to the Edwon Wilcox whom her friend Philomela Wood married. BDP.

37. Philena Wilcox to Charity Bryant, October 27, 1838; Philena Wilcox to Charity Bryant, May 20, 1839. BDP.

38. Philena Wilcox to Charity Bryant, September 14, 1839. BDP.

39. Philena Field to Charity Bryant, March 14, 1840. BDP.

40. Philena Wilcox to Charity Bryant, October 27, 1838. BDP.

41. Lucy Hurlbut to Charity Bryant, May 18, 1832. BDP.

42. SDD, February 7, 1836.

43. Lucy Hurlbut to Charity Bryant, December 1, 1832. BDP.

44. Lucy Hurlbut to Charity Bryant, November 18, 1832. BDP.

45. Charity Bryant to Sally Bryant, September 16, 1801. BBFP.

46. Vesta Guild to Charity Bryant, January 8, 1816. BDP.

47. Hannah Mitchell to Charity Bryant, January 10, 1840. Hannah reports Vesta "told me many things respecting you and Miss Drake the labour you performed with your feeble health which I could not have credited had it not come from lips sacred to the truth." BDP.

48. Eli Moody to Sylvia Drake, February 6, 1839. BDP.

49. Mark A. Noll, ed., *God and Mammon: Protestants, Money, and the Market, 1790–1860* (New York: Oxford University Press, 2001).

50. For two contrasting outlooks on the new economy, see Charles Sellers, *The Market Revolution: Jacksonian America, 1815–1846* (New York: Oxford University Press, 1994); Daniel Walker Howe, *What Hath God Wrought: The Transformation of America, 1815–1848* (New York: Oxford University Press, 2009), chapter 14.

51. "12 Tailoress Girls," *Semi-Weekly Eagle* [Vermont], September 18, 1848.

CHAPTER 18

1. Charity Bryant to niece [unaddressed and undated, ca. 1851]. BDP.

2. Sally Field to Charity Bryant, May 1841; Lydia Richard Snell to Charity Bryant, May 11, 1842; Cyrus Bryant to Charity Bryant, August 23, 1851. BDP. William Cullen Bryant to Cyrus Bryant, November 6, 1851. BBFP.

3. Sally Field to Charity Bryant, May 1841. BDP.

4. SDD, September 10, 1822; March 17, 1823.

5. Charity Bryant to niece [unaddressed and undated, ca. 1851]. BDP. See also SDD, April 16, 1836.

6. Charity Bryant to Sarah Snell Bryant, October 19, 1802. BBFP. A yellow fever plague struck both the Caribbean and North American port cities including Charleston, Philadelphia, New York, and Boston in 1802; "Yellow Fever," *The Telescope: or American Herald*, September 16, 1802.

7. "Fever," *Boston Commercial Gazette*, September 20, 1802; *Second Annual Report of the State Board of Health of Massachusetts* (Boston, 1871), 2:136.

8. Conevery Bolton Valencius, *The Health of the Country: How American Settlers Understood Themselves and Their Land* (New York: Basic Books, 2002).

9. William Cullen Bryant, *Letters of a Traveller*, 136.

10. Lydia Richards to Charity Bryant, May 22, 1825. BDP.

11. Charity Bryant to Sarah Snell Bryant, January 9, 1825. BBFP.

12. SDD, May 24, 1821. For similar remarks see June 2, 1821; September 18, 1822; January 13, 1822; January 3, 1835.

13. SDD, April 8–10, 1822.

14. SDD, April 26, 1822.

15. SDD, April 27, 1823; February 19, 1836.

16. SDD, August 8, 1838.

17. Caroline Rankin to Charity Bryant, February 3, 1847. BDP. See also SDD, December 20, 1823.

18. SDD, February 27, 1821; May 26, 1822; July 29, 1822; August 27, 1822; September 22, 1822; March 7, 1835; March 21, 1835; November 26, 1835; August 24, 1823; January 24, 1823.

19. Sylvia noted in February 1823 that Charity was menstruating for the first time since the previous June; SDD, February 24, 1823. A reference to Charity experiencing a "change in nature" comes from Lydia Richards to Charity Bryant, April 16, 1824. BDP. When Sylvia went through menopause over a decade later she suffered frequent bleeding and headaches. In 1840, niece Caroline Bryant wrote to ask "How is Aunt S? Does her troublesome visitor continue to make her as frequent calls as formerly?" Caroline A. Bryant to Charity Bryant, July 26, 1840; Caroline A. Bryant to Charity Bryant, February 17, 1840; Silence Bryant to Charity Bryant, February 17, 1840. BDP. The word "visitor" has often been used for menstruation, Janice DeLaney, Mary Jane Lupton, and Emily Toth, *The Curse: A Cultural History of Menstruation* (Springfield: University of Illinois Press, 1988).

20. Lydia Richards to Charity Bryant, April 16, 1824. BDP.

21. William G. Rothstein, *American Physicians in the Nineteenth Century: From Sects to Science* (Baltimore: Johns Hopkins University Press, 1985), chapter 3.

22. Ibid., 45–48; John S. Haller, *American Medicine in Transition, 1840–1910* (Urbana: University of Illinois Press, 1981), 86.

23. See, for example, Susan E. Klepp, *Revolutionary Conceptions: Women, Fertility, & Family Limitation in America, 1760–1820* (Chapel Hill: University of North Carolina Press, 2009), chapter 5.

24. SDD, April 27, 1821; May 12, 1821; April 28, 1822; May 1, 1822; May 5, 1822; July 13, 1822; August 3, 1822. John Monroe, *The American Botanist and Family Physician* (Wheelock [Vt.]: Silas Gaskill, 1824), 36, 57, 76, 95, 111.

25. SDD, May 31, 1821; May 22, 1822; August 23, 1822; Monroe, *American Botanist*, 19–20, 36, 37, 40, 48. Hiram Harvey Hurlburt Jr. recalled digging sweet flag root on the women's property and sharing the harvest with them; Diary of Hiram Harvey Hurlburt Jr.

26. SDD, May 2, 1822; July 27, 1822; August 27, 1822; September 21, 1823; June 26, 1836. Monroe, *American Botanist*, 45, 57, 87; Samuel North, *The Family Physician and Guide to Health, Together with Some Remarks on Surgery* (Waterloo [N.Y.]: Wm. Child, 1830), 215, 70.

27. Rothstein, *American Physicians in the Nineteenth Century*, 49.

28. SDD, August 27, 1823.

29. SDD, August 27, 1838.

30. SDD, May 6, 1822.

31. SDD, August 28, 1823.

32. SDD, May 1, 1822; July 28, 1822; August 11, 1822.

33. Rothstein, *American Physicians in the Nineteenth Century*, 159.

34. SDD, June 23, 1821.

35. Lydia Richards Snell to Charity Bryant, May 8, 1846; Lydia Richards Snell to Charity Bryant, May 29, 1846. BDP.

36. SDD, September 20, 1823.

37. SDD, April 28, 1822; September 7, 1835; September 23, 1835.

38. "Dr. Coits Family Pills," *The Times* [Charleston], September 18, 1812. Language about the female uses of the pill may have been intended to signal the medicine's helpfulness as an abortifacient, an application that likely held little interest to Sylvia.

39. Sylvia likely weighed less than 100 pounds for much of her adult life; see Eli Moody to Sylvia Drake, July 30, 1824. Moody also referenced Drake's "frail body" in Eli Moody to Sylvia Drake, April 21, 1851. BDP.

40. SDD, May 14, 1822. See also May 17, 1836.

41. SDD, October 31, 1822; June 7, 1835; June 16, 1835; September 3, 1838.

42. Silence Bryant to Charity Bryant, November 6, 1838. BDP.

43. SDD, November 7, 1823. BDP. They also used rum as a topical treatment; SDD, November 19, 1835.

44. SDD, May 24, 1822.

45. SDD, March 15, 1835.

46. SDD, May 16, 1822.

47. SDD, May 31, 1823; December 11, 1835.

48. SDD, May 22, 1822.

49. SDD, May 28, 1822.

50. Brown, *Foul Bodies*, chapter 7; Valencius, *Health of the Country*, 133–58.

51. SDD, July 10, 1822.

52. SDD, July 14, 1822.

53. SDD, July 22, 1822.

54. SDD, July 25, 1822; North, *Family Physician*, 224, 97.

55. SDD, July 26, 1822.

56. SDD, July 27, 1822.

57. SDD, July 28, 1822.

58. SDD, August 3, 1822; August 5, 1822; August 9, 1822; August 20, 1822; August 23, 1822.

59. SDD, August 11, 1822.

60. SDD, August 18, 1822. Two months later she sought a third opinion, from Dr. Fullers in nearby New Haven; SDD, October 26, 1822.

61. "Doctor Uriel Linsley," *Connecticut Herald*, November 10, 1810. See also "Doctor L. Sprague," *The Newburyport Herald*, May 19, 1812.

62. "Medical School," *The New-Hampshire Sentinel*, January 12, 1822.

63. SDD, August 27, 1822; September 3, 1822; September 5, 1822; September 12, 1822; September 14, 1822; September 15, 1822.

64. SDD, September 14, 1822.

65. SDD, August 25, 1823; September 23, 1823. See also Lilian Baker Carlisle, "Adult Cradles," *Spinning Wheel* (1982): 46–48.

66. SDD, August 20, 1821.

67. David C. Humphrey, "Dissection and Discrimination: The Social Origins of Cadavers in America, 1765–1915," *Bulletin of the New York Academy of Medicine* 49, no. 9 (1973): 819–27; Michael Sappol, *A Traffic of Dead Bodies: Anatomy and Embodied Social Identity in Nineteenth-Century America* (Princeton, N.J.: Princeton University Press, 2002); Lester S. King and Marjorie C. Meehan, "History of the Autopsy," *American Journal of Pathology* 73, no. 2 (1973): 514–44.

68. SDD, March 12, 1835.

69. Charity Bryant to Peter Bryant, January 30, 1820. BBFP.

70. SDD, March 12, 1835.

71. Vesta Guild to Charity Bryant, January 5, 1833. BDP.

72. Lydia Richards to Charity Bryant, March 28, 1821; July 22, 1822; December 5, 1822. BDP.

73. Lydia Richards to Charity Bryant, April 16, 1824. BDP.

74. Rothstein, *American Physicians in the Nineteenth Century*, 152–61.

75. Cyrus Bryant to Charity Bryant, January 14, 1851; Cyrus Bryant to Charity Bryant, March 28, 1851. BDP.

76. SDD, February 7, 1835; February 17, 1835.

77. SDD, August 11, 1838.

78. William Cullen Bryant to John Howard Bryant, April 22, 1850. BBFP.

79. William Cullen Bryant to Charity Bryant, September 25, 1843. BDP; Voss and Bryant II, *Letters of William Cullen Bryant*, 2:247–49.

80. Charity Bryant, "A Midnight Prayer," August 7, 1809. BDP.

81. SDD, June 3, 1821. See also SDD, July 21, 1822; January 19, 1822; February 26, 1835.

82. SDD, May 11, 1835. Once Charity smoked Sylvia with hot wool; SDD, October 31, 1822.

83. SDD, May 1, 1821.

84. SDD, September 26, 1823; May 3, 1835.

85. SDD, April 1, 1823.

86. Charity Bryant to Peter Bryant, January 30, 1820. BBFP.

87. For example, SDD, August 30, 1822.

88. Elizabeth Mavor, biographer of the Ladies of Llangollen, explores the same possibility for Eleanor Butler and Sarah Ponsonby; Mavor, *Ladies of Llangollen*, 104–5.

89. Bullough and Voght, "Homosexuality and Its Confusion with the 'Secret Sin,' " 143–55. For a period example, see Mary S. Gove, *Lectures to Ladies on Anatomy and Physiology* (Boston: Saxon & Pierce, 1842).

90. Lefkowitz Horowitz, *Rereading Sex*, chapter 5.

91. Buchan, *Domestic Medicine*, 346; Joseph J. Fraumeni et al., "Cancer Mortality among Nuns: Role of Marital Status in Etiology of Neoplastic Disease in Women," *Journal of the National Cancer Institute* 42, no. 3 (1969): 455–68.

92. Kara A. Britt and Roger B. Short, "The Plight of Nuns: Hazards of Nulliparity," *The Lancet* 379, no. 9384 (2012): 2322–23.

93. William Whitty Hall, *Health at Home, or Hall's Family Doctor* (Hartford, Conn.: James Betts & Co., 1876), 523.

94. SDD, March 1, 1835.

95. SDD, July 21, 1821.

96. SDD, December 9, 1835.

97. SDD, March 4, 1821.

98. SDD, March 17, 1822.

99. SDD, April 7, 1822.

100. SDD, February 21–22, 1822.

101. Perry Miller, *The New England Mind: The Seventeenth Century* (Cambridge, Mass.: Harvard University Press, 1983).

102. Charity Bryant to Peter Bryant, March 21, 1813. BBFP.

103. SDD, November 18, 1821. Sylvia also referred to Jesus as "the Physician God" in March 9, 1823. These beliefs were common in their community. A member of their church advised the women of the efficacy of prayer as a curative; SDD, September 16, 1835.

104. SDD, August 10, 1835.

105. SDD, November 7, 1823.

106. "Recipe for Lameness." BDP.

107. SDD, September 17, 1835. Cyrus Bryant Drake's health is discussed in "Cyrus Bryant Drake" in *Minutes of the Eighty-Third Annual Meeting*, 59–60.

108. SDD, August 7–8, 1835.

109. SDD, May 25, 1822. Azel had recovered from having the mumps two weeks before; SDD, May 10, 1822.

110. SDD, September 6–7, 1838.

111. Clarissa Moody to Charity Bryant, November 7, 1823; Susan P. Bryant to Charity Bryant, March 16, 1840, enclosed within Oliver Bryant to Charity Bryant, February 25, 1840. BDP.

112. SDD, August 7, 1838.

113. SDD, January 11, 1835. See also July 3, 1835.

114. SDD, August 11, 1822.

115. SDD, March 19, 1836; March 27, 1836; May 1, 1836; May 27, 1836.

116. SDD, June 1, 1836.

117. SDD, July 21–23, 1821.

118. Clara E. Hudson, "The Romances of a Country Doctor" (October 7, 1947), Shaw-Hudson House, Plainfield, Massachusetts.

119. SDD, January 7–8, 1822. See also SDD, May 27, 1822; June 19, 1822; May 30, 1823.

120. SDD, February 11–12, 1822.

121. SDD, May 25, 1822.

122. SDD, August 14, 1823.

123. SDD, October 8, 1823.

124. SDD, April 26–27, 1822. On laundry in early America, see Brown, *Foul Bodies*, 215–21. See also SDD, January 17, 1835; February 5, 1835; July 6, 1835.

125. SDD, January 13–14, 1822.

126. Peter Bryant to Philip Bryant, February 7, 1811. BBFP.

127. SDD, June 25, 1836.

128. SDD, June 29–July 6, July 20, and August 3, 1838.

129. SDD, July 17, August 11, and August 21, 1838.

130. Roland Howard to Charity Bryant, September 18, 1839. BDP.

131. For example, Sally Field to Charity Bryant, March 7, 1841; Caroline Bryant to Charity Bryant, March 27, 1841; Oliver Bryant to Charity Bryant, December 10, 1844; Hayward Marshall to Charity Bryant, 1846. BDP.

132. Sally Field to Charity Bryant, April 14, 1844. BDP.

133. Lydia Richards Snell to Charity Bryant, April 14, 1846; Ebenezer Snell to Charity Bryant, June 27, 1846. BDP.

134. Daniel Bryant to Charity Bryant, February 20, 1847; Justin Olds and Charity Louisa Olds to Charity Bryant, May 9, 1847. BDP.

135. Sarah J. Purcell, "Commemoration, Public Art, and the Changing Meaning of the Bunker Hill Monument," *The Public Historian* 25, no. 2 (2003): 55–71.

136. Silence Bryant to Charity Bryant, August 23, 1843. BDP.

137. William Cullen Bryant to Cyrus Bryant, November 6, 1851. BBFP.

138. Eli Moody to Charity Bryant and Sylvia Drake, May 14, 1851; "Letter Record, 1849–1851"; Caroline Rankin to Charity Bryant, October 2, 1850. BDP.

139. Caroline Rankin to Sylvia Drake, October 7, 1851. BDP.

140. William Cullen Bryant to Cyrus Bryant, November 6, 1851. BBFP.

CHAPTER 19

1. Charity did compose two early poems to Sylvia discussing the prospect of separation. The first separation was averted when Sylvia decided to accompany Charity to Massachusetts in spring 1808. The second poem was written in March 1810; Sylvia's company on Charity's 1810 trip to Massachusetts suggests that this separation was averted as well. Charity Bryant, "On the Prospect of Separation," March 18, 1808; Charity Bryant, "Acrostic written by firelight on the prospect of a speedy separation," March 1810; Account of her Travels by Charity Bryant, April 9, 1844. BDP.

2. Eli Moody to Sylvia Drake, October 20, 1851; Caroline Rankin to Sylvia Drake, October 7, 1851; Emma Rankin to Sylvia Drake, September 25, 1852. BDP.

3. William Cullen Bryant to Cyrus Bryant, November 6, 1851. BBFP. No condolence letter from William Cullen Bryant to Sylvia Drake is archived at the Henry Sheldon Museum, but since the museum sold off many of the poet's letters this absence does not prove that William Cullen Bryant failed to send one. A condolence letter may be in the hands of a private collector.

4. Cyrus Bryant Drake to Sylvia Drake, October 11, 1851; Eli Moody to Sylvia Drake, October 20, 1851; D. D. Cook to Sylvia Drake, December 20, 1851. BDP.

5. Eli Moody to Sylvia Drake, October 20, 1851; Polly Drake to Sylvia Drake, November 4, 1851. See also Almira Reed to Sylvia Drake, December 6, 1851. BDP.

6. Diann Smith to Sylvia Drake, March 8, 1853; Cyrus Bryant Drake to Sylvia Drake, October 11, 1853; D. D. Cook to Sylvia Drake, December 20, 1851. BDP.

7. Premo, *Winter Friends*, 29–38.

8. Charity Bryant, "Swiftly our moments pass away" [ca. 1835]. BDP. Although undated, the poem appears on a sheet of paper with acrostics written for Lucy Hurlbut and Philomela Wood, who worked as assistants for the women in 1835. For Sylvia's diary entry, see SDD, August 6, 1835.

9. Charity Bryant, "Swiftly our moments pass away" [ca. 1835]. The phrase "all our years" also echoes the wording of Psalm 128, a longtime favorite at wedding ceremonies, which Sylvia used in a diary entry in December 1835 to thank God for the mercy he had shown to Charity and herself "all the days of our lives"; SDD, December 5, 1835.

10. Charity Bryant, "To a Friend on her *Birth Day*. October 31, 1847." BDP.

11. For Sylvia's widow's weeds, see Sylvia Louisa Drake to Polly Shaw, June 23, 1854. SDP. For Charity's will, see Charity Bryant Administration Account, ACPR 25:78. A fire in February 1852 burned all probate records from before that time (including Charity's original will). However, the tax records' valuation of the women's property in 1851 and 1852, combined with the Administration record, demonstrate that Charity's will described the women's cottage as common property; WTR, 1851–1852. For the distribution of Charity's clothing and the approval of the Bryant family, see Oliver Bryant to Sylvia Drake, February 12, 1853; Emma Rankin to Sylvia Drake, February 11, 1853; Almira Reed to Sylvia Drake, March 5, 1853. BDP.

12. Sylvia Drake to Elijah Fish, March 30, 1853. BGP.

13. Sylvia Drake to Asaph Drake, February 1853; Sylvia Louisa Drake to Polly Shaw, January 1859; Dela D. Willard to Polly Shaw, June 7, 1860. SDP. WTR, 1852–1860.

14. Sylvia Drake to Polly Shaw, September 30, 1859; Sylvia Drake to Asaph Drake, September 30, 1859. SDP; Record of Asaph Drake's life. DFP. For Sylvia's conflict with Fordyce Shaw see Diary of Hiram Harvey Hurlburt Jr.

15. Orpha Jewett diary, January 31–February 18, 1868. James Family Diaries and Accounts. HSM.

16. Orpha Jewett diary, January 31–February 18, 1868. James Family Diaries and Accounts. HSM.

17. W. N. Oliver to F. M. Shaw, July 14, 1868. SDP.

18. Sarah Pierce, founder of the Litchfield Academy in Connecticut, expressed the desire to be buried "in one grave" with her beloved Abigail Smith; Moore, *Sister Arts*. The famous Ladies of Llangollen share a grave; Mavor, *Ladies of Llangollen*. The name of Gertrude Stein's life partner, Alice B. Toklas, is engraved on the back of her gravestone in Paris's Cimetière Père-Lachaise; visited by the author, August 2013.

19. Probate of Sylvia Drake will, March 9, 1868. ACPR 32:618–19.

20. Linda Kerber, "The Paradox of Women's Citizenship in the Early Republic: The Case of *Martin vs. Massachusetts*, 1805," *American Historical Review* 97, no. 2 (1992): 349–78.

21. Basch, *In the Eyes of the Law*.

22. Probate of Sylvia Drake will, March 9, 1868; Executor's Inventory of Sylvia Drake property; Appraiser's Inventory of Sylvia Drake property. ACPR 32:618–19; 687; 148–49. For accounts of Harriet E. Bowdish and Lauren Drake see "Memoir written by Mrs. H. Child Chrysler." For the distribution of Sylvia's personal effects, which inspired some conflict among her nieces, see unsigned letter to Emmeline Drake, January 28 [1869?]. DFP.

23. Woody Holton, *Abigail Adams* (New York: Atria Books, 2009), 406–9. Of course, Adams had far more property to distribute than Sylvia.

24. Administrator's Inventory of Asaph Drake property; Division & Partition Warrant for Asaph Drake property. ACPR 33:115; 37:228–43.

25. Probate of Oliver Drake will. ACPR, 2:140–46.

26. "Cyrus Bryant Drake," in *Minutes of the Eighty-Third Annual Meeting*, 59–60; "Thomas S. Drake," in Carleton, *Genealogical and Family History of the State of Vermont*, 555; "Nelson Asaph Drake," in Howard L. Conard, ed., *Encyclopedia of the History of Missouri: A Compendium of History and Biography for Ready References* (New York: The Southern History Company, 1901), 2:314–15. Also, "Memoir written by Mrs. H. Child Chrysler"; Asaph Drake Autobiography. DFP.

27. "Memoir written by Mrs. H. Child Chrysler."

28. "Memoir written by Mrs. H. Child Chrysler"; "Cyrus Bryant Drake," in *Minutes of the Eighty-Third Annual Meeting*, 59–60.

29. Frances Fairchild Bryant to John Howard Bryant, December 15, 1833. William Cullen Bryant Collection, B6. The Trustees of Reservations Research and Archives Center, Sharon, Massachusetts; "Might have been Tilden's wife," *Globe*, October 6, 1907; *Report on the Progress and Condition of the United States National Museum* (Washington, 1911), 62; "Leaves $250,000 to Chum," *New York Times*, August 2, 1907; "Historical Society Gets Bryant Relics," *New York Times*, November 6, 1910.

30. Leslie Choquette, "Homosexuals in the City: Representations of Lesbian and Gay Space in Nineteenth-Century Paris," *Journal of Homosexuality* 41, no. 3–4 (2008): 149–67.

AFTERWORD

1. Godwin, *A Biography of William Cullen Bryant*, 1:410; Charles Henry Brown, *William Cullen Bryant: A Biography* (New York: Scribner, 1971), 90, 288; Gilbert H. Muller, *William Cullen Bryant: Author of America* (Albany: State University Press of New York, 2008), 28–29, 57, 342.

2. Godwin, *Biography of William Cullen Bryant*, 1:410.

3. Diary of Hiram Harvey Hurlburt Jr.

4. This story is included within Washington, *History of Weybridge*, 45.

5. Heys, "Two Seamstresses of Weybridge."

6. Merrit P. Allen to Mrs. Walter Painter, November 8, 1953. Parmalee Allen Papers. HSM. Allen's biography is taken from "Along Boy's Life Trails," *Boys' Life*, August 1935.

7. Blanche Wiesen Cook, "The Historical Denial of Lesbianism," *Radical History Review* 20 (1979): 60–65.

8. Martin Bauml Duberman, "Reclaiming the Gay Past," *Reviews in American History* 16, no. 4 (1988): 515–25.

9. Andy Christiansen, "Take Back Vermont—Let History Show Us the Way," in *Take Back Vermont* (2000), http://www.speakeasy.org/~jessamyn/tbvt/tbvtart6.html.

10. Jan Albers, "Sylvia and Charity: A Vermont Love Story for the Ages," *Past Times: Stories from the Sheldon Museum* (April 2009).

11. "Sylvia Drake," in "Painter/Drake/Parmalee/Smith Ohio Vermont USA" index on www.rootsweb.ancestry.com. Updated January 4, 2012.

12. Faderman, *Odd Girls and Twilight Lovers*, 1–2.

13. Local historian Jan Albers used this approach in her 2000 history of the Vermont landscape, which described Charity Bryant as Sylvia Drake's "lady friend." See Albers, *Hands on the Land*. However, Albers subsequently corrected this euphemism. In 2009, she published an article in the Henry Sheldon Museum's newsletter that described the women's relationship as a marriage; Albers, "Sylvia and Charity: A Vermont Love Story for the Ages."

ACKNOWLEDGMENTS

GREAT THANKS ARE due to the many archivists, librarians, amateur historians, grant organizations, research assistants, colleagues, readers, listeners, friends, and family who supported the writing of *Charity and Sylvia*.

This book began with a fortuitous trip to the Henry Sheldon Museum in Middlebury, Vermont, and it is only fitting that the acknowledgments begin with a recognition of the institution's many archivists and volunteers who assisted my multiple visits. Thanks to Jane Ploughman, Mary Epright, Marjorie Robbins, Orson Kingsley, Eva Garcelon-Hart, and Jan Albers. Thanks also to Maureen Mulligan and Probate Judge Missy Smith of the nearby Addison County Probate Court and to Virginia Lazarus of the Vermont Supreme Court.

Down the road in Weybridge, I was equally fortunate to receive assistance from local historians Ida and Larry Washington. Town Clerk Karen Brisson gave me full run of Weybridge's records and of the town photocopier. Pat Fiske shared a manuscript in her possession that had been passed down through the Drake family. Millicent Rooney, of the Monument Farm Dairy, showed me around town and shared her knowledge of local history. Also the farm's chocolate milk is amazing.

In Massachusetts, Charity and Sylvia's birthplace, I received extraordinary help from local citizens, amateur historians, and professional librarians. Judy Williams gave me a tour of Plainfield. She showed me the house where Lydia Richards had grown up, and which Charity so often visited, and she showed me inside the house where Lydia Richards died, now Judy's home. She also helped to arrange my visit to the Shaw-Hudson house, home of Charity's greatniece Sarah Bryant Shaw, which is preserved exactly as it stood in the 1860s. In nearby Cummington thanks are due to Carla Ness at the Community House Archives.

I encountered similar generosity on the eastern side of the state, in the towns where Charity and Sylvia were born and raised. Frank Meninno of the Easton Historical Society helped explain to me the geography and traditions of this venerable town, giving me a far greater grasp of the Drake family's origins. Karen Tucker of Easton let me look inside her home, which used to be a tavern kept by friends of Charity and Sylvia's. Cynthia Ricciardi at the Old Taunton Historical Society also went out of her way to help me find information about Easton. In West Bridgewater, Marlene Howell opened the Old Bridgewater Historical Society for my visit and pointed out where to find the forgotten cemeteries in which Charity's relations were buried.

Thanks are also due to the many archivists who keep Boston's impressive research facilities running smoothly. Elizabeth Bouvier helped to guide my fruitful hours at the Court and Judicial Archives at the Massachusetts Archives. Thanks as well to librarians and archivists at the American Congregational Association Library, the Massachusetts Historical Society, and Houghton Library of Harvard University. In the neighboring state of New York, thanks to the archivists at the Long Island Studies Institute at Hofstra University and the New York Public Library.

When Peter Bryant's descendants moved west to Illinois they carried with them many important papers relating to the family's history. Thank you to Sarah Cooper and Pam Lange at the Bureau County Historical Society who showed me their wonderful collection and encouraged my research. Thanks also to Cindy Ditzler and Joan Metzger at Northern Illinois University's Regional History Center, which contains a great collection of material relating to the Bryant family.

A couple of generous individuals shared private manuscripts that had been passed down in their families. Randy Hayward, a descendant of Sylvia's sister Polly Hayward, sent me scans of numerous wonderful eighteenth- and nineteenth-century documents, one of which can be seen in the book's illustration pages. Samuel Minter shared scans of his ancestor Hiram Harvey Hurlburt Jr.'s handwritten memoir, with its description of Charity and Sylvia that I quote from so many times in the book. I am sure that there are more documents out there filed away in descendants' attics that could shed more light on Charity and Sylvia's story. If any readers are in possession of said papers, please get in touch with me! The book might be finished but my curiosity about the women's lives continues.

Two research assistants made important contributions. Meleisa Ono George counted, compiled, and charted the evidence in Sylvia's diaries and the women's business accounts, giving me a new way to look at the research. Amy Glemann Goldin served as a great companion in the archives and on the road during a particularly fruitful weeklong journey through Massachusetts.

Amy Glemann Goldin also read many draft chapters of the manuscript and gave helpful feedback. Thanks for reading drafts are also due to Amanda Littauer, Aaron Bobrow-Strain, and Ilana Stanger-Ross. Tom Foster and the second anonymous reader for Oxford University Press read almost the whole book and gave great comments. To them I offer not only thanks but apologies for not including the final chapter in my submission; I wanted to put off writing Charity's and Sylvia's death scenes as long as possible.

I also received feedback on specific chapters from numerous scholars. Participants and audience members at the May 2012 Early American Biographies workshop hosted by the *William and Mary Quarterly* and the Early Modern Studies Institute had a spirited discussion of Chapter 5. Thanks especially to Annette Gordon-Reed, convener of the workshop; James Sidbury and James H. Sweet who responded to the chapter; and Karin Wulf who shared photos and insights from her own research. The conversation really pushed me to consider the potential limits of historical prose. Members of the Pacific Northwest Early American Group read and commented on Chapter 14. Thanks especially to Daniel Vickers and Jennifer Spear who had great suggestions. Beatrix Hoffman answered questions on the history of medicine as I wrote Chapter 18 and read the draft when I was finished. Lynne Marks read Chapters 1 and 2. Lizzie Reis gave me great encouragement on the preface, which has been through far more drafts than I care to tell.

Through all those drafts the preface has always begun with the same paragraph, which is the very first paragraph I wrote for the book, drafted in my History 491 class at Northern Illinois University during the spring of 2009. We had a five-minute in-class writing exercise that I took part in, and I might have trashed the paragraph but my students encouraged me to hold onto it. Thanks! Thanks also to my students at the University of Victoria whose classroom insights have greatly expanded my understanding of the history of sex and gender.

My colleagues at both universities have been equally generous with their support. I began the project while working at Northern Illinois University, with the support of a Faculty Artistry and Research Summer Grant. I have also received research support from the University of Victoria where I now teach. The greatest source of funding for *Charity and Sylvia* came from the Social Science Humanities Research Council of Canada.

Research grants and institutional support enabled me not only to visit archives but also to discuss *Charity and Sylvia* at a number of conferences. The community of scholars who have contributed their insights at meetings of the Society of Historians of the Early American Republic, the Canadian Committee on Women's History, the Organization of American Historians, the American Historical Association, the Western Association of Women Historians, and numerous other venues have my gratitude. Andrew Burstein and Carol Groneman went out of their way to provide encouragement.

One fellow historian and friend has been at more of those conference talks than anyone else excepting me. She was at the very first talk I gave about Charity and Sylvia, to the "Bodies of Knowledge: Sexuality in the Archives" conference at the University of Queensland in 2007, and she has been my companion at many universities and conference hotels throughout the United States and Canada in the years that followed. Throughout, she has been a constant source of advice, feedback, encouragement, and love. Amanda Littauer has been my best comrade in arms since graduate school. Her example led me into the history of sex and gender in the first place. This project would have been much less pleasurable without her.

It hardly seems possible, but there is one person who has been an even bigger booster of *Charity and Sylvia* than Amanda, my father, Jonathan Sinnreich. He believed in this book from the very beginning. He has read more drafts than anyone else and told me that each one was perfect. That support has meant the world to me. Other family members have also read drafts and given encouragement, including Masha Zager, Emily Pines, Carol Sinnreich, and Aram Sinnreich.

Last but not least, my husband, Timothy Cleves, has been there from the very beginning, by my side on the summer day I first set foot in the Henry Sheldon Museum, and sitting in the next room now. His belief in me and my work is a great source of strength. The care he takes of me and of our children has given me the time and space to write this book. His excellence as a husband is a great argument for why marriage should be an equal right for all people.

Paris
October 2013

INDEX